On Being and What There Is

On Being and What There Is

Classical Vaiśeṣika and the History of Indian Ontology

Wilhelm Halbfass

STATE UNIVERSITY OF NEW YORK PRESS

Production by Ruth Fisher

Marketing by Dana E. Yanulavich

Published by
State University of New York Press, Albany

Printed in Canada

For information, address the State University of New York Press,
State University Plaza, Albany, NY 12246

Library of Congress Cataloging-in-Publication Data
Halbfass, Wilhelm.
On being and what there is : classical Vaiśeṣika and the history of Indian ontology / Wilhelm Halbfass.
p. cm.
Includes bibliographical references and index.
ISBN 0-7914-1177-X (alk. paper). — ISBN 0-7914-1178-8 (pbk. : alk. paper)
1. Vaiśeṣika. 2. Ontology—History. I. Title.
B132.V2H27 1992
111′.0954—dc20 91-43295
CIP

10 9 8 7 6 5 4 3 2 1

Contents

Preface

The following chapters are fragments of a much larger project, a comprehensive history of Indian thinking about "being" and "what there is." In the course of more than twenty years I have learned to scale down this impossible dream. Appropriately, I am now presenting some preliminary results of my work on one single system, the Vaiśeṣika system, which is commonly considered the lowest and, in a sense, crudest of the "orthodox" systems of Hindu thought. However, I still hope to be able to complete a corresponding volume on the concepts of being, or the forms of transcendence of such conceptualization, in Advaita Vedānta. Even within the development of the Vaiśeṣika school, I have focused on the older period up to Udayana, whose work paves the way for Navyanyāya. In spite of many references to Nyāya literature, this is primarily a study of the classical Vaiśeṣika system as such and not of later forms of combination or integration of the Nyāya and Vaiśeṣika systems. More specifically, it is an attempt to uncover movements of thought and unanswered questions under the petrified surface of the classical system.

Over the years, my methodological positions and philosophical allegiances have changed. The result has been a certain eclecticism and growing doubts concerning the meaning and relevance of the topic itself. We do not know whether the "question of being" is a meaningful question. But once this question is gone, or reduced to certain linguistic, semantic, or logical technicalities, what else could provide us with a comparable sense of philosophical wonder and perplexity? What would happen to philosophy itself?

The book combines specialized philological and conceptual investigations with general philosophical and comparative reflections. Some of its sections may seem easily accessible to the general reader; others may appear remote even to the specialist. But we may repeat here what we said in an earlier publication (*Tradition and Reflection*, p. VIII): "Such differences reflect the nature of the sources and our state of research. In some central instances, the resolution of technical problems, and the attention to minute philological details, are indispensable in order to approach the broader issues. Philology and philosophical reflection cannot be separated in such cases."

For several sections of the book, I have used and reworked materials published before. In particular, parts or preliminary versions of Chapters 5, 6, 7, and 8 have appeared in *WZKS* 19 (1975), 20 (1976), 24 (1980); *Adyar Library Bulletin* 50 (1986); *JAOS* 109 (1989); and elsewhere. The responses to these preliminary publications, as well as to numerous oral presentations, have been encouraging and stimulating. At important junctures, my work on the Vaiśeṣika system and on Indian ontology in general has received generous financial support from different sources. Specifically, I want to mention a combined fellowship of the National Endowment for the Humanities and the American Institute of Indian Studies in 1982–83. Most of the final draft of the book was completed during the academic year 1989–90, while I was a fellow of the Wissenschaftskolleg (Institute for Advanced Study) in Berlin. Here, I enjoyed excellent working conditions, a stimulating intellectual environment, and the competent secretarial help of Firooza Kraft. Some final additions were made after my return to the University of Pennsylvania, with the support of David Fern and the Department of South Asia Regional Studies.

1

Introduction: The Question of Being

1. Do we know what we mean when we speak about nonbeing or that which is not? Do we know what we mean when we speak about being or that which is? Is there a difference between being and what there is; that is, the entities which exist? The dialogue partners in Plato's *Sophist*, Theaetetus and the stranger from Elea, share their perplexity (*aporía*) about what once seemed to them most familiar and obvious, and they agree that those who still believe to know what they are saying should explain what they mean when they talk about being or that which is.[1] According to the stranger from Elea, the unquestioned familiarity of the "is" and "is not" has been shattered once and for all by the bold and paradoxical statements of "father Parmenides"; that is, by his thesis that only being is, that nonbeing is not, and that there is no becoming and change. The most obvious has become most confusing and perplexing; and in such perplexity, philosophy itself has its origin and natural habitat. What is being? What is really real? Plato sees an intellectual "battle of giants" (*gigantomachía*) being fought over these questions.[2]

In the following generation, Plato's greatest disciple and critic,

Aristotle, refers once again to the question "what being is," and he says that it is an old question which continues to be the subject of inquiry and perplexity.[3] Aristotle postulates "a science which investigates being as being, and what belongs to it according to its own nature";[4] that is, a science which, unlike other, "regular" sciences, does not focus on mere sections or subdivisions of what there is. Approximately two thousand years later, in the early seventeenth century, this very special, yet all-comprehensive "science," which Aristotle himself called *first philosophy* (*prṓtē philosophía*), became known as *ontology.* Christian Wolff defined it as "science of being in general, or insofar as it is being" ("scientia entis in genere, seu quatenus ens est").[5] In his system, it was the first and foremost part of "metaphysics" (another term *not* used by Aristotle), and it was distinguished from "theology" ("theologia"); that is, the science of the highest being.

Aristotle's phrase *on hēi on*, "being as being," is as suggestive as it is ambiguous. Does it mean being in its abstract universality, the common denominator of whatever there is, or does it mean an entity which is what it is by virtue of the sheer fact that it is; i.e., a divine and absolute being? The concept of "first philosophy" reflects such ambiguity and renders it more conspicuous. On the one hand, "first philosophy" has the task of investigating being as such and in general (*kath'hólou*); but on the other hand, Aristotle presents as its domain the "first essence" (*prṓtē ousía*) and what is "separate" (*chōristón*) as well as "unchanging" (*akínēton*). In this second sense, "first philosophy" coincides with "theology" (*theología*). The relationship between the two definitions of "first philosophy" has not been clarified by Aristotle himself; it has, however, been debated by generations of Aristotle scholars. Do these definitions represent different stages in the development of Aristotle's thought? Are they indeed as different and unrelated as they appear to be? Does the divine essence or substance of "theology" provide the necessary focus for an "ontological" inquiry into the unity and universality of being in general?[6]

The "unity" of being remains elusive. It is, according to Aristotle, not the unity of a genus; being is not the highest genus of what there is. And the usages of the word *being* are neither entirely synonymous nor merely homonymous. Being has more than one sense, "is said in many ways" (*to on légetai pollachṓs*). There is "being per accidens" (*katá symbebēkós*, i.e., in an "accidental," nonessential manner of predication) and "being per se" (*kath'hautó*). There is being in the sense of truth, and being that may be divided into "potential" and "actual being" (i.e., *dýnamis* vs. *enérgeia*). And again, "being per se" is "said in many ways"; that is, in accordance with the ten "categories" or "modes of predication" (*schēmata tēs katēgorías*) "substance" (*ousía*), "quality" (*poión*), and so forth.[7] It is substance in the sense of the concrete individual entity which provides an exemplary and prototypical meaning of being and a focus and tenuous unity for its different usages.

Aristotle's thought about being is deeply aporetic, and it cannot be confined to the apparent clarity and simplicity of Wolff's science of ontology.[8] Aristotle's science of being qua being has not been a channel of orderly progress and an unambiguous accumulation of knowledge and insight. But together with the problems and paradoxes raised by Parmenides and Plato, it has remained alive throughout the history of Western thought, in numerous reinterpretations, transformations, adaptations, tentative solutions, and above all, unanswered questions. The question of "what being is" may be present in different ways, at different levels of thematicity, not only in explicit and programmatic "ontologies" and definitions of being. Speculations on "levels of reality," reflections on the usage of words and the conditions of true knowledge, debates whether certain entities exist (such as universals or God)—all this may reflect the question of being; and in general, the ways in which it has been asked are at least as relevant as the explicit answers.

2. Aristotle's aporetic ontology, as well as the paradoxes of Plato and Parmenides, find their way into the philosophy of Plotinus and the tradition of Neo-Platonism. Here, they are absorbed by a metaphysics of emanation, which resolves conceptual problems by postulating not only different levels of reality, but also a hierarchy of experiential realization and corresponding transformations of the knowing subject. Being (the realm of the intellect) and nonbeing themselves are superseded and transcended by the One (*to hen*), the ultimate goal of mystical realization.[9]

The great theistic philosophies of Christianity, Islam and Judaism adopt and transform the traditions of Plato, Aristotle, and Plotinus. Aristotle himself becomes the recognized master of High Scholasticism. The relationship between theology and ontology, "highest being" and "universal being," assumes new dimensions and appears in a variety of interpretations. In the history of Christianity, the most exemplary and comprehensive integration of ontology and theology has been achieved in the system of Thomas Aquinas, in particular in his doctrine of the "analogia entis," that is, the "analogy" of divine and dependent being, and his twofold correlation of the finite entities with "universal being" ("esse commune") on the one hand and the divine "subsistent being" ("esse subsistens") on the other hand.[10]

Greek ontological concepts have been inherited and assimilated not only by different religious philosophies, but also by different cultural and linguistic traditions. The corresponding terms have been translated into numerous languages, in particular Latin (beginning in pre-Christian Rome), Arabic, and various European vernaculars. In this process, they have been reinterpreted and supplemented in a variety of ways. Available words in the various languages have assumed new terminological functions, and numerous new terms have been created (such as *essentia* and *entitas* in Latin). Significant details of this process of transmission, transformation, and continuation still await historical clarification.

In Latin, Aristotle's *ousía* is rendered both as "essentia" (which seems to be a terminological creation of Cicero) and "substantia." Subsequently, "essentia" as well as "quidditas" may also correspond to Aristotle's suggestive and elusive "what it means to be something" (*to ti ēn einai*).[11] Other terms, though not entirely without precedent or counterparts in Greek thought, represent more independent and innovative conceptual developments in Latin. The word *existentia,* which appears in its characteristic role in the writings of the Christian Neo-Platonist Marius Victorinus (fourth century) is introduced as a Latin translation for Greek *hýparxis;* but its Greek prehistory is only of minor conceptual importance.[12] For its further development and its conspicuous juxtaposition and contrast with "essentia," the impact of Islamic thought and Arabic terminology, and of the Islamic renaissance of Greek thought, have to be taken into consideration. The Arabic language, with its verbs of being, such as *kāna* and *wajada* (*mawjūd, wujūd*), provides linguistic conditions and devices that differ significantly from those of the Greek language; they may have favored a more rigorous and pervasive distinction between essence and existence.[13] The Middle Ages add several important innovations to the ontological vocabulary in Latin, for instance *quidditas* and *realitas* (since John Duns Scotus).[14]

Among the European vernaculars, German is conspicuous by its numerous additions to the classical ontological terminology, such as *Wirklichkeit, Wesen, Dasein,* as well as by the ease with which it employs both the nominalized infinitive ("Sein") and the participle ("seiend," "Seiendes"); this suggestive distinction, which is also available in Greek and Latin, has no equivalent in French or English. Meister Eckhart (ca. 1260–1327) and Christian Wolff (1679–1754) are among the most important contributors to the German ontological vocabulary.[15]

3. The distinction between "essence" and "existence" is particularly conspicuous in the Western ontological tradition; in its various transformations, it is among the most pervasive and persistent themes and problems of Western thought in general. In spite of its connections with the Greek concepts of *ousía* and *hýparxis,* on the one hand, and *dýnamis* and *enérgeia,* on the other hand, this theme assumes its characteristic dimensions in its association with later, theistic thought and with speculations on the process of creation and the contingency of the world. An influential and controversial model of thought, which presents essences as possibilities to which God adds existence or actuality in the act of creation, found its classical articulation in the *Metaphysics* of Avicenna (ibn Sīnā, 980–1037).[16]

> Existence becomes a problem when the possibility of non-existence is taken seriously. But contingency, or the possibility of non-existence, was not regarded as an ultimate fact by the Greek thinkers. . . . It was in the context of a theistic philosophy, a doctrine of creation, among the Jewish, Christian and Mohammedan thinkers of the Middle Ages, that the question of contingency, and therefore, of existence, became acute. . . . The discussion of existence, then, emerges from an earlier condition of thought in which the existence of things is taken for granted and the problem of being is the problem of what really is as opposed to what is merely apparent, or of what is permanent as opposed to what is transitory.[17]

For the time being, we may disregard the historical and conceptual problems associated with such broad statements.[18]

The theme of essence and existence may appear under a variety of titles; the common usage of this terminology is relatively late. For instance, Thomas Aquinas does not use this pair of terms. Instead, he correlates and contrasts *essentia* with *ens/esse,* or *quidditas* with *actus essentiae,* without assuming an additive relationship between the two.[19] Even his disciple Aegidius Romanus, who taught the "real" distinction between essence and existence in created, finite beings, uses *esse* instead of *existentia* in his *Theoremata de esse et essentia*.

The further development of the topic through Suarez to Wolff and others has been characterized as a development toward essentialization. In Wolff's terminology, *being* ("ens") is defined as what is possible; that is, compatible with existence: "Ens dicitur quod existere potest, consequenter cui existentia non repugnat. . . . Quod possibile est, ens est." Existence itself is a mere supplement to the essential possibilities, a "complementum possibilitatis."[20] A rich and independent tradition of debate on essence and existence (*māhiyya-wujūd*, etc.) is found in medieval as well as later Islamic thought.[21]

The idea of "first philosophy" assumes a new role and meaning in the thought of Francis Bacon and René Descartes. In Descartes' *Meditationes de prima philosophia*, "first philosophy" does not deal with being qua being, but with the principles of human knowledge, with certainty, method and ideas. Whereas Avicenna's theory of creation postulates the addition of actual existence to the mere possibility of things, Descartes' method requires proof for the existence of things over and above their appearance in the ideas of his own mind. In the following century, Immanuel Kant states that "the proud name of an ontology" has to be replaced by the more "modest one of an analytic of pure understanding."[22] *Transzendentalphilosophie* ("transcendental philosophy"), which "contains the conditions and first elements of all our knowledge a priori," takes the place of first philosophy.[23] Existence cannot be deduced from ideas or intelligible essences; its only indicator is sensation ("Empfindung"). There is no rational ontological proof for the existence of God; being is no "real predicate" that could be added to the essential qualifications implied in the concept of God: "Sein ist offenbar kein reales Prädikat, d.i. ein Begriff von irgend etwas, was zu dem Begriffe eines Dinges hinzukommen könnte. Es ist bloss die Position eines Dinges, oder gewisser Bestimmungen an sich selbst."[24]

The Cartesian search for certainty and the Kantian replacement of ontology with transcendental philosophy have set the scene for the modern attempts to redefine and reestablish "first philosophy." Edmund Husserl's subordination of ontology to phenomenology is an example, and even Alexius von Meinong's "theory of objects" ("Gegenstandstheorie"); Meinong proposes an elaborate theory and terminology of "objectivity," that is, of entities as well as nonentities, to account for the possibility of positive and negative predication and to solve problems and paradoxes that had first been articulated in the Western tradition by Parmenides and Plato.[25]

4.

> Many volumes might be filled with the frivolous speculations concerning the nature of Being (to on, ousia, Ens, Entitas, Essentia, and the like), which have arisen from overlooking the double meaning of the word *to be*. . . . The fog which rose from this narrow spot diffused itself at an early period over the whole surface of metaphysics.[26]

John Stuart Mill's reference to the double function of *to be* as copula and verb of existence is symptomatic and programmatic: In recent and contemporary ontological debate, the focus shifts from the question "what being is" to the conditions of speaking about it and the confusions in what others have said about it. The methods of modern conceptual and linguistic analysis and the tools of symbolic logic are used to articulate semantic distinctions, to resolve traditional ontological difficulties by uncovering underlying grammatical and conceptual confusions and to eliminate meaningless questions concerning "being."[27]

According to W. V. Quine, the "ontological problem" is conspicuous by its simplicity. "It can be put in three Anglo-Saxon monosyllables: 'What is there?' It can be answered, moreover, in a word—'Everything' . . ."[28] Of course, this all-comprehensive answer leaves much "room for disagreement over cases; and so the issue has stayed alive down the centuries." What Quine calls the *issue* involves several questions: What in particular ought to be accepted as existent? What is the criterion of its acceptance? What is the meaning of "existence"? Quine does not answer these questions as such. Instead, he deals with the ontological commitment implied in various systems of thought and discourse, at the level of common sense as well as in scientific and philosophical theories. He tries to determine what they accept as existent and to produce a consistent method of how to achieve such determination. Existence in this sense, that is, as existential commitment in given bodies of discourse, is defined as "the value of a bound variable." It is implied in quantification, in terms like (*at least*) *one, some, all*—these variables of quantification provide a semantic framework that enables us to establish the ontological implications of what we and others say.[29]

Others associate the whole enterprise of ontology with certain characteristics, usually with what they consider to be defects, of the natural languages employed for the purpose. *To be* appears as a word with "odd jobs" (Wittgenstein) and deceptive functional analogies with "full verbs" that have misled philosophers into false depths. More specifically, it is the role of *being* as a noun that has been criticized; the use of *being* and *reality* as subjects of statements, or of *real* as a predicate, appears as a prime example of G. Ryle's notion of "systematically misleading expressions."[30]

A. C. Graham states: "The concept of Being is a good test for the thesis of Benjamin Whorf that the grammatical structure of language guides the formation of philosophical concepts." He sees words such as *to be,* which serve both as copula and indicator of existence and fail to distinguish between essence and existence, almost exclusively "confined to Indo-European languages." Graham contrasts this with the uses of *shih/fei* and *yu/wu* in Chinese thought; he seems to envy the good fortune of the Chinese, whose language saved them from the confusions of Western ontology. Similarly, he credits the Arabic language with an inherent distinction between essence and existence.[31] Ultimately, and especially for speakers of Indo-European languages, symbolic logic has to take care of the necessary distinctions and to overcome the deficiencies of the natural languages: "In symbolic logic the verb 'to be' dissolves into the sign of existence ($\exists$), which is not a predicate but a quantifier, and three separate copulae, the signs of identity ($=$), class membership ($\in$) and class inclusion ($\subset$)." In accordance with the views of B. Russell and others, we should not even search for a single and unitary concept of being behind these distinctions.[32]

J. W. M. Verhaar, editor of the series of studies on "the verb 'be' and its synonyms" from which the preceding quotes are taken, expresses the hope that his series "will provide some of the necessary foundational material for research in logic, the theory of knowledge and ontology."[33] What was once regarded as "first philosophy" would thus be based on, and perhaps reduced to, empirical research in linguistics.

All this has not prevented numerous attempts to renew the ideas of "first philosophy" and ontology, to redefine and resume Aristotle's project of a science of being qua being, and to "update" the Aristotelian doctrine of categories.[34] Not only Thomists and other Neo-Scholastics have continued to refer to "being qua being" and tried to determine what it means to be an entity: "For something to be an entity, it must exist and be identifiable. But to exist and be identifiable, it must have a character, a content, properties through which it could be identified and thus acknowledged as an existent."[35] Metaphysicians, linguists, and even some logicians have questioned the adequacy of Mill's and Russell's distinctions and resumed the search for an underlying unity, or at least coherence, in the uses of *to be* and its synonyms.[36]

5. What has happened to Aristotle's "science of being qua being" and Plato's perplexities? Is being still a significant topic of inquiry and perplexity? Is the "question of being" still a meaningful one? Has it ever been a meaningful question? Has there been progress? Is there scope for progress, is there a subject matter of ontology? Does being have a meaning that would be susceptible of methodic inquiry and progressive clarification? Have we gone beyond Parmenides, Plato, and Aristotle only insofar as we understand better why they were puzzled? Have we learned not to be puzzled any more? Has the modern analytical approach, has the approach of linguistic analysis reduced the "question of being" to its true and legitimate dimensions? Or is this approach a symptom of what Martin Heidegger has called the *oblivion of being?*

Heidegger's own insistence on the "question of being" has been stubborn, almost obsessive, and highly idiosyncratic. Again and again, he proclaims the significance and urgency of this question. He asserts that it is the "proper and sole theme of philosophy" and the hidden focus and destiny of the entire history of Western thought. He invokes the perplexities of Plato and Parmenides, as well as Aristotle's aporetic "science of being qua being," and calls for their rediscovery and renewal. The logical demarcation of the various functions of *to be* as copula and verb of existence, and the elimination of its "natural" ambiguity, may produce greater conceptual clarity and still amount to a further obscuration of the "question of being."[37] Looking back at the tradition of European metaphysics and Western philosophy and science in general, Heidegger sees a progressive "Seinsvergessenheit," "oblivion of being," a growing preoccupation with "entities" ("Seiendes") instead of "Being" ("Sein"), and with objectification, calculation, theoretical and technical mastery. This process culminates in the globalization of modern science and technology and the nihilism by which it is accompanied; yet at the same time, and out of the depth of oblivion, it opens a new sense and dimension of the significance and urgency of the question of being.

Heidegger's "path" has led him away from the anthropocentric focus of *Sein und Zeit* (*Being and Time,* 1927) into intense, yet tentative and elusive efforts to read the history of Western thought and the oblivion of Being as an event of Being itself and to face Being through its oblivion and concealment. Such thought is not committed to tangible results and applicable methods. It is a reaction against calculative and representational thought, against conceptual precision, a withdrawal into poetry, myth, and capricious etymologies. Its aimlessness and futility are deliberate. It does not even attempt that kind of historical and systematic clarification that we find in Heidegger's earlier statements, for instance in his *Einführung in die Metaphysik* (*Introduction to Metaphysics*), probably his most accessible contribution to the "question of being."[38]

Here, he delineates some of the characteristic features of Western thought about being, in particular the four forms of the so-called limitations of being, symptomatic correlations in which *being* has become thematic in European thought.

> Just as in the "is" we have a thoroughly familiar mode of discourse of being, so in the noun "being" we run into very definite modes of discourse that have even taken on a quality of formulas: being and becoming; being and appearance; being and thinking; being and the ought. . . . This "and" does not mean only that we casually throw in something else; no, we are adding something from which "being" is distinguished: being *and not*. . . . But in these formula-like titles we also mean something which, differentiated from being, somehow belongs intrinsically to it, if only as its Other.[39]

Heidegger finds the first and second distinctions "at the beginning of the inquiry into being," that is, in ancient Greece; the third distinction is "foreshadowed as early as the first two," but "it took its actual form only at the beginning of the modern era." And finally, "the fourth distinction . . . belongs wholly to the modern era."[40]

These four "limitations" provide significant perspectives of interpretation; but they have to be transcended by more fundamental distinctions, in particular by the correlation of being and time and the "ontological difference" between being itself and the entities (essents). In another context, Heidegger says: "This distinction is not arbitrary; rather, it is the one by which the theme of ontology and thus of philosophy itself is first of all attained. . . . We call it the *ontological difference*—the differentiation between being and beings."[41]

Heidegger himself has become a favorite target of criticism and ridicule from the side of analytical philosophy. His use and misuse of "systematically misleading expressions" is notorious. He seems to represent the consummation of all that is questionable in Western ontology. His assertion that the "question of being" is the one and only question of philosophy seems as excessive as his stubborn insistence that not only ontology, but philosophy in general, is a uniquely Greek-European phenomenon. Quite obviously, Heidegger's thought about being does not represent the "latest state" of "ontological research" or of an orderly "science of being." Instead, it epitomizes the questionability of the "question of being"; and in this sense, it illustrates the contemporary condition of ontological thinking.[42]

6. We cannot treat the history of Western ontology as the mere prehistory of its current status. Its progress has been elusive; it does not provide us with a reliable platform of "latest research." The question of being, which includes the question whether there is such a question, is still open. We do not know what being is; nor do we know how much sense it makes to ask this question. We are not sure of the direction of Western thought about being. We cannot discount the possibility of losses and obscurations.

What does this mean for the study of non-Western ontologies and traditions of thought about being which leave us without the guidance of our own familiar ontological terminology? How does it affect our approach to the Indian tradition of thought about being? Does it mean that there is no direction for our following investigations, and that they will be without philosophical commitment? What can, what should, we expect? Can we expect genuine discoveries and clarifications from the Indian texts? Should we expect nothing more than exotic cases of conceptual and grammatical confusion and exemplifications of linguistic and cultural relativity? Do these texts deal with questions that are still significant for us? Can they teach us about different questions and about other types of significance? Have we gone beyond the Indian questions and answers, or may we hope to rediscover dimensions of the problem of being that have been neglected, obscured, or buried by the development and ostensible progress of Western philosophy and science? In what sense are we open for the Indian answers and questions and for a reexamination of our own premises? Can we expect to clarify our own tradition of ontological thought, its meaning and limits, by comparing and contrasting it with the Indian tradition? Can comparison teach us about the unity and identity of the question of being or only about a variety of human approaches and confusions? Will the comparative study of ontologies ultimately liberate us from any attachment to "being itself" and to the unity and identity of the "question of being"?

> Just as the botanist divides the plants into classes and investigates the laws of their development, so the analytic investigator of philosophy has to search for the types of world views and recognize the lawful nature of their formation. Such a comparative approach raises the human mind above the confidence (a confidence rooted in its own limiting conditions) to have grasped in any of these world views truth itself.[43]

Is such relativistic detachment the goal of comparison? Should we try to avoid this kind of comparison and focus on Indian thought as such? We cannot repeat ancient Indian thought and self-understanding; we cannot rethink it in its own context and horizon. Can we rethink it in a way that does justice to its own aspirations *insofar as* it affects and redirects our own thought? Can ancient Indian thought *live* in the medium of modern Western thinking? Does it have a dormant potential that we might try to actualize, which would then provide our own thought with new perspectives and directions?

7. Whatever our answer to these questions may be, it is our first responsibility to understand the Indian statements. But this in itself is a complex and elusive process. It requires, first of all, much learning, familiarization and assimilation. We have to be able to translate the texts into our own languages; we have to listen to them as carefully and patiently as possible; we have to be aware of their traditional cultural context and background. But we also have to be aware of our own background; we have to comprehend the Indian texts in accordance with our own modes of thought and discourse. We have to explore their meaning by using the means of interpretation and analysis available in our natural languages, as well as those developed by Western philosophical thought. Mere familiarization and assimilation are not enough; this has to be supplemented by conceptual analysis and clarification. We are not just dealing with words. We have to think about what we mean by our own words, as well as about the meaning of the original terms we are trying to translate and comprehend.

The relationship and transition between familiarization and clarification is complex and elusive. Clarification implies a commitment to objective standards of precision and analysis. It is not just assimilation to one's own context and level of understanding. But does it imply the possession of a superior level of insight and understanding? Does it imply genuine progress beyond those ideas and doctrines which are the object of clarification? Of course, we have to recall our earlier observation that ontology does not provide us with a secure platform of latest research. We may, indeed, have more efficient tools of analysis. But this does not mean that we know more about being than Plato, Aristotle, or the great thinkers of ancient India, or that we have surpassed and superseded their questions and insights. Nor does it mean that our ontological terms and concepts will reduce the Indian concepts to their true and ultimate meaning.

What is more, in dealing with Indian thought we are dealing with a vast tradition which has had its own origins, undergone its own peculiar transformations, and developed its own characteristic tensions between past and present. Without exaggerating the distance, we have to be aware of the difference: In dealing with India, we are not dealing with our own past. This is a very simple and obvious fact. Yet there has been a strong, if not pervasive tendency in the European historiography of philosophy to relegate Indian (and "Oriental") thought in toto to the past or even to the prehistory of European philosophy. This tendency, which has precedents in Greek thought and doxography, has found its most powerful and provocative expression in the system of Hegel.[44] In a less obvious fashion, the retrospective and subordinating perspective is still widespread in the post-Hegelian approaches to non-Western traditions. In a sense, it pervades the whole enterprise of "understanding" not just the past, but also all foreign traditions; that is, the attempt to explore what they really mean,[45] to reveal their implied structures, premises, and intentions. Implicitly or explicitly, this entails the idea of a privileged viewpoint, a higher level or more comprehensive horizon of awareness and reflection. We cannot simply discard this perspective; to some extent, it has become factually unavoidable. But we have to be aware of its background and historical ramifications.

More recently, the advocates of "comparative philosophy" have tried to rectify the inadequacies of historical *sub*ordination and replace or supplement it with a *co*ordinating method which places its objects, that is, the philosophies produced by different cultural traditions, on an equal level.[46] "Comparative philosophy" is still in a nascent state; there is no reason to question its great potential and promise for the future. But once again, we have to be aware that there is a problem concerning the standpoint of the observer. Its neutrality cannot simply be declared. The "comparative method," as an explicit project, has its roots in certain specific constellations of modern Western thought. Although it was frequently associated with anti-Hegelian movements and sentiments and rejected by Hegel himself, its freedom from Hegelian premises and its intercultural neutrality and universality should not be taken for granted.[47]

8. Is there a truly common ground for a comparison of different traditions of thought and a neutral, universal medium through which they can communicate? One important recent suggestion is that such a common basis is provided by logical and linguistic analysis and exemplified by the methods of modern analytical philosophy of the Anglo-Saxon type.[48] As a matter of fact, the claim has been made that these methods, in particular the use of symbolic logic, are "separated from the restrictions of the various existing languages," as well as the traditions by which they are used, and conducive to a truly universal understanding of the different philosophical traditions.[49]

Once again, we have to see the merits as well as the inherent limits of this approach. We should not underrate the extraordinary instrumental value of modern formal and analytical methods, including symbolic logic, in the interpretation of philosophical texts and traditions; their uses may be compared to those of a microscope. Nor should we minimize the extent to which the formal and analytical dimension is actually present within the Indian tradition; in its own way, this tradition calls for such instruments of interpretation. In a sense, analysis itself is a hermeneutic response to Indian thought and a manner of fulfilling its own inherent aspirations. We may also acknowledge the potential of orderly scientific progress, of conceptual refinement in the development of logic and analytical philosophy. Insofar, it is very appropriate to approach Indian as well as Western forms of reasoning and argumentation from the vantage point of "latest research." However, we should not construe the perfection of formal methods as the implicit telos of Indian philosophy or as the goal and essence of philosophy in general. In particular, we should not take it for granted that conceptual differentiation, terminological refinement, and the perfection of our tools of analysis constitutes progress in the "science of being." Nor should we use Indian and other texts about being as mere occasions for the employment and display of the "latest achievements" in logic and epistemology.[50] Clarity and precision are indispensable; yet they have to be pursued with caution and discretion. Analysis and the search for conceptual precision can be obtrusive and interfere with the task of translating and understanding, and with our obligation to respect the Indian tradition in its own context and dimensions. A certain well-tempered vagueness may, indeed, be a hermeneutic virtue.

We have to be aware of the place of formal methods within the whole texture of the Indian philosophical tradition. Precision, analysis, and conceptual differentiation play a very significant role in Indian philosophical thought. Yet it cannot be measured by these standards alone. It has also produced an extremely rich, and ultimately more powerful, tradition of transcending analysis, differentiation, and conceptualization. And this cannot be dismissed as mysticism and irrationalism; it is itself motivated and guided by thought and reflection and by an intense awareness of the limits of reasoning and argumentation.[51]

At the end, we do not have a well-defined method, and perhaps not even a definite perspective, for our exploration of the Indian texts and teachings. Our procedure will be eclectic. We will ask different kinds of questions and borrow our heuristic and exegetic devices from different sources. Whenever it seems appropriate, we will try to derive interpretive perspectives and hermeneutic guidance from the Indian tradition. But, of course, such derivation itself requires understanding and interpretation.

Conceptual devices that have been developed by Western philosophical thought will be indispensable tools of translation, interpretation, and analysis; but we will have to use them cautiously. We have to be constantly aware that our own ontological concepts and premises are problematic. We have to be willing and able to question, modify, or withhold familiar concepts and conceptual distinctions. We cannot simply "apply" such notions as substance, quality and universal, essence and existence, actuality and potentiality, or even extension and intension. We must be ready to see them not just as tools of analysis or interpretation, but also as open problems and objects of comparison.

Using such terms does not mean that we know the true and precise meaning of their Indian counterparts; we can only say that we are dealing with comparable areas of thought, debate, and potential confusion. Inevitably, exegesis and translation will lead us into these open areas of philosophical reflection and debate. On the other hand, historical and philological problems will often interfere with conceptual problems. Philology, exegesis, and philosophical reflection may seem to be inseparable; we cannot always be sure what we are doing. This may be frustrating; but it can also be a philosophical challenge.

Chapter 1: Notes

1. See *Sophist*, 244a (. . . ἡμεῖς δὲ πρὸ τοῦ μὲν ᾠόμεθα, νῦν δ'ἠπορήκαμεν). Heidegger cites this passage from the *Sophist* in the prologue to *Sein und Zeit* (1927).

2. *Sophist*, 237a; for the expression "father Parmenides," see 241d; on the γιγαντομαχία περὶ τῆς οὐσίας, see 246af.

3. See *Metaphysics*, 1028b: καὶ δὴ καὶ τὸ πάλαι τε καὶ νῦν καὶ ἀεὶ ζητούμενον καὶ ἀεὶ ἀπορούμενον, τί τὸ ὄν. For an analysis and interpretation of this statement, see M. Frede and G. Patzig, *Aristoteles, 'Metaphysik Z'. Text, Übersetzung und Kommentar* (Munich, 1988), vol. 2, p. 24. Frede and Patzig emphasized that the twofold ἀεὶ should be construed in a distributive manner with both πάλαι and νῦν, and that there is no need to read this as a prediction that ontology would forever be aporetic.

4. *Metaphysics*, 1003a: ἐπιστήμη τις ἣ θεωρεῖ τὸ ὂν ᾗ ὄν, καὶ τὰ τούτῳ ὑπάρχοντα καθ' αὑτό.

5. See *Philosophia prima sive Ontologia* (Frankfurt, 1730; 2d ed., 1736), ed. J. Ecole (Darmstadt, 1962), p. 1. In his German works, Wolff used the term *Grundwissenschaft;* see *Hist. Wb. Phil.*, vol. 3, pp. 925ff. The oldest recorded usage of the word *ontology* is found in R. Goclenius, *Lexicon philosophicum* (Frankfurt, 1613; reprint, 1964), art. "Abstractio" (p. 16, margin: "ὀντολογία seu philosophia de ente"). J. Clauberg used the term *ontosophy;* see *Metaphysica de ente, quae rectius Ontosophia* (Amsterdam, 1656).

6. For discussion of the relation between the two meanings of *first philosophy,* and on the role of *theology* in Aristotle's thought, see H. Flashar, *Die Philosophie der Antike,* vol. 3, pp. 376–389; H. Happ, *Hyle. Studien zum aristotelischen Materie-Begriff* (Berlin, 1971), pp. 316 ff.

7. Cf. F. Brentano, *Von der mannigfachen Bedeutung des Seienden nach Aristoteles* (Freiburg, 1862; reprint Hildesheim, 1960), pp. 6ff. (English trans. R. George; Berkeley, 1976). For further literature on the "meaning of being" and its basic divisions in Aristotle's *Categories* and *Metaphysics*, see H. Flashar, *Die Philosophie der Antike*, vol. 3, pp. 294f.; 310 ff.; 437 ff.

8. For characteristically different approaches to Aristotle's thought about being, see J. Owens, *The Doctrine of Being in the Aristotelian Metaphysics* (Toronto, 1951; 3d ed., 1978); P. Aubenque, *Le problème de l' être chez Aristote* (Paris, 1962; 2d ed., 1977); G. Patzig, "Theologie und Ontologie in der Metaphysik des Aristoteles," *Kant-Studien* 52 (1960–61):185–205 (English trans. in *Articles on Aristotle*, vol. 3. *Metaphysics*, ed. J. Barnes, M. Schofield, and R. Sorabji (London, 1979).

9. Cf. E. Booth, *Aristotelian Aporetic Ontology in Islamic and Christian Thinkers* (Cambridge, 1983), p. 38: "Whatever is aporetic in Aristotle is made soluble by its direct dependence on higher realities and therefore higher certainties." See also Plotinus, *Enneads* VI, 9, 2; 6; and J. M. Rist, *Plotinus. The Road to Reality* (Cambridge, 1967).

10. Cf. *Hist. Wb. Phil.*, vol. 2, articles "Esse commune/esse subsistens" and "Essenz, essentia"; J. de Vries, *Grundbegriffe der Scholastik* (Darmstadt, 1980; 2d ed., 1983); G. P. Klubertanz, *St. Thomas Aquinas on Analogy* (Chicago, 1960).

11. Cf. R. Eucken, *Geschichte der philosophischen Terminologie* (Leipzig, 1879; reprint Hildesheim, 1964), pp. 51ff.; E. Gilson, *L'être et l'essence*, 2d ed. (Paris, 1972), pp. 339ff. For the interpretation of Aristotle's τὸ τί ἦν εἶναι, see M. Frede and G. Patzig (cited in n. 3), pp. 34f.

12. E. Gilson, *L'être et l'essence*, pp. 344ff.; P. Hadot, *Porphyre et Victorinus* (Paris, 1968), pp. 267ff.; *Hist. Wb. Phil.*, vol. 2, art. "Existenz, existentia."

13. Cf. S. M. Afnan, *Philosophical Terminology in Arabic and Persian* (Leiden, 1964); F. Shehadi, "Arabic and 'To Be'," Verhaar, vol. 4, 112–125; A.-M. Goichon, *Vocabulaires comparés d'Aristote et d'Ibn Sīna* (Paris, 1939); K. Georr, *Les Catégories d'Aristote dans leurs versions syro-arabes* (Beirut, 1948); A. C. Graham, "'Being' in Linguistics and Philosophy," Verhaar, vol. 5, 225–233.

14. Cf. R. Eucken (cited in n. 11), p. 68; Duns Scotus also introduced *actualitas* and *haecceitas*. A. C. Graham (cited in n. 13), p. 230, suggests that *quidditas* was modeled on Arabic *māhiyya* but concedes that this may entail chronological problems.

15. Cf. R. Eucken, pp. 118ff.; B. Schmoldt, *Die deutsche Begriffssprache Meister Eckharts* (Heidelberg, 1954); K. Albert, *Eckharts Lehre vom Sein* (Saarbrücken, 1976); P. Piur, *Studien zur sprachlichen Würdigung Christian Wolffs* (Halle, 1903).

16. Cf. J. Moreau, "L'être et l'essence dans la philosophie d'Aristote," *Autour d'Aristote, Recueil d'études de philosophie ancienne et médiévale offert à Monseig-*

neur A. Mansion (Louvain, 1955), pp. 181–204; G. Smith, "Avicenna and the Possibles," *New Scholasticism* 17 (1943): 340–357 (especially 348); P. Morewedge, *The Metaphysica of Avicenna (ibn Sīnā)* (New York, 1973). See also the collection of articles in *Philosophies of Existence—Ancient and Medieval*, ed. P. Morewedge (New York, 1982).

17. D. J. B. Hawkins, *Being and Becoming* (New York, 1954), pp. 36f.; Hawkins' study is not always adequate.

18. On the problems concerning radical contingency and the origins of the idea of a "creation from nothing," see, for instance, G. Scholem, *Über einige Grundbegriffe des Judentums* (Frankfurt, 1970), pp. 53–89.

19. Cf. E. Booth, *Aristotelian Aporetic Ontology* (cited in n. 9); E. Gilson, *Being and Some Philosophers*, 2d ed. (Toronto, 1952), pp. 188f.; see also n. 10 above.

20. C. Wolff, *Philosophia prima sive Ontologia* (cited in n. 5), § 134f.; 174.

21. See n. 13; 16 above.

22. I. Kant, *Kritik der reinen Vernunft*, A247 (B304).

23. I. Kant, *Welches sind die wirklichen Fortschritte, die die Metaphysik seit Leibnizens und Wolffs Zeiten in Deutschland gemacht hat?* ("Preisschrift 1791"), A11 ("weil sie die Bedingungen und ersten Elemente aller unsrer Erkenntnis a priori enthält").

24. *Kritik der reinen Vernunft*, A598 (B626). Kant adds that no existential conclusions ought to be drawn from the use of the copula.

25. Cf. J. N. Findlay, *Meinong's Theory of Objects and Values*, 2d ed. (Oxford, 1963).

26. J. S. Mill, *Logic* I,4,1.

27. Cf. B. Russell, *The Principles of Mathematics* (London, 1903), p. 64 n.: "The word *is* is terribly ambiguous, and great care is necessary not to confound its various meanings." See also R. Carnap, *Meaning and Necessity*, 2d ed. (Chicago, 1956), pp. 205ff.; E. K. Specht, *Sprache und Sein* (Berlin, 1967).

28. *From a Logical Point of View*, 2d ed. (Cambridge, Mass., 1961), p. 1.

29. Cf. ibid., p. 15: "We look to bound variables in connection with ontology not in order to know what there is, but in order to know what a given remark or doctrine, ours or someone else's, *says* there is."

30. Cf. G. Ryle, "Systematically Misleading Expressions," *Proceedings of the Aristotelian Society* 32 (1931/32): 139–170, especially 143ff: "Quasi-ontological statements"; see also E. K. Specht, *Sprache und Sein*, pp. 22f.

31. See A. C. Graham, "'Being in Classical Chinese," Verhaar, vol. 1, pp. 1–39; Chinese, according to Graham, "does not permit one to make these particular mistakes" (36). See also "'Being' in Linguistics and Philosophy: A Preliminary Inquiry," Verhaar, vol. 5, pp. 225–233, especially 228f.: "It is a misplaced compliment to credit Al-Fārābī (died 950) and Ibn Sīnā (Avicenna, 980–1037) with the discovery of the ontological difference between essence and existence; it was impossible for an Arab to confuse them." For a strong rejection of such views, see the statements by A. H. Basson and D. J. O'Connor, "Language and Philosophy: Some Suggestions for an Empirical Approach," *Philosophy* 22 (1947): 49–65, especially 61: "There is absolutely nothing to suggest that a 'better language' might solve our philosophical problems for us."

32. See A. C. Graham, Verhaar, vol. 5, p. 233; B. Russell, *Introduction to Mathematical Philosophy* (London, 1919), pp. 170ff.

33. Verhaar makes this statement in the "editorial preface" that appears at the beginning of every volume in his series.

34. See, for instance, R. Grossmann, *The Categorial Structure of the World* (Bloomington, 1983), p. xv.

35. P. Butchvarov, *Being qua Being* (Bloomington, 1979), p. 122.

36. Cf. C. Kahn, "The Greek Verb 'To Be' and the Concept of Being," *Foundations of Language* 2 (1966): 245–265; idem, *The Verb 'Be' in Ancient Greek* (Dordrecht, 1973; Verhaar, vol. 6). Kahn refers specifically and extensively to the "ontology" of the logician S. Leśniewski, and also to E. Gilson's interpretation of the verb *be* (cf. ch. 1, § 3f.). Kahn gives a very cautious and thoughtful assessment of the influence of natural languages on philosophical thought.

37. See, for instance, *Sein und Zeit (Being and Time)*, pp. 1f.; *Die Grundprobleme der Phänomenologie* (Frankfurt, 1975), p. 3 (trans. A. Hofstadter, *The Basic Problems of Phenomenology;* Bloomington, 1982, p. 11: "We assert now that *being is the proper and sole theme of philosophy*"); *Die Grundbegriffe der Metaphysik* (Frankfurt, 1983), pp. 468–483.

38. *Einführung in die Metaphysik,* based upon university lectures delivered in 1935, was first published in 1953; trans. R. Manheim, *An Introduction to Metaphysics* (New York, 1961; 1st ed., New Haven, 1959).

39. *An Introduction to Metaphysics,* p. 79.

40. Ibid., pp. 80ff.

41. *The Basic Problems of Phenomenology* (cited in n. 37), p. 17 (§4); cf. pp. 318ff. (§22).

42. The East Asian, specifically Japanese, reception of Heidegger has been extraordinary: see *Heidegger and Asian Thought,* ed. G. Parkes (Honolulu, 1987);

Japan und Heidegger, ed. H. Buchner (Sigmaringen, 1989). For a penetrating and sensitive response from one of the most subtle thinkers of modern India, see J. L. Mehta, *Martin Heidegger: The Way and the Vision* (Honolulu, 1976).

43. See W. Dilthey, *Die geistige Welt*, vol. 1, ed. G. Misch (Stuttgart and Göttingen, 1961), p. 380; translated in *India and Europe*, p. 430.

44. Cf. *India and Europe*, ch. 6.

45. Cf. ibid., pp. 166f.

46. Cf. ibid., pp. 422ff. (on B.N. Seal).

47. Cf. ibid., pp. 426ff. (on A. Comte and P. Masson-Oursel), 433.

48. We may mention here the work of D. H. H. Ingalls and some of his disciples, in particular B. K. Matilal.

49. See H. Nakamura, "Buddhist Logic Expounded by Means of Symbolic Logic," *JIBSt* 7 (1958–59): 395–374, especially 394. See also the pioneering contributions by S. Schayer, especially "Studien zur indischen Logik", parts 1 and 2 (1932–33); "Über die Methode der Nyāya-Forschung" (1933) in *O filozofowaniu Hindusów* (Warsaw, 1988), pp. 410–432.

50. See, for instance, F. Staal, *Universals* (Chicago, 1988), pp. 59–139.

51. Cf. *Tradition and Reflection*, ch. 5; and later, Chapter 10.

2

The Question of Being in India: General Historical Perspectives

1. There is no equivalent to the Aristotelian project of a "science of being qua being" in the Indian philosophical tradition, nor to the Platonic perplexity about being and nonbeing; nor is there an explicit counterpart to Wolff's conception of "ontology." Yet being is one of the central and pervasive themes of Indian thought. It is the object of intense reflection, discussion, and disagreement, and a catalyst of debate among the competing schools of Hinduism, Buddhism, and Jainism. Although it is true that there are no systematic monographs on ontology, there is a rich, coherent, and clearly identifiable documentation of thought and debate about being. For identifying Indian ontological literature, our first lead has to come from the thematic use of certain words; that is, the Indian (primarily Sanskrit) synonyms or cognates of the verb *to be* and their various derivatives. Sanskrit is an Indo-European language, and it has several roots etymologically related to the Western ontological vocabulary.

Two verbal roots are usually presented as lexicographic equivalents of *to be: as/asti* (corresponding to Latin *est,* Greek *estí,* English *is,* etc.) and *bhū/bhavati* (which has an intriguing etymological kinship with Greek *phýō/phýsis.* Both *bhū* and *as* have more prominent existential and veridical functions than *to be; bhū* has, moreover, dynamic implications. Accordingly, they are commonly treated as verbs expressing a peculiar kind of process or action. Nonetheless, both *bhū* and *as* may also take the function of copula, although the copula is generally quite rare in Sanskrit and particularly uncommon in the nominal style of classical theoretical and philosophical literature. Here as well as in related cases, the differences between Sanskrit and other Indo-European languages are a matter of degree, not of principle.[1]

The nominal derivatives of the roots *as* and *bhū,* together with numerous compound word formations, account for the major part of the Indian ontological terminology. For *as,* we have *sat, satya, sattva, sattā, astitva,* etc.; for *bhū,* we have *bhāva, bhava, bhāvin, bhavitṛ, bhāvana, bhavana, bhūta, bhūti, bhāvatva,* etc.; and as relevant compounds, or words with prefixes, we may mention *svabhāva, sadbhāva, sanmātra, sattāsambandha, svarūpasattā, svātmasattva, sambhava, udbhava.* In addition to *as* and *bhū,* there are various other significant roots, such as *vṛt* (noun: *vṛtti,* referring to "occurrence" in a temporalized and localized sense) and *vas* (nouns: *vastu, vāsana;* referring to "dwelling," that is, a durable presence, and etymologically related to German *gewesen* and *Wesen,* that is, "essence," and the English past tense *was*). Together with various other terms, for instance abstracts from words meaning "this," "that," or "thus" (*idaṃtā, tattva, tathātva, tathatā*), and numerous increasingly complex compounds and abstracts, these terms constitute an ontological vocabulary that is no less extensive, diversified, scholastic, and ambiguous than its Western counterpart.[2] In dealing with this terminology, we have to be ready to revise and adjust our own terminological premises and expectations.

Within the domain of the philosophical systems, the entire terminology of "genesis," "change," "manifestation," "actuality/potentiality" (i.e., *utpatti, pariṇāma, vyakti, śakti,* etc.) is, of course, related to, and relevant for, the ontological debate.[3]

2. Other terms and concepts are more or less directly affiliated with, or related to, this primary vocabulary of "being." First of all, we have to refer to the rich and complex terminology of nonbeing and negation, which is inseparable from that of being and assertion. From an early time, *asat, abhāva,* and so forth, as well as *tuchya, tuccha, alīka,* and so on have played a role comparable and supplementary to that of their positive counterparts; in some respects, it is even more basic.[4]

Another set of relevant ideas may be described as "horizon concepts"; that is, as concepts or mythical projections under which being itself is subsumed or which are said to constitute, include, and transcend both being and nonbeing. As examples from different periods and partly mythical, partly philosophical contexts, we may mention *kāla,* "time," *brahman, ātman, skambha,* various deities or divine principles, but also "suchness" (*tattva*), the concrete entity (*vastu*), "object of knowledge" (*prameya*), and "object of speech" or "meaning" (*abhidheya*).[5]

It would be very inappropriate to dismiss the various mythological and theological ideas that have been associated with being, nonbeing, and their transcendence as philosophically and "ontologically" irrelevant. They may, indeed, be mythical, culturally bound, untranslatable, and not part of an abstract, universal ontology. But the role of abstractness, universality, translatability is itself a problem for any comparative and transcultural approach to the question of being. Moreover, the separation of mythology, theology, and philosophy is elusive not only in the older Indian texts relating to the question of being, but also in various later traditions. The tension and relationship between "mythological," "culturally bound," "untranslatable" ideas and the "abstract" ontological terms is thus a major historical and philosophical issue. In particular, this is true when we are dealing with such central, fundamental, and "typically Indian" notions as *brahman, ātman, akṣara* and even *dharma.* The "ontological" significance of these terms is undeniable, although it is obviously different from that of *sat, sattā,* and *bhāva.*[6]

The meaning of words like *brahman* and so on is not only of cultural and historical interest, just as the meaning of *sat, bhāva,* and so forth, is not of purely philosophical interest. Even in its seemingly abstract notions, Indian ontology, or the Indian approach to the question of being, is a symptom of the Indian tradition.

Whatever its general conceptual significance may be, it is also the reflection of specific cultural and historical realities.

Finally, we have to refer to the extensive literature that exists in non-Indian translations, especially in Buddhism. It may be helpful and sometimes indispensable to consider the terminology in those languages, in particular Chinese and Tibetan, into which ontologically relevant texts were translated. For this, we have also to be aware of the linguistic peculiarities of these languages, their different capabilities for ontological distinctions, and so forth. For instance, Tibetan distinguishes more clearly than Sanskrit between *to be* as copula (*yin*) and *to exist* (*yod*), as well as between their negations (*min; med*). This may remind us of the relationship between Greek and Arabic.[7]

3. Relevant texts come from the entire recorded history of Indian thought, beginning with the Veda, and in particular from the classical systems of Hinduism, Buddhism, and Jainism. Being becomes thematic at various levels and in different contexts, for instance in debates and controversies concerning the status of certain representative entities, such as the soul, God, substances, universals. Does the soul exist, and in what sense? Do wholes exist over and above their parts? What would that mean? What do entities as entities have in common? What does it mean to be an entity? Do things remain identical in time? Is being compatible with change and impermanence? Does it imply change? This question is the topic of vast debates between the Buddhist process philosophers and their Hindu opponents, just like the question of the ontological status of universals and related issues.[8]

Being becomes also thematic in linguistic and grammatical analysis. What do the words *to be, being, entity,* and so forth imply for those who use them? How do *as* and *bhū* function as verbs? Do they denote acts or activities, just like other verbs? How should it be explained grammatically, semantically, and metaphysically that we posit something, think and speak in terms of *being* even if we think and speak about what *is not?*[9]

What is an acceptable criterion to distinguish being from nonbeing, reality from illusion? How does real existence relate to, or differ from, being thought, meant, or perceived? How does it relate to truth, meaning, and practical efficiency? In the eleventh century, the Buddhist philosopher Ratnakīrti presented a list of attempts to define being (*sattva*): "inherence of (the universal) reality" (*sattāsamavāya*); "being subject to origination, decay and stability" (*utpādavyayadhrauvyayogitva*); "being the domain (and condition) of valid cognition" (*pramāṇaviṣayatva*), and others. He rejected all of them and advocated instead the Buddhist notion of *arthakriyākāritva,* "effectiveness," "making a difference in practice," "functioning toward an effect or purpose."[10] In his view, this definition was not just theoretically superior to the other definitions; but it was also the one that all the other schools unknowingly and unwillingly recognized: Whatever somebody may say about the theoretical nature of reality, practical efficiency is the criterion one adopts when it comes to deciding what to accept as real and what not. This implies a far-reaching critique of the ordinary worldly orientation toward reality that stands in the way of final liberation; but it also implies a critique of all attempts to establish entities and their being in a purely theoretical fashion. Theory and conceptualization themselves appear as projections of a primeval desire or thirst (*tṛṣṇā*), a will to posit and preserve one's self and identity and to find identity and durability in the world. This Buddhist approach, especially in its Mahāyāna versions, has significant parallels in the tradition of Advaita Vedānta.[11]

At this point, there is no need for an explicit comparison with Heideggerian ideas, in particular with his critique of the role of representational and objectifying thinking; nor do we have to discuss the applicability of his four "limitations" (being and becoming; being and appearance; being and thinking; being and the ought).[12] There is, however, no good reason to adopt Heidegger's own exclusion of his ideas from the interpretation of non-Western traditions.[13]

4. In accordance with the general character of the Indian tradition, there are no such conspicuous and programmatic opening events in Indian ontology as the declarations of Parmenides, Plato, and Aristotle. Indian thought about being, just as Indian philosophy in general, develops gradually out of mythical and anonymous sources. In the oldest extant documents of presystematic and pre-Buddhistic thought in India, that is, in the Vedas and older Upaniṣads,[14] being and nonbeing (*sat* and *asat*) emerge as themes of inquiry and speculation in cosmogonic contexts; that is, in connection with myths and speculations concerning the origin and primeval status of the world in which we live.[15]

J. A. B. van Buitenen and others have suggested that the first reference to being (*sat*) in such cosmogonic contexts, that is, the beginning of the so-called *sadvidyā*, constitutes the transition from a "mythological stage to a more or less philosophical one," or simply the beginning of philosophy in India.[16] The sixth chapter of the *Chāndogya Upaniṣad* contains the most famous and familiar Vedic-Upaniṣadic text on being. The teacher Uddālaka Āruṇi, instructing his son Śvetaketu, declares that nothing could have arisen from what is not and that the world, insofar as it is, must have its origin and its unity in being (*sat*) itself:

> In the beginning, my dear, this world was just Being (*sat*), one only, without a second. To be sure, some people say: "In the beginning this world was just Nonbeing (*a-sat*), one only, without a second; from that Nonbeing Being was produced." But verily, my dear, whence could this be? . . . How from Nonbeing could Being be produced? On the contrary, my dear, in the beginning this world was just Being, one only, without a second.[17]

The attempt to identify the *sadvidyā* that this text epitomizes as the beginning of Indian philosophy, or even the very idea that there is such an identifiable beginning, must remain questionable. What is beyond question is the fact that this is one of the most seminal texts in the history of Indian thought. Yet it is by no means representative of Vedic thought about being, or even of the Upaniṣadic way of dealing with being. The text itself indicates that it was preceded by earlier discussions and speculations about being, nonbeing, and the origin of "this world". The theory of the origination of being from nonbeing, to which it refers and which it rejects, is, in fact, found in the older Upaniṣads (including the third chapter of the Chāndogya Upaniṣad) as well as the Brāhmaṇas and even in the *Ṛgveda*.[18] This theory not only precedes Uddālaka Āruṇi's doctrine, but constitutes its indispensable background and counterpart. Whether we call it *philosophy* or not, this elusive and discarded cosmogony from nonbeing is of great significance for the beginnings of Indian thought about being. In a sense, it is more fundamental than the "theory of being" (*sadvidyā*) that van Buitenen tried to identify as the origin of Indian philosophy.

5. *Ṛgveda* X, 72 and a variety of other sources up to and beyond *Chāndogya Upaniṣad* III, 19 teach that nonbeing, *asat*, "was" in the beginning, and that *sat* arose from nonbeing.[19] What does this mean? In what sense does it differ from Uddālaka's position? It has been emphasized that the origin from *asat* should not be interpreted as a creation from nothing (*creatio ex nihilo*) and that *sat* and *asat* should not be taken as "existence" and "nonexistence" in an abstract sense. Various authors (for instance, H. Oertel) suggest "chaos" as an equivalent for *asat;* that is, an undifferentiated, unstructured substrate out of which the structured and orderly world of *sat,* a cosmos with natural and moral regularities, arose. The contrast between *sat* and *asat* would thus amount to the contrast between the determinate and the indeterminate, the differentiated and the undifferentiated.[20] W. N. Brown even suggests that *asat* is the Ṛgvedic equivalent of "hell"; that is, the chaotic underworld out of which the Gods formed the structured cosmos.[21]

J. A. B. van Buitenen emphasizes that one should not credit the Vedic authors with an abstract notion of existence; in his view, this would be an anachronism. After adopting the view that the "first occurrence of the term *sat* in cosmogonical Veda texts" marks the transition from mythology to philosophy, he states: "On the other hand, the strictly philosophical import of the notion of *sat* should not be exaggerated: It is anachronistic to render it as 'being' in the sense of *esse.* It is a very concrete term . . ."[22] Van Buitenen's statements show that he sees abstraction as the proper and constitutive achievement of philosophy. The Vedic-Upaniṣadic conception of *sat* appears as a significant, yet incomplete, step toward abstraction; it is philosophical only to the extent that it is abstract.

Is this adequate? Can being as a principle of cosmogony be measured by the standard of abstraction? Cosmogony deals with origins, not with abstractions. It is concerned with the origin of what there is, not with its common denominator. The question is: What was all this in the beginning? Where does it come from? How did it come into existence, or into its present state of being? The answers vary. *Sat* and *asat* appear among many other, more or less "concrete" examples; they are not even the most frequent or conspicuous ones. *Prajāpati, ātman, brahman,* the "one" (*eka*) and the "mind" (*manas*) are among the alternatives; they all appear as predicate nominatives in the familiar formula "this was in the beginning . . ." (*idam agra āsīt*).[23]

What does the expression *in the beginning* mean? How does the concept of *sat* relate to those concepts with which it competes or which it replaces? Is it really a progression in terms of abstractness? What does it mean that this world "was" (*āsīt*) something else in the beginning; that is, something different from what it is now? To what extent was it this world, to what extent was it something else? What kind of transformation has taken place? Is that which "was" in the beginning no longer present in the world as it is now, or does it remain present as its underlying cause and substrate? If this should be the case, the question what this world was in the beginning would amount to the question what it ultimately is; that is, what its irreducible substance or substrate is. It would correspond to the kind of question that was asked by the Pre-Socratics, such as Thales, Anaximander, and Anaximenes.

6. According to the sixth chapter of the *Chāndogya Upaniṣad,* this is, indeed, the meaning of *agra āsīt:* The beginning is the lasting essence, the root, the basis, the ultimate support (*pratiṣṭhā, mūla, āyatana*) of what there is. Being itself is the ultimate irreducible substance in which all entities are a priori contained and with which they are ultimately identical. Nothing can ever come into being; in reality, there is no creation. Cosmogony amounts to cosmology of substance. Brahman itself is often presented as the ultimate everlasting "support" (*pratiṣṭhā*).[24] There seems to be no room for genuine cosmogony. This is even more obvious in conjunction with the cyclical way of thinking, which came to dominate post-Vedic Indian thought and which regards the cosmos as an infinite sequence of periodic destructions and regenerations.

The so-called *satkāryavāda,* that is, the theory of the preexistence of the effect or product in its cause,[25] is the systematic unfolding of Uddālaka Āruṇi's substantialism and eternalism. But even the rejection of such preexistence by the *asatkāryavāda* traditions does not provide a genuine alternative: It recognizes only temporarily "new" configurations of preexistent constituents, such as the atoms. It is just a different type of substantialism and eternalism.[26] If we adopt the familiar interpretation of *asat* as primeval chaos, undifferentiated, unstructured substrate, and so on, the more ancient Vedic cosmogonies from "nonbeing" would not provide an alternative either. The position of *Chāndogya Upaniṣad* VI would not really be the rejection of an entirely different cosmogony, that is, of a *creatio ex nihilo,* but it could be reduced to a disagreement concerning the semantics of *sat* and *asat.* The apparent introduction of a new cosmogony would amount to a change in the meaning of *being* and *nonbeing.* The cosmogony of Uddālaka Āruṇi would thus not be incompatible with the kind of cosmogony he rejected.

This is, indeed, the interpretation of Śaṅkara and his followers, as well as of other harmonizers of the Vedic teachings. The apparent contradiction is resolved by assigning the different statements to two different levels of discourse and truth, with a corresponding variation in the meaning of *sat* and *asat*. *Asat*, "nonbeing", as used in *Chāndogya* III and elsewhere, simply means unevolved, undifferentiated, not particularized into different "names and forms" (*avyākṛtanāmarūpa*, etc.).[27] In *Chāndogya* VI, *sat* itself is undifferentiated pure being, "prior" to entering into the process of particularization.[28] In both cases, we would deal with an absolute, irreducible foundation.

The apparent absence of a genuine notion of creation, that is, of *creatio ex nihilo*, and of a corresponding notion of the uniqueness and contingency of cosmic and individual existence has led to sweeping statements about the general character of Indian thought, which has been characterized as fundamentally substantialist and cyclical. This has been contrasted with the biblical idea of creation, and with Judaeo-Christian linear notions of time and history. We do not have to discuss the ambiguous and problematic role of "creation from nothing" in Western thought and specifically in the Bible.[29] Instead, we have to refer once again to the Vedic fascination with the "beginning" (*agra*) and with cosmogony, and we have to ask whether this can indeed be reduced to an interest in the basic substance and foundation (*pratiṣṭhā*) of the world. In other words, is Vedic cosmogony and cosmology ultimately committed to an "ontology of substance"?[30]

7. Vedic cosmogony is very complex and elusive, and it would be presumptuous to reduce it to certain "basic outlines." The cosmogonic myths, metaphors, and paradigms may vary and merge with one another even within one single text, such as *Ṛgveda* X, 129. Here, the cosmogonic process is characterized as birth or germination, but also as transformation and emanation; the author himself indicates his uncertainty and ultimate ignorance.[31] *Ṛgveda* X, 129 is a late and retrospective hymn. Numerous other ideas are found in other texts; metaphors of birth and biological formation occur side by side with conceptions that present the world as an artefact.[32] There is no need for us to go into further details or to discuss the attempts of modern scholars to identify and clarify the central ideas and underlying premises in the apparent chaos of Vedic cosmogony.[33] Regardless of all complexities, and regardless of the absence of a coherent cosmogonic doctrine, the reader of the older Vedic texts, in particular the Ṛgveda itself, will easily notice certain recurrent themes and perspectives of Vedic cosmogony and of the Vedic sense of reality in general: Creation myths are often presented as separation myths, as myths about the creation of livable space, the open horizon in which we live.[34] This is combined with a sense of amazement and wonder about such openness itself, as well as the things that appear in it, and the precarious nature of their existence. In most cases, Indra is the central figure in the creation myths of this type; he is the one who accomplishes the separation of heaven and earth and creates the indispensable intermediate space, as well as the polarities that go with this primeval cosmic dichotomy.[35]

We need not, we cannot discuss in detail how significant and original the connection between Indra and the idea of cosmogonic separation is. Varuṇa, too, is at times credited with the separation of heaven and earth.[36] Elsewhere, the separation is described as a spontaneous event.[37]

What is decisive is the opening, the separation as such, a separation that implies not only the creation of free space, but also the establishment of firm boundaries, of distinguishability and bipolarity. Of course, F. B. J. Kuiper observes correctly that Indra's act presupposes the existence of an undifferentiated totality: "Indra does not create anything but acts as a kind of magnetic force . . ."[38] Yet the fascination is not with the amorphous primeval substance or substrate as such, but with the open space that is its negation, as well as the condition of all particularized existence that occurs in it.

8. The old Vedic texts, in particular the *Ṛgveda,* leave no doubt as to Vedic man's fascination with openness and unobstructed space. The vocabulary to express such fascination is rich and manifold, and it includes a number of words that in later Sanskrit usage have lost this particular connotation. The word *loka,* commonly translated as "world," would be a conspicuous example. Its Vedic usage can be paraphrased as "room to exist freely and without hindrance and obstruction." In the Vedic texts, it is often accompanied by such adjectives as *uru,* "broad, wide."[39] Sanskrit words that appear as lexicographic equivalents for *earth,* such as *pṛthivī, mahī, urvī,* and even *bhūmi,* have basic Vedic connotations of "extended," "wide," "great," "open." *Ākāśa, vyoman,* and so forth, also exemplify the Vedic sense of the openness of space and what we may call a primeval metaphysical *clearing.* The Vedic word *māyā* itself, which has far-reaching implications in later Indian thought about the ontological status of the spatiotemporal world, is associated with "measurement," "extension," "projection into space." There is also a sense of wonder and amazement about that which appears in this extended openness, the spatial and temporal things that emerge in it, as visible, extended, measurable, identifiable entities—mountains, rivers, living creatures. They are experienced in the sheer amazing presence and inexplicable contingency of their existence. This seems to be an essential part of the Vedic meaning of *māyā*.[40]

The experience of openness is also an experience of separation and apartness. The open space is an intermediate space (*antarikṣa*) between the poles of heaven and earth. The upholding of the open space is at the same time an upholding of the polarities to which it owes its existence; it is also an upholding of the polarities and distinctions that exist within this space. It means preventing them from collapsing, merging in an undifferentiated and unidentifiable unity and totality, from becoming *saṃśliṣṭa* and *avyākṛta* again.[41] *Sat* itself, in its distinction from *asat* and as the very realm of distinctions, has to be upheld against such collapse; that is, against the disappearance of openness. The cosmogonic acts or events have to be repeated in the rituals; that is, the acts of *dharman/dharma*. The connection of *dharma* with *dhṛ* (*dhāray;* cf. also *vi-dhṛ*), "to support," "to uphold," is not only an etymological one.[42]

9. The distinct entities that appear in the Vedic openness cannot be described as mere modifications of a primeval substance or substrate. Rather, their appearance implies the negation of such substantiality. It implies novelty and contingency. The Vedic "creation," the primeval opening may not be a "creation from nothing." Yet it implies a first beginning, an event that remains unique in spite of all the ritual repetitions by which it is followed. The "opening," the cosmogonic separation, presupposes a primeval "something," whatever its nature may be. But at the same time, it is the creation of that very "nothing" in which contingent existence is possible—the amazing appearance of those entities or phenomena which constitute the realm of *māyā*, and the continuity of which is subject to an active upholding through the human enactment of *dharma*.[43]

This is not the place for a comparison between biblical and Vedic thought. It is, however, important to remember that those broad generalizations which characterize Indian thought as fundamentally "cyclical" and "substantialist" and contrast it with the Judaeo-Christian tradition are thoroughly inadequate as far as Vedic thought is concerned.[44] There is, indeed, the search for the ultimate basis and substance of what there is and the identification of being itself with this substance. Being itself is forever present in all entities; that is, its modifications. The instruction of Śvetaketu in the sixth chapter of the *Chāndogya Upaniṣad* contains the most exemplary presentation of this view: Being is the ultimate cause and substance, and the anticipation of all entities. There is no room for contingency and no need for creation. Yet in numerous older texts, we find a pervasive fascination with the "beginning," the cosmogonic act, the primeval event of separation and opening, with openness itself, and with the appearance of contingent entities in it. In this sense, and without drawing a strict line between "philosophy" and "mythology," we may speak of two different Vedic "ontologies" or, more cautiously, of different, though perhaps supplementary, perspectives on the reality of the world.[45] Whereas the "ontology of substance" may play a more conspicuous role in later Indian, specifically Hindu, philosophy, the philosophical significance of the mythology and ontology of openness should by no means be underestimated.

10. Uddālaka Āruṇi's "science of being" (*sadvidyā*) does not recognize anything over and above "being" (*sat*). But according to other Vedic-Upaniṣadic texts, "being" and "nonbeing" themselves presuppose a more fundamental ground, or a more comprehensive horizon. They are included in, or subordinated to, such principles as *ātman*, *brahman*, or the mythical "world frame" (*skambha*).[46] *Ṛgveda* X, 129 and other, less famous texts invoke the idea of an original state and a primeval "One" (*tad ekam*) beyond being and nonbeing.[47] The most important Vedic-Upaniṣadic concept associated with such transcendence of being and nonbeing is the concept of *brahman*. In a number of texts, *brahman* is presented as transcending both *sat* and *asat*,[48] or as including and superseding both that which is (*sat*) and what is beyond (*tyat*).[49] The distinction between *sat* and *tyat* is sometimes explained as a distinction between the formed and the formless (*mūrta*, *amūrta*), the mortal and the immortal (*martya*, *amṛta*), the speakable and the inexpressible.[50]

It would not be appropriate to describe such transcendence of all polarities as the inclusion and disappearance of all distinctions in an undifferentiated primeval substance. We are dealing here with a transcendence of a higher conceptual order; it includes and supersedes the polarity between distinction and nondistinction, differentiation and nondifferentiation itself, and provides important suggestions for later conceptual thought and systematic philosophy.[51]

Even being or reality itself, that is, *sat* and other derivatives of the root *as,* may be associated with such transcendence. *Being* in this sense transcends itself and its distinction from that which is not. The *Taittirīya Upaniṣad* says that *satya* includes both itself and its opposite, *anṛta: satyaṃ ca-anṛtaṃ ca satyam abhavat.*[52] This implies different levels of meaning for the terminology of *being, truth,* and *reality.*

There is no explicit debate on the semantics of *sat* and on the different functions of *to be* (*as, bhū*) in the Vedic texts; nor do we find a theory of levels of truth or discourse comparable to the one used by Śaṅkara.[53] *Sat* in the sense of "entity" is not systematically and thematically distinguished from *sat* as primeval Being; nor do we find an explicit formulation of the "ontological difference" between *esse* and *ens, Sein* and *Seiendes.* However, this can hardly justify T. Vetter's suggestion that Vedic-Upaniṣadic thought was confined to entities and that the "ontological difference" remained entirely unknown in the Indian tradition prior to Maṇḍanamiśra (approximately 700 A.D.).[54]

11. What kind of precedent does the Veda set for later Indian thought about being? What kind of beginning does it provide? It is well known that the relationship between the Veda and Hinduism is ambivalent, even paradoxical, and that it involves complex problems of continuity and change. According to Louis Renou, reverence for the Veda, even in the most orthodox circles of Hinduism, was nothing more than a "tipping of the hat," a ceremonial gesture without genuine affinity or commitment.[55]

Indeed, the Vedic texts do not contain a "Hindu creed," nor do they provide us with a clearly recognizable doctrinal basis for later Hindu thought. "They offer only vague and questionable analogues to those ideas and ways of orientation which have become basic premises of later Hinduism. It may suffice to recall here the cyclical world view, the doctrine of karma and rebirth, the ethical principle of *ahiṃsā* and the soteriology of final liberation."[56] Nonetheless, classical Hindu philosophy invokes the Veda as the criterion of "orthodoxy" and tends to find its own teachings anticipated by, or at least fully compatible with, the Veda. Is this essentially a fiction and projection, or is the Veda indeed a real and significant source of classical Indian philosophy? Renou himself found "real extensions" of the Veda in later Hinduism.[57] Is Hindu ontology—or more generally, Indian thought about being—among these "extensions"?

Bhartṛhari, the great teacher of the "nondualism of the word" (*śabdādvaita*), claims that the various traditions of monistic or dualistic and pluralistic thought have their origin in certain suggestive Vedic and Upaniṣadic statements, which were subject to different interpretations.[58] Most of the examples which Bhartṛhari cites in support of this thesis have to do with the notions of "being" and "nonbeing" and the question of the "origin" (*agra*) of the world.

We cannot accept such claims as historically accurate statements nor can we accept the systematic notions of Advaita Vedānta as philologically adequate exegesis. Yet it would be entirely inappropriate to dismiss the real connections between the Veda and these later developments as irrelevant. Śaṅkara's philosophy of nondualism may not be a historically adequate interpretation of the Upaniṣads. Nonetheless, it is a genuine continuation and transformation. Even if we do not accept van Buitenen's thesis that the Upaniṣadic *sadvidyā* marks the beginning of Indian philosophy, we cannot deny the extraordinary significance of the sixth chapter of the Chāndogya Upaniṣad for the systematic philosophies of Sāṃkhya, Vedānta, and so on.

In a more general and elusive sense, ancient patterns of Vedic mythology, its schemes of immanence-in-transcendence, unity-in-diversity, and identity-in-difference have become basic precedents and presuppositions of later philosophical thinking.[59] The pervasive fascination with a transcending horizon of being and nonbeing, or a principle in which they are united, the associations of *sat* with permanence, light, awareness, and so forth, or simply certain strong and exemplary usages of *asti*[60]—all this has opened important perspectives. And in spite of all subsequent oblivion and obscuration, the Vedic cosmogonies of separation and opening, as well as the associated idea of an "upholding" (*dhṛ; dharma/dharman*) of such openness and the polarities and distinctions that appear in it, have had their echoes and "extensions" in the systematic philosophies of Buddhism as well as Hinduism.[61]

12. Indian philosophy is less susceptible of historical demarcations and periodizations than its European counterpart. However, the following broad division (a modified version of suggestions made by E. Frauwallner[62]) will provide us with a basic framework for our historical orientation:

1. Presystematic thought, as documented in the Vedas, Upaniṣads, epics, and early texts of the Buddhists;
2. The philosophy of the classical systems of Hinduism (such as Sāṃkhya, Yoga, Vaiśeṣika, Nyāya) and Buddhism (for instance, Sarvāstivāda and Yogācāra);
3. The philosophies of the theistic groups, in particular of the Vaiṣṇavas and Śaivas, which take a leading role in the second millenium A.D.;
4. Modern Indian philosophy, which responds to the Western challenge (after 1800).

Our following investigations will deal primarily with the philosophy of the systems, which began in the centuries after the death of the Buddha, reached its culmination in the first millenium A.D., and has been continued up to the modern era. Unlike presystematic thought, the philosophy of the systems is committed to formal criteria of coherence, the avoidance of contradictions, methods of proof and argumentation, and so on. Epistemology and dialectics play an increasingly conspicuous role.

The challenge of Buddhism and other non-Vedic or anti-Vedic movements has been of great importance for the development of systematic philosophy; and this has had special implications for the history of ontology in India.

Change and impermanence, and the illusory nature of self and substance, appear as characteristic Buddhist teachings in the earliest canonical documents. Later on, we find more systematic and technical conceptions of "momentariness" (*kṣaṇikatva*) and "voidness" (*śūnyatā*). In the ontological debates of the classical period, that is, the Indian "giants' battle about being," the Buddhists appear generally as advocates of change and becoming, of nonself and nonidentity, and as critics of reification and essentialization, if not of ontological commitment and conceptualization per se.[63] The Buddha teaches a "middle way" between "eternalism" (*śāśvatavāda*) and "destructionism" (*ucchedavāda*) or simply between the metaphysical positions of "is" (*asti*) and "is not" (*nāsti*).[64] Ontological and metaphysical commitment of this kind appears as a (positive or negative) reflection of that primeval "thirst" (*tṛṣṇā*) which Buddhism tries to overcome.

However, this does not mean that conceptualizations of being or cosmological speculations play no role in Buddhism. For instance, the Sarvāstivāda tradition has produced extensive speculations on the ontological status of past, present, and future entities and on potentiality and actuality. It has also produced elaborate enumerations and classifications of entities, or types of entities. Debates on the status of the effect before its actual manifestation (i.e., the positions of *satkārya* and *asatkārya*) are also part of the Buddhist tradition.

But even the critics of the Sarvāstivāda are by no means indifferent with regard to ontological questions. Such concepts as *dharmatā* and *tathatā*, or *śūnyatā*, may not be "regular" ontological concepts; yet in their own peculiar way, they have to do with the question of being.[65]

In its own way, the tradition of the Jainas has made very significant contributions to the debate about being. It may suffice to mention the works of Siddhasena Divākara and Mallavādin, which are among the most exemplary documents of Indian ontology.

13. In the Hindu defense against the Buddhist process philosophy and "negative ontology," the schools of Vaiśeṣika, Nyāya, and Pūrvamīmāṃsā take a leading role. The concept of substance, the doctrine of universals and the assumption of a well-structured universe of durable and identifiable entities, and clearly distinguishable categories of reality, are at the heart of this defense. Within Hinduism, the debate between *satkāryavāda* and *asatkāryavāda,* the competing theories of the preexistence or nonexistence of the effect in its material cause, is of obvious relevance for the history of Indian ontology. The Sāṃkhya, Vaiśeṣika, and other schools participate in the debate. In the context of this debate, as well as in the defense against the Buddhists, the Vaiśeṣika school develops and explicates its conceptualizations of being.

The tradition of Advaita Vedānta affiliates itself with the "revelation" of the Upaniṣads and its teachings concerning *ātman, brahman, sat,* and *asat.* As we have seen, Śaṅkara tries to reconcile the different cosmogonic and cosmological statements by assuming two levels of truth and discourse in the Upaniṣads. In general, he uses ontological terminology, in particular the idea of a universal "being" or "beingness," with some caution. Other Vedāntins, for instance Maṇḍana, are less cautious.[66]

The meaning of being is questionable not only in its application to *brahman*, but also with regard to the status of the empirical world of time and space, which is often said to be "inexpressible" (*anirvacanīya*) in terms of being as well as nonbeing (*sadasadbhyām*).[67] Some of the most extensive debates concerning "being" and "nonbeing" are associated with the concept of *māyā*. The great controversies between the nondualistic followers of Śaṅkara and the Dvaita Vedānta school of Madhva concerning the status of the world are among the most significant contributions to the ontological debate in the second millenium A.D.[68] We should also mention the Viśiṣṭādvaita tradition and the Śaivite Pratyabhijñā system of Kashmir, as represented by Abhinavagupta.

Bhartṛhari, the metaphysician of the Vedic revelation and teacher of the "nondualism of the word" (*śabdādvaita*), is of special importance for the history of Indian ontology. In a unique manner, he combines metaphysics with grammar and linguistic reflection. In particular, he connects the investigations of the grammarians concerning the meaning and function of such verbal roots as *as* and *bhū* with speculations on the nature of universals and the metaphysical structure of the world. His concepts of *mahāsattā*, *upacārasattā*, and so on, illustrate this dual orientation of his thought. In general, the grammatical tradition is among the major sources of Indian ontology.[69]

14. In conclusion, and in an inevitably simplifying classification, we may say that three different, yet interlinked and complementary sources have contributed to the development of ontological thought and debate in India:

1. Cosmogony and cosmological speculation;
2. Grammar and linguistic analysis and reflection;
3. Soteriological ideas concerning the liberation from, and transcendence of, being as well as nonbeing.

Vedic cosmogony and cosmology are very obvious, yet equally ambiguous, roots of Indian ontology. Cosmogony has to be distinguished from cosmology, and both of these have to be distinguished from conceptually explicit ontology. However, in their own way, cosmogony and cosmology may be anticipations of an understanding of being that ontology articulates through explicit conceptualizations of being. It seems to be natural for ontology in this specific sense of the word to occur historically later than cosmogony and cosmology; however, this does not eo ipso imply a more advanced understanding or a superior access to being. In a complex metamorphosis, the Vedic speculations on the origin and nature of the world evolve into theories of elements and doctrines of categories, as exemplified by the Vaiśeṣika system. In this process, ontology in the strict sense, as explicit thematization of being, may be affiliated with reflections on the meaning of origination, destruction, and transformation or it may have to do with projects of comprehensive enumeration and classification; that is, with the question *What is there?*[70]

The grammatical and linguistic approach to the question of being, which we find in the tradition of the great grammarians Pāṇini, Patañjali, and so forth, is clearly different from the cosmogonic, cosmological, and "enumerative" approach. It deals not with the world per se, but with our ways of speaking about it. It does not try to determine which entities exist or "what being is," but what such words as *to be* and *to become* (*as, bhū,* etc.) mean and how they function in our speech and thought. Yet in spite of this obvious difference, the links between the two approaches have been close and extensive, not only in those traditions of Indian thought that assume an archetypal cosmological role of language and believe in a fundamental correspondence between language and the real world or between linguistic and cosmological categories.[71]

The practical, soteriological, and transformational dimensions of Indian thought would not seem to be conducive to, nor even compatible with, ontology as a theoretical, conceptual enterprise. Yet as a matter of fact, some of the more antitheoretical and anticonceptual movements of Indian thought, especially in Buddhism and nondualistic Vedānta, have nevertheless made intense and far-reaching contributions to the "question of being" or to ontology insofar as it is inherently questionable. We may speak here not only of a critique of inadequate conceptualizations of being, of a "negative ontology," or of a desire to transcend the fundamental dichotomy of being and nonbeing and the attachment to objectifiable reality. This is, in a sense, thought about being that is rooted in and motivated by a desire for absolute liberation, a kind of "soteriontology." Even Nāgārjuna's doctrine of voidness (*śūnyavāda*) may be classified not only as a "negative ontology," but also as a "soteriontology" of this kind.[72] Concerning Śaṅkara's Advaita Vedānta, his concept of liberation, that is, of coinciding with the absolute reality and identity of *brahman* (*brahmabhāva*), has an undeniably ontological dimension.[73] Familiar distinctions of "philosophical theory" and "soteriological practice" are not well suited to describe Śaṅkara's peculiar "soteriontology."[74]

The tradition of thinking about being to which these three sources have contributed is clearly different from that of Western ontology. Yet in its own way, it responds and corresponds to those basic problems and perplexities that we have presented in our general introduction.

Chapter 2: Notes

1. B. Delbrück, *Altindische Syntax.* (Halle, 1888), p. 273, describes the copulative uses of both *as* and *bhū* as later, historically derivative developments; but see also J. Canedo, *Zur Wort- und Satzstellung in der alt- und mittelindischen Prosa* (Göttingen, 1937), pp. 36; 77ff. (examples from Vedic literature). On general problems concerning the concept of copula in linguistics, see H. Gipper, *Bausteine zur Sprachinhaltsforschung,* 2d ed. (Düsseldorf, 1969), pp. 135–214; 502ff. (bibliography). The Tibetan translators, whose language provided them with a choice between the existential *yod* and the more copulative *yin,* would make the different functions of *bhū* and *as* more explicit. However, it would hardly be appropriate to impose a rigorous distinction between the copulative and existential uses of *to be* on the Sanskrit materials; see also the pertinent observations by C. Kahn, "The Greek Verb 'To Be' and the Concept of Being," *Foundations of Language* 2 (1966): 245–266 (especially 247, on the lack of distinction in Greek).

2. Numerous other derivatives of *bhū* (such as *vibhava, vibhūti, anubhava,* etc.) are not part of the technical ontological vocabulary, but have, nonetheless, potential ontological implications.

3. See later, Chapters 3, 8.

4. See later, Chapter 7; *tuchya* in the sense of utter voidness appears already in *Ṛgveda* X, 129, 3.

5. See later, section 10; *skambha* is the mythical "world pillar" (cf. *Atharvaveda* X, 7–8). The emergence of such terms as *prameya* and *abhidheya* reflects a growing emphasis on epistemology, logic, and semantic analysis. *Tattva* appears in different roles in Nyāya, Buddhism, Bhartṛhari's *Śabdādvaita,* etc.

6. On *akṣara*, see J. A. B. van Buitenen, "Akṣara," *JAOS* 79 (1959): 176–187; on *dharma*, see *India and Europe*, pp. 317ff.

7. See earlier, Chapter 1, section 2 (especially n. 13). Although the translators were fully aware of the different ontological capacities of Sanskrit on the one hand and Chinese or Tibetan on the other, they did not suggest any "linguistic relativity" of ontological concepts and theories. For an early attempt to establish a correspondence between the ontological terminology in Sanskrit and Latin, see Paulinus a S. Bartholomaeo, *Vyacarana* (Rome, 1804), p. 155; *tatvam, svabhavam*, etc., appear as equivalents of *essentia*, whereas *satvam, sattā, stiti* are given for *existentia*.

8. See, for instance, D. N. Shastri, *Critique of Indian Realism* (Agra, 1964); N. V. Joshi, *Indian Philosophy from the Ontological Point of View* (Bombay, 1977; using the term *ontology* in a loose sense).

9. Reflection on these questions can be traced back to our oldest extant sources in grammar and etymology (i.e., Pāṇini and Yāska) and is fully explicit in Patañjali's *Mahābhāṣya* and Bhartṛhari's *Vākyapadīya*.

10. See *Ratnakīrtinibandhāvalī*, ed. A. Thakur (Patna, 1957), p. 62, (*Kṣaṇabhaṅgasiddhi*, Introduction): *yadi nāma darśane darśane nānāprakāraṃ sattvalakṣaṇam uktam āste, arthakriyākāritvaṃ sattāsamavāyaḥ, svarūpasattvam, utpādavyayadhrauvyayogitvaṃ, pramāṇaviṣayatvaṃ, sadupalambhakapramāṇagocaratvaṃ, vyapadeśaviṣayatvam ityādi* . . . The second edition (*Ratnakīrtinibandhāvaliḥ*; Patna, 1975, p. 67), introduces some misprints into the text (for instance, *tadupalambhaka-* instead of *sadupalambhaka-*).

11. See later, Chapter 10. The Vedānta commentator Prakāśātman (ca. A.D. 1000) uses the term *arthakriyāsāmarthyasattva* to describe the level of empirical, worldly reality more commonly known as *vyāvahārikasattva;* see *Pañcapādikāvivaraṇa* (Benares, 1892; Vizianagram Sanskrit Series), p. 31; also K. Cammann, *Das System des Advaita nach der Lehre Prakāśātmans* (Munich, 1965), pp. 46f.

12. See earlier, Chapter 1, section 5 (especially n. 38ff.).

13. See later, Chapter 10; cf. also J. L. Mehta, "Heidegger and the Comparison of Indian and Western Philosophy," *PEW* 20 (1970): 303–317; also in *Philosophy and Religion. Essays in Interpretation* (New Delhi, 1990), pp. 1–19.

14. For a stimulating, though somewhat idiosyncratic and speculative, discussion of some of these developments, see C. A. Scharbau, *Die Idee der Schöpfung in der vedischen Literatur* (Stuttgart, 1932).

15. Cf. J. Gonda, "In the Beginning," *ABORI* 63 (1982): 43–62.

16. See J. A. B. van Buitenen, *Rāmānuja's Vedārthasaṃgraha* (Poona, 1956), p. 3.

17. The translation follows R. E. Hume, *The Thirteen Principal Upanishads*, 2d ed. (London, 1931; reprint, 1971), p. 241.

18. See *Chāndogya Upaniṣad* III, 19, 1 (*asad eva-idam agra āsīt*); *Ṛgveda* X, 71, 2–3; see also *Bṛhadāraṇyaka Upaniṣad* I, 2, 1 (*na-eva-iha kiṃcana agra āsīt*); *Taittirīya Upaniṣad* II, 7; and *Ṛgveda* X, 129, 4 (*sato bandhum asati niravindan*).

19. Altogether, the word *asat* occurs seven times in the Ṛgveda; five times, we find *āsat* (with accentuated lengthened first vowel). For further references, see H. Oldenberg, *Die Weltanschauung der Brāhmaṇa-Texte* (Göttingen, 1919), pp. 177ff. Oldenberg suspected a confusion between "being" as copula and "being" as existence in these texts.

20. See H. Oertel, "Asat = 'Undifferentiated', 'Formless', 'Incapable of Perception by the Senses' in Vedic Prose," *New Indian Antiquary* 1 (1938–39): 317–321; see also J. Gonda, *Die Religionen Indiens*, vol. 1 (Stuttgart, 1960), p. 181.

21. See W. N. Brown, "The Rigvedic Equivalent for Hell," *JAOS* 61 (1941): 76–80; see also "The Creation Myth of the Rig Veda," *JAOS* 62 (1942): 85–98 (also in *India and Indology, Selected Articles* by W. N. Brown, ed. R. Rocher. Benares, 1978, pp. 20ff.).

22. *Rāmānuja's Vedārthasaṃgraha* (cited in n. 16), p. 3.

23. Cf. J. Gonda, "In the Beginning" (cited in n. 15).

24. *Chāndogya Upaniṣad* VI, 8, 4 describes all creatures as having their root, their abode and their support in pure being (*sanmūla, sadāyatana, satpratiṣṭhita*); according to VII, 24, the absolute self or "plenum" (*bhūman*) is established (*pratiṣṭhita*) "in its own greatness" (*sve mahimni*). See also J. Gonda, "Pratiṣṭhā," *Selected Studies*, vol. 2 (Leiden, 1975), pp. 338–374; "Āyatana," ibid., pp. 178–256.

25. The *satkāryavāda* is, of course, most commonly associated with the Sāṃkhya and Yoga schools of thought.

26. See later, Chapter 3.

27. See Śaṅkara on *Chāndogya Upaniṣad* III, 19, 1: *asad avyākṛtanāmarūpam idaṃ jagad aśeṣam agre prāgavasthāyām utpatter āsīn, na tv asad eva*. For a comprehensive discussion and harmonization of exemplary cosmogonic references to being and nonbeing in the Upaniṣads, see *BSBh* I, 4, 14–15.

28. See *Chāndogya Upaniṣad* VI, 3, 2 (*nāmarūpe vyākaravāṇi*); 3 (*nāmarūpe vyākarot*); see also the extensive references to "differentiation" (*vyākṛ*) in *BU* I, 4, 7 (with *BUBh*).

29. Cf. G. Scholem, *Über einige Grundbegriffe des Judentums* (Frankfurt, 1970), pp. 53–89.

30. This has, of course, significant parallels in ancient Greek thought, for instance in the cosmologies of Thales and Anaximander.

31. For other exemplary paradigms and modalities of origination or production, see, for instance, the well-known Ṛgvedic hymns X, 72; X, 90; and X, 121; see also R. N. Dandekar, *Universe in Hindu Thought* (Bangalore, 1972).

32. See, for instance, *Ṛgveda* X, 81–82 (Viśvakarman, the divine sculptor or carpenter).

33. Cf. H. von Glasenapp, *Entwicklungsstufen des indischen Denkens* (Halle, 1940), p. 23: "das chaotische Durcheinander der im Veda entwickelten zahllosen Schöpfungslehren." J. Varenne, *Cosmogonies védiques* (Paris, 1982), seems to assume variations of one basic myth; see also F. B. J. Kuiper, *Ancient Indian Cosmogony,* ed. J. Irwin (Delhi, 1983), pp. 9–22 ("The Basic Concept of Vedic Religion").

34. For a comparative survey of separation myths in different ancient traditions, see W. Staudacher, *Die Trennung von Himmel und Erde* (Tübingen, 1942; reprint Darmstadt, 1968); on the "openness" of the world, cf. J. Gonda, *Loka. World and Heaven in the Veda* (Amsterdam, 1966), especially pp. 7ff.; 25ff.

35. See, for instance *Ṛgveda* X, 89; also II, 12. The act of opening is usually associated with the killing of Vṛtra, the covering, enclosing force.

36. Cf. *Ṛgveda* V, 85; VII, 86.

37. On the role of various deities in the cosmogonic process, see also R. N. Dandekar, *Universe in Hindu Thought* (Bangalore, 1972), pp. 4ff.; 12ff.; 32ff.

38. *Ancient Indian Cosmogony* (cited in n. 33), 11. Kuiper sees the separation or opening as the "second stage" in the cosmogonic process; cf. also pp. 103ff.

39. Cf. J. Gonda, *Loka* (cited in n. 34), pp. 18ff. Sāyaṇa's commentary uses the terms *avakāśa* (on VIII, 100, 12) and *prakāśa* (on X, 104, 10) to express the sense of open space and light that seems to be at stake in these texts. The concept of *prakāśa,* as used by later thinkers (for instance, Abhinavagupta) associates the sense of primeval openness with ideas about absolute awareness as the condition of the possibility of all manifestation.

40. Cf. B. Hager, *Die Entwicklung des Māyā-Begriffes im Indo-Arischen* (Freiburg, 1983; Diss. Tübingen, 1942), especially pp. 11ff.; J. Gonda, "The 'Original' Sense and the Etymology of Skt. *māyā,*" *Four Studies in the Language of the Veda* (The Hague, 1959), pp. 119–193; for later developments, see L. T. O'Neil, *Māyā in Śaṅkara* (Delhi, 1980). *Māyā* is the power of ("magical") projection, as well as the projection itself. The derivation of the word from the root *mā,* "to measure" (cf. also *nirmāṇa*) seems basically acceptable and would be compatible with the important connotations of spatial extension and spatial projection.

41. Cf. F. B. J. Kuiper, *Ancient Indian Cosmogony* (cited in n. 33), p. 104.

42. Cf. *India and Europe,* ch. 17 (especially pp. 317ff.).

43. Both *dharman/dharma* and *māyā* suggest a "dynamic universe" whose very existence and continuity depend on acts and powers of upholding and projection; for a challenging, though somewhat speculative, presentation of this "dynamic universe," see L. Silburn, *Instant et cause. Le discontinu dans la pensée philosophique de l'Inde* (Paris, 1955), especially chs. 1–3.

44. On Hegel's claim that Indian thought is fundamentally "substantialist," see *India and Europe,* ch. 6.

45. Once again, this statement involves a certain degree of simplification and questionable generalization.

46. On *skambha,* see *Atharvaveda* X, 7–8. All-inclusiveness and transcendence of all distinctions is ascribed to a variety of divine or sacrificial principles, and it serves often as a device of glorification; see, for instance, *Atharvaveda* XI, 4 (*prāṇa*); XI, 7 (*ucchiṣṭa*).

47. See, for instance, *Atharvaveda* X, 8, 6.

48. Cf. *Muṇḍaka Upaniṣad* II, 2, 1: also *Śvetāśvatara* IV, 18; on *brahman* in general, see J. Gonda, *Notes on brahman* (Utrecht, 1950).

49. Cf. *Taittirīya Upaniṣad* II, 6.

50. Cf. *Bṛhadāraṇyaka Upaniṣad* II 3, 1ff.

51. Cf. also the concept of the *bhūman* ("plenum"), *Chāndogya Upaniṣad* VII, 24f.

52. *Taittirīya Upaniṣad* II, 6.

53. However, the distinction between "higher" and "lower" knowledge (*parā, aparā vidyā* in *Muṇḍaka Upaniṣad* I, 2, 4f. was available to provide scriptural support for Śaṅkara's distinction between the "absolute" (*pāramārthika*) and conventional (*vyāvahārika*) levels of truth and discourse.

54. See T. Vetter, *Erkenntnisprobleme bei Dharmakīrti* (Vienna, 1964), pp. 89–98; especially p. 98: "Das Merkwürdige an der Entwicklung der indischen Philosophie ist eben, dass erst seit Maṇḍana der Ausdruck '*sat*' dazu dient, *das* Seiende vom einzelnen Seienden so abzuheben, dass es mehr ist als ein nur ontisches Prinzip. Ab diesem Zeitpunkt haben wir in Indien das 'Seiende' in einer ontologischen Bedeutung wie bei einigen europäischen Systemen das 'Sein'." Regardless of all merely terminological questions, this does not seem to do justice to the sense of transcending the entire "ontic" realm, which we find not only in Vedic-Upaniṣadic thought, but also, though in a radically different style, in Buddhism (most notably in Nāgārjuna's *Śūnyavāda*).

55. See L. Renou, *Le destin du Veda dans l'Inde* (Paris, 1960), p. 1: "un simple 'coup de chapeau' donné en passant à une idole . . ."

56. See *Tradition and Reflection*, p. 1.

57. Ibid., pp. 2f.

58. See Bhartṛhari, *VP* I, 8 (with his own *Vṛtti*).

59. Cf. *Tradition and Reflection*, pp. 39ff.

60. See, for instance, *Śatapatha Brāhmaṇa* X, 4, 2, 21: *asty etad dhy amṛtaṃ, yad dhy amṛtaṃ, tad dhy asti; Ṛgveda* VIII, 100, 3f. (on Indra): *yadi satyam asti; Kaṭha Upaniṣad VI,* 12f.: *asti-iti bruvato 'nyatra kathaṃ tad upalabhyate . . . asti-ity eva-upalabdhavyaḥ*).

61. Cf. L. Silburn, *Instant et cause* (cited in n. 43); and F. E. Reynolds, "Multiple Cosmogonies and Ethics: The Case of Theravada Buddhism," *Cosmogony and Ethical Order*, ed. R. W. Lovin and F. E. Reynolds (Chicago, 1985), pp. 203–224.

62. See E. Frauwallner, *Gesch. d. ind. Phil.*, vol. 1, pp. 28f. Frauwallner has only three basic periods; but it seems advisable to separate presystematic thought from the philosophy of the systems.

63. This tendency has found many different expressions in the history of Buddhist thought, especially in Mahāyāna Buddhism; in a very radical form, it appears in the Prajñāpāramitā literature and in Nāgārjuna's Madhyamaka school.

64. See, for instance, *Saṃyuttanikāya* II, 17 (Kaccāyana/Kātyāyana); this important text on the "extremes" of *atthitā* and *natthitā* (i.e., *astitā* and *nāstitā*) is cited by Nāgārjuna, *MK* XV, 7. Nāgārjuna himself described *nirvāṇa* as the disappearance of, or liberation from, the ideas of being and nonbeing; cf. *Ratnāvalī* I, 42ff.

65. Cf. G. Nagao, *Mādhyamika and Yogācāra* (Albany, 1991), pp. 155–187: "Ontology in Mahāyāna Buddhism" (especially pp. 155–159, "Buddhism and Ontology").

66. Cf. Maṇḍana, *Brahmasiddhi*, ed. S. Kuppuswami Sastri (Madras, 1937; reprint Delhi, 1984), pp. 37f.; the absolute *ātman* is called *sattālakṣaṇa*, and *sattā* itself is referred to as *prakṛtiḥ parā*. Maṇḍana's use of *sattā* seems indebted to Bhartṛhari's *Vākyapadīya*. Unlike Śaṅkara, Maṇḍana also tried to establish "reality as such," or "pure being" (*vastumātra, sanmātra*), as the datum of pure, prepredicative perception.

67. On Śaṇkara's use of *anirvacanīya* (in his *BSBh*, it is usually accompanied by *tattvānyatvābhyām*), see P. Hacker, *Kl. Schr.*, pp. 84ff.

68. On the side of Advaita Vedānta, this debate culminated in the *Advaitasiddhi* by Madhusūdana Sarasvatī (ca. 1600).

69. See also later, Chapter 9, on being and time according to Bhartṛhari and the tradition of grammatical philosophy.

70. See later, Chapter 4.

71. This correspondence is basically taken for granted in the Nyāya and Vaiśeṣika systems.

72. Such terms as *dharmatā, tathatā,* and above all, *śūnyatā* express a radical commitment to an identity (*svabhāva*) which is not the identity of particular entities (*bhāvānāṃ svabhāvaḥ*); see, for instance, Nāgārjuna, *MK* XV (*Svabhāvaparīkṣā*) with Candrakīrti's commentary; see also *Tradition and Reflection,* p. 253. Such texts as the *Ratnagotravibhāga* have a more positive view of ultimate being, as coinciding with "Buddha nature" and liberation; cf. E. Frauwallner, *Die Philosophie des Buddhismus* (Berlin, 1956), pp. 256ff.

73. See, for instance, *BSBh* I, 1, 4 (*Works,* vol. 2, 18): liberation is the nature and being of *brahman,* and not something to be brought about (*brahmabhāvaś ca mokṣaḥ, tasmān na saṃskāryo 'pi mokṣaḥ*).

74. Cf. *India and Europe,* pp. 270ff.; *Tradition and Reflection,* pp. 254ff.

3

Genesis, Enumeration, and the Question of Being

1. In the history of Indian thought, the Vedic fascination with the "beginning," that is, the initial cosmogonic event or primeval state of the world, was replaced by, or transformed into, a preoccupation with schemes of recurrent evolution and involution and with the permanent foundations of such regular and cyclical processes. The generally unchallenged assumption of cosmic cycles leaves little room for the question of a first beginning. This is true for the philosophical systems as well as for religious and mythological speculation. In the Purāṇas, the cosmogonic question in the strict sense has disappeared. What is called *original creation* (*prākṛtasarga*) and distinguished from the "re-creation," or "secondary creation" (*pratisarga*), is not a first and absolute beginning, but only a more fundamental event in a wider, but still cyclical framework of time.[1]

Moreover, the increasingly soteriological orientation of classical Indian thought favors the orientation toward a future goal and solution; that is, a final, irreversible liberation from all cyclical existence. The question of the first beginning appears as the very prototype of a useless, unanswerable question.[2] The familiar statement that the world and its cycles are without beginning (*anādi*) is not only, and perhaps not even primarily, a cosmological and metaphysical thesis, but also a dismissal of the cosmogonic question itself. In accordance with this attitude, there is not much explicit interest in the manner in which the cycles succeed each other in time. Is it a recurrence of identical worlds or world structures? Does the sequence of cycles constitute a linear development which implies that the successive worlds or world phases are somehow different from each other? Reflection on these questions, though certainly not entirely absent, remains somewhat marginal.[3]

The "origin" becomes a recurrent event. The question now is: What is the origin *and* decay of this world? In other words, what is the regular course of events, the underlying scheme and structure in the dissolution and reappearance of this visible and organized world, and what is the firm ground from which it emerges and to which it returns again and again? The old mythical question: What *was* all this in the beginning? is translated into the question: What *is* it, in the ultimate analysis? In other words, what are the ultimate ingredients of the cycles, those constituents or elements of the world that are not affected by the recurrent cosmic processes?

2. In the preceding chapter, we noted that cosmological speculation has produced at least two basically different perspectives on the question of being. On the one hand, an explicit ontological interest evolves through questions concerning the meaning of genesis, origination and change; on the other hand, it manifests itself through an interest in comprehensive enumeration and classification and reflection on the question *What is there?* In the context of the cyclical world-view, enumeration itself may have different implications. It may be an enumerative description of cosmic schemes, that is, a "vertical" enumeration of stages of evolution, or a "horizontal" classification of ultimate entities and classes of entities. In the history of classical Indian philosophy, Sāṃkhya and Vaiśeṣika exemplify these different types of cosmological enumeration.

Both of these systems present elaborate lists of world constituents. However, the Sāṃkhya does so in a "vertical" manner; that is, in an enumeration of successive stages (i.e., the primeval "nature," *prakṛti*, and its twenty-three evolutes).[4]

The Vaiśeṣika, on the other hand, is the most representative case of a "horizontal" enumeration and classification of world constituents. It lists its cosmic factors and "categories" of reality not as successive stages in a scheme of evolution, but in a horizontal, synchronic arrangement, which includes, however, certain structures of dependence and subordination. The ultimate constituents of the world never merge with one another nor do they emerge from one common ground; they are irreducibly distinct. The emphasis on what is ultimately separate is, indeed, one of the associations of the name *Vaiśeṣika*.[5]

The Vaiśeṣika system, just like other traditions, lists the ultimate substances (*dravya*) of the world, including four types of atoms (*paramāṇu*). But it incorporates this list in a more comprehensive enumeration of types or classes of entities; that is, the so-called categories (*padārtha*) "substance," "quality," "motion," "universal," and so forth. From the cosmological interest in the ingredients of evolution and the irreducible elements of the world, it proceeds to the more comprehensive as well as more elusive question *What is there?* According to Quine's familiar and provocative statement, this deceptively simple question articulates "the ontological problem." In the words of G. Bergmann, "an ontology is an inventory of what exists (is there)."[6]

3. Both Sāṃkhya and Vaiśeṣika exemplify the ancient Indian predilection for elaborate enumerations, classifications, and numerical schemes. E. Frauwallner called it "das indische Streben nach Systematik und zahlenmässiger Erfassung der Dinge."[7] Since Vedic times, we find long lists of phenomena of the most diverse kind, such as physical entities, deities, events, natural regularities, ritual phenomena, and abstract notions. Cosmological enumerations are just one exemplary type of such lists; we find them in Hinduism as well as Buddhism and Jainism.

The older cosmological enumerations are usually of the vertical type or at least affiliated with schemes of evolution or emanation. This includes the oldest lists of "elements" in the Upaniṣads, most conspicuously in *Chāndogya Upaniṣad* VI; here, "fire," "water," and "earth" appear as successive emanations from the ultimate substance, *sat* or pure "being."[8]

E. Frauwallner has suggested that the most ancient Sāṃkhya did not have a theory of evolution and that it had a list of elements *not* included in a scheme of evolution or emanation nor derived from a more basic source. He saw this as the "simple and natural" way of cosmological thinking.[9] The texts do not provide much evidence for Frauwallner's thesis, which implies that the Sāṃkhya theory of evolution is a secondary phenomenon, nor do they support his more general assumption that the nonevolutionary approach would have been "simple and natural" in Vedic-Upaniṣadic and early Epic thought.

In the earlier Vedic-Upaniṣadic texts, which are committed to cosmogony instead of cosmology, it seems quite difficult to find unambiguous cases of "horizontal," static, nonevolutionary enumeration of equally irreducible, nonderivative world constituents. Texts that suggest a division of one fundamental entity, such as *Ṛgveda* X, 90, are neither unambiguous cases of "horizontal" classification, nor are they typical of Vedic-Upaniṣadic thought. The "doctrine of Yājñavalkya" ("Yājñavalkyalehre") that Frauwallner cites from the *Bṛhadāraṇyaka Upaniṣad* does not provide conclusive evidence. The same may be said about the *Aitareya Upaniṣad,* which gives us the oldest extant list of five elements; although it does not present the elements as successive emanations, it includes them in, and derives them from, *brahman.*[10] The traditional term for "element," *bhūta/mahābhūta,* which emerges in the Upaniṣads, seems to have an evolutionary connotation insofar as it suggests something that "has become." We may recall here the etymological connection of its root *bhū* with Greek *phýo/phýsis.* The individual elements are, of course, not necessarily presented as successive stages. From an early time on, they may be coordinated "horizontally" *within* "vertical" schemes of evolution. This is an example of "horizontal evolution" or "ramification" at one level of cosmic development. Even in the *Mahābhārata,* our most important source for the early history of the Sāṃkhya tradition, the basic tendency is still evolution-oriented, if not fully "vertical." For the parallel texts *Mahābhārata* XII, 187 and XII, 239f., which Frauwallner claimed as main evidence for a "nonevolutionary" early Sāṃkhya, that is, a coordination of equally irreducible elements, J. A. B. van Buitenen has convincingly argued that they do, indeed, presuppose an "evolutionary" perspective, although of the type he called "horizontal" evolution.[11] For the majority of the other cosmological schemes and enumerations in the Mahābhārata, we may say that they are unambiguously "vertical."[12]

4. The vertical cosmological perspective that tends to view different kinds of entities as successive stages in a process of evolution or emanation has, to a certain extent, also determined the interpretation of what later on came to be known as categorial distinctions, in particular the distinction between "substances" and their "qualities." Among the characteristic features of classical Sāṃkhya, we find its enumeration of five "subtle elements" (*tanmātra*) in addition to the five "gross elements" (*mahābhūta*). As a matter of fact, these so-called subtle elements are the hypostatized characteristics and, in accordance with the literal meaning of *tanmātra,* "pure essences" of the elements. Following the precedent of the *Chāndogya Upaniṣad* and other ancient texts, they are seen as cosmologically prior to the elements themselves, which are merely less refined and more concrete versions or mixtures of the original essences.

However, once qualities in general were considered as subordinate to and dependent on their substance-substrates (and finally classified as a different "category"), these essential and elemental qualities, too, had to be subordinated to their substance-elements and repositioned in the scheme of evolution. Accordingly, various texts preserve the scheme that gives priority to the "pure essences" (*tanmātra*), but then also add a corresponding series of derivative "qualities" (*guṇa*), presenting them as products or emanations of their "gross" elemental substrates.[13] Elsewhere, for instance in some of those texts which Frauwallner cites as evidence for a "preevolutionary" Sāṃkhya, the *tanmātra* do not appear at all; instead, "qualities" such as color, taste, and smell are presented as emanations of their elemental substances and genetically subordinate phases in the evolutionary scheme. Most conspicuously, we find this in the dialogue between Bhṛgu and Bharadvāja in the Mahābhārata, and in its elaborate list of quality emanations.[14] With reference to such texts, we may say that the "horizontal" and "categorial" distinction between "substance" (*dravya*) and "quality" (*guṇa*) that culminates in the Vaiśeṣika system was either preceded or echoed by a genetic, "vertical" distinction and correlation between the elemental substances and their characteristic essences.

5. To be sure, other texts in the Mahābhārata come much closer to the kind of horizontal, nonevolutionary enumeration that Frauwallner seems to postulate as the natural or ideal type of cosmological enumeration. The instruction of Asita Devala in the Mahābhārata provides a good example. Asita presents the five "great elements" (*mahābhūta*) as the material out of which the Lord produces this whole world and all beings in it. These elements are called *eternal* and *unchanging.* Time (*kāla*), "being" or "becoming" (*bhāva*) and "nonbeing" or "destruction" (*abhāva*) are added in a horizontal fashion to the list of five elements. Together, they are said to be the external constituents of all beings.[15] Yet even in this text, we find traces of the "vertical," evolutionary perspective.[16]

Another type of "horizontal," nonevolutionary enumeration of elements may be characterized as materialistic. The references found in the Mahābhārata are supplemented by old Buddhist and Jaina sources. We hear about a teacher, Ajita Keśakambala, allegedly a contemporary of the Buddha, who proclaimed that only the four material elements—that is, earth, water, fire, and air—exist. Subsequently, we find the same list of four elements in the well-known tradition of systematic materialism (Cārvāka, Lokāyata) associated with such names as Bṛhaspati, Uśanas, and Purandara.[17] Another contemporary of the Buddha Gautama and the Jina Mahāvīra, Kakuda Kātyāyana (Pakudha Kaccāyana), added "pleasure, pain, and souls" to Ajita's list of elemental entities (*kāya*).[18]

Other cosmological enumerations of a more or less horizontal type have been produced by the Buddhists and Jainas. In particular, Jainism has been linked with Vaiśeṣika pluralism—not only by modern scholars, but also by the Jaina tradition itself.[19] However, the nature of the relationship between Jainism and early Vaiśeṣika has not yet been established. The age, origin, and background of cosmological enumeration in Jainism, in particular of its fundamental list of "basic entities" (*astikāya*), continue to be problematic. K. K. Dixit states "that the tradition of discussing the nature of *loka* and *aloka*, matter and soul was comparatively old, that of discussing the nature of five *astikāyas* comparatively recent. It seems that the tradition of discussing the nature of reality in general is still more recent."[20] Whereas the debate about "reality in general" (*satsāmānya*), that is, the phenomena of origination (*utpāda*) and so forth and the distinction between the substance (*dravya*) and its modes (*paryāya*) seems to have no real precedent in the Āgamas and apparently gained prominence only with Umāsvāti's *Tattvārthasūtra*, the notion of *astikāya* does occur in the canonical *Viyāhapaññatti* (often referred to as *Bhagavatīsūtra*).

> Mahāvīra's chief disciple Gautama, when asked to justify his belief in the existence of the five *astikāyas*, naively pleads that only that which exists is called by his camp an existing entity, only that which does not a non-existing entity (*savvam atthibhāvam atthi-iti vadāmo, savvaṃ natthibhāvaṃ natthi-iti vadāmo*)."[21]

Whatever the original meaning of *astikāya* may be, it does not become a central and programmatic term in Jainism, but remains one item of enumeration among many others. It appears among the twenty-three *anuyogadvāra,* topics of debate and investigation, which include *pṛthivī, dvīpa, śarīra, dṛṣṭi,* and *jñāna.*[22] Evidently, it does not indicate any special or exclusive interest in the "ontological" question *What is there?*

6. Extensive schemes of enumeration and classification are found in the Buddhist Abhidharma traditions. The five "groups" (*skandha*) of physical and mental factors, the six "elements" (*dhātu*), and the twelve "realms" (*āyatana*) are the most conspicuous and familiar categories of enumeration in Buddhism, not to mention the causal links (*nidāna*) in the twelvefold chain of dependent origination (*pratītyasamutpāda*). Not only the existence of different schemes of enumeration, but also the role and relevance of enumeration *per se* have been a matter of concern and debate in Buddhism. The coexistence of the three competing lists of *skandha, dhātu,* and *āyatana* is explained as an accommodation to different types of disciples.[23] However, this cannot vindicate enumeration, classification, and conceptualization in general.

The fundamental motivation of the Buddhists is practical and soteriological. Enumeration and classification should serve a soteriological purpose. They should focus on soteriologically relevant causal relations and on the conceptual mastery of the conditions of worldly existence, and thus contribute to the goal of liberation from this condition. But such interest in comprehensive enumeration and conceptual mastery may again produce attachment to the world and one's own deceptive identity. The enumerative, objectifying approach itself calls for transcendence and detachment.

The word *dharma* indicates the ultimate units of enumeration, classification, analysis, and identification. It is at the same time one of the most central and most elusive terms of Buddhism in general. The debates about the meaning of *dharma* have been intense and far-reaching, and they reflect basic differences in the interpretation of Buddhism. Numerous translations and explanations have been suggested, for instance, "element," "object," "phenomenon," "datum," and "element of existence."[24]

We do not have to determine the full semantic range of the term *dharma* or its various functions in different contexts. Our question is: What is the role of *dharma* as a category of enumeration and classification? What is it that is being enumerated, classified, and identified in the *dharma* lists? But can we determine the meaning of *dharma* as such, regardless of the fact that it is the ultimate unit of enumeration and identification? In a sense, enumeration and identification, or rather enumerability and identifiability, constitute the meaning of *dharma*. Dharmas are essentially "identifiables," basic, irreducible units of identification. They are supposed to emerge at the end of a process of analysis and division that reduces all false units and apparent identities to their true and ultimate constituents.

The Abhidharma tradition itself supports this interpretation. It refers to the etymological affiliation of *dharma* with the root *dhṛ*, "to uphold," and derives its meaning from the fact that it upholds its own identity and distinctness (*svalakṣaṇadhāraṇād dharmaḥ*).[25] An analogous explanation is proposed for *dhātu*, "element."[26] However, the idea of ultimate identifiables remains elusive and controversial. According to the Mahāyāna, one should not enumerate and classify dharmas. One should not be attached to the "identity" (*svabhāva*) of any particular entities, not even to the identifiability and objectifiability of these ultimate identifiables.[27]

7. What is there? How can it be classified and enumerated? What does it mean to deal with the totality of what there is? What is the relationship between the enumeration and classification of different types of entities and the semantic analysis of being? What deserves to be listed as a separate item of ontological enumeration? Should being itself, insofar as it can be distinguished from, and predicated of, what there is, somehow be added to it? Is the assertion of being or existence, and its distinction from nonbeing, an act of enumeration and classification? Does the distinction between being and nonbeing presuppose a definition of being? Does the definition of being require a previous understanding of nonbeing? Can being be defined as the common denominator of what there is? But to what extent is an understanding of "being itself" the condition of the possibility of referring to what there is? In what sense does it determine the extent of enumeration and the enumerability of enumerables?

According to W. V. Quine, the ontological problem *What is there?* can be answered in one word: "everything," although this answer may leave "room for disagreement over cases."[28] The Vaiśeṣika system of "categories" (*padārtha*), with its inherent claim of comprehensive enumeration, is obviously committed to this answer; but it also illustrates its ambiguity and questionability, and the scope of what Quine called "room for disagreement." This becomes more obvious if we compare the Vaiśeṣika project of enumeration with other approaches to "everything" (*sarvam*), or the totality of what there is, for instance in the Buddhist Sarvāstivāda-Vaibhāṣika school.

Apart from other significant differences concerning the systematic premises and the psychological as well as soteriological orientations of Vaiśeṣika and Sarvāstivada, their notions of "everything" are characteristically different. Above all, this has to do with the role of time in these two traditions. In Vaiśeṣika, time itself is thoroughly integrated into the system of horizontal enumeration: It is one of nine substances (*dravya*), an enumerable item on a par with other world constituents. Time is an entity, not the horizon in which entities exist nor the abyss in which they disappear. There is not much room for reflections concerning "being and time," or "being-in-time," nor for speculations on past, present, and future as modes of existence or on potentiality and actuality.

In the Sarvāstivāda-Vaibhāṣika list of seventy-five basic enumerables (*dharma*), time as such does not appear at all.[29] Yet temporality is a far more prominent and pervasive theme than in the Vaiśeṣika. The four Sarvāstivāda masters Dharmatrāta, Ghoṣaka, Vasumitra, and Buddhadeva are associated with basically different positions concerning the relationship and distinction between past, present, and future.[30] The Sarvāstivāda is not a system of evolution comparable to the Sāṃkhya. Yet there are significant affinities. Actuality and potentiality, manifestation and latency are pervasive themes in both traditions.

This brings us back to the distinction between evolutionary and nonevolutionary, vertical and horizontal schemes of cosmology, and more specifically, to the systematic relationship and confrontation between Vaiśeṣika and Sāṃkhya-Yoga that constitutes the main topic of this chapter.

8. In traditional Indian doxography as well as in the modern histories of Indian philosophy, the systems of Vaiśeṣika and Sāṃkhya are often presented as characteristic examples of two different theories of causality, that is, of *asatkāryavāda* and *satkāryavāda*. These doxographic titles are very familiar. But is their meaning as clear, and their opposition as unambiguous, as it appears to be?

Satkāryavāda is commonly defined as the theory that the effect (*kārya*), or rather the product, already exists in its material cause; and hence nothing new is brought into existence or produced in the process of causation. *Asatkāryavāda,* on the other hand, is defined as the theory that the product does not preexist in its material cause, and hence is produced; that is, brought into existence in the process of causation.

In the extant Sāṃkhya literature, the locus classicus for the *satkāryavāda* is verse 9 of Īśvarakṛṣṇa's *Sāṃkhyakārikā:*

> *asadakaraṇād upādānagrahaṇāt sarvasambhavābhāvāt/*
> *śaktasya śakyakaraṇāt kāraṇabhāvāc ca satkāryam//*

The verse gives us five reasons why the effect has to preexist in its material cause: what is not cannot be produced; the effect requires a material cause; not everything arises from everything; the cause produces only what corresponds to its potential; and the effect has the nature of the cause. The first reason states that it is impossible to produce something out of nothing; the following reasons postulate a more specific correspondence between the nature of the product and its cause. Although these two types of reasons seem easily compatible and, in fact, complementary, their coordination is not without problems.[31]

The Sāṃkhya "theory of the preexistent effect" has to be seen in connection with the concept of *prakṛti,* the inherently dynamic primeval nature (and ultimate material cause, *pradhāna*) that contains the entire spatiotemporal universe in a "nonmanifest" (*avyakta*) state. The undifferentiated *prakṛti* evolves periodically into the manifest world through a process of internal modification (*pariṇāma*) and by producing out of and yet within itself a series of "differentiations" (*vikāra, vikṛti*). This process is at the same time a process of manifestation and presentation for the "spirit" (*puruṣa*); that is, pure, passive, yet actualizing awareness. The basic premise of this explanation is that nothing can come out of nothing and that the undifferentiated totality of *prakṛti* anticipates the existence of all particular entities. This is the universal cosmological and metaphysical application of the first reason for the *satkāryavāda.* The following reasons are more specific, but also more problematic if applied to the concept of *prakṛti.* They presuppose not just an undifferentiated preexistence of differentiated entities nor the preexistence of differentiated effects in a nondifferentiated cause; instead, they postulate special causes for special effects. Particularity and differentiation themselves cannot be "new"; that is, originating out of nonparticularity and nondifferentiation. A special product, such as sesame oil, requires a special material cause: sesame seeds. But this process of specified derivation cannot be traced back to the ultimate material cause, *prakṛti* itself, which is by definition nonspecific, nonmanifest, and undifferentiated.[32]

9. For the Vaiśeṣika *asatkāryavāda,* there is no analogous locus classicus. In the Vaiśeṣikasūtras, the issue is repeatedly referred to, specifically in several Sūtras of *Adhyāya* IX, as well as in *Sūtra* I, 1, 8.[33] In Praśastapāda's authoritative systematization of the Vaiśeṣika, the *asatkāryavāda* receives very little explicit attention. On the one hand, this may suggest that it is basically taken for granted, or, as B. Faddegon notes, "considered a settled tenet of the Vaiśeṣika system."[34] On the other hand, one gets the impression that Praśastapāda avoids the issue or considers it somewhat obsolete.[35]

According to its standard interpretation, the *asatkāryavāda* teaches the production of new entities out of their constituents; that is, the origination of wholes (*avayavin*) that are genuinely new units with an identity of their own and something over and above the sum total of their parts. The Vaiśeṣika does not recognize a nonmanifest, potential state of the world. In general, it tends to avoid the ideas of potentiality and latency, as well as the assumption of different "modes of being."[36] Instead, it tries to understand the world in terms of a combination, aggregation, and separation, but also substitution and replacement of definite, actual, distinct entities. In the terminology of the *Mahābhāṣya,* it emphasizes *ādeśa* instead of *vikāra.*[37]

The historical process of debate has led to an increasingly confrontational articulation of the two positions, but also to interaction and mutual accommodation. The idea of aggregation gains some significance in Sāṃkhya. Some Sāṃkhya thinkers even try to explain the transition from potentiality to actuality, or latency to manifestness, in terms of *asatkāryavāda* premises, although few go as far a Mādhava, who interprets "manifestation" (*abhivyakti*) itself as a new, additional factor. Mādhava and others also adopt a form of atomism for the Sāṃkhya.[38] On the other hand, the Vaiśeṣika has made concessions to the idea of potentiality; the concept of *śakti* itself has its own peculiar history in

Vaiśeṣika. In their rejection of the Buddhist theory of momentariness (*kṣaṇikatva, kṣaṇabhaṅga*), which implies a far more radical notion of universal actuality, the Naiyāyikas and Vaiśeṣikas (including Śrīdhara and Udayana) have invoked various ideas of latent causality, potentiality, and manifestation.[39]

Yet, in spite of much dialectical interaction and various tacit accommodations, what characterizes the debate most is a certain refusal to address each other's basic premises concerning the nature of being and the different meanings in which the words *sat* and *asat* are used. The transition from "nonbeing" to "being" that the Vaiśeṣika accepts is not identical with the one that the Sāṃkhya rejects. With the appropriate semantic adjustment and clarification, the Vaiśeṣika theory itself could easily be called *satkāryavāda*. The disagreement is as much about the meaning and usage of words, as it is about the nature of reality and causality. Nonetheless, the debate between *satkāryavāda* and *asatkāryavāda* is a genuinely ontological debate.[40] The familiar doxographic labels, which present this as a debate concerning different theories of causality, hide rather than reveal this underlying ontological significance.

10. The Sāṃkhya concept of *prakṛti*, or of the unevolved, nonmanifest (*avyakta*) cause and substance of our manifest, actual universe, is among the most familiar notions of Indian philosophy. But do we understand its ontological implications? Do we know what the Sāṃkhya means when it speaks of a latent, unevolved, nonmanifest preexistence of the product in its cause, and of the world in *prakṛti*? Do we know what we mean when we speak about "being" in a latent, nonmanifest, potential state?

Various ancient and popular metaphors illustrate such withdrawal into latency (and reemergence from it): The world disappears in, and emanates from, *prakṛti* in a manner that may be compared to the way in which a tortoise protrudes, retracts, and hides its limbs.[41] But what is the ontological and cosmological meaning of such hiding? In their own way, modern Sāṃkhya scholars have tried to paraphrase and explain the latent preexistence of all products, including the manifest universe itself, in their causes. We hear, for instance, that the cosmic products preexist in the sense "that they are specifications of the inherent generativity of primordial materiality" and, furthermore, "that the emergence of the various effects together with the causal matrix from which they derive is characterized in terms of continuing dynamic transformation."[42] Whatever this may mean, it does not address the fundamental ontological issue.

Regardless of all specific causal processes and all specific functions ascribed to the three *guṇa,* we have to proceed from and return to the basic ontological premise, as it is found in the Sāṃkhya teachings and in related texts: "There is no existence for that which is not; nor is there nonexistence for that which is" (*na-asato vidyate bhāvo, na-abhāvo vidyate sataḥ*).[43] "That which is cannot arise in what is not; nor can that which is loose its reality" (*na-asati sataḥ sambhavaḥ, na sata ātmahānam*).[44] "That which is, is once and for all; that which is not, is not (i.e., nonexistent) once and for all. There is no origination for what is not, nor destruction for what is" (*yad asty asty eva tad, yan na-asti na-asty eva tad. asato na-asti sambhavaḥ, sato na-asti vināśaḥ*).[45]

The last of these three statements is attributed to the Sāṃkhya teacher Vārṣagaṇya. According to another fragment ascribed to this teacher, the entire threefold world may withdraw from manifestness, but not from reality; even in the state of withdrawal, it continues to exist, because destruction is unacceptable. Because of its merger (*saṃsarga*) with *prakṛti,* the world is "subtle"; and because of such subtleness, it cannot be perceived. Therefore, destruction is nothing but withdrawal from manifestness (*tad etat trailokyaṃ vyakter apaiti na sattvād, apetam apy asti vināśapratiṣedhāt. saṃsargāc ca-asya saukṣmyam, saukṣmyāc ca-anupalabdhis. tasmād vyaktyapagamo vināśaḥ*).[46] This is the state of the world when it is entirely without "transformation" or "differentiation" (*vikāra, vikṛti*).

11. Classical Sāṃkhya shares its basic term *vikāra* with the "science of being" which Uddālaka Āruṇi presents in the Chāndogya Upaniṣad and which forms the background of the *satkāryavāda.* According to Uddālaka's teaching, all entities are differentiations, transformations (*vikāra*) of pure being (*sat*), the universal substrate. They are identifiable particulars and have a reality and identity of their own, insofar as they can be named. "Name and form" (*nāmarūpa*) are the vehicle, if not the principle, of differentiation (*vyākṛ*) and particularization. The manifestation of the world coincides with the differentiation of the absolute.[47]

To what extent does this describe the position of Sāṃkhya? Is manifestation nothing else than differentiation of one underlying substrate?[48] Here, we have to remember that, unlike Uddālaka's "science of being" (*sadvidyā*), classical Sāṃkhya is a dualistic system, which recognizes the "spirit" (*puruṣa*), that is, pure, objectless, awareness, as the second irreducible principle. Evolution and differentiation, so we are told, are "for the sake of the spirit" (*puruṣārtha*). What then is the role of awareness in the process of manifestation and actualization? What is its cosmological role and its ontological meaning? To what extent does it contribute to, or perhaps even constitute, actuality and manifestness (*āvirbhāva, prādurbhāva*)?[49]

The statements of the Sāṃkhya texts tend to be metaphorical and somewhat elusive; but the basic position seems to be clear: The presence of the *puruṣa,* pure awareness, does indeed "solicit" the process of differentiation and actualization; yet, it does not in any way contribute to the process as such. Neither does it supply any of the specific features or structures of the world of experience, nor does it generate the character of manifestness or actuality. "Manifestness" (*vyakti*) as well as differentiation are produced *for* the *puruṣa.* The process is entirely objective: *prakṛti* generates its own visibility, transforms itself into a content of experience. It does so through the mediating presence of the three *guṇa,* which are psychological as well as physical and cosmological principles, "threads" that extend from the state of potentiality into the actual, manifest, differentiated universe.[50] Without this, there would be nothing to be experienced.

In its "subtle," nonmanifest state, the world is inherently imperceptible; its imperceptibility is not due to any incapacity of the perceiving subjects. Even Kapila, the greatest sage and seer, could not see and identify entities in their latent, potential state; he could not see the world in *prakṛti,* because it is objectively nonmanifest.[51] On the other hand, classical Sāṃkhya does not admit any movement between different states of being, any fluctuation between actuality and potentiality, in awareness itself. The spirit is unchanging, contentless, absolute awareness and presence per se, unaffected by what is presented to or withdrawn from it.

12. The allied Yoga system also recognizes the immutability of the pure "spirit" (*puruṣa*), but leaves much room for "actuality" and "potentiality" within the "mind" (*citta*). Transition from potentiality (*śak-*

ti) to actuality (*abhivyakti*) in the mental sphere means change from an unconscious, "unnoticed" (*aparidṛṣṭa*) state to a conscious, "noticed" (*paridṛṣṭa*) one.[52] Furthermore, the Yoga associates the conceptions of actuality and potentiality, manifest (*vyakta*) and subtle (*sūkṣma*) with time and temporality: Present phenomena are manifest, that is, actual; past and future phenomena are subtle, that is, potential (*vartamānā vyaktātmāno, atītānāgatāḥ sūkṣmātmānaḥ*).[53] The concepts of actuality and potentiality are thus used in an attempt to clarify the nature of time and its three "routes" (*adhvan*); that is, past, present, and future.

The connection of these reflections with Sarvāstivāda ideas about "being" and "time" is as obvious as the affinity that the Yoga teachings concerning actuality and potentiality in the mental sphere have with the Yogācāra-Vijñānavāda tradition.[54] This tradition distinguishes the subconscious, latent traces stored in the "base consciousness" (*ālayavijñāna*) from the actuality of present experience; that is, the actual functioning (*pravṛtti*) of awareness. The mind itself is the substrate and "seed" of all phenomena (*sarvabīja*); through a process of internal transformation (*vijñānapariṇāma*), it evolves into the manifoldness of actual experiences and objects of awareness.[55] The great Vedānta (and Mīmāṃsā) philosopher Maṇḍanamiśra applies this idea in his own way; he speaks of an apparent unfolding (*vipariṇāma, vivartana*) of the pure subject (*draṣṭṛ*) or self (*ātman*).[56] In general, the tradition of Advaita Vedānta has adopted important suggestions from Buddhism as well as Sāṃkhya and Yoga, and it has transformed them into its own complex theories of "apparent transformation" (*vivarta*) and "objective illusion" (*māyā*).

Unlike Yogācāra, classical Yoga does not attempt to reduce *esse* to *percipi*, or "being" to "being experienced." Yet, it tends to ascribe a more constitutive role to awareness or experience than the Sāṃkhya and to interpret it as an efficient factor of manifestation and actualization.

The correspondences between the *satkāryavāda*, especially in its Yogic version, and certain ideas of Sarvāstivāda and Yogācāra are undeniable. On the other hand, there are significant Buddhist parallels of the *asatkāryavāda*. In general, the Buddhists have asked challenging questions concerning the relationship between wholes and their parts, and the ontological status of aggregates (such as the famous chariot discussed in the *Milindapañha*).[57] Implicitly or explicitly, the Nyāya and Vaiśeṣika have responded to this challenge.

In their own way, the Buddhists have articulated the idea of the "prior nonexistence" (*prāgabhāva*) of the product in its cause. The formula that epitomizes the precarious fact that something exists that did not exist before—*abhūtvā bhavati, abhūtvā bhāvaḥ*—is typically Buddhist and most familiar in the Sarvāstivāda debates.[58] As a matter of fact, some Sāṃkhya texts refer explicitly to the *asatkāryavāda* of the Buddhists.[59]

The debate between the two theories that the product does, or does not, preexist in its material cause, that is, *satkāryavāda* and *asatkāryavāda*, fades away without a clear victor and without a generally recognized solution of basic ontological problems. It remains, of course, a familiar doxographic issue and is referred to as such by numerous later authorities, including Udayana.[60] Up to the end of the living debate, its protagonists fail to address each other's divergent concepts of being. Yet, this debate has exemplary significance in the history of Indian ontology. Although it has not produced definitive solutions, its results are by no means negligible. What it has left behind is a rich legacy of problematic concepts, questions, and suggestions concerning actuality and potentiality and the enigmatic relationship between being and time.[61]

Chapter 3: Notes

1. Cf. M. Biardeau, *Études de mythologie hindoue*, vol. 1. *Cosmogonies purāṇiques* (Paris, 1981), p. 8, n. 1: "un recommencement plus radical." See, on the other hand, *Ṛgveda* VI, 48, 22: *sakṛdd ha dyaur ajāyata, sakṛd bhūmir ajāyata.*

2. In particular, this is the case in Buddhist thought, but also in Advaita Vedānta and other Hindu systems.

3. Cf., for instance, Bhartṛhari, *VP* III/9, 51ff. with Helārāja's commentary; this text rejects a strictly cyclical view of time and the possibility of returning to an identical past; see later, Chapter 9, n. 10.

4. On the other hand, *puruṣa* is coordinated with *prakṛti* in a "horizontal" fashion.

5. This would apply most specifically to *viśeṣa,* "ultimate particularity," the fifth category of the system.

6. G. Bergmann, *Logic and Reality* (Madison, 1964), p. 127; on Quine, see earlier, Chapter 1, n. 28f.

7. E. Frauwallner, *Gesch. d. ind. Phil.*, vol. 2, p. 27; cf. vol. 1, p. 313.

8. See *Chāndogya Upaniṣad* VI, 2; *Aitareya Upaniṣad* III, 3, has a list of five elements (adding air and ether).

9. See E. Frauwallner, *Kl. Schr.*, p. 64 (originally in *Wiener Zeitschrift für die Kunde des Morgenlandes* 32, 1925): "In einem Dualismus . . . ist zu der Annahme einer Entstehung der Elemente gar keine Nötigung vorhanden, sondern sie erscheint vielmehr recht gekünstelt. Einfach und natürlich ist es, dass Welt und Einzelwesen aus den ewigen Elementen hervorgehen und wieder in sie zurürckkehren."

10. *Kl. Schr.*, pp. 96ff. (originally in *Zeitschrift für Indologie und Iranistik* 4, 1926); see also *Aitareya Upaniṣad* III, 3.

11. See J. A. B. van Buitenen, "Studies in Sāṃkhya (I)" *Studies in Indian Literature and Philosophy,* ed. L. Rocher (Delhi, 1988), pp. 43–51 (originally in *JAOS* 76, 1956, 153–157); on "horizontal evolution" or "ramification," cf. van Buitenen's "Studies in Sāṃkhya (II)" ibid., pp. 53–73; especially p. 55 (originally in *JAOS* 77, 1957, 15–25).

12. Cf. *Mahābhārata* XII, 175ff. (Bhṛgu and Bharadvāja): XII, 239ff. (Śuka and Vyāsa); XIV, 42 (*Anugītā;* Brahmā presents an evolutionary scheme of the elements and the emergence of our empirical world).

13. Cf. M. Biardeau, *Cosmogonies purāṇiques* (cited in n. 1), p. 20f. (on *tanmātra* and *bhūta,* with reference to *Kūrmapurāṇa* I, 4, 24f.); see also P. Chakravarti, *Origin and Development of the Sāṃkhya System of Thought* (Calcutta, 1951; reprint Delhi, 1975), p. 242 (on cumulative and noncumulative concepts of *tanmātra*).

14. See *Mahābhārata* XII, 175ff. (Bhṛgu and Bharadvāja).

15. *Mahābhārata* XII, 267, 4ff. (Asita Devala).

16. See XII, 267, 7ff.

17. Cf. E. Frauwallner, *Gesch. d. ind. Phil.*, vol. 2, pp. 27f.; 301ff.; see also F. O. Schrader, *Über den Stand der indischen Philosophie zur Zeit Mahāvīras und Buddhas* (Leipzig, 1902; Diss. Strassburg), pp. 52ff. Materials concerning the philosophy of the materialists (Bārhaspatya, Cārvāka) have been collected by M. Namai in two articles in Japanese; see *Indological Review* 2 (1976): 33–74; 3 (1981): 59–78; and by D. P. Chattopadhyaya and M. K. Gangopadhyaya in the anthology *Cārvāka/Lokāyata* (New Delhi, 1990).

18. Cf. E. Frauwallner, ibid., and F. O. Schrader, ibid.; see also C. Vogel, *The Teachings of the Six Heretics* (Wiesbaden, 1970).

19. Cf. H. Ui, *The Vaiśeṣika Philosophy,* pp. 36ff., 65ff.; A. Thakur, Introduction to *VS,* ed. Jambuvijaya, pp. 6ff. (on the tradition of Ṣaḍulūka Rohagupta, a schismatic Jaina teacher who apparently adopted Vaiśeṣika teachings).

20. See K. K. Dixit, *Jaina Ontology*, p. 28; for an example of a comprehensive classification in Jainism, see also *Uttarādhyayanasūtra*, ch. 36.

21. *Jaina Ontology*, p. 27.

22. Cf. ibid., pp. 18ff.

23. Cf. Vasubandhu, *AKBh* I, p. 20 (ed. P. Pradhan, 2d ed., Patna, 1975, p. 14): *mohendriyarucitraidhāt tisraḥ skandhādideśanāḥ*). Other broad categories of classification include the juxtaposition of *saṃskṛta* ("conditional") and *asaṃskṛta* ("unconditional") elements; cf. O. Rosenberg, *Die Probleme der buddhistischen Philosophie* (Heidelberg, 1924; reprint San Francisco, 1976), pp. 120–140 (Russian edition, Petrograd, 1918); Nyanatiloka, *Guide Through the Abhidhamma Piṭaka*, 3d ed. by Nyanaponika (Colombo, 1957); J. Takasaki, *An Introduction to Buddhism*, trans. R. W. Giebel (Tokyo, 1987), pp. 107–127.

24. Cf. O. Rosenberg, *Die Probleme*, p. 83; J. R. Carter, *Dhamma: Western Academic and Sinhalese Buddhist Interpretations* (Tokyo, 1978); T. Stcherbatsky, *The Central Conception of Buddhism and the Meaning of the Word Dharma* (London, 1923; reprint Delhi, 1974).

25. Cf. Vasubandhu, *AKBh* I, 2 (ed. P. Pradhan, p. 2); Candrakīrti, *Prasannapadā* on *MK* XVII, 1 (ed. L. de La Vallée Poussin, p. 304); XXIII, 7 (457); see also Buddhaghosa, *Atthasālinī*, (commentary on *Dhammasaṅgaṇi*), §94: *sabhāvaṃ dhārenti*.

26. Cf. Vasubandhu, *AKBh* III, p. 3 (ed. P. Pradhan, p. 112): *svalakṣaṇadhāraṇād dhātuḥ*.

27. Cf. E. Conze, *Buddhist Thought in India* (London, 1962), pp. 204ff., 220ff. (dharmas as *svabhavaśūnya*); see also *The Large Sūtra on Perfect Wisdom*, part 1, trans. E. Conze (London, 1961), p. 98 (I, 4, 13): "A Bodhisattva should therefore be trained in non-attachment to all dharmas, and in their unreality—in the sense that he does not construct or discriminate them."

28. See earlier, Chapter 1, no. 28. See also P. M. Williams, "On the Abhidharma Ontology," *JIPh* 9 (1981): 227–257; Williams cites Quine's ontological question and discusses its implications and problems with reference to the Sarvāstivāda views on being, time, and intentionality.

29. See earlier, n. 24; see also S. Schayer, *Contributions to the Problem of Time in Indian Philosophy* (Cracow, 1938), pp. 19f.

30. See S. Schayer, *Contributions*, pp. 28ff.; L. de La Vallée Poussin, "Documents d'Abhidharma," *Mélanges chinois et bouddhiques* 5 (1936–37): 75–158; P. M. Williams, "Buddhadeva and Temporality," *JIPh* 4 (1976–77): 279–294.

31. On the ambiguities of "production" and "manifestation," see later, Chapter 8; on the interpretation of *SK*, v. 9, see also Y. Wadhwani-Shah, "A New Plausible Explanation of Sāṅkhya-Kārikā 9," *JIPh* 17 (1989): 211–224.

32. However, one might say that the theory of the three *guṇa* addresses the problem in its own, mythical fashion.

33. Cf. *VS* I, 1, 8: *dravyāṇi dravyāntaram ārabhante;* see also Candrānanda's commentary on this Sūtra.

34. See B. Faddegon, *The Vaiçeṣika System*, p. 29; cf. also Vyomaśiva, *Vy.*, p. 602 (*vaiśeṣikaśāstre hy asad utpadyata iti prasiddham*); and Mallavādin, *DNC*, vol. 2, pp. 502f. (*asatkāryatvasiddhi* and the lost *Kaṭandī* on *VS*).

35. Likewise, Praśastapāda has very little to say about nonbeing (*asat, abhāva*) in general. This is, of course, very different with his successors. Praśastapāda himself notes that for a Vaiśesika to accept the preexistence of the product would be contrary to the premises of his school (*svaśāstravirodhin*); see PBh, p. 234. Cf. also Śrīdhara's paraphrase, *NK*, p. 237; and Vyomaśiva, *Vy.*, p. 602.

36. Vācaspati explains that according to the Vaiśeṣika the manifest (actual) arises from the manifest and that the atoms are manifest (actual); see *Tattvakaumudī* on *SK* 15 (Introduction): *vyaktāt vyaktam utpadyate . . . paramāṇava hi vyaktāḥ*).

37. For *ādeśa* in the sense of "substitution," "substitute," see *Mahābhāṣya* I, 1, 56 (on *Vārttika* 11f.; vol. 1, pp. 136f.). Patañjali further paraphrases: *yo 'bhūtvā bhavati.*

38. Cf. Bhāsarvajña, *NBhūṣ*, p. 569; see also Uddyotakara, *NV* IV, 1, 48 (Calc. S.S., p. 998; on the production of *abhivyakti*, "manifestation," but without explicit reference to Mādhava). On Mādhava in general, see E. A. Solomon, *The Commentaries of the Sāṃkhya Kārikā—A Study* (Ahmedabad, 1974), pp. 153–169.

39. The Vaiśeṣika commentators use terms such as *sāmarthya* and *yogyatā* (capability, capacity) which have obvious connotations of potentiality; cf. Śrīdhara, *NK*, p. 144 (*kāraṇasāmarthya*); Udayana, *Kir.*, GOS, pp. 93–97 (*sāmarthya* and the Buddhist doctrine of momentariness and pure actuality). For implications of "potentiality" in the Vaiśeṣika "universals," including *sattā*, see later, Chapter 8, sections 6, 12.

40. Cf. W. Liebenthal, *Satkārya in der Darstellung seiner buddhistischen Gegner* (Stuttgart, 1934), p. 50: "Der satkārya-vāda ist die letzte theoretische Spitze einter Diskussion ontologischen Inhalts."

41. Cf. P. Chakravarti, *Origin and Development* (cited in n. 13), p. 220.

42. G. J. Larson in *Sāṃkhya. A Dualist Tradition in Indian Philosophy*, ed. G. J. Larson and R. S. Bhattacharya (Princeton, 1987; *EIPh*), p. 68.

43. *Bhagavadgītā* II, 16.

44. *YBh* IV, 12; cf. *NBh* I, 1, 29: *na-asata ātmalābhaḥ, na sata ātmahānam.* For

all this, we have to recall the instruction of Śvetaketu, *Chāndogya Upaniṣad* VI, 1ff.

45. Cf. Vasubandhu, *AKBh* V, p. 27 (ed. P. Pradhan, p. 301); see also A. Wezler, "Remarks on the Sarvasarvātmakatvavāda," *Philosophical Essays*, A. Thakur Felicitation Vol., (Calcutta, 1987), pp. 166–181 (especially pp. 178f.).

46. See *YD*, ed. R. C. Pandeya, p. 57. Pandeya reads *asaṃsargāc* instead of *saṃsargāc*, but this seems hardly tenable; on this term and the meaning of the statement, cf. A. Wezler, "Remarks" (n. 45), pp. 176ff. A very similar statement appears in *YBh* III, 13; but unlike *YD*, this text does not mention the name of Vārṣagaṇa/Vārṣagaṇya. See also Helārāja on *VP* III/9, p. 55.

47. Cf. *Chāndogya Upaniṣad* VI, 1–4; especially the recurrent formula *vācārambhanaṃ vikāro nāmadheyam*, and VI, 3, 2: *nāmarūpe vyākaravāṇi*.

48. Cf. the presentation by Śaṅkara, *BSBh* II, 1, 4.

49. Whether only one *puruṣa* is assumed or (as in certain Sāṃkhya schools) many is not relevant in this particular context.

50. The guṇas, *sattva*, *rajas*, and *tamas* constitute and differentiate the realm of feelings and other mental phenomena (*pleasure*, *pain*, *passion*, *dullness*, etc.) as much as the physical, material realm. Even cognition and detachment are ultimately administered by the guṇas for the pure, unaffected *puruṣa*.

51. Cf. *YD*, p. 70: *śrīkapilabrāhmaṇair api pradhānapuruṣāv apratyakṣāv iti naḥ śāstram*. The text contrasts this with the Nyāya-Vaiśeṣika theory that atoms are accessible to "yogic perception" (*yogipratyakṣa*).

52. See *YBh* III, 15: *cittasya dvaye dharmāḥ*; Vyāsa uses the terms *śakti* vs. *abhivyakti*, *aviśeṣa* vs. *viśeṣa*, etc.; cf. also *YBh* II, 19; IV, 13.

53. See *YBh* IV, 13; cf. also III, 13; IV, 12. Accomplished yogins know past and future objects; accordingly, these have to be ontologically validated.

54. For a comparative study, see B. M. Sinha, *Time and Temporality in Sāṃkhya-Yoga and Abhidharma Buddhism* (New Delhi, 1983).

55. Cf. Vasubandhu, *Triṃśikā*, v. 1 (with commentary by Sthiramati); see also v. 18.

56. See Maṇḍana, *Brahmasiddhi*, ed. S. Kuppuswami Sastri (Madras, 1937; reprint Delhi, 1984), p. 7; cf. also P. Hacker, *Vivarta*, (Wiesbaden, 1953; Ak. Wiss. Lit. Mainz), especially pp. 34ff., on the relation between *vivarta* and *pariṇāma*.

57. See *Milindapañha*, ed. V. Trenckner, (London, 1880; Pali Text Society; reprint 1962), pp. 26ff.

58. Cf. Nāgārjuna, *MK* XXVII, 12: *na-apy abhūtvā samudbhūto*; see also *MK*, ed. L. de La Vallée Poussin, p. 263, n. 2: "La formule *abhūtvā bhavati* . . . est

caractéristique du Bouddhisme; elle joue un grand rôle dans la controverse du *sarvāstivāda*."

59. Cf. Gauḍapāda's commentary on *SK*, 9; see also *NBh* IV, 1, 14.

60. See, for instance, Udayana, *Kir.*, GOS, p. 227.

61. See later, Chapters 8 and 9.

4

The Vaiśeṣika Categories: An Introductory Survey

1. In his *Vyomavatī,* the Vaiśeṣika commentator Vyomaśiva describes the basic intention of Kaṇāda, the mythical founder of the Vaiśeṣika system: "I shall enumerate everything in this world that has the character of being" (*yad iha bhāvarūpam, tat sarvaṃ mayā-upasaṃkhyātavyam*). In a later section of the same work, Kaṇāda's project appears in a somewhat different formulation: "I shall name everything that has the character of being" (*yad bhāvarūpam, tat sarvam abhidhāsyāmi*).[1] A similar statement is found, approximately two centuries later, in Udayana's *Kiraṇāvalī.*[2]

Erich Frauwallner has suggested that Vyomaśiva and Udayana knew an "original beginning" of the Vaiśeṣikasūtra not found in the currently available versions of the text and that their statements are quotes from, or paraphrases of, this "original beginning." This thesis is challenging, but not convincing; already Bhartṛhari took the allegedly new beginning *atha-ato dharmaṃ vyākhyāsyāmaḥ* for granted.[3] Vyomaśiva's description of Kaṇāda's project may go back to older sources;

but it seems to be a retrospective and explanatory statement, instead of an actual quote. It ascribes to the author or compiler of the Vaiśeṣikasūtra an all-inclusive ontological project and perspective, and the idea of enumerating the totality of what there is within one comprehensive horizon of being. By the time of Vyomaśiva, Kaṇāda had been raised to the status of an omniscient (*sarvajña*) seer and sage whose intention to enumerate and classify all entities could be invoked as evidence for the completeness of the Vaiśeṣika table of categories. Śrīdhara and Udayana, too, speak repeatedly of the omniscient "great sage who was determined to enunciate all objects."[4] Such completeness of enumeration, and not (as suggested by Anantalal Thakur) the exclusion of nonbeing, seems to be at stake in Vyomaśiva's references to Kaṇāda's intentions.[5]

At any rate, Vyomaśiva's and Udayana's statements are expressions of classical Vaiśeṣika self-understanding. The project of a comprehensive inventory, not just of a particular type of entities but of whatever there is, and the idea of an enumeration that includes and supersedes all other enumerations are central to this self-understanding. On the other hand, this idea has been criticized as internally inconsistent, theoretically unfeasible, and above all, as soteriologically irrelevant or counterproductive. Even the allied Nyāya system has raised the charge of soteriological irrelevance against the Vaiśeṣika project of exhaustive enumeration.[6]

Regardless of all specific historical and philological questions, and whatever the "original beginning" of the Vaiśeṣikasūtra may have been, it is safe to say that, in its own way and in accordance with its own self-understanding, classical Vaiśeṣika deals with the fundamental ontological question *What is There?*

2. The Vaiśeṣika answer to the question *What is there?* is well known and easily accessible in traditional Indian presentations or modern surveys. A few brief and general reminders will be sufficient. The basic claim is that all entities can be listed and classified under certain fundamental "titles" or "categories" (*padārtha*). The classical version of this list of categories, which is found in Praśastapāda's *Padārthadharmasaṃgraha* and reproduced in numerous later documents of the Vaiśeṣika or of the allied Nyāya and Vaiśeṣika systems can be summarized as follows.

There are six fundamental categories, or divisions of reality: substance (*dravya*), quality (*guṇa*), motion (*karman*), universal (*sāmānya*), particularity (*viśeṣa*), and inherence (*samavāya*). Nonbeing (*abhāva*) does not appear in Praśastapāda's list. These six categories are further specified and subdivided as follows.

There are nine substances or classes of substances: earth, water, fire, air, ether (*ākāśa*), space, time, souls (*ātman*), and mental organs (*manas*). The first four of these are elemental substances; they consist of indivisible, invisible, and indestructible atoms (*aṇu, paramāṇu*). The atoms form aggregates and constitute those composite and noneternal material things with which we are dealing in our practical and empirical lives. Ether, space, and time are nonatomic, unitary, all-pervasive, indestructible substances. The souls, too, are omnipresent and eternal, whereas the "mental organs" (*manas*) are equally eternal, but of atomic dimension, that is, infinitely small.

There are twenty-four qualities: color, taste, smell, and touch; number, dimension, separateness (*pṛthaktva*), conjunction, and disjunction; proximity (i.e., priority in space or time) and distance (posteriority); cognition, pleasure, pain, desire, aversion, and effort; gravity, liquidity, viscidity, disposition (*saṃskāra*); merit and demerit (i.e., good and bad karma); and sound. Some of these qualities are coextensive and coeval with their substrates, whereas others have only a momentary existence. Some can occur in all substances, whereas others are confined to specific substrates. Most qualities reside in one individual substrate, but some, such as conjunction and number, may reside in several entities jointly and simultaneously; all are nonrecurrent quality-particulars.

Motion (*karman*), which may inhere in atoms and their aggregates (i.e., composite physical bodies), but also in the mental organs, is of five different types: moving upward, moving downward, bending, stretching, and simple locomotion (*gamana*).

Universals (*sāmānya*), such as "substanceness," "qualityness," "horseness," "whiteness," and so on, are recurrent generic properties in substances, qualities, and motions. They account for the fact that numerically different individual entities can be associated with an identical concept, referred to by a common term, identified as members of the same class, and distinguished from members of other classes. The supreme, that is, most inclusive, universal is "beingness" or reality (*sattā*); it inheres in all substances, qualities, and motions. Lower, more specific universals (*sāmānyaviśeṣa*) have an exclusive as well as inclusive function.

Particularities (*viśeṣa;* more specifically, *antyaviśeṣa*) are ultimate factors of individual identity. They reside exclusively in the eternal, noncomposite substances, that is, in the individual atoms, souls, and mental organs, and in the unitary substances ether, space, and time. They account for the irreducible identity and distinctness of each of these entities.

Inherence (*samavāya*) is the relationship between entities that cannot occur separately. It is the one omnipresent principle of cooccurrence and coalescence that integrates parts and wholes, particulars and universals, substances, qualities, and motions. It accounts for the fact that we are dealing with concrete things, instead of isolated world constituents.[7]

Śrīdhara says that the structure of Praśastapāda's system involves basically two levels: enunciation or enumeration (*uddeśa*) and characterization or definition (*lakṣaṇa*), which may or may not include a more detailed examination (*parīkṣā*). He defends this twofold structure against those (i.e., primarily Naiyāyikas) who argue that the third element, *parīkṣā,* should always be involved. Prior to Praśastapāda, this threefold division appeared already in Vātsyāyana Pakṣilasvāmin's *Nyāyabhāṣya.*[8]

3. The list of categories is supposed to provide a complete inventory of our world, in accordance with the presumed omniscience of its originator, Kaṇāda. However, there are some noticeable differences between Praśastapāda's inventory and the presentation in Kaṇāda's Sūtras. Apart from the fact that an enumeration of all six categories appears only in one single, somewhat dubious Sūtra, the Vaiśeṣikasūtras list only the first seventeen of Praśastapāda's twenty-four qualities. On the other hand, they pay more attention to nonbeing and its subdivisions than Praśastapāda. The commentators found, of course, ways to deal with such variations. More radical discrepancies are found in other, though less authoritative, Vaiśeṣika texts.

Candramati's *Daśapadārthī* (or *Daśapadārthaśāstra*) is the most conspicuous example. In addition to Praśastapāda's six categories, this short text lists four other basic items: universality per se (i.e., existence); potentiality and nonpotentiality (*śakti, aśakti*); and nonbeing (*abhāva*). Erich Frauwallner has argued that Candramati preceded Praśastapāda, and that Praśastapāda's more conservative teachings are a response to Candramati's radical innovations.[9] Frauwallner's argumentation is persuasive, but not conclusive. The available evidence seems insufficient to establish Candramati's priority; nonetheless, we may adopt it as an attractive hypothesis. Whereas Praśastapāda became the most authoritative systematizer of the school, Candramati found no recognition. Curiously, his work survived in Hsüan-tsang's Chinese translation.

The categorial status of *śakti* has been subject to some debate within the Vaiśeṣika itself, as well as in the Mīmāṃsā.[10] Other debates tried to determine whether *tamas,* "darkness," should be added to the list of substances and whether the "Lord" (*īśvara*) should be accorded the status of a special substance.[11]

Classification and subdivision are obviously problematic with regard to the third category, "motion." How can the different types of motion be distinguished from, and demarcated against, each other? How can they be affiliated with genuine universals, distinctive generic properties? Would it be possible to subsume all motions under one basic class; that is, "locomotion" (*gamana*)?[12] The concept of "motion" (*karman*) itself is unclarified. Its first four subdivisions involve a partial overlap with "action."

The Nyāya author Bhāsarvajña, who sought to reverse Uddyotakara's wholesale adoption of the Vaiśeṣika list of categories, suggested that motion should be removed from the basic list of categories and instead be subsumed under the category "quality."[13] In addition, Bhāsarvajña tried to introduce other, more or less radical changes, most conspicuously in the list of qualities; he also questioned the status of time and space as substances.[14] More than other categories, the list of guṇas was subject to a certain fluctuation. While Jinabhadra (sixth century) still listed Kaṇāda's seventeen qualities, another Jaina author, Haribhadra (eighth century), mentioned twenty-five instead of Praśastapāda's twenty-four. Later authors introduced further revisions.[15] In the following period of coalescence between Nyāya and Vaiśeṣika, nonbeing (*abhāva*) was finally established as the seventh category. It appears in works of the combined systems as well as in pure Vaiśeṣika works, for instance, in Śivāditya's *Saptapadārthī.*

The most sweeping changes were suggested centuries later by one of the greatest representatives of Navyanyāya, Raghunātha Śiromaṇi. They affect the basic list of categories as much as numerous subdivisions. Old items are removed, new ones are added. *Saṃkhyā,* "number," was raised to the rank of a separate category; likewise, such notions as the "status of cause" and "effect" (*kāraṇatva, kāryatva*) appeared as categories.[16] Obviously, the basic orientation has changed; this is no longer a simple extension or modification of the old list. However, Raghunātha's innovations did not have any lasting impact in the history of Nyāya and Vaiśeṣika.

4. The two last items in the classical list, *viséṣa* and *samavāya*, constitute the most peculiar and idiosyncratic Vaiśeṣika categories. They appear somewhat marginal and controversial; nonetheless, they are central and symptomatic. Whereas Praśastapāda ascribed "ultimate particularity" to all eternal substances and specifically to the individual atoms, Candramati reserved it for the three all-pervasive unitary substances ether, space, and time (*ākāśa, dikkāla*).[17] The position of the *Vaiśeṣikasūtra* was more elusive and open to different interpretations. Praśastapāda had the ostensible support of an ancient commentator like Ātreya, who described the "ultimate particularities" as something that remains at the end of all processes of origination and destruction (*utpattivināśayor ante vartate*). Ātreya's formula, which implied the presence of *antyaviśeṣa* in atoms, was cited by Praśastapāda's commentators Vyomaśiva and Śrīdhara.[18]

Not only the opponents of the Vaiśeṣika system,[19] but also some of its allies and advocates have viewed *viśeṣa* as dispensable and redundant. Why should a special principle "particularity" be added to the very own nature (*svarūpa*) of the ultimate individual substances; that is, to what they are by themselves? Raghunātha Śiromaṇi drew the radical conclusion and simply rejected *viśeṣa*.[20] The fact that, in spite of all difficulties, classical Vaiśeṣika insists in keeping this item in its list of categories illustrates the central role of individuation and irreducible distinguishability in its understanding of being.[21]

The elusive history of the concept of *samavāya* cannot be discussed in this brief "introductory survey." M. Hiriyanna says:

> The conception of *samavāya* is described as the cornerstone of the Vaiśeṣika in modern works on that system of philosophy. While the description shows that the importance of *samavāya* is recognized, the terms employed in rendering it into English such as "inherence", "inhesion", "inseparable relation" and "intimate union" raise a doubt whether its exact nature is well understood.[22]

It seems that the idea of *samavāya* has undergone certain modifications or reinterpretations in early Vaiśeṣika. Its earlier meaning was primarily associated with the cooccurrence of material causes and products, with the presence of the "new" thing in its causes and conditions, and with a relationship between cause and effect that coincides with production.[23] Later on, the meaning, or at least the focus of the meaning, shifted toward a more static "inherence" of attributes (i.e., qualities, etc.) in their substrates.

At any rate, classical Vaiśeṣika considers *samavāya* as a principle that is supposed to account for the cooccurrence and coalescence of different and ontologically distinct world constituents within concrete things. In a sense, it restores the unity and concreteness of things after their categorial decomposition.[24]

5. As we have noted earlier, a complete list of all six categories as well as the term *padārtha* itself is found only in one single Sūtra of questionable authenticity. In the version of the Vaiśeṣikasūtra that forms the basis of Śaṅkaramiśra's commentary *Upaskāra,* it appears as I, 1, 4. It is missing, however, in the versions used by several apparently older commentaries; that is, Candrānanda's *Vṛtti,* Bhaṭṭavādīndra's *Vārttika,* and the anonymous commentary edited by Anantalal Thakur.[25]

What does this mean? Is it merely a textual, philological problem, or does it have deeper historical and systematic significance? Does the absence of *Sūtra* I, 1, 4 in some versions of the text reflect a stage of development at which the list of six categories (which is taken for granted not only in Vātsyāyana's *Nyāyabhāṣya* but also by Caraka and Āryadeva[26]) had not been finalized? The Sūtras that follow I, 1, 4 provide a systematic and coherent presentation of substances, qualities, and motions. Universals, particularities, and inherence are introduced later, in a somewhat casual and erratic fashion. Could this be an indication that there was an earlier version of the Vaiśeṣika that dealt only with the first three of Praśastapāda's six categories?

We do not know whether any ancient Vaiśeṣika teachers did, indeed, present the first three categories and their subdivisions as a complete inventory of the world, although the Mahābhārata refers somewhat casually to the "knowers of substances, qualities, and motions" (*dravyaguṇakarmajña*).[27] Yet it is obvious that the two sets of categories are heterogeneous in more than one respect, and that they reflect different questions and viewpoints. In the versions of the Vaiśeṣika system that we have today, they constitute different levels of the systematic structure, and they seem to represent different layers of historical development. The system itself is, in a sense, petrified history. The Vaiśeṣika teachers themselves recognized the difference through an inconspicuous, yet significant terminological distinction: Only the first three categories may be called *objects* (*artha*), but not the universals, and so forth.[28]

Several modern scholars have tried to pursue what we may call the *archaeology of the Vaiśeṣika system*, for instance, R. S. Bodas, Barend Faddegon, Harsh Narain, and above all, Erich Frauwallner.[29] Frauwallner saw basically four stages in the development of the system: (1) an ancient enumerative philosophy of nature; (2) the formulation of new ideas, such as the theory of atoms and a mechanistic view of the physical world; (3) the emergence of the doctrine of categories; and (4) the reorganization of the old philosophy of nature in accordance with the doctrine of categories.[30] Frauwallner was fully aware that his reconstruction was largely hypothetical; yet he insisted that without such an attempt the system could not be rendered intelligible: "Aber der Versuch musste einmal gemacht werden. Denn erst so wird vieles, was im erhaltenen System zunächst seltsam anmutet, verständlich und begreiflich."[31] Frauwallner was convinced that Praśastapāda himself was responsible for a thorough reorganization of the system, which had an impact upon subsequent recensions of the Vaiśeṣikasūtra. He also thought that Praśastapāda's soteriological commitment was foreign to, if not incompatible with, the purely theoretical attitude of ancient Vaiśeṣika. As we have seen, he tried to support this interpretation with his questionable hypothesis of a forgotten or suppressed "original beginning" of the Vaiśeṣikasūtra.[32]

6. We have used the term *padārtha* and translated it as "category." We have noticed Frauwallner's distinction between "philosophy of nature" ("Naturphilosophie") and "doctrine of categories" ("Kategorienlehre"). We have also seen that the Vaiśeṣika itself distinguishes *padārtha* terminologically from *artha*, "object." What then is a *padārtha*, and what do we mean by *category?*

Henry Thomas Colebrooke, the European pioneer of the study of Indian philosophy and the first to summarize in English the basic teachings of the Vaiśeṣika system, rendered *padārtha* as "predicament" or "category."[33] James R. Ballantyne, too, used "category."[34] Max Müller, in one of his earliest publications, made the association with Aristotle more explicit. In his view, Kaṇāda's list of padārthas and Aristotle's doctrine of categories have the same purpose and meaning: They try to establish "what can ultimately be predicated of the objects" ("was in letzter Instanz von den Gegenständen ausgesagt werden kann").[35] The precise meaning and function of Aristotle's concept of *katēgoría* continues to be controversial and elusive. In one sense, his categories are "the highest genera," *ta genikṓtata,* the most fundamental and most pervasive classes and types of entities. But they appear also as forms of predication and even as different meanings of being. There are, of course, many other, supposedly less ambiguous versions of the doctrine of categories in the history of Western thought. In some versions, the categories appear as forms of thought or speech or as conditions of the possibility of experience; in other versions, they are presented as divisions of reality itself.[36] There is no need for us to adopt any specific doctrine of categories or to eliminate all ambiguity from the concept. "Categoriology," just as ontology itself, does not have an authoritative state of latest research nor a clearly recognizable direction of progress. What is important is to be aware that the concept of category suggests an approach to reality that is not direct and straightforward, but involves an awareness of, or reference to, linguistic and cognitive structures. Language, thought, and reality meet in the philosophical concept of category. Categories may be "highest genera," but they do not simply classify elements, natural species, or other groups of individual entities. They involve a different sense of distinction and analysis.[37]

The linguistic reference is clearly present in the literal meaning of *padārtha;* that is, "meaning" or "object of a word." In this sense, *padārtha* is, indeed, a key word of semantic reflection in the Nyāya and other traditions.[38] However, it is also used in a less literal and more casual sense, as "basic issue" or "topic of discourse."[39] As far as its role in classical Vaiśeṣika is concerned, the linguistic connotation is important, but not very conspicuous at the explicit level. Formal definitions, or explanations of the word, are found in later texts,[40] but not in Praśastapāda's *Padārthadharmasaṃgraha.*

For Praśastapāda, the *padārthas* are the most comprehensive units of enumeration, the ultimate divisions of reality, and the most basic correlates of thought and speech. They are not structures or projections of language and thought. Praśastapāda himself says that *astitva,* "isness" (i.e., factuality, objectivity), *jñeyatva,* "knowability," and *abhidheyatva,* "nameability," "denotability" are common denominators of all six categories. The categories are the direct correlates of *uddeśa,* "enunciation," "listing"; that is, the first step in Praśastapāda's twofold procedure. They are not the products of definition, abstraction, and analysis (*lakṣaṇa, parīkṣā*). The categories are not natural species; yet they are supposed to represent divisions that are equally real and objective. Praśastapāda does not discuss the relationship of the Vaiśeṣika padārthas with the grammatical categories "noun," "adjective," "verb," and so on, and he does not consider the possibility of a linguistic derivation of his categories. The actual correspondences are, nonetheless, intriguing, and they have been noticed by traditional Indian grammarians and philosophers as well as by modern scholars.[41]

7. We may now return to our observations concerning the "archaeology" of the Vaiśeṣika system and the manner in which it combines different types and levels of discourse; that is, the cosmological enumeration of elements and other ingredients of the world and the categoriological distinction of modes of being. To illustrate the peculiarity of this approach, a comparison with classical Jaina thought will be helpful.

The Jainas, too, distinguish between "categories" of entities, in particular substance (*dravya*), quality (*guṇa*), and mode or transformation (*paryāya, pariṇāma*). But they do not try to develop this list into a complete inventory of all entities. In addition to the categories, they preserve their doctrine of five fundamental constituents of the world (*astikāya*). No attempt is made to combine the two lists or to integrate cosmological enumeration and categorial distinction.[42] In the Vaiśeṣika, on the other hand, the enumeration of elements and other cosmic factors is subsumed under the list of categories, while at the same time the list of categories appears as a continuation and extrapolation of the enumeration of elements, and so forth. This is a distinctive achievement, but it also accounts for some of the basic problems and difficulties the system has to face.

The list of categories is supposed to provide an all-comprehensive framework under which all significant phenomena recognized by common sense or postulated by preceding traditions of Indian thought can be subsumed. We find the elements of ancient Upaniṣadic and Epic cosmology together with various later ideas of natural forces, and so on, but also, for instance, "merit" and "demerit"; that is, the two types of *adṛṣṭa*, the "invisible" power of past deeds.

The integration and subsumption functions differently if we compare the first and second group of categories. While there is a numerically explicit list of specific substances, qualities, and motions, no such enumeration is offered for the universals (*sāmānya*)—not to mention the ultimate particularities (*viśeṣa*). Nonetheless, Praśastapāda considers the universals as genuine enumerables or objects of enunciation (*uddeśa*). They are "nameable" (*abhidheya*) and identifiable entities, objective ingredients of the world, real subjects of predicates and loci of attributes (*dharmin*).[43] However, the enterprise of enumeration stops at this point. The attributes or predicates (*dharma*) of universals, and so forth, are not recognized as a further set of nameable entities. They are ingredients or results of *lakṣaṇa* and *parīkṣā*, abstractions.[44]

Praśastapāda does not have much to say about the order and sequence of the categories or about the procedures by which they may be derived and justified. To a certain extent, this is done by later commentators, for instance Udayana.[45] That *dravya*, substance, is the central and most fundamental category, is usually taken for granted.[46] For the opponents of the system, such as the Advaita Vedāntins, this priority (*prādhānya*) of substance indicates one of the basic problems of the Vaiśeṣika categories. How can any other entities be listed separately, if substance (*dravya*) is the substrate and essence of everything?[47] The Buddhists, on the other hand, do not recognize any substances at all.

8. The literature concerning classical Vaiśeṣika and its ontology is substantial, but not overwhelming. We have, of course, to start with the Vaiśeṣikasūtra attributed to Kaṇāda. This text continues to pose major philological and chronological problems. We may assume that the bulk of the work was in existence toward the beginning of the Christian era, but that the text continued to undergo revisions and modifications for a number of centuries. Until a few decades ago, Śaṅkaramiśra's *Upaskāra* (late fifteenth century) was the oldest available commentary, and its version of the Vaiśeṣikasūtra was the only available version of the text.[48] In 1957, A. Thakur published an anonymous *Vyākhyā*, which may be several centuries older than the *Upaskāra;* in 1961, Jambuvijaya published his edition of Candrānanda's *Vṛtti,* which may have been written before 1000.[49] Both commentaries contain versions of the text that are significantly, though not dramatically, different from Śaṅkaramiśra's version. In 1985, Thakur's edition of Bhaṭṭavādīndra's *Vaiśeṣikavārttika* was published.[50] Some pandits of the nineteenth century added their own commentaries to their editions of the Sūtra text, in particular Jayanārāyaṇa Tarkapañcānana and Candrakānta Tarkālaṅkāra.[51] Further Sanskrit commentaries were produced in the twentieth century, for instance by Brahmamuni Vidyāmārtaṇḍa, Vīrarāghavācārya, and Tirumalai Tātācārya.[52] Udayavīra Śāstrī's presentation of the Sanskrit text is accompanied by a very detailed explanation in Hindi.[53]

For the exploration of classical Vaiśeṣika ontology, Praśastapāda's *Padārthadharmasaṃgraha* and its commentaries are far more significant than the Vaiśeṣikasūtra commentaries. As we have noted earlier, Praśastapāda's work, which belongs to the period around A.D. 500, is an independent reorganization of the traditional Vaiśeṣika teachings. It became so successful and authoritative that it overshadowed even the Sūtra itself and provided the basis for numerous extensive commentaries. Apart from such late works as Padmanābha Miśra's *Setu* (sixteenth century) and Jagadīśa Tarkālaṅkāra's *Sūkti* (seventeenth century), three older commentaries are our most important sources: Vyomaśiva's *Vyomavatī* (around 800); Śrīdhara's *Nyāyakandalī* (tenth century); Udayana's *Kiraṇāvalī* (eleventh century).[54] These materials are supplemented by numerous digests and more or less independent treatises on the Vaiśeṣika, or the combined Nyāya and Vaiśeṣika systems. Among these, the *Lakṣaṇāvalī* by Udayana, the *Saptapadārthī* by Śivāditya, the *Nyāyalīlāvatī* by Vallabha, and the *Mānamanohara* by Vādivāgīśvara deserve special attention.[55] The basic teachings are also reproduced in numerous manuals of the combined Nyāya and Vaiśeṣika systems.[56] In general, such Nyāya works as Uddyotakara's *Nyāyavārttika* are indispensable for the study of Vaiśeṣika ontology.

In addition, we have to consult the presentation of the Vaiśeṣika by its opponents. This applies, above all, to the so-called dark period of the school between the Vaiśeṣikasūtra and Praśastapāda, and even to a lost Vaiśeṣika commentary by Praśastapāda himself. Most of what we know about this period comes from Buddhist and Jaina sources, such as Dignāga's *Pramāṇasamuccaya*, Bhavya's *Tarkajvālā*, Jinabhadra's *Viśeṣāvaśyakabhāṣya*, and above all, Mallavādin's *Dvādaśāranayacakra*.[57]

9. In the traditional Indian doxographies, the Vaiśeṣika system ranks low. Its commitment to the Veda and its soteriological orientation have been questioned.[58] Advaita Vedāntins have emphasized its distance from the standpoint of nondualism. In Śaṅkara's *Brahmasūtrabhāṣya,* the followers of the Vaiśeṣika appear as "seminihilists" (*ardhavaināśika*).[59]

On the other hand, the realistic, physicalistic, and analytical orientation of the Vaiśeṣika and the allied Nyāya system has attracted the special attention of modern Western and Indian scholars. It has been claimed as an exemplary expression of the nonmystical, secular, analytical, and scientific potential of Indian thought. James R. Ballantyne was convinced that the rediscovery and propagation of Nyāya-Vaiśeṣika in India would provide a basis and framework for the introduction of modern Western science.[60] In Brajendranath Seal's *The Positive Sciences of the Ancient Hindus* (1915), the two systems play an important part. More recently, Indian authors have made renewed efforts to demonstrate in detail the scientific achievements, and the inherent scientific method, in the Vaiśeṣika. This has been done not only in English and Indian vernaculars, but also in Sanskrit.[61]

In his own, philologically committed way, Erich Frauwallner has shown a special fascination with the scientific and secular aspects of the Vaiśeṣika and Nyāya. For him, the approach of ancient Vaiśeṣika exemplified the ideal of pure theory and knowledge for the sake of knowledge, and it provided an Indian counterpart and equivalent to the attitude of classical Greek philosophy and science.[62]

In a different, less historically oriented fashion, the tradition of Nyāya-Vaiśeṣika has appealed to modern analytical philosophers of the "Anglo-Saxon" type. The following statement by Karl H. Potter exemplifies this affinity and appeal:

> Nyāya-Vaiśeṣika offers one of the most vigorous efforts at the construction of a substantialist, realist ontology that the world has ever seen. It provides an extended critique of event-ontologies and idealist metaphysics. It starts from a unique basis for ontology that incorporates several of the most recent Western insights into the question of how to defend realism most successfully. This ontology is "Platonistic" (it admits repeatable properties as Plato's did), realistic (it builds the world from "timeless" individuals as well as spatio-temporal points or events), but neither exclusively physicalistic nor phenomenalistic (it admits as basic individuals entities both directly known and inferred from scientific investigations). Though the system has many quaint and archaic features from a

modern point of view, as a philosophical base for accommodating scientific insights it has advantages: its authors developed an atomic theory, came to treat numbers very much in the spirit of modern mathematics, argued for a wave theory of sound transmission, and adapted an empiricist view of causality to their own uses.[63]

Another leading representative of the analytical approach to Indian thought, Bimal K. Matilal, says that the Nyāya-Vaiśeṣika writers were "critical and positive thinkers, and genuinely interested in logic, analysis of human knowledge and language, and descriptive metaphysics." He adds that their teachings provided an "antidote" to the world-negating attitudes found in Vedānta and Buddhism.[64]

For Potter and Matilal, the latest achievements of Western analytical and scientific thought provide the standards of evaluation. In our introductory observations, we have briefly discussed the validity and the problems of this approach, as far as the "question of being" is concerned. To use modern analytical tools as means of clarification is, indeed, very appropriate if it is not based upon the premise that there is a state of latest research in ontology that would allow us to assess all previous attempts as more or less successful approximations.[65]

Chapter 4: Notes

1. See *Vy.*, p. 47 (ed. Gaurinath Sastri, vol. 1, p. 21): *tathā sarvajñena muninā pṛthivyādisaṃjñāvyatirekeṇa saṃjñāntarānabhidhānād dravyāntarāsattvam iti. yad iha bhāvarūpaṃ tat sarvaṃ mayā-upasaṃkhyātavyam iti hi pratijñā muneḥ;* p. 492 (ed. G. Sastri, vol. 2, p. 73).

2. See *Kir.*, GOS, p. 148 (Bibliotheca Indica, pp. 482f.): *pratijñataṃ hi tena, yad bhāvarūpam tat sarvam abhidhāsyāma ita.* Unlike Vyomaśiva, Udayana does not invoke the intention of Kaṇāda in his commentary on the phrase *saṃjñāntarānabhidhānāt* ("because no other term is mentioned"), which concludes Praśastapāda's list of substances; he simply says (*Kir.*, p. 11): *sūtrakṛtā-iti-śeṣaḥ; lokena-iti vā.*

3. See E. Frauwallner, "Der ursprüngliche Anfang der Vaiśeṣika-Sūtren," *Nachgelassene Werke,* vol. 1, ed. E. Steinkellner (Vienna, 1984), pp. 35–41, especially pp. 37ff. Frauwallner himself admits that Vyomaśiva was aware of the current version of *VS* I, 1, 1 (cf. *Vy.*, p. 20c; ed. Gaurinath Sastri, p. 12). Bhartṛhari's *Mahābhāṣyadīpikā,* which cites this same version in its introductory

portion, was first published in 1965 (ed. V. Swaminathan) and not accessible to Frauwallner during the period of his Vaiśeṣika studies. See also my review of Frauwallner's *Nachgelassene Werke*, *JAOS* 106 (1986):857f.

4. See Vyomaśiva, *Vy.* p. 47 (*sarvajñena muninā*); 492 (*pratijñātaṃ ca maharṣiṇā*); Śrīdhara, *NK*, pp. 8f.; 149 (*sarvajñena maharṣiṇā sarvārthopadeśāya pravṛttena*); Udayana, *Kir.*, p. 148 (*sarvārthopadeśapravṛttena maharṣiṇā pratijñātam*). Praśastapāda mentions the "completeness of enumeration" more casually (cf. *PBh*, p. 8: *tadvyatirekeṇa-anyasya saṃjñānabhidhānāt;* variant reading *saṃjñāntarānabhidhānāt*). For a critical discussion of Kaṇāda's "omniscience", and its compatibility with that of the founders of other systems (e.g., Bādarāyaṇa and Kapila), see Bhāsarvajña, *NBhūṣ*, pp. 162f.

5. Cf. *Vaiśeṣikadarśana of Kaṇāda with an Anonymous Commentary*, ed. A. Thakur (Darbhanga, 1957), Introduction, p. 15. Thakur characterizes Vyomaśiva's and Udayana's statements as a declaration "that only positive (*bhāva*) categories will be explained in the Vaiśeṣika-darśana." Justifying the exclusion of *abhāva* in *VS* and *PBh* became, indeed, increasingly significant for the commentators; however, the statements under discussion (cf. n. 1f.) are *not* invoked in such contexts (see, for instance, *Vy.*, p. 20j; ed. Gaurinath Sastri, p. 14).

6. Cf. *NBh* I, 1, 9: *asty anyad api dravyaguṇakarmasāmānyaviśeṣasamavāyāḥ prameyam, tad bhedena ca-aparisaṃkhyeyam*. Critique is also implied in the reference to *VS* I, 1, 1, which appears in Bhartṛhari's *Mahābhāṣyadīpikā* and, much later, in Durvekamiśra's *Arcaṭāloka* (as quoted by E. Frauwallner, *Nachgelassene Werke*, p. 37; see earlier, n. 3).

7. For a good survey of the systematic structure and the historical precedents of classical Vaiśeṣika, see E. Frauwallner, *Gesch. d. ind. Phil.*, vol. 2.

8. Cf. Śrīdhara, *NK*, p. 26; see also Vātsyāyana, *NBh* I, 1, 3 (Introduction): *trividhā ca-asya śāstrasya pravṛttiḥ uddeśo lakṣaṇaṃ parīkṣā ca-iti;* and B. Faddegon, *The Vaiçeṣika System*, pp. 24f.

9. See E. Frauwallner, "Candramati und sein Daśapadārthaśāstram," *Studia Indologica*, Festschrift W. Kirfel (Bonn, 1955), pp. 65–85; also in: *Kl. Schr.*, pp. 202–222.

10. See E. Frauwallner, *Gesch. d. ind. Phil.*, vol. 2, pp. 154f.

11. On darkness (*tamas*) see, for instance, *VS* V, 2, 21f.; Śrīdhara, *NK*, pp. 9f.; on the Lord (*īśvara*), see Uddyotakara, *NV* IV, 1, 21 (Calc. S.S., pp. 951f.).

12. Cf. *PBh* with *NK*, pp. 296ff. Earlier (*PBh*, p. 293), Praśastapāda introduced the concept of *jātisaṃkara*, overlap or confusion of universals; this illustrates the problematic nature of his classification of motions.

13. See *NBhūṣ*, p. 158; cf. also L. V. Joshi, *A Critical Study of the Pratyakṣa Pariccheda of Bhāsarvajña's Nyāyabhūṣaṇa* (Ahmedabad, 1986), pp. 509ff.; 522ff.

14. Cf. *NBhūṣ*, pp. 590ff.; see also later, Chapter 9, section 7. For revisions in the list of qualities, see *NBhūṣ*, pp. 160ff.

15. Cf. Gaṅgādharasūri, *Kaṇādasiddhāntacandrikā*, ed. T. Gaṇapati Śāstrī (Trivandrum, 1913), pp. 1ff. On Jinabhadra, see Chapter 6, n. 66; for Haribhadra, cf. *Ṣaḍdarśanasamuccaya with Commentaries*, ed. M. K. Jain (New Delhi, 1981), pp. 407, 412ff. (v. 61ff., with commentary by Guṇaratna). Haribhadra lists *vega*, "momentum", separately.

16. See *Padārthatattvanirūpaṇa*, ed. and trans. K. H. Potter (Cambridge, Mass., 1957), p. 27.

17. See H. Ui, *The Vaiśeṣika Philosophy*; and M. Hattori in *Indian Metaphysics and Epistemology*, ed. K. H. Potter (Princeton, 1977; EIPh, vol. 2), p. 280; for further details, see later, Appendix 2.

18. See A. Thakur, "The Problem of the Vaiśeṣikabhāṣya," *Proceedings of the International Congress of Orientalists* 26, Delhi 1964, III/1 (Poona, 1969), pp. 489–493; ibid., p. 491. B. K. Matilal, *Nyāya-Vaiśeṣika* (Wiesbaden, 1977), p. 61, suggests that Ātreya may have been identical with the author of the *Kaṭandī*.

19. See, for instance, Śāntarakṣita, *TS*, v. 813–822. *Viśeṣa* was also rejected or questioned by the Mīmāṃsakas, who otherwise borrowed freely from the Vaiśeṣika list of categories.

20. Cf. *Padārthatattvanirūpaṇa* (cited in n. 16), p. 43.

21. On *viśeṣa* in the philosophy of Madhva, see S. Siauve, *La doctrine de Madhva* (Pondicherry, 1968), pp. 54ff.

22. See M. Hiriyanna, "What Is Samavāya?" *Recent Indian Philosophy*, Papers Selected from the Proceedings of the Indian Philosophical Congress, 1925–34), vol. 1, ed. K. Bhattacharya (Calcutta, 1963), pp. 212–222; ibid., p. 212.

23. See later, Chapter 7, section 6.

24. Cf. Bhartṛhari's characterization of the Vaiśeṣika as *saṃsargavāda*, "theory of amalgamation"; see *VP* III/7 (*Sādhanasamuddeśa*), 9 (with Helārāja's commentary). For an elaborate critique of *samavāya*, see Mallavādin, *DNC*, vol. 2, pp. 523ff.; cf. also Śāntarakṣita, *TS*, v. 823–866.

25. See earlier, n. 5. See also *Vaiśeṣikadarśanam*, ed. A. Thakur (Darbhanga, 1985), pp. 58–253: Bhaṭṭavādīndra on *VS* I, 1, 4–II, 2, 41; pp. 254–316: reprint of the "anonymous commentary" first published in 1957. Both works are indebted to Udayana and use similar versions of the Sūtra text.

26. Cf. *NBh* I, 1, 9 (cited in n. 6); H. Narain, *Evolution of the Nyāya-Vaiśeṣika Categoriology*, vol. 1 (Benares, 1976), p. 219.

27. Cf. H. Narain, *Evolution*, p. 123.

28. See *VS* VIII, 14 (VIII, 2, 3 *Upaskāra*): *artha iti dravyaguṇakarmasu*. The precise meaning of this Sūtra is, however, controversial.

29. Cf. H. Narain, *Evolution*, pp. 119ff.; B. Faddegon, *The Vaiçeṣika System*, pp. 107f.

30. Cf. E. Frauwallner, *Gesch. d. ind. Phil.*, vol. 2, pp. 314ff.; and the explicit presentation, pp. 29–197.

31. Ibid., p. 316.

32. See earlier, n. 3.

33. Cf. H. T. Colebrooke, *Miscellaneous Essays*, vol. 1 (London, 1837), pp. 261ff. (first published in the *Transactions of the Royal Asiatic Society* 1, 1824); the translation "category" ("Kategorie") was adopted by Hegel; see *Vorlesungen über die Geschichte der Philosophie. Einleitung*, ed. J. Hoffmeister (Leipzig, 1940), pp. 328f.

34. J. R. Ballantyne, "On the Nyāya System of Philosophy," *Benares Magazine* (1849). Ballantyne also refers to the etymological sense "that which is meant by a word".

35. M. Müller, "Beiträge zur Kenntnis der indischen Philosophie I," *ZDMG* 6 (1852): 1–34; see especially pp. 11, 32ff.

36. The most radical reinterpretation of the term since Aristotle was, of course, presented by Kant.

37. For a survey of the historical and systematic problems, see *Hist. Wb. Phil.*, vol. 4, art. "Kategorie, Kategorienlehre"; also *The Encyclopedia of Philosophy*, ed. P. Edwards, vol. 2, art. "Categories".

38. Cf. *NS* and *NBh* II, 2, 66 (Calc. S.S., pp. 670f.).

39. See the commentaries on *NS* I, 1, 1ff.; the Nyāyasūtra itself never uses the term *padārtha* in the general sense of "basic issue" or "topic."

40. See, for instance, Annaṃbhaṭṭa's *Dīpikā* on his own *Tarkasaṃgraha*, 2: *padasya-arthaḥ padārtha iti vyutpattyā-abhidheyatvaṃ padārthasāmānyalakṣaṇam*. Śivāditya opens his *Saptapadārthī* with the statement: *pramitiviṣayāḥ padārthāḥ;* Udayana's *Lakṣaṇāvalī* has: *abhidheyaḥ padārthaḥ*.

41. H. von Glasenapp, *Die Philosphie der Inder* (Stuttgart, 1949), p. 62, sees the classification of words, as found in Patañjali, as the condition of the "ontological distinction of things, qualities and actions." K. A. Subramania Iyer, "The Conception of Guṇa Among the Vaiyyākaraṇas," *New Indian Antiquary* 5 (1941–43): 121–130, suggests that the Vaiśeṣika categories were already available to the early grammarians, including Pāṇini himself. Either suggestion appears questionable.

42. Cf. E. Frauwallner, *Gesch. d. ind. Phil.*, vol. 2, pp. 261f.

43. See *PBh*, p. 15: *evaṃ dharmair vinā dharmiṇām uddeśaḥ kṛtaḥ*.

44. See later, Chapter 6.

45. Cf. H. Narain, *Evolution* (cited in n. 26), p. 98; also p. 94.

46. Cf. Śrīdhara, *NK*, p. 7: *ādau dravyasya-uddeśaḥ, sarvāśrayatvena prādhānyāt*.

47. Cf. Śaṅkara, *BSBh* II, 2, 17: Everything has the nature and identity of the substance (*dravyātmakatā*), i.e., participates in the essence of the substance.

48. It was first published in 1861 (Calcutta, Bibliotheca Indica); excerpts had been translated by J. R. Ballantyne in 1851.

49. See later, Appendix 1, section 1.

50. In: *Vaiśeṣikadarśanam*, ed. A. Thakur (Darbhanga, 1985).

51. Jayanārāyaṇa added his own commentary *Vivṛti* to the edition of 1861; Candrakānta's commentary (in *Vaiśeṣikadarśanam*, ed. R. Chaudhuri, Calcutta, 1887) presents itself as the first real *Bhāṣya* (p. 2).

52. Cf. *Vaiśeṣikadarśanaṃ brahmamunibhāṣyasametam* (Baroda, 1962); T. Vīrarāghavācārya, *VS* with *Rasāyaṇa* (Madras, 1958); Deśika Tirumalai Tātācārya, *Sugamā vaiśeṣikavṛttiḥ* (Prayāga, 1979).

53. Cf. *Vaiśeṣikadarśanam* (Gaizabad, 1984). Āryamuni produced a Hindi commentary inspired by the Ārya Samāj (Lahore, 1907; reprint 1982); see also the Sanskrit commentary *Vedabhāskara* in: K. N. Sharma, *Vaisheshikadarshana* (Barchhwar, 1972).

54. See later, Appendix 1.

55. We may also mention that, in addition to his *Upaskāra*, Śaṅkaramiśra produced a more systematic survey of the system: *Kaṇādarahasya*, ed. V. P. Dvivedin (Benares, 1917).

56. See, for instance, Keśavamiśra's *Tarkabhāṣā*, Laugākṣi Bhāskara's *Tarkakaumudī*, or Annaṃbhaṭṭa's *Tarkasaṃgraha*.

57. On Mallavādin, see later, Chapter 8.

58. See earlier, n. 6.

59. Cf. Śaṅkara, *BSBh* II, 2, 18.

60. See, for instance, "On the Nyāya System of Philosophy," *Benares Magazine* (1849); the article has the subtitle "and the correspondence of its divisions with those of modern science."

61. See, for instance, Nārāyaṇagopāla Doṅgare, *Vaiśeṣikasiddhāntānāṃ gaṇitīyapaddhatyā vimarśaḥ* (Benares, 1979).

62. Cf. *India and Eruope*, pp. 158; 271.

63. See *Indian Metaphysics and Epistemology*, ed. K. H. Potter (Princeton, 1977; *EIPh*, vol. 2), p. 1.

64. See B. K. Matilal, *Nyāya-Vaiśeṣika* (Wiesbaden, 1977; History of Indian Literature VI/2), p. 112.

65. See earlier, Chapter 1.

5

The Vaiśeṣika Concept of Substance

1. Since the early days of Western Indology, in particular since Colebrooke's pioneering studies in Indian philosophy, the Sanskrit word *dravya* has usually been rendered as "substance."[1] Most of those who have used this European term as an instrument of translation and interpretation have taken its meaning and intelligibility for granted.[2] Yet it does not require much historical and systematic reflection to see that the concept of substance in itself and in its Western context is one of the most ambiguous and elusive of all philosophical concepts and that its familiarity should not be mistaken for clarity and intelligibility.

In a recent critical review of the problem of substance, we read: "Substance is the oldest topic of philosophical inquiry, and it is also one of the most entangled."[3] The history as well as the basic ambiguities of the topic can be traced back to Greek thought, specifically to the philosophy of Aristotle. The term *substance* ("substantia") itself is affiliated with the Aristotelian terms *ousía,* on the one hand, and *hypokeímenon,* on the other hand. A modern encyclopaedia of philosophy distinguishes six notions of substance: "(1) the concrete individual, (2) a core of essential properties, (3) what is capable of independent existence, (4) a center of change, (5) a substratum, and (6) a logical subject"; it adds that these were "never thoroughly worked out and reconciled in Aristotle."[4] There is no need to discuss the details of this list. In the history of European thought, the concept of substance covers, indeed, the entire semantic range from concrete empirical things to bare particulars and basic substrates. In applying the word *substance* to the Indian philosophical tradition, and in using it as a translation of *dravya,* it is important to be aware of the questions and ambiguities with which it has been associated. Rendering *dravya* as "substance" does not tell us what its meaning is; it only introduces us to the kind of problem we have to expect.

Dravya, too, is a complex, controversial, and elusive concept. Its uses and implications in Nyāya and Vaiśeṣika, Mīmāṃsā and philosophy of grammar, Jainism, Buddhism, and Vedānta vary widely. Its meanings range from "concrete individual" to "bare substrate" and "ultimate essence." In various ways, it is distinguished from, as well as associated with, qualities, universals, and logical subjects and correlated with such concepts as *guṇa, jāti, sāmānya, ākṛti, vyakti, piṇḍa, āśraya, ādhāra,* and *dharmin.* The different approaches to this elusive notion of *dravya* exemplify historically different levels of reflection as well as fundamental distinctions in conceptual and soteriological orientation.

2. Patañjali's *Mahābhāṣya* (secondary century B.C.) documents some of the early debates concerning the semantic and categorial status of *dravya.* This presentation already reflects basic conceptual problems and ambiguities. Patañjali tries to clarify in a general sense what the meaning of words (*śabda*) is. More specifically, he deals with the question whether such generic terms as *cow* or *tree* refer to individual "substances" (*dravya*) or to generic "forms" (*ākṛti*).[5] Here as elsewhere, Patañjali summarizes centuries of earlier debates. He refers not only to earlier grammarians, such as Kātyāyana and Vyāḍi, but also, though less explicitly and specifically, to conceptual developments in the early, scarcely documented history of the philosophical systems.

Patañjali was aware of different uses and meanings of both *dravya* and *ākṛti* and of corresponding variations in the relationship between the two concepts. According to one usage, *dravya* refers to the underlying stuff; that is, to the shapeless, yet by no means indeterminate material of which things are made. In correlation to this meaning, *ākṛti* means the particular and transitory "shapes" or forms that such material may assume.[6] According to another usage discussed by Patañjali, *dravya* means the individual object that has its generic identity or class membership because of a permanent generic "form" (*ākṛti*) inhering in it.[7] The second meaning of *dravya* is explained, in an etymologizing and somewhat ambiguous fashion, as *guṇasaṃdrāva*, "confluence of qualities."[8] Although this seems to suggest a mere aggregation of qualities, without an underlying substrate, Kaiyaṭa nevertheless uses the term *āśraya*, "substrate," to paraphrase this idea of a "confluence of qualities."[9] We do not have to discuss the more specific problems in Patañjali's two notions of substance. In a general sense, they correspond to one of the fundamental ambiguities in the Aristotelian conception of substance; that is, the dichotomy of *hypokeímenon*, "substrate," and *tóde ti*, "individual thing."

For Patañjali's linguistic and semantic approach, *dravya* in the sense of "individual entity" is more important. In other texts, the term *vyakti* represents this meaning of *dravya*; there are, of course, different interpretations of the terminological relationship between *dravya* and *vyakti*.[10] Detailed discussions concerning the "meaning of words" (*padārtha*) and the semantic status of *vyakti*, *ākṛti*, and *jāti*, are found not only in grammatical literature, but also in Nyāya and Mīmāṃsā.[11]

The suggestion has been made that the concept of *guṇasaṃdrāva*, "confluence of qualities," implies a reference to early Sāṃkhya.[12] Others have argued that Patañjali's grammatical categories presuppose a knowledge of the Vaiśeṣika categories.[13] However, the available sources do not provide conclusive evidence for these suggestions.

A fuller and more explicit integration of philosophical and grammatical reflection can be observed many centuries later, in the *Vākyapadīya* of Bhartṛhari (ca. A.D. 500). Bhartṛhari was obviously aware of early Vaiśeṣika, Sāṃkhya, and other systems. His own concept of empirical substance was inseparable from the concept of grammatical subject. Substance in this sense is anything that can be referred to by a noun or even a pronoun.[14] However, this functional and empirical concept of substance is superseded by the idea of an absolute substance, which coincides with the nondual *brahman*, the ultimate ground of language and the world. The commentator Helārāja states explicitly that Bhartṛhari has a twofold notion of substance, the absolute (*pāramārthika*) and the empirical and conventional (*sāṃvyavahārika*) one.[15] This corresponds to Bhartṛhari's fundamental distinction between a "superimposed being" (*upacārasattā*) that is a correlate and function of language and an absolute reality and identity (*mahāsattā, ātman, svabhāva*) that is the condition and ground of language itself.[16] Nonetheless, because language is an emanation of *brahman*, even the functional and conventional remains embedded in the absolute.

3. Although the Vaiśeṣika calls its fundamental categories of reality *padārtha*, it does not do so in an explicit search for the "meaning of words." In general, linguistic and semantic perspectives are less significant in this tradition than in other schools, in particular the Nyāya and the Mīmāṃsā. In spite of its obvious grammatical correlations and its general linguistic implications, the Vaiśeṣika doctrine of categories is not rooted in, nor guided by, explicit linguistic and grammatical reflection. As we have noted earlier, the roots of the Vaiśeṣika are in cosmology; its basic interest is in the enumeration of irreducible elements and world constituents. The cosmological orientation of ancient Vaiśeṣika also determines its access to the problem of substance. The exposition of this problem proceeds not from a definition of "substance," but from an enumeration of substances; *uddeśa* precedes *lakṣaṇa*.[17]

The Vaiśeṣikasūtra first enumerates all substances, qualities (*guṇa*), and motions (*karman*); then it lists certain properties shared by these three categories. Finally, it lists the characteristic attributes of substances, qualities, and motions.[18] Substances are described as having motions and qualities, and as inherential causes (*kriyāvad guṇavat samavāyikāraṇam iti dravyalakṣaṇam*).[19] A thoroughly revised and enlarged, though basically similar definition appears in Praśastapāda.[20]

This approach is clearly and conspicuously different from the presentation in Patañjali's *Mahābhāṣya*. It is also different from what we find in the *Nyāyabhāṣya*, or in various classical Jaina works. Umāsvāti's authoritative *Tattvārthasūtra* (probably fourth century A.D.) states: "What exists has the nature of substance" (*sad dravyalakṣaṇam*); it adds that substances are endowed with qualities (*guṇa*) and modes (*paryāya*).[21] The commentaries provide further specifications. Substances appear as substrates of attributes and as stable cores of being that preserve the identity of things through processes of change. Kundakunda, the second major authority in ancient Jaina philosophy, also emphasizes these two implications of the concept of substance.[22] Although classical Jaina thought seems to be indebted to the Vaiśeṣika doctrine of categories, its definition of substance does not appear as a mere appendix to an enumeration of substances. The dividing line between categorial distinction and cosmological enumeration is drawn more clearly than in ancient and classical Vaiśeṣika.[23]

In accordance with the growing emphasis on the formal perfection of definitions, later Nyāya and Vaiśeṣika philosophers have tried to work out more concise and rigorous, but also more playful and puzzling definitions of *dravya* than those provided by Kaṇāda or Praśastapāda. After 1000, these efforts reach a culmination in such works as Udayana's *Lakṣaṇāvalī*. Here, we find a series of alternative definitions, beginning with "what is not the locus of the utter absence of qualities" (*guṇātyantābhāvānadhikaraṇa*) and ending with "the substrate of three layers of inherence" (*samavetasamavetasamaveta*).[24]

4. The group of entities that have been subsumed under the category of substance (i.e., earth, water, fire, air, ether, time, space, souls, mental organs) is heterogeneous in more than one sense. Its composition poses historical as well as systematic problems; the meaning and role of such items as souls (*ātman*), time, and space (*kāla, diś*) in this list would deserve special attention.[25]

For our present context, the division of the category *dravya* into "eternal" (*nitya*) and "noneternal" (*anitya*) substances is most relevant. Whereas all nine substances (or classes of substances) are essentially irreducible, indestructible constituents of the world, the elemental substances (i.e., earth, water, fire, and air) occur not only in their eternal, irreducible form, as atoms (*aṇu, paramāṇu*), but also as destructible compounds of such atoms, as concrete empirical objects of our daily practical acquaintance. Obviously, the division into "eternal" and "noneternal" substances is quite different from the distinction between fire and earth or water and souls. It involves more fundamentally different functions of the word *dravya* and historically and systematically different approaches to the problem of substance.[26] The noneternal substances are not theoretically irreducible cosmic substrates, but things with which we deal in our ordinary linguistic and practical behavior. They cannot be listed or enumerated in the same sense as the elements. Noneternal substances are transitory constellations. They come and go. They cannot be codified in a permanent list. "The universe thus consists of 1) a primary one that subsists always . . . ; and 2) a derivative one which is dependent on it and which is the world we ordinarily know."[27]

Whereas the Vaiśeṣika considers the noneternal substances to be effects of, and derived from, the eternal substances, it does not regard them as less real. They, too, are real substrates of real qualities and other attributes. They have their irreducible identity and reality as long as they last. The Vaiśeṣika tries to explain and defend their precarious ontological status in its peculiar and controversial theory of the "whole" (*avayavin*) as an entity over and above its constituent parts (*avayava*).[28]

The eternal substances generate other, additional substances: *dravyāṇi dravyāntaram ārabhante*.[29] The effect does not preexist in its material cause (*asatkāryavāda*). The *avayavin*, such as a tree, has an identity and individuality of its own; it is a real referent of language and cognition, of words and thoughts. It is the product of parts; it does not consist of parts. In a strict sense, the word *total* or *complete* (*kṛtsna*) cannot be applied to the *avayavin*.[30]

5. The reality of the *avayavin* is required by its identity in thought and speech. But this does not mean that it can be reduced to a merely cognitive or semantic identity. It is, according to the Vaiśeṣika, reality in the fullest, that is, physical and cosmological, sense. The *avayavin* has its own qualities, caused by, yet different from, those of the parts. The champions of the theory even go so far as to argue that the *avayavin* should have a weight of its own, over and above the combined weights of the parts.[31]

The Vaiśeṣikas and Naiyāyikas defend the reality of the *avayavin* stubbornly against all critics, above all against the Buddhists who try to demonstrate that the identity and reality of wholes, such as a tree or a chariot, is nothing but a false belief based upon a linguistic label.[32] On the other hand, they do not want to defend all kinds of aggregates as genuine wholes. Not all aggregates have an identity over and above their parts. Only certain types of composite entities qualify for this status.

Vātsyāyana discusses various examples and criteria and suggests that genuine wholes require a certain homogeneity of the parts. Likewise, Vaiśeṣika authors, for instance Śrīdhara, note that normally the conjunction of homogeneous (*samānajātīya*) parts constitutes genuine wholes.[33] However, the definition and demarcation of "real" wholes cannot be a matter of sheer physical compatibility or homogeneity. The basic premise of the system of categories is that what is real should be knowable (*jñeya*) and nameable (*abhidheya*); it should be identifiable in thought and speech. However, there are different types of linguistically identifiable wholes, corresponding to the distinction between "individual nouns", such as *cow, man, tree,* and "mass nouns," such as *water, milk,* or (though less characteristically) *cloth,* the most familiar example in the debates about the whole. In particular, this distinction implies a different role for the "intermediate wholes" (*avāntarāvayavin*); that is, identifiable segments which may be combined and included in larger wholes. Any piece of cloth is still cloth, and any amount of water is still water. This can obviously not be said about trees and cows.[34]

Generally, the *avayavin* should be an identifiable member of a recognizable class; it should have an identifiable generic property, that is, a real universal inhering in it. The problem of the reality and identity of the *avayavin* is thus inseparable from that of the reality and identity of universals (*sāmānya, jāti*), although this may not be very visible and explicit in the texts.[35]

Various problems, both epistemological and ontological, suggest themselves with regard to the generic identity and identifiability of an *avayavin*. How much of it, how many of its constituent parts do we have to see to identify it as an entity belonging to a particular class? How much of it, how many parts can be removed before it loses its generic identity or class membership? When and how does a composite entity cease to be what it is? The Nyāya-Vaiśeṣika philosophers discuss such questions, perhaps somewhat reluctantly, mainly in response to Buddhist and other criticism.[36]

In addition to the problems of generic identity, there are other problems relating to the numerical identity of an *avayavin*. When does one individual "whole" turn into another individual of the same type? When and how is it replaced by a numerically different member of the same class? The *Nyāyabhāṣya* states, against the assumptions of common sense, that the removal of small sections of a tree is sufficient to turn it into another tree.[37] This view is radicalized by Udayana and others to the extent that any increase or decrease, and perhaps even rearrangement, of parts would imply the genesis of a new individual *avayavin*.[38]

Composite, "noneternal" (*anitya*) substances have no lasting numerical identity; their continuity is an illusion. The Nyāya-Vaiśeṣika champions of permanence and continuity, the uncompromising opponents of the Buddhist "doctrine of momentariness" (*kṣaṇabhaṅgavāda*), thus adopt their own version of discontinuity and momentariness.

Unlike the Jainas, the Vaiśeṣikas and Naiyāyikas do not have a notion of "vertical universal" (*ūrdhvatāsāmānya*) that would accompany an individual substance through nonessential modifications and codify its numerical identity in time.[39] Unlike Kant's or Aristotle's concepts of substance, the Vaiśeṣika notion of the "noneternal substance" (*anityadravya*) does not emphasize, and not even imply, the idea of continuity in change or the demarcation of an essential core against nonessential modifications.[40]

Numerically different "noneternal substances" succeed each other within the time frame of one apparently identical empirical thing, each being the substrate of "its own" qualities or motions. This is the most important characteristic the "noneternal substance" shares with its "eternal" counterpart: to provide a locus for the inherence of attributes.

6. As we have noted earlier, Praśastapāda gives a revised definition of *dravya*. Instead of the formulation of Sūtra I, 1, 14 (*kriyāvad guṇavat samavāyikāraṇam iti dravyalakṣaṇam*), we find the following statement: *pṛthivyādīnāṃ navānām api dravyatvayogaḥ svātmany ārambhakatvaṃ guṇavattvaṃ kāryakāraṇāvirodhitvam antyaviśeṣavattvam.*[41]

Praśastapāda omits *kriyāvat*, "possessing motion," as it applies to only a limited group of substances. Instead, he adds the following characteristics that he found implied in various other Sūtras dealing with substances: *dravyatvayoga*, "connection with (the universal) substanceness"; *svātmany ārambhakatva*, that is, the capability of substances to initiate (and support) new, dependent entities; *kāryakāraṇāvirodhitva*, "compatibility of effects and causes," that is, the coexistence of the material cause and its product; and *antyaviśeṣavattva*, "possession of ultimate particularities."[42] In the case of the elemental substances, this last characteristic can apply only to the atoms. The possession of qualities (*guṇavattva*) is central in both definitions.

Apart from all specific variations, the following observation seems most significant: Praśastapāda distinguishes more clearly between the levels of *uddeśa*, "enunciation," "(cosmological) enumeration," and *lakṣaṇa*, "definition." At the level of definition, he presents "common and specific characteristics" (*sādharmya, vaidharmya*); that is, abstract attributes that do not constitute additional enumerables. The transition from *uddeśa* to *lakṣaṇa* involves a peculiar kind of "semantic ascent."[43] In Praśastapāda's view, the list of categories represents the divisions of the real world in the medium of language. It provides the nomenclature of the world; it does not say anything "about" the world. In a literal sense, this nomenclature, this "naming" of the fundamental constituents of the world, does not involve predication.

The predicates or abstract attributes that appear at the level of *lakṣaṇa*, "definition," are not part of the basic nomenclature of the world. In his definition of the category *dravya*, Praśastapāda uses such terms as *dravyatvayoga* and *guṇavattva*, not *guṇa*. The difference is significant. In its relation to *guṇa*, "quality," *dravya* is a cosmological substrate (*āśraya*); in relation to *guṇavattva*, "possession of qualities," *dravya* is nothing but a logical subject (*dharmin*). The manner of qualification is essentially different in both cases.

Praśastapāda's procedure thus implies a separation of the logical and the cosmological dimension. Yet this does not mean that there is no room for ambiguity and overlap.[44]

7. *Guṇavattva*, "possession of qualities," is the most characteristic, but also most problematic "common attribute" (*sādharmya*) of all substances. What does it mean for a substance to "have" qualities? How is its own nature or being determined not just by its qualities as such, but by the fact that it (actually or potentially) supports or possesses them? And furthermore, how can it be what it is, a substance, without having its qualities and other attributes? Is the substance as such, and divested of its inherent qualifiers, an identifiable and distinguishable something? Is there a "bare substance," stripped of and apart from its attributes, a "qualificand" (*viśeṣya*) without "qualifiers" (*viśeṣaṇa*)? Such and similar questions are suggested by the Vaiśeṣika juxtaposition of substances and qualities; and they are reflected in the critique of the Buddhists and other opponents of the Vaiśeṣika system.[45]

According to Uddyotakara, the "possessive" relationship between substances and qualities can be illustrated by other possessive relationships between clearly distinguishable entities, for instance between a man and his vessel; and he argues that such genitive constructions that speak of "the *color of* something" reflect a real state of affairs, a real relationship between distinct relata.[46] The Jaina teachers Mallavādin and Siṃhasūri discuss the problem of "bare substances," and the problem of how a mere qualificand can be a specific substrate for a particular qualifier, in great detail. Their sources include Vaiśeṣika texts that are no longer extant. One of these sources states explicitly that even "bare things" (*vastumātra*), without any connection with qualifiers, are different from one another and can thus account for the specificity and limitation of their relationship with particular qualifiers: *athavā viśeṣaṇasambandham antareṇa-api vastumātrāṇāṃ parasparātiśayo 'sti, tena viśeṣaṇasambandhaniyamasiddhiḥ.*[47] Although Praśastapāda can hardly reject this kind of statement, he tries to avoid or circumvent the commitment it involves.

As we have seen, Praśastapāda's procedure implies a separation of the logical and the cosmological dimension. In accordance with this separation, a *dravya* can be seen as an *āśraya,* a cosmological substrate of other, ontologically separable world constituents, such as the qualities (*guṇa*); or it can appear as a *dharmin,* a logical and grammatical subject of predicates. There is a twofold relationship of "having." As a *dharmin,* a substance is characterized by such abstract and inseparable attributes as "possession of qualities" (*guṇavattva*); as an *āśraya,* it is characterized and supplemented by ontologically separable, additional factors, such as the qualities. The problem of a "bare substance," an attributeless substrate, has thus been circumvented or rather disguised by the structure of Praśastapāda's system. There is no utterly indeterminate, featureless substance. Even as a mere substrate (*āśraya*), apart from its qualities and other "additional" attributes, the substance is a determinate and identifiable entity, insofar as it is a specific *dharmin.*

Praśastapāda's attempt to resolve or circumvent the problem of substance and the paradoxes of the qualifier-qualificand relation by assigning the concept of *dravya* to different semantic levels reflects his historical situation. It also exemplifies his peculiar method of integrating cosmology with logic and epistemology and his attempt to preserve and defend the cosmological heritage of old Vaiśeṣika in a new atmosphere of thought.[48]

In Chapter 3, we referred to a cosmological theory that regards the qualities (*guṇa*) as emanations of their substrates; that is, the elemental substances. In particular, we find this view in the Mahābhārata. Here, the elemental qualities color (*rūpa*), taste (*rasa*), and so forth, as well as certain other qualities, appear as a further stage of cosmic evolution.[49] It would certainly be uncautious to postulate a direct connection between such theories and early Vaiśeṣika. In general, our knowledge of early Vaiśeṣika is quite insufficient. Yet we may assume that it had its origin in an atmosphere of thought that tended to reify the qualities and to assume an external and additive relationship between substances and qualities. Of course, we have no documentation of the Vaiśeṣika as a purely cosmological system. But, even as a fully developed "system of categories," it remains a hybrid philosophy of nature. As a later reflection of this fundamentally additive and "naturalistic" approach, we may recall the theory that a newly produced composite substance (*kāryadravya*) is without its proper qualities during the first moment of its existence and that there is an equally minute interval between the destruction of a substance and its quality.[50]

8. In the debate about the concept of substance, epistemological issues become increasingly significant and conspicuous. In their own way, they illustrate the underlying ontological and metaphysical problems.

The assumption that the cognition, in particular the perception, of a concrete qualified entity presupposes the cognition and (at least implicit) identification of the qualifying factors has an old tradition in the Vaiśeṣika school. It seems to be taken for granted in the explanation of perception in the Vaiśeṣikasūtra.[51] However, the text does not tell us whether or in what sense the qualificand and its qualifiers are actually separable data of perceptual awareness; nor does it raise the question whether there is an awareness of substance per se and without its qualities. The Sūtra postulates that we perceive a substance with reference to and in accordance with (*apekṣam*) its attributes, such as the qualities and universals; we see it as being qualified and specified by its attributes. The Sūtra also tells us that the perception of a white object results from the whiteness residing in the appropriate substrate and from the perception of such whiteness.[52] This statement does not explicitly distinguish between the perception of the color and the colored thing; nor does it try to isolate "mere substance" as a datum or perception.[53] In general, color is supposed to be among the conditions of the visibility of a substance.[54] This seems to imply that an object is visible only insofar as it is colored, and that there is no room for the perception of a substance apart from its color. On the other hand, there is the unquestioned premise that the substance itself appears in and through the colored phenomenon.[55]

Praśastapāda articulates the problem in his own fashion. In his analysis of perception, he refers to an awareness of the qualifying factors, but also to an intuition of the substance as such (*svarūpālocanamātra*).[56] This seems to imply that he postulates, as a part or phase of the perception of the concrete thing, an awareness of the substance merely as such, as bare substrate and particular. However, no further details are given; no attempt is made to show that or how a substance can actually appear in perception without any qualities. To be sure, the careful systematizer Praśastapāda could hardly have presented such an argument after emphasizing (in accordance with Vaiśeṣikasūtra IV, 1, 6) the indispensability of color for the perception of a substance.[57]

Praśastapāda does not make a clear distinction between an immanent phenomenological description and analysis of the contents of awareness and the causal explanation of the physical and psychological processes of perception; external factors and internal data are not always kept apart.

With regard to color, this implies the following ambiguity: on the one hand, *rūpa* has to be present as a datum in the perceptual awareness of a substance; on the other hand, it has to be present as one of the causal factors that make perception possible.[58] The distinction between these two aspects, however, receives more serious attention in response to Buddhist criticism.

9. In what sense does a "bare substance," without its qualifying factors, have a "nature of its own" (*svarūpa*)?[59] The very idea of *svarūpa* seems to be much more appropriate with reference to the qualifying factors. Praśastapāda himself associates it primarily with "specific universals" (*sāmānyaviśeṣa*).[60]

The cognition of the concrete qualified thing results from the intuition of such specific universals and other qualifying factors. Praśastapāda describes this "cognitive result" as knowledge that has the substance and so forth as its domain (*pramitir dravyādiviṣayaṃ jñānam*).[61] Obviously, this qualified knowledge of the substance cannot be identical with the *svarūpālocanamātra* of the bare substrate, but presupposes it as one of its own ingredients. As a matter of fact, the intuition of the qualifiers themselves presupposes an immediate awareness of an undefined something, an "undifferentiated intuition" (*avibhaktam ālocanamātram*) of a bare particular. The commentator Śrīdhara identifies this immediate, undivided awareness as the contact between the senses and the object (*ālocyate 'nena-ity ālocanam indriyārthasaṃnikarṣas tanmātram, avibhaktaṃ kevalaṃ jnānānapekṣam*).[62]

Once again, we see the ambiguous role of substance as qualified thing (*viśiṣṭa*) and bare qualificand (*viśeṣya*), that is, substrate of qualifications,[63] as well as the elusive distinction between causal factors and cognitive ingredients.

The "contact" (*saṃnikarṣa*) between the senses and objects poses a number of problems that we cannot discuss in detail. One basic historical reminder may suffice: The old conception of *saṃnikarṣa* was apparently based on the assumption of a concrete "thing" that included its attributers. Once the Vaiśeṣika had divided and analyzed this concrete something in accordance with its doctrine of categories, what remained as the direct and primary object of the "contact" was the "substrate" (*āśraya*).[64] Other complex and indirect modes of contact were required for the other categories. The fully developed version of this theory of "modes of *saṃnikarṣa*" is found in Uddyotakara's *Nyāyavārttika*. The perception of the substance per se, as substrate, is due to simple contact or connection (*saṃyoga*), that of its quality to "inherence in what is connected" (*saṃyuktasamavāya*), that of the quality-universal to "inherence in what is inherent in what is connected" (*saṃyuktasamavetasamavāya*), and so on.[65] Prior to Uddyotakara, Bhartṛhari used the same kind of terminology in a different context.[66] The theory was generally adopted by the Vaiśeṣika commentators, in particular Vyomaśiva and Śrīdhara.[67] The Nyāya commentators, on the other hand, used Praśastapāda's ideas of *ālocanamātra* and *svarūpālocanamātra* to explain the problematic term *avyapadeśya* ("not to be designated," "undesignated") in *Nyāyasūtra* I, 1, 4.[68]

10. Praśastapāda postulates the apprehension of the bare "substance itself" as a theoretically indispensable ingredient of the "predicative" and conceptually explicit awareness of concrete things; that is, of that kind of awareness which identifies its objects in accordance with their inherent qualities, generic properties, and so forth. This corresponds basically to the manner in which other Nyāya and Vaiśeṣika writers, including Praśastapāda's commentator Vyomaśiva, infer an underlying "pre-predicative perception" (*nirvikalpakapratyakṣa*) from the phenomenon of "predicative perception" (*savikalpakapratyakṣa*).[69] Praśastapāda does not make an explicit attempt to identify the bare substances as a separate and specific datum of actual perceptual experience. This can be seen from another section of his work, in which he gives a more phenomenologically oriented analysis of the process of perception; that is, of the identification and specification of an object of perception. Praśastapāda himself describes this process as a progression from "indeterminate awareness" (*anadhyavasāya*) to identification and ascertainment (*adhyavasāya*).[70]

Although the expression *mere intuition* (*ālocanamātra*) appears in the text, no reference is made to the bare substance as such. Praśastapāda states that the first step in our perception of both familiar and unknown objects is an indeterminate apprehension, a "mere intuition" of an unidentified something that finds its expression in the question *What is it?* (*kimityālocanamātra*). Subsequently, we notice a series of increasingly specific attributes or qualifiers, from the highest universal "reality" (*sattā*) to such specific universals as *panasatva,* which enable us to identify an object as a member of a particular class, such as the class of *panasa* trees. Praśastapāda does not try to clarify the relationship between the indeterminate awareness, *What is it?* (*kim ity*), and the identification of the highest universal, *sattā*. His presentation seems to imply that the awareness of the universal "reality" is the most immediate consequence of the "indeterminate awareness" of a bare something, but not identical with it. As we have seen, Śrīdhara is more explicit; he interprets Praśastapāda's expression *avibhaktam ālocanamātram* as a reference to the contact between objects and senses that is supposed to actualize the awareness of the appropriate qualifying factors (*viśeṣaṇa*), which would invariably include "reality" (*sattā*).[71] We may recall here the theory of some Advaita Vedāntins (for instance, Maṇḍana and, several centuries later, Prakāśātman) that the first moment of immediate, unadulterated perception reveals to us the "mere something" (*vastumātra*) in its true reality and undifferentiated identity, that is, as pure, undifferentiated being (*sanmātra*); according to this view, the absolute *brahman,* the "great universal" (*mahāsāmānya*), manifests itself in the undivided and unspecified presence of prepredicative perception.[72]

To be sure, Praśastapāda does not try to describe and specify what is given to us as "bare substance" in the mode of immediate, prepredicative awareness (*ālocanamātra*). But according to the premises of his system, it cannot be "pure being" nor an utterly indeterminate something. It has to be a specific entity that, even "without" its qualifying factors, is capable of providing an identifiable and distinguishable locus for the inherence of specific attributes. As we have seen, this conception of a "bare," yet irreducibly specific, substance and substrate involves a peculiar "semantic ascent"; that is, its status as a *dharmin*.[73]

11. Soon after Praśastapāda, some Naiyāyikas, in particular Uddyotakara, Bhāvivikta, and Aviddhakarṇa, tried to do what the author of the *Padārthadharmasaṃgraha* had not done and perhaps deliberately avoided. They tried to show that the bare substance, as a separable or actually separate substrate of qualities, appears as an identifiable datum of perception and that it can be experienced even without its qualities.[74]

Uddyotakara argues in detail against the Buddhist critique of substance, in particular against the attempt to reduce substances to mere aggregates of perceivable qualities. As part of his defense, he cites the following case: When a crystal is placed in the vicinity of a dark object, we see the crystal (i.e., the substance) as such, but without its proper, i.e. bright, color. Instead, we see it as being associated with the dark color superimposed by the object in its vicinity.[75] Later on, Uddyotakara repeats this argument and adds what he considers to be further evidence; that is, the observation that a crane may be visible at night and identifiable as a bird even if its white color cannot be seen.[76]

Śāntarakṣita's *Tattvasaṃgraha,* together with the commentary by Kamalaśīla, cites and refutes these arguments. It also deals with the claim that a man covered by armor (*kañcuka*) can be identified as such, although his color and other attributes cannot be seen. The names of Uddyotakara and Bhāvivikta are mentioned in this connection.[77] In his commentary *Vipañcitārthā* on Dharmakīrti's *Vādanyāya,* Śāntarakṣita mentions Aviddhakarṇa and ascribes to him the thesis that in dim light, which allows no perception of colors and other attributes, a substance can be identified as a cow or horse.[78]

There is no need to enlarge on the insufficiency of these arguments and their ineffectiveness against the Buddhist critics. Their circular nature is obvious. No serious attempt is made to describe what is actually given in perception. Only those who take the existence of ontologically and epistemologically separable substrates for granted will be able to "see" substances in the various instances cited by the Naiyāyikas.[79]

The visibility of a substance in dim light, without an identifiable color, still presupposes the visibility of its shape or configuration (*saṃsthāna*). According to the Buddhist opponents, this phenomenon of "mere shape" (*saṃsthānamātra*) constitutes no better evidence for an underlying substance than color itself.[80] Uddyotakara is aware of this kind of objection. But he insists that "colorless" shape provides us with a direct perceptual access to an underlying substance.[81] Vyomaśiva seems to agree; in dim light, so he argues, the composite substance (*avayavin*) is visible as "mere shape" (*saṃsthānamātra*).[82]

Śrīdhara, too, invokes shape in his defense of the concept of substance. Against the attempt to explain all entities as aggregates of perceivable qualities, he insists that qualities such as color cannot account for the particularity of individual entities. Only *saṃsthāna* which is recognizably different in different instances (*pratyekavilakṣaṇa*) can indicate the indispensable particularity of the underlying substance.[83] We should, however, not forget that *rūpa*, specifically in its older usages, may not only mean "color," but also "figure" and "shape."

12. The concept of shape or configuration (*saṃsthāna*) is equally significant, though not immediately obvious in the debate about the "perceptibility by two senses" (*dvīndriyagrāhyatva*) which we find documented in Nyāya and Vaiśeṣika literature beginning with the Nyāyasūtra.[84] The observation that the same entity can be the object of seeing and feeling is used as evidence for the existence of an identical substrate of the different visual and tactile qualities. No sensuous quality is accessible to more than one sense organ. Therefore, what is accessible to more than one sense organ must be different from the qualities. The conclusion is that only the substance itself, the substrate of the different sensuous qualities, can be the common referent of seeing and feeling: "I touch the pot that I have seen; I see that same pot that I have touched."[85] The pot itself has to be there to account for this coordination and "identifying referral" of qualitative impressions that have nothing in common or for its recognition (*pratisaṃdhāna*) through such different types of qualities.

However, closer epistemological and phenomenological analysis shows that once again we are not dealing with an underlying substrate, but with shape (*saṃsthāna*) as the common datum of tactile and visual perceptions. Accordingly, Śrīdhara states that one has to assume a "specific shape" (*saṃsthānaviśeṣa*) to explain the fact that vision and touch can have an identical object.[86] In this version, the notion of *dvīndriyagrāhyatva* may remind us of "Molyneux' problem," a symptomatic question discussed by J. Locke and others: Can somebody who has been born blind and knows a particular shape through his sense of touch identify this same shape visually once he has gained the capacity of seeing? Of course, in this case we are not dealing with the numerical identity of a substance, but only with the generic identity of a shape.

In a series of related arguments, the Naiyāyikas and Vaiśeṣikas also try to prove that the phenomena of coordination and recognition (*pratisaṃdhāna*) presuppose the existence of a coordinating and recognizing subject; that is, the soul or self (*ātman*).[87] According to the Vaiśeṣika table of categories, the *ātman* is among the eternal, noncomposite substances, with a characteristic set of qualities. The clear understanding of its true nature is supposed to be the condition of final liberation.

In the debates between Hindus and Buddhists, the *ātman* is the substance par excellence, the most representative and most controversial exemplification of a "substratum," a durable "center of change," and a core of irreducible identity.[88] According to the Buddhists, it is the most significant symptom and projection of attachment and desire, of a soteriologically harmful commitment to existence. Implicitly or explicitly, the Buddhist critique of substances in general is aimed at this substance par excellence. In this sense, the debate about substance has important soteriological implications. It is part of what we have called *soteriontology*.[89]

It is not difficult to see the problems and ambiguities in the Vaiśeṣika concept of substance. Nonetheless, this concept reflects a remarkable analytical and systematic effort. Moreover, it has been of major significance in the history of Indian thought. Its impact can be felt even in those systems by which it has been rejected, criticized, or superseded. In particular, it has been an important catalyst for the critique of the empirical world as we find it in Advaita Vedānta and Mahāyāna Buddhism.[90]

Chapter 5: Notes

1. Cf. H. T. Colebrooke, *Miscellaneous Essays*, vol. 1 (London, 1837), pp. 261–294. A. Dow, who did not know Sanskrit, used the term *substance* for what he called *dirba* (i.e., *dravya*) and *quality* for *goon* (i.e., *guṇa*) in his *History of Hindostan*, vol. 1 (London, 1768); see *The British Discovery of Hinduism in the Eighteenth Century*, ed. P. J. Marshall (Cambridge, 1970), p. 131.

2. Other translations appear rarely and mostly in works that may be considered obsolete. M. Müller, "Beiträge zur Kenntnis der indischen Philosophie. I." *ZDMG* 6 (1852): 1–34, uses *Gegenstand* (see pp. 10ff.); J. C. Chatterji, *The Hindu Realism* (Allahabad, 1912), speaks of nine "realities."

3. See A. Quinton, *The Nature of Things* (London, 1973), p. 1; but see also E. Cassirer, *Substanzbegriff und Funktionsbegriff* (Berlin, 1910), p. 200: "Der logische Gedanke der Substanz steht an der Spitze der wissenschaftlichen Weltbetrachtung überhaupt."

4. See *Encyclopedia of Philosophy*, ed. P. Edwards, vol. 8, art. "Substance and Attribute"; see also *Aristotle. A Collection of Critical Essays*, ed. J. M. E. Moravcsik (Garden City, N.Y., 1967), pp. 75–145.

5. Cf. M. Biardeau, *Théorie de la connaissance et philosophie de la parole dans le brahmanisme classique* (Paris, 1964), pp. 43ff.; 57ff.; 229ff.; and P. Scharf, *The Denotation of Generic Terms in Ancient Indian Grammar, Nyāya, and Mīmāṃsā* (Diss. University of Pennsylvania, 1990), pp. 27ff.

6. Cf. B. K. Matilal, *Epistemology, Logic, and Grammar in Indian Philosophical Analysis* (The Hague, 1971), pp. 113f. (Vyāḍi's notion of substance).

7. See *Mahābhāṣya*, vol. 1, pp. 7; 246f.; vol. 2, p. 366.

8. See *Mahābhāṣya*, vol. 2, p. 366; also p. 200 (*guṇasamudāya*). For a somewhat different, yet related approach, cf. Vyāsa, *YBh* III, 44: *sāmānyaviśeṣasamudāyo 'tra dravyam*; subsequently, Vyāsa refers to the *grammarian* Patañjali.

9. Kaiyaṭa probably wrote his *Pradīpa* on Patañjali's *Mahābhāṣya* in the eleventh century.

10. Cf. *NS* II, 2, 67: *vyaktir guṇaviśeṣāśrayo mūrtiḥ;* see also Jayanta, *NM*, pp. 297ff.; and M. Spitzer, *Begriffsuntersuchungen zum Nyāyabhāṣya* (Leipzig, 1927), pp. 76ff.

11. Cf. M. Biardeau, *Théorie de la connaissance* (cited in n. 5), pp. 161ff.; and P. Scharf, *The Denotation* (cited in n. 5).

12. Cf. A. Wezler, "A Note on Mahābhāṣya II, 366. 26: *guṇasaṃdrāvo dravyam*," *Buddhism and Its Relation to Other Religions: Essays in Honour of Dr. Shozen Kumoi* (Kyoto, 1985), pp. 1–33. However, Wezler's references to Mallavādin are intriguing, and they deserve most careful consideration.

13. See, for instance, K. A. Subramania Iyer, "The Conception of Guṇa Among the Vaiyyākaraṇas," *New Indian Antiquary* 5 (1942–43): 121–130.

14. Cf. Bhartṛhari, *VP* III/4, 3 (*vastūpalakṣaṇaṃ yatra sarvanāma prayujyate / dravyam ity ucyate, so 'rtho bhedyatvena vivakṣitaḥ*); see also K. A. Subramania Iyer, *Bhartṛhari*, pp. 78f.; 262f.; and B. K. Matilal, *Logic, Language, and Reality* (Delhi, 1985), pp. 381f. (substances and pronouns); 385 (substance as "anything that is expressible by a noun or a substantive").

15. See Helārāja on *VP* III/1 (*Dravyasamuddeśa*), 1.

16. Cf. K. A. Subramania Iyer, *Bhartṛhari*, pp. 209; 215f.; 259; 312f. The fact that *upacārasattā*, functional, predicative, "figurative" being, can be "imposed

upon," or applied to, all meanings or intentional objects (including nonentities), reflects the absolute transcendence implied in *mahāsattā.*

17. See earlier, Chapter 4, section 2.

18. Cf. *VS* I, 1, 4ff. (*Upaskāra:* I, 1, 5ff.).

19. *VS* I, 1, 14 (15).

20. See later, section 6.

21. See *Tattvārthasūtra* V, 29; 37; the definition of *guṇa* in V, 40 seems to reflect *VS* I, 1, 15 (*Upaskāra:* I, 1, 16).

22. For some comparative observations on the different concepts of substance, see B. K. Matilal, *Logic, Language and Reality* (cited in n. 14), pp. 294ff.; also "Ontological Problems in Nyāya, Buddhism and Jainism. A Comparative Analysis," *JIPh* 5 (1977): 91–105.

23. See earlier, Chapter 4, section 7. Siddhasena and Mallavādin represent a somewhat different approach.

24. *Lakṣaṇāvalī* 9; 12; cf. M. Tachikawa, *Structure of the World*, pp. 56f.; see also S. Bhaduri, *Studies in Nyāya-Vaiśeṣika Metaphysics* (Poona, 1947; reprint, 1975), pp. 36ff.

25. On time, see Chapter 9.

26. Cf. E. Frauwallner, *Gesch. d. ind. Phil.*, vol. 2, pp. 44ff.; 162ff.

27. See M. Hiriyanna, *Outlines of Indian Philosophy* (London, 1932; reprint, 1967), p. 240.

28. For a survey of the development of this theory, see O. Grohma, *Die Lehre vom avayavī in Nyāya und Vaiśeṣika vor Udayana* (Diss. Vienna, 1971). Vigorous objections came not only from the Buddhists, but also from the Sāṃkhya; cf. *YD*, ed. R. C. Pandeya, pp. 48ff.

29. *VS* I, 1, 8 (*Upaskāra:* I, 1, 10); Candrānanda explains: *svātmavyatiriktaṃ kāryadravyam.*

30. Cf. *NBh* and *NV* II, 1, 32 (Calc. S.S., pp. 471f.; especially *NV*, p. 472: *na-avayavī kṛtsno na-ekadeśaḥ*).

31. Cf. the elaborate discussion of this topic in Uddyotakara, *NV* II, 1, 33 (Calc. S.S., pp. 492–496). See also later, Chapter 6, on the color of the whole (especially sections 8f., on the color *citra*, "variegated").

32. See, for instance, the famous simile of the chariot, *Milindapañha* (see Chapter 3, n. 57), pp. 26ff.

33. Cf. *NBh* II, 1, 35ff.; Śrīdhara, *NK*, p. 148 (*samānajātīyasaṃyogasya dravyāntarotpattihetutvāt*); cf. also O. Grohma (cited in n. 28), pp. 138ff. The inadequa-

cies in the criterion of "homogeneity" became increasingly obvious, and it was modified or abandoned by later authors; see, for instance, Bhāsarvajña, *NBhūṣ*, pp. 129f.

34. For the terms *individual noun* and *mass noun*, see B. L. Whorf, *Language, Thought, and Reality*, ed. J. B. Carroll (Cambridge, Mass., 1956), pp. 140ff. Whorf says: "Mass nouns denote homogeneous continua without implied boundaries." The concept of the "individual noun" seems implied in the notion of *antyāvayavin* ("ultimate whole") that emerges in later discussion about wholes (see Śivāditya, *Saptapadārthī*, section 121; ed. D. Gurumurti, p. 90: *dravyānārambhakaṃ kāryadravyam antyāvayavī*). Such "ultimate wholes" are distinct individual entities whose aggregation does not produce further wholes.

35. But see *NBh* II, 1, 36 (Calc. S.S., p. 512): a whole must be different from its parts, because it provides a basis for the manifestation of specific universals (*jātiviśeṣābhivyaktiviṣayatvād avayavy arthāntarabhūta iti*). On the one hand, we have a merely physicalistic, naturalistic notion of the whole; on the other hand, we have a notion that accommodates epistemiological and semantic criteria. The tension and ambiguity between these two concepts (or perspectives) has never been fully resolved or clarified in Nyāya or Vaiśeṣika.

36. On the history of critique, cf. O. Grohma (cited in n. 28), pp. 33–92.

37. See *NBh* III, 1, 10f. (Calc. S.S., pp. 729ff.); cf. also Śrīdhara, *NK*, p. 34. Śrīdhara states that the "recognition" (*pratyabhijñāna*) of a substance (specifically an organic body) does not prove its unity and identity, because it may be based upon the similarity (*sādṛśya*) of successive entities.

38. Cf. C. Ramaiah, *Change and Identity in Indian Philosophy* (Tirupati, n.d.), pp. 61ff. Grohma, p. 137, notes that, unlike the Buddhist "momentariness," such instability is not inherent in the very nature of reality, but the result of the causal influences to which a thing is exposed. Nonetheless, the temporal status of the "whole" according to the Nyāya-Vaiśeṣika is highly precarious and obviously incompatible with those basic assumptions of common sense and practical life to which the school is otherwise committed. According to the so-called *Yogasūtrabhāṣyavivaraṇa* attributed to Śaṅkara (cf. *Tradition and Reflection*, ch. 6), such more or less constant loss of identity and replacement of one thing by another would, for instance, make ownership regulations impossible and in general lead to a complete breakdown of ordinary worldly life; see *Vivaraṇa* on *YS/YBh* I, 43.

39. On *ūrdhvatā-* and *tiryaksāmānya*, ("horizontal universals"), see Māṇikyanandin, *Parīkṣāmukha* IV, 3–5 (*sāmānyaṃ dvedhā*); and the commentary by Prabhācandra, *Prameyakamalamārtaṇḍa*, ed. Mahendra Kumar (Bombay, 1941); other terms for the "vertical" and "horizontal" universals are *vistārasāmānya* and *āyatasāmānya*; see Kundakunda, *Pravacanasāra* II, 1, with commentaries.

40. Cf. I. Kant, *Kritik der reinen Vernunft*, A 182: "Alle Erscheinungen enthalten das Beharrliche (Substanz) als den Gegenstand selbst, und das Wan-

delbare, als dessen blosse Bestimmung, d.i. eine Art, wie der Gegenstand existiert." On this definition of substance, see J. Bennett, *Kant's Analytic* (Cambridge, 1966), pp. 183ff.

41. *PBh*, 20.

42. Cf. *VS* I, 1, 8 (*Upaskāra* I, 1, 10): *dravyāṇi dravyāntaram ārabhante;* I, 1, 11: *kāryāvirodhi dravyaṃ kāraṇāvirodhi ca* (*Upaskāra* I, 1, 12: *na dravyaṃ kāryaṃ kāraṇaṃ ca vadhati*); on *antyaviśeṣa*, see I, 2, 6.

43. Cf. W. V. Quine, *Word and Object* (Cambridge, Mass., 1960), pp. 271ff. (for the term, not necessarily the interpretation of "semantic ascent").

44. On the historical background of such ambiguity, and the "archaeology" of the Vaiśeṣika system, see earlier, Chapter 4, section 5.

45. Nāgārjuna provided a precedent and model for such critique in his reductive analysis of the Sarvāstivāda concepts *lakṣya* and *lakṣaṇa* in *MK*, ch. 5 (*Dhātuparīkṣā*).

46. See, for instance, *NV* I, 1, 14 (Calc. S.S., p. 210); here, statements about qualities of things (*tasya śvetaṃ rūpam*, etc.) are correlated with a statement about a water-jar owned by a brahmin (. . . *yathā brāhmaṇasya kamaṇḍalur iti*).

47. See Mallavādin, *DNC*, vol. 2, p. 486.

48. See Chapter 4, section 5.

49. Cf. Mahābhārata (crit. ed.), XII, 224, 35ff.; 225, 1ff.; 177, 26ff.; and earlier, Chapter 3, section 4.

50. A fully explicit, nonambiguous statement of this theory seems to be missing in *PBh*. According to Candrānanda, it is implied in *VS* VII, 1, 12: *aguṇavato dravyasya guṇārambhāt karmaguṇā aguṇāḥ*. This Sūtra is not found in Śaṅkaramiśra's version. Later Vaiśeṣika authors had to defend the theory against various objections; see, for instance, Vallabha, *Nyāyalīlāvatī*, ed. Harihara Śāstrī and Ḍhuṇḍhirāja Śāstrī (Benares, 1927–1934; ChSS), pp. 752ff.; see also Śrīdhara, *NK*, pp. 104f.; Keśavamiśra, *Tarkabhāṣā*, ed. D. R. Bhandarkar and Kedarnath (Bombay, 1937), pp. 29ff.

51. Cf. *VS* VIII, 1, 6: *sāmānyaviśeṣāpekṣaṃ dravyaguṇakarmasu;* VIII, 1, 7: *dravye dravyaguṇakarmāpekṣam;* cf. also II, 2, 19 (17); and Śrīdhara, *NK*, p. 199: *viśeṣyajñānaṃ hi viśeṣaṇajñānasya phalaṃ, viśeṣaṇajñānaṃ na jñānāntaraphalam*.

52. See *VS* VIII, 9: *samavāyinaḥ śvaityāc chvaityabuddheḥ śvete buddhis te kāryakāraṇabhūte*. The *Upaskāra* has some minor variants.

53. However, Candrānanda's commentary emphasizes the implied distinction between the universal "whiteness" (*śvaityasāmānya*) and the quality "white" (*śvetaguṇa*).

54. Cf. *VS* IV, 1, 6: *mahaty anekadravyavattvād rūpāc ca-upalabdhiḥ*. This Sūtra is often quoted and appears in a number of variants or combinations with IV, 1, 9 (8). It found its way into the Nyāya commentaries and was even counted as a *Nyāyasūtra;* cf. K. Preisendanz, *Studien zu Nyāyasūtra III, 1 mit dem Nyāyatattvāloka Vācaspati Miśras* II (Stuttgart, forthcoming), n. 173. The Buddhist commentator Yaśomitra cites it as evidence for the Vaiśeṣika theory that substances per se are perceptible; cf. *Vasubandhu et Yaśomitra,* ed. L. de La Vallée Poussin (*Bouddhisme. Études et matériaux: Cosmologie,* 1913), p. 222: *rūpadarśane hi tadāśrayadravyopalabdhir iṣyate vaiśeṣikaiḥ.*

55. We may recall at this point that the perception of other sensible qualities, such as smell, does not entail a perception of the substance itself. The case of touch (*sparśa*) and tactile qualities is particularly problematic. In the case of the invisible substance wind or air (*vāyu*), it only provides a basis for inferring the underlying substance (cf. *VS* II, 1, 8ff.; and IV, 1, 8: *rūpasaṃskārābhāvād vāyāv anupalabdhiḥ; Upaskāra* IV, 1, 7: *saty api dravyatve mahattve rūpasaṃskārābhāvād vāyor anupalabdhiḥ*). But for visible substances, the *dvīndriyagrāhyatva* theory (see later, section 12) postulates that they can also be felt (*spṛś*) as substances.

56. See *PBh,* pp. 186ff.; cf. also M. Hattori, "Two Types of Non-Qualificative Perception" *WZKS* 12–13 (1968–69; *Beiträge zur Geistesgeschichte Indiens,* Festschrift E. Frauwallner): 161–169; L. Schmithausen, "Zur Lehre von der vorstellungsfreien Wahrnehnung bei Praśastapāda," *WZKS* 14 (1970): 125–129.

57. See also W. Slaje, *Die Wahrnehmungslehre bei Vyomaśivaḥ* (Diss. Vienna, 1983), pp. 81ff.; on Aviddhakarṇa and "bare substances," see later, section 11.

58. Cf. *PBh,* 186: *udbhūtarūpaprakāśacatuṣṭayasaṃnikarṣād dharmādisāmagrye ca.* Praśastapāda distinguishes, of course, between "means of valid cognition" (*pramāṇa*) and "cognitive result" (*pramiti*); see *PBh,* p. 187; cf. also Vyomaśiva's distinction between *ālocana* and *ālociti, Vy,* pp. 560f.

59. Cf. H. N. Randle, *Indian Logic in the Early Schools* (London, 1930), p. 108, n. 2: the term "*svarūpa* means that the object, whatever it may be, is intuited 'in itself', i.e., not as related in any way to anything else."

60. See *PBh,* p. 187: *tatra sāmānyaviśeṣeṣu svarūpālocanamātraṃ pratyakṣam pramāṇaṃ, prameyā dravyādayaḥ padārthāḥ, pramātā-ātmā, pramitir dravyādiviṣayaṃ jñānam. sāmānyaviśeṣajñānotpattāv avibhaktam ālocanamātraṃ pratyakṣaṃ pramāṇam, asmin na-anyat pramāṇāntaram asti, aphalarūpatvāt.*

61. See ibid., p. 187.

62. *NK,* p. 198; see also p. 199: *ato viśeṣaṇajñāne indriyārthasaṃnikarṣamātram eva pramāṇam.*

63. Cf. *NK,* p. 117 (*pūrvapakṣa*): *yadi dravyasvarūpamātram eva viśeṣyajñānasya-ālambanam, asaty api viśeṣaṇe tathā pratyayaḥ syāt.*

64. Cf. PBh, 186: *rūparasagandhasparśeṣv anekadravyasamavāyāt svagataviśeṣāt svāśrayasaṃnikarṣān niyatendriyanimittam* (sc. *jñānam*) *utpadyate.*

65. See *NV* I, 1, 4 (Calc. S.S., pp. 94f.): *saṃnikarṣaḥ punaḥ ṣoḍhā bhidyate. saṃyogaḥ, saṃyuktasamavāyaḥ, saṃyuktasamavetasamavāyaḥ, samavāyaḥ, samavetasamavāyaḥ, viśeṣaṇaviseṣyabhāvaś ca-iti.*

66. Cf. *VP* III/3 (*Sambandhasamuddeśa*), 13ff.

67. See *Vy*, pp. 558f.; *NK*, p. 195; in a different context, the term *saṃyuktasamavāya* appears in *VS* X, 18 (*Upaskāra:* X, 2, 7; quoted in *PBh*, p. 139).

68. See the sequence of commentaries (Vātsyāyana, Uddyotakara, Vācaspati, Udayana) on *NS* I, 1, 4. The expression *ālocanamātra* occurs also in *SK*, v. 28; *YD* paraphrases *grahaṇa.*

69. The underlying "pre-predicative" awareness can *only* be inferred, and not simply be ascertained by perception or introspection; cf. *Vy.*, p. 557: *sadbhāve* (sc. *nirvikalpakajñānasya*) *kiṃ pramāṇam? savikalpakajñānotpattir eva.* For a survey of these conceptual developments, see B. Gupta, *Die Wahrnehmungslehre in der Nyāyamañjarī* (Bonn, 1963), pp. 69ff.; 97ff.

70. See *PBh*, p. 182; on *adhyavasāya*, cf. also *NS/NBh* II, 1, 1ff.

71. See earlier, n. 62.

72. Cf. B. Gupta, *Die Wahrnehmungslehre* (cited in n. 69), pp. 81; 84; Maṇḍana, *Brahmasiddhi*, ed. S. Kuppuswami Sastri (Madras, 1937), pp. 58; 71; K. Camman, *Das System des Advaita nach der Lehre Prakāśātmans* (Wiesbaden, 1965), pp. 57f.

73. See n. 43. Cf. also B. Gupta. *Die Wahrnehmungslehre*, pp. 69ff.; 98ff.; 115f., on the idea of a particular something, a substance with an identity of its own, to be isolated from its qualifying factors. Vācaspati states on *NS* I, 1, 4 (*Nyāyadarśana*, vol. 1, ed. A. Thakur; Darbhanga, 1967, p. 232): *svabhāvo hi dravyasya upādhibhir viśiṣyate na tu-upādhayo vā tair viśiṣṭatvaṃ vā tasya svabhāvaḥ.*

74. Others, such as Jayanta, are more cautious; cf. *NM*, p. 286: *yathā rūpādyasambaddhā na vyaktir upalabhyate / tathā-eva jātyayuktā* . . . On the perception of substances according to Bhāsarvajña, see L. V. Joshi, *A Critical Study of the Pratyakṣa Pariccheda of Bhāsarvajña's Nyāyabhūṣaṇa* (Ahmedabad, 1986), pp. 493ff.

75. See *NV* I, 1, 14 (Calc. S.S., pp. 208f.; ed. A. Thakur, p. 421).

76. See *NV* III, 1, 1, (Calc. S.S., p. 711): *yadā-ayam anupalabhyamānarūpādikaṃ vastu-upalabhate, tadā-asya tadviśiṣṭaḥ pratyaya upajāyate, yathā nīlādyuparisthitasphaṭike pratyayo rūpādyanupalabdhau bhavati, rātrau ca balākāyāṃ śuklādirūpāgrahaṇāt pakṣipratyayaḥ. tasmād rūpasparśavyatirikte ghaṭapratyayaḥ.*

77. See *TS*, v. 556ff.; especially 557: *kañcukāntargate puṃsi tadrūpādyagatāv api puruṣapratyayo dṛṣṭaḥ.*

78. See *Dharmakīrti's Vādanyāya with the Commentary of Śāntarakṣita*, ed. R. Sāṅkṛtyāyana, Appendix to *Journal of the Bihar and Orissa Research Society* 21–22 (1935–36): 35: *aviddhakarṇas tv āha rūpādyagrahe 'pi dravyagrahaṇaṃ asty eva, yato mandaprakāśe 'nupalabhyamānarūpādikaṃ dravyam upalabhyate 'niścitarūpaṃ gaur aśva vā-iti.*

79. Śāntarakṣita, *TS*, v. 566, says that the recognition of the person in armor is in reality inferential (*ānumānika*).

80. In his reference to Aviddhakarṇa (see n. 78), Śāntarakṣita notes: *nanu ca tatra-api saṃsthānamātram upalabhyate.* See also *TS*, v. 566 (*saṃniveśa*, paraphrased as *saṃsthānaviśeṣa* by Kamalaśīla).

81. See Uddyotakara, *NV* I, 1, 14 (Calc. S.S., pp. 205f.; ed. A. Thakur, pp. 419); cf. also Śāntarakṣita's *pūrvapakṣa* (see n. 78): *satyam upalabhyate* (sc. *saṃsthānam*), *na tu tad rūpādyātmakam.*

82. See *Vy*, p. 46 (ed. Gaurinath Sastri, vol. 1, p. 20): *mandamandaprakāśe sati saṃsthānamātrasya-avayavino grahaṇād.* The text preceding this statement is obviously corrupt in the ChSS edition; it has been partially corrected by Gaurinath Sastri.

83. See *NK*, p. 41: *pratyekavilakṣaṇasaṃsthānasaṃvedanāt, rūpādisvabhāvasya sarvatra-aviśeṣāt;* cf. also Kumārila, *ŚV*, p. 438 (*Vanavāda*, v. 17): *anyad anyac ca saṃsthānaṃ pratipiṇḍaṃ pratīyate.*

84. See *NS* III, 3, 1ff. with commentaries.

85. See *NBh* IV, 1, 36 (Calc. S.S., p. 974): *yaṃ kumbham adrākṣaṃ taṃ spṛśāmi, yam eva-asprākṣaṃ taṃ paśyāmi;* cf. also *NBh* III, 1, 1; and Vyomaśiva, *Vy.*, p. 44: *na ca dvābhyām indriyābhyām ekārthagrahaṇaṃ vinā pratisaṃdhānaṃ nyāyyam.*

86. See *NK*, p. 41: *saṃsthānaviśeṣaḥ kalpanīyaḥ, yena darśanasparśanābhyām ekārthagrahaṇam api sidhyati.*

87. In the Nyāya texts, *ātman* appears as the first in the list of relevant "objects of knowledge" (*prameya*); see *NS* I, 1, 9; on proofs for the existence of the *ātman*, including the argument from *pratisaṃdhāna*, see *NBh* and *NV* I, 1, 10.

88. For a thorough and comprehensive analysis of these debates, see C. Oetke, *"Ich" und das Ich. Analytische Untersuchungen zur buddhistisch-brahmanischen Ātmankontroverse* (Stuttgart, 1988).

89. See earlier, Chapter 2, section 14.

90. See later, Chapter 10.

6

The Vaiśeṣika Concept of Guṇa *and the Problem of Universals*

1. The relationship and distinction between *sāmānya/jāti* and *guṇa*—that is, between "universal" or "generic property," on the one hand, and "quality" on the other—is one specific chapter of what we may call the Indian version of the problem of universals. It represents an aspect of this problem that, though not completely absent, has been less conspicuous and explicit in the Western philosophical tradition. Here, the very notion of an attribute or quality is commonly associated with repeatability and universality; qualities, as repeatable attributes of individual things, seem to coincide with universals. It is symptomatic that one of the leading modern theoreticians of the problem of universals in the West, W. V. Quine, defines this problem as "the question whether there are such entities as attributes, relations, classes, numbers, functions."[1] The question whether and to what extent the dichotomy of the "universal" and the "particular" applies to the qualities themselves has remained a minor and somewhat marginal concern. By and large, and particularly in the earlier periods of Western philosophy, it is difficult to find an equivalent to the strict and comprehensive distinction between *sāmānya* and *guṇa* as it has been developed in the Vaiśeṣika and Nyāya systems.

Referring to this conceptual and terminological discrepancy, K. H. Potter has asked the question: "Are the Vaiśeṣika guṇas qualities?"[2] He answers his question as follows: "the English word 'quality' usually suggests repeatability. . . . Qualities are properties shared among the objects of everyday life. But this is not the view expounded in the Nyāya-Vaiśeṣika system. Since it is not, as I shall proceed to show, the translation of 'guṇa' as 'quality' is highly misleading." The alternative translations offered by Potter are "particular character," as used by G. F. Stout, "abstract particular" in D. C. Williams' sense, and finally G. Santayana's "trope," as redefined by D. C. Williams.[3] In a further contribution, "More on the repeatability of guṇas,"[4] Potter defends his interpretation against the objections raised in an article by D. M. Datta[5] and recapitulates his arguments: "My arguments, as presented before, were of two kinds: a) the demonstration that a contradiction arises if guṇas are construed as repeatable, and b) the incidental citation of at least one passage (from Viśvanātha's *Siddhāntamuktāvalī*) evidently defending the unrepeatability of guṇas against an objector."[6] More recently, Potter's interpretation of the "unrepeatability" issue was criticized by H. Narain with reference both to its Indian and its Western implications. Narain, who did not question the basic connotation of "unrepeatability" in the Vaiśeṣika conception of *guṇa,* suggested "attribute" as the most suitable translation of term *guṇa.*[7] By 1977, Potter himself adopted the translation "quality," though with some reservations.[8]

The basic merit of Potter's interpretation is obvious and can hardly be questioned. In a philosophically committed manner, it focuses on an issue that the more historically and philosophically oriented presentations of the Vaiśeṣika system tend to disregard. However, its textual basis and its historical horizon are too narrow. It does not integrate the "unrepeatability" issue in its Indian context and setting, nor does it explore its wider historical and conceptual implications. In the following, we shall try to clarify some of these implications, to provide a broader textual basis, and to suggest some further viewpoints for relating the Vaiśeṣika concept of *guṇa* to the concepts of *sāmānya* and *jāti,* and to the general "problem of universals."

2. In the Western presentations of the Vaiśeṣika system, the fourth and fifth categories, *sāmānya* and *viśeṣa,* appear in a wide variety of translations.[9] H. T. Colebrooke uses "community" and "difference" or "particularity";[10] another pioneer in this field, J. R. Ballantyne, has "community" and "distinction."[11] In F. Max Müller's early German writings, we find "das Allgemeine" and "das Besondere";[12] later, he uses "community" or "genus" for *sāmānya*, and paraphrases *viśeṣa* as "that which constitutes the individuality or separateness of an object."[13] Other suggestions include "generality" and "particularity" (P. Tuxen);[14] "generality or genus" and "specific individuality" (Ganganatha Jha);[15] "genus" and "species" (Nandalal Sinha);[16] "Gattung" and "Besonderheit" (A. Winter);[17] "Begriff" or "Universale" and "Unterschied" (G. Patti);[18] "Allgemeinbegriff" and "Besonderheit" (E. Hultzsch and O. Strauss);[19] "Gemeinsamkeit" and "Besonderheit" (E. Frauwallner).[20] As far as *viśeṣa* is concerned, some of the discrepancies are due to the fact that this term has two different functions in classical Vaiśeṣika; "ultimate *viśeą*" (*antyaviśeṣa*) and "intermediate species" or "specific universal" (*sāmānyaviśeṣa*).

In more recent studies in English, "universal" is the most common translation for *sāmānya;* it appears, for instance, in the writings of S. Bhaduri, N. Smart, P. K. Mukhopadhyay, and B. K. Matilal.[21] The term "universal" is sometimes paraphrased as, or replaced by, "generic property" or "generic characteristic."[22] The translations of *viśeṣa* continue to vary more widely, sometimes with explicit reference to its different functions in the system. In addition to such familiar terms as "individuality" and "particularity,"[23] various other, less common terms, for instance "individuator" and "differential,"[24] have been used to translate *viśeṣa* in the sense of *antyaviśeṣa*.

For the following discussion, we will adopt the translation "universal" for *sāmānya*, and "particularity" (or "ultimate particularity") for *viśeṣa* in the sense of *antyaviśeṣa;* instead of "universal," we may also occasionally say "generic property." In general, the term *universal* recommends itself because of its rich historical associations, even if some of these associations are potentially misleading. Here as elsewhere, translation should not be confused with definition and systematic analysis.

To introduce our discussion, we may recall here the basic meaning of *sāmānya* and *viśeṣa* (i.e., *antyaviśeṣa*) according to classical, "standardized" Vaiśeṣika: Universals are recurrent and indestructible generic properties in substances, qualities, and motions. They account for the fact that numerically different individual entities can be associated with an identical concept, referred to by a common term, and identified as members of the same class. Particularities are ultimate factors of individual identity. They reside exclusively in the eternal, noncomposite substances and account for the irreducible identity of each of these entities.[25] Although these definitions are sufficiently clear and familiar, some historical reflection and differentiation is, nonetheless, called for. Once again, our retrospective has to begin with the Vaiśeṣikasūtra.

3. Kaṇāda does not introduce *sāmānya* with a definition. Apart from the dubious Sūtra I,1,4, it is not even listed, or referred to, as a category (*padārtha*). After a first occurrence of the expression *sāmānyaviśeṣa* in Sūtra I,1,7, the explicit discussion of the topic begins, in a somewhat abrupt fashion, in Sūtra I,2,3: *sāmānyaṃ viśeṣa iti buddhyapekṣam*. The following two Sūtras give some examples: Existence or reality is sheer inclusiveness or universality, or the universal par excellence (*bhāvaḥ sāmānyam eva*); "substanceness," "qualityness," "motionness" (*dravyatva, guṇatva, karmatva*) are universals, but also specific features. Sūtra I,2,6 (*anyatra-antyebhyaḥ viśeṣebhyaḥ*) refers to the ultimate particularities.[26] The remainder of the Āhnika (i.e., I,2,7–18) presents further arguments and specifications concerning the status of the universals "reality," "substanceness," and so on. The term *sāmānya* occurs again in a number of other Sūtras. Its uses are not always terminological. In several cases, it appears in the general sense of "similarity," or as a synonym of *sādharmya;* it occurs also as an adjective in the sense of "common" or "general".[27]

The entire section suggests a hierarchy of more or less inclusive universals, with "reality" as the ultimate, that is, most inclusive, generic property. The first Sūtra in this series of statements, I,2,3, is also the most controversial one. It seems to imply that it depends on our understanding whether we identify something as *sāmānya* or *viśeṣa;* that is, whether we consider its inclusive or exclusive function. However, some modern scholars have argued that not just the inclusive or exclusive aspect, but the universals or generic properties as such, are "relative to our understanding" (*buddhyapekṣa*) and thus mind-dependent. According to this interpretation, Kaṇāda would have held a conceptualistic, if not nominalistic, view of the universals. "The notions sāmānya and viśeṣa are relative notions and represent notional or logical categories rather than ontological ones."[28]

Although Kaṇāda's text is, indeed, elusive and problematic, we may safely say that it does not warrant such an interpretation. Kaṇāda's commentators and successors never even consider it. Instead, they offer thoroughly realistic interpretations of the concept of *sāmānya*. For a more coherent and systematic presentation, we have to turn once again to Praśastapāda. Here, the doctrine of universals is fully integrated into the system. Kaṇāda's idea that the inclusive or exclusive functions of universals can be a matter of perspective is no longer significant in this presentation.

Praśastapāda opens his discussion of universals with a series of characteristic phrases: *sāmānyaṃ dvividhaṃ, param aparaṃ ca; svaviṣayasarvagatam abhinnātmakam anekavṛtti; ekadvibahuṣv ātmasvarūpānugamapratyayakāri, svarūpābhedena ādhāreṣu prabandhena vartamānam anuvṛttipratyayakāraṇam.*[29] We may paraphrase this as follows: Universals are of two kinds, ultimate and nonultimate; they are present in all appropriate objects (i.e., their instances), residing in many individual entities without losing their essential unity, that is to say, they are, in their undivided identity, simultaneously present in any number of substrates and produce the notion of recurrence or inclusion.

The following sections illustrate and expand these introductory statements. "Reality" (*sattā*) constitutes the "ultimate universal" or "supreme generality." It is all-inclusive and pervades all substances, qualities, and motions. Nonultimate universals, on the other hand, pervade and include certain entities and exclude others. Praśastapāda leaves no doubt that he regards the universals as real factors in the real world. They are by no means mere concepts and abstractions; instead, they are the condition of the possibility of general ideas and generic terms. They explain and justify the fact that we identify numerically different entities as members of the same class.

4. If we compare Praśastapāda's exposition with the relevant sections of the Vaiśeṣikasūtra, we notice a number of additions, but also one conspicuous absence. The elusive term *buddhyapekṣa* ("dependent on cognition"), as used in Sūtra I,2,3, is missing. However, in an earlier section of his work, Praśastapāda mentions *buddhilakṣaṇatva*, "having cognition as its mark," as a characteristic of the three categories *sāmānya*, *viśeṣa*, and *samavāya*.[30] This seems to be his interpretation of *buddhyapekṣa*. It was adopted and made more explicit by his commentators.

Śrīdhara explains: *buddhir eva lakṣaṇaṃ, pramāṇaṃ. vipratipan-*

nasāmānyādisadbhāve buddhir eva lakṣaṇam, na-anyat. dravyādisadbhāve tv anyad api tatkāryaṃ pramāṇam syāt.[31] We paraphrase: Cognition alone serves as a mark or criterion; that is, as evidence. Cognition alone, and nothing else, provides evidence for the objective existence of universals, and so forth, an existence that has been contested. For the existence of substances, and so forth, there is also other evidence: their products or effects. However, Śrīdhara adds that the lack of causality (*akāraṇatva*), which Praśastapāda ascribes to the universals, has to be specified.[32] It means that they cannot function as "inherential and noninherential causes" (*samavāyyasamavāyikāraṇa*); it does not imply a total negation of "efficient" causality (*nimittakāraṇatvapratiṣedha*). Universals can be "causes" of mental occurrences (*pratyayakāraṇa*); they can have cognitive effects.[33] Likewise, Vyomaśiva states that "efficient," "instrumental" causality is acceptable, and that it is the inclusive (*anugata*) and exclusive (*vyāvṛtta*) character of cognitions (*buddhi*) that indicates the presence of *sāmānya* or *viśeṣa*.[34] Accordingly, Śaṅkaramiśra's explanation of Sūtra I,2,3 paraphrases *buddhyapekṣa* as "that which has cognition as its reference, i.e., as mark or criterion" (*buddhir apekṣā liṅgaṃ lakṣaṇaṃ vā yasya*).[35]

As we have seen, classical Vaiśeṣika assumes a perception of universals even without an explicit awareness of repetition or recurrence. Any perceptual identification of concrete and specific entities presupposes an awareness of universals as qualifying factors (*viśeṣaṇa*) and as conditions of predication.[36] The difference between this simple perceptual awareness (*ālocanamātra*) of universals and their identification through recurrent cognition is that only the latter makes their character as universals (i.e., their identical presence in many particular entities) fully explicit.

Later followers of the Nyāya and Vaiśeṣika describe the universals as indispensable conditions for the determination and regulation of causal linkages (i.e., as *kāraṇatāvacchedaka* and *kāryatāvacchedaka*). At this point, we do not have to discuss these and other arguments for the existence of universals, which emerge in the writings of Udayana and his successors.[37] In general, the Naiyāyikas and Vaiśeṣikas continue to insist that neither language nor inferential reasoning could operate without universals.[38]

5. The Buddhists and other opponents raised numerous objections against the Nyāya-Vaiśeṣika theory of universals. In response to such criticism, the proponents of the school adopted various modifications and specifications, and they were forced to deal with problems not explicitly addressed in the oldest texts.

In particular, they had to specify and clarify the relationship between recurrent cognitions and general terms, on the one hand, and real universals, on the other. "Not all general terms yield objective universals. In fact most do not, unless they are in line with what is accepted in the system as the 'natural' classification. The meanings of a large number of general terms in our language are construed as *upādhis*, i.e., 'nominal' properties, not objective universals."[39]

Kaṇāda and Praśastapāda did not really address this issue. It was, above all, Udayana who tried to provide a set of formal criteria for the exclusion of invalid or counterfeit universals, such as "cookness" (*pācakatva*) or "being an inhabitant of Ayodhyā" (*ayodhyāvāsitva*); the most important and characteristic of these invalidating factors (*jātibādhaka*) is mixture or overlap (*saṃkara*).[40] Universals may be juxtaposed at the same level of generality, with clearly distinct areas of extension; or they may be subordinated to one another. But there can be no partial crossing or overlap of their spheres. There has to be a well-ordered hierarchy of higher and lower, more or less inclusive generalities. It is obvious that this hierarchy of real universals includes not only cosmological divisions, natural species, types of qualities and motions, and so forth, but also, for instance, social divisions (specifically the four main castes) and various types of "normal" or "natural" artefacts (such as pots and garments). In this sense, the universals, together with the other basic categories, constitute the structure of the real world.[41]

The simultaneous presence of identical universals in numerically different substrates, their eternity, and so on, are further targets of intense criticism and ridicule. How can a universal preserve its unity and identity while residing in many particulars? Does it inhere in every particular in its entirety? Can it divide itself? According to the Buddhists, both alternatives are equally absurd.[42] Does a universal move with its substrates? Does it come into being with the genesis of its instances? What happens to a universal if all its actual, temporal substrates have perished?[43]

Somewhat reluctantly, the Vaiśeṣika commentators, such as Vyomaśiva, discuss the case of "disappearance of all substrates" (*samastāśrayavināśa*),[44] and they are obliged to postulate some state of continued existence for the universals. But unlike Plato, they do not have any supramundane realm for such continued existence; and unlike Bhartṛhari, they cannot interpret the universals or genera (*jāti*) as inherent forces (*śakti*) of the absolute brahman or "word-principle" (*śabdatattva*), nor as patterns and prototypes for its expansion into the empirical world.[45] "Nyāya-Vaiśeṣika universals exist nowhere but in this very world of ours, and particulars do not 'copy' but 'manifest' them, or allow the universals to *reside* in them."[46] Some Naiyāyikas, for instance Jayanta, compare the concrete individuals (*piṇḍa*), transitory "manifestors" (*vyañjaka*) of the eternal, but nonmanifest universals, to the ephemeral "sounds" (*dhvani*) that, according to the Mīmāṃsā metaphysics of language, manifest the eternal, indestructible "words" (*śabda*).[47] Accordingly, they postulate (as Bhartṛhari did centuries earlier) a nonmanifest potential presence of all universals in all particulars (*sarvasarvagatatva*).[48] However, the concepts of potentiality and nonmanifestness play only a marginal role in Nyāya and Vaiśeṣika. The Vaiśeṣika commentators are generally reluctant to adopt such models as that of *śabda* and *dhvani*.[49] Yet in spite of all problems, they continue to describe the universals (*sāmānya, jāti*) as entities that are eternal (*nitya*), unitary (*eka*), and present in many particulars (*anekavṛtti*).[50]

6. From an early time, the Nyāya joins the Vaiśeṣika in the defense of the universals. Even prior to the formation of a combined Nyāya-Vaiśeṣika school, their strategies were often indistinguishable. We should not forget, however, that the two systems start from somewhat different premises and with a clearly distinguishable terminology. In the Nyāyasūtra, the relevant term is *jāti,* not *sāmānya.*[51] In the Vaiśeṣikasūtra, *jāti* is never used in the sense of "universal." Even Praśastapāda uses it only somewhat casually and avoids it altogether in his chapter on universals.[52]

An important, but elusive statement appears in Nyāyasūtra II,2,69: *samānaprasavātmikā jātiḥ.* The Sūtra says that it is the nature of *jāti* to produce what is common or similar. It does not specify the content of such similarity or the type of entities or phenomena it considers as common. Some modern scholars have suggested that this is a reference to natural species and the homogeneousness of their members.[53] However, Vātsyāyana Pakṣilasvāmin's *Nyāyabhāṣya* does not even consider this possibility. Instead, it interprets *jāti* as that "which produces common cognition" (*yā samānāṃ buddhiṃ prasūte*). It also cites the concept of *sāmānya*, as "cause of the recurrence of ideas" (*pratyayānuvṛttikāraṇa*), and explains *jāti* as *sāmānyaviśeṣa* "specific universal."[54] The Vaiśeṣika influence, probably from some lost source between the Vaiśeṣikasūtra and Praśastapāda, seems obvious in this interpretation.

According to the *Nyāyabhāṣya*, *jāti* would correspond to what Praśastapāda calls *lower* or *nonultimate universal (aparaṃ sāmānyam); sāmānya* would have a somewhat wider application than *jāti*. Although this distinction has some relevance, it is not universally observed by the Naiyāyikas and Vaiśeṣikas. In general, the Vaiśeṣika commentators continue to favor *sāmānya*. Some later authors introduce more specific terminological distinctions and reserve the term *jāti*, unlike *sāmānya*, for "real" universals.[55] Although *jāti*, with its connotations of "birth" and "natural species", does, indeed, favor such specification, the uses of *jāti* and *sāmānya* tend to coincide in classical Nyāya and Vaiśeṣika.

Some significant differences are found in the use of the term *ākṛti*, "form." In Vaiśeṣika, its role is negligible. But in early Nyāya, *ākṛti* is defined as the "mark" (*liṅga*) of the universal (*jāti*). Patañjali's *Mahābhāṣya* notes a similar relationship.[56] In classical Mīmāṃsā and some grammatical traditions, *ākṛti* can be used as a synonym of *jāti/sāmānya* and refer to the universal itself. Kumārila states such synonymy explicitly; Śabara does not even use the term *jāti*.[57] Vājapyāyana, an ancient grammarian cited by Kātyāyana and Patañjali, defines "form" as "one, but residing simultaneously in many substrates" (*ekam anekādhikaraṇasthaṃ yugapad*).[58] The analogy with the Nyāya-Vaiśeṣika definition of *sāmānya/jāti* (*ekaṃ nityam anekavṛtti*) is obvious.

In general, the tradition of grammatical thought, as documented in Patañjali's *Mahābhāṣya*, provides very significant counterparts and potential precedents for the Nyāya-Vaiśeṣika debates on universals and qualities. This is true even if early Vaiśeṣika did not directly borrow from these sources and may, indeed, predate them to some extent. In addition to its observations concerning *jāti* and *ākṛti*, Patañjali's *Mahābhāṣya* also discusses in detail the various meanings and implications of *guṇa*.[59]

Classical Mīmāṃsā, on the other hand, borrows freely from the teachings of early Vaiśeṣika and tries to adjust them to its own systematic needs. We find this process first documented in Śabara's *Mīmāṃsābhāṣya*. In the works of Kumārila, it is much more conspicuous and pervasive. Yet in spite of his free and somewhat eclectic borrowing, Kumārila keeps his critical distance and draws his inspiration from other sources as well, including the Jaina perspectivism. He avoids the additive approach of the Vaiśeṣika and its reification of juxtaposable attributes. For him, all categories, including qualities and universals, remain embedded in the complex and ambiguous unity of the concrete thing (*vastu, piṇḍa*), the paradigm of reality.[60]

7. The basic contrast between qualities and universals seems to be taken for granted in the Vaiśeṣikasūtra. Sūtra I,2,14 (*guṇe bhāvād guṇatvam uktam*) postulates a different categorial status for the qualities and the universal "qualityness." What occurs in the qualities cannot be a quality itself. Accordingly, Praśastapāda presents both "connection with qualityness" (*guṇatvābhisambandha*) and "being without qualities" (*nirguṇatva*) among the defining characteristics of all qualities.[61] The distinction applies also to specific qualities, such as the colors (*rūpa*) or the instances of the color red (*rakta*). What they have in common (i.e., *rūpatva* and *raktatva,* respectively) must be of a different nature than the qualities themselves.

The *guṇas* must be regarded as "abstract particulars" or particularized *qualia;* that is, as particular spatiotemporal occurrences of colors, tastes, dimensions, and so on. This view is implied in, and exemplified by, Praśastapāda's division of the guṇas into those "which reside in one substance only" (*ekadravyavṛtti*), and those "which inhere in more than one substance" (*anekāśrita*).[62] That there are guṇas that are supposed to be located in more than one substance does, of course, not mean that they are quasi-universals. On the contrary, they always remain "unrepeatable" particulars. But as relational guṇas, such as "connection" (*saṃyoga*), "separation" (*vibhāga*), or "number" (*saṃkhyā*), they involve a plurality of substances that are related to each other, or grouped together in relation to a perceiving subject.[63] We may say that in such cases quality-particulars are shared by, or distributed over, numerically different substances.

The Naiyāyika Uddyotakara, a champion of the Vaiśeṣika system of categories whose lifetime was not far from that of Praśastapāda, illustrates the meaning of the term *ekadravyavṛtti* and its bearing upon the problem of universals in a passage of his *Nyāyavārttika.* Referring to Nyāyasūtra I,1,23, which associates doubt (*saṃśaya*) with the "occurrence of a common attribute" (*samānadharmopapatti*), an opponent asks about the exact meaning and character of this "common attribute" (*samānadharma*). What is it that is common in the familiar example of the man and the post? What constitutes the misleading similarity of shape that provides the occasion for our doubt? What is the role of the quality *parimāṇa*, "dimension," in this case? Is the common and confusing factor a quality (*guṇa*) or a universal (*sāmānya*)? It cannot be a quality, because a quality resides in one substance only (*ekadravyavṛtti*) and cannot be common to (*sādhāraṇa*), or simultaneously present in, two numerically different substances.[64] In another passage, Uddyotakara notes that the "property" (*dharma*) of one thing cannot also exist in another thing. But he adds that linguistic usage tends to neglect the difference between identity in the strict sense and mere equality or homogeneity: *tattulyaḥ sa eva ucyate*.[65]

The case for "inherence in one substance only" (*ekadravyavṛttitva*), that is, for particularity and unrepeatability, is still more obvious if we consider some of the other items in the Vaiśeṣika list of guṇas, such as "gravity" (*gurutva*) or "liquidity" (*dravatva*). These are not static attributes, but powers and forces in nature, which have their actuality and effectivity at particular points in time and space and in particular substances only. The final list of twenty-four qualities includes also *dharma* and *adharma* (under the common title *adṛṣṭa*); that is, good and bad karma which is by definition the exclusive property and responsibility of the individual soul by which it has been produced and for which it will bear fruit.[66] Other qualities of the soul, such as "pleasure" (*sukha*), "pain" (*duḥkha*), or "effort" (*prayatna*), appear as equally "private" and individually restricted phenomena.[67]

However, the most explicit and controversial statements concerning the ontological distinction between qualities and universals have not been made with reference to mental attributes, but with reference to colors; in this case, the distinction would seem to be far less obvious and natural.

8. One obvious reason for the special attention paid to color is the fact that it is traditionally listed as the first in the series of guṇas and that it serves as their most familiar exemplification and as a kind of model case. Accordingly, Śrīdhara's commentary illustrates Praśastapāda's general statement about those qualities that reside in single substances only (*śeṣās tv ekaikadravyavṛttayaḥ*) by referring specifically to the colors: "The remainder (of qualities), i.e., color-particulars, etc., reside in one particular (substance) only; unlike connection, one color-particular does not reside partially in two substances" (*śeṣā rūpādivyaktaya ekasyām eva vyaktau vartante, na punar ekā rūpavyaktiḥ saṃyogavad ubhayatra vyāsajya vartate*).[68]

The expression *rūpavyakti* is symptomatic: Color-particulars, particular instances of color, inhere in particular substances; they are (to borrow a phrase from Bhartṛhari's commentator Helārāja) "different from substrate to substrate" (*pratidravyaṃ bhinnāḥ*). They manifest and exemplify universals that are different from those inhering in their substrates; accordingly, they are particulars (*vyakti*) of a different kind. We find this use of the word *vyakti* also in Vyomaśiva and even in Kumārila.[69] In older Nyāya literature, *vyakti* is explained as a "substratum of specific qualities" (*guṇaviśeṣāśraya*) and as a concrete perceptible substance.[70] In its role as a *vyakti*, a guṇa obviously assumes some of the connotations of "substance," in particular certain connotations of individuality and numerical identity. The distinction between quality-universal and quality-particular implies a distinction between generic and numerical unity and identity. As a matter of fact, we hear about "*one* color-particular" (*ekā rūpavyaktiḥ*).[71] Within the framework of the system, this is problematic insofar as "number" (*saṃkhyā*), including numerical unity, is listed as a quality itself and therefore should not inhere in other qualities.[72]

The unity and numerical identity of a color-particular, a *rūpavyakti*, is a derivative one, borrowed from the unity and numerical identity of the substance-particular in which it inheres. A color is present in a "pervasive" manner of inherence (*vyāpyavṛtti*) in the whole colored thing, permeating its unity and totality; through such presence, it has a unity of its own. This view is illustrated and pursued to extreme consequences in the notorious Nyāya and Vaiśeṣika theory of the color *citra*, "variegated." Because there are unitary things that are variegated or multicolored, this character in itself must constitute *one* color, *one* particular instance of *one* color-species, *citratva*. The numerical identity of the color-particular is supposed to entail qualitative and generic unity; that is, the presence of a real universal. The theory of the color *citra* and its stubborn defense against Buddhist criticism and ridicule[73] is a curious, but symptomatic episode in the history of Nyāya and Vaiśeṣika. Apart from other problems connected with the system of categories, it illustrates and dramatizes some of the basic difficulties inherent in the Vaiśeṣika conception of the whole (*avayavin*).[74]

9. It is Udayana who states the reality of a species, or a "specific universal" (*jātiviśeṣa*), "variegatedness" (*citratva*) in the most concise and unambiguous manner: *nīlatvādivac citratvam api jātiviśeṣa eva.*[75] In general, he offers some of the most incisive observations on the Nyāya-Vaiśeṣika theory of qualities and on the conceptual analysis of colors in particular.

The basic characterization of the universals as "eternal, one, and residing in many substrates" (*nityam, ekam, anekavṛtti*)[76] is not applicable to the qualities. In his Vaiśeṣika commentary *Kiraṇāvalī,* Udayana defends this premise of his guṇa theory against a view that does not recognize the distinction between color-particulars and color-universals. According to this view, the colors themselves would be eternal and identically present in different substrates and thus coincide with the universals. Whatever the direct target of Udayana's arguments may be, there is no doubt that it represents an understanding of guṇa that has its place in the tradition of grammatical thought and that we find documented in Patañjali's *Mahābhāṣya.* Referring to Pāṇini's Sūtra V,1,119, Patañjali cites Kātyāyana's view that the abstract suffixes *-tva* and *-tā,* which the Vaiśeṣika would associate with universals, signify qualities (*guṇa*).[77] Patañjali himself discusses in detail the following questions: Are colors, such as white or whiteness (*śauklya*), one or many? If they are one, what is the meaning and character of such unity? How is it compatible with the difference of shades and degrees of color, such as "white" (*śukla*) and "whiter" (*śuklatara*)? Patañjali suggests various possibilities. The color white may be one, but differentiated in terms of less and more (*alpatvamahattva*); or it may be one without such internal differentiation, but more or less overshadowed and obscured by other colors; or what we call *one* color may in fact be a certain spectrum, a plurality of similar colors.[78] It is obvious that this discussion is not concerned with the numerical difference of "unrepeatable" color-particulars, but with the difference of shades and degrees that are still "repeatable" types or subspecies of color.

In his *Kiraṇāvalī,* Udayana discusses the problem of degrees (*tāratamya*) of color in his own way, and he offers a solution that is in accordance with his systematic premises. He postulates a plurality of intermediate species or subspecies (*avāntarajāti*) of colors, manifested by the different color-shades that inhere only in the substance earth and not in any other kind of substance: *kiṃca śuklaśuklataraśuklatamādyavāntarānan-*

tajātimad rūpaṃ kṣitāv eva, na-anyatra.[79] Other explanations of the qualitative gradation (*tāratamya*) of colors, such as the "mixture of substrates" (*āśrayamiśratā*), corresponding to Patañjali's second suggestion, are rejected.[80]

Against the attempt to raise the colors themselves to the level of universals, Udayana argues that this would lead to an inadmissable overlap or mixture of universals (*jātisaṃkara*).[81] Such a defect can be avoided only if quality-universals do not inhere directly in substances, side by side with substance-universals such as "cowness" (*gotva*), but indirectly, through quality-particulars. Udayana's commentator Vardhamāna summarizes this issue in the phraseology of Navyanyāya: What we observe in the case of substances is the possession of qualities that are equipped with universals, such as whiteness, but not the possession of universals that would be identical with qualities, such as white (*śuklatvādijātimadguṇavattvaṃ dravye 'nubhūyate, na tu śuklādijātimattvam eva*).[82] Later commentators, for instance Padmanābha in his commentary *Setu* on Praśastapāda's *Padārthadharmasaṃgraha*, continue the discussion about colors and color-universals.[83]

10. The theory that qualities as such, specifically colors, are eternal, unitary, and "repeatable" is also found in the Pūrvamīmāṃsā, both in the school of Kumārila and that of Prabhākara. Kumārila himself adopts this view in the *Śabdanityatā* chapter of his *Ślokavārttika*.[84] But in his *Tantravārttika*, he also invokes the distinction between general colors, or even color-universals, and their particular instances (*vyakti*).[85]

Prabhākara's follower Śālikanātha states that a quality inheres in substances just like a universal "form" (*ākṛtivad dravyeṣu guṇaḥ samavaiti*) and that there is only one redness in all substances, which is signified by the word *red* (*sakaladravyeṣv eko 'ruṇimā aruṇapadābhidhānīya iti*).[86] Unlike the Naiyāyikas and Vaiśeṣikas, the Prābhākaras do not recognize the disappearance and replacement of colors in a persisting substance as evidence for the existence of color-particulars. In their view, it is the variability and plurality of "inherence" (*samavāya*) that accounts for the presence or absence, the appearance or disappearance of one eternal color at different times and in different substances. In Nyāya and Vaiśeṣika, *samavāya* is defined as one and eternal (in Vaiśeṣika also as imperceptible), and it cannot account for disappearances and changes. By rejecting this understanding of *samavāya*, the Prābhākaras also reject the claim that the disappearance of a color implies the destruction of a manifesting color-particular.[87]

Extensive discussions focus on the last item in Praśastapāda's list of guṇas: "sound" (*śabda*).[88] Unlike color, taste and the other sensuous qualities, sound has only a partial presence (*pradeśavṛtti*) in its substrate, the one and indivisible ether (*ākāśa*). The particularity of sound-particulars is obviously of a different type than the particularity of color-particulars, which is somehow coextensive with and derived from the particularity of the underlying substances. In Western discussions concerning individuality and particularity, the role of sounds is conspicuously different from that of colors; as an example in modern thought, we may mention the influential work of P. F. Strawson.[89] In India, the controversies between Nyāya-Vaiśeṣika and Mīmāṃsā concerning the nature of *śabda* have lasted for many centuries; they have implications that go far beyond the limited scope of this chapter. It may suffice to refer to the presentation in Jayanta's *Nyāyamañjarī,* which relates this topic explicitly to the questions concerning the particularity of colors and other qualities.

Jayanta argues against the Mīmāṃsā thesis that there is only one identical "*g*-letter" (*gakāra, gaśabda*), and so forth, that is variously revealed or manifested by certain appropriate acoustical events (*dhvani*). He advocates the Nyāya view that there are many perishable "letter-particulars," individual instances of such letters as *g*, with one universal "*g*-ness" (*gatvasāmānya*) inhering in all of them. If *g* were one and eternal per se, the "*g*-universal" would not have a locus of inherence.[90] Just as there is a plurality of instances of the quality white, which may be more or less radiant, so there are many instances of particular letters, articulated sounds, which may be of higher or lower pitch: *yathā ca śuklaguṇasya bhāsvaradhūsarādibhedavato nānātvam, tathā varṇasya-apy udāttādibhedavataḥ.*[91]

Moreover, Jayanta insists that a "plurality of *g*-sounds" (*gakāranānātva*) and other "letter-particulars" (*varṇavyakti*) is attested by an awareness of distinction (*vicchedagrahaṇa*) even if we notice no qualitative differences.[92]

11. According to the Nyāya and Vaiśeṣika conception of *guṇa*, there is no such immediate affinity between quality and universal as is widely assumed in the European philosophical tradition. However, we should not see this phenomenon as evidence for fundamental differences between Indian and Western thought in general.[93] What we are dealing with in this case has a specific association with the Vaiśeṣika system and its peculiar background and prehistory. As we have seen, the Vaiśeṣika system began as a cosmology and philosophy of nature.[94] Its understanding of the qualities, and its characteristic tendency to reify them and to treat them as particulars in their own right, reflect this origin. In spite of the growing preoccupation with logical and epistemological questions and perspectives, the old cosmological and physicalistic basis is never completely abandoned.

In its Western context, the problem of qualities and universals has a tradition that goes back to Plato's theory of ideas, or eidetic forms, and to Aristotle's criticism of it. In the Aristotelian scheme of ten categories, quality (*tò poión*) is usually listed as the second.[95] Starting with H. T. Colebrooke, Western students of the Nyāya and Vaiśeṣika systems have noticed a basic analogy between *guṇa* and *poión*. However, the differences are at least as relevant and obvious.[96] We cannot go into a detailed comparison; but a few reminders concerning Aristotle's understanding of qualities and universals will be appropriate.

The basis of Aristotle's analysis of reality is the *tóde ti*, the concrete individual "something". Only such a concrete thing, a "primary substance," can really be an "individual and numerically one."[97] Whatever can be "said of many things," be it an "essential qualification" or a "mere quality," should not be regarded as a *tóde ti*.[98] General terms like *white* or *man* are applicable to many concrete individuals, but do not signify any separate particular "something." Concerning "mere qualities," such as "white," Aristotle says: "These predicates which do not signify substance must be predicates of some other subject, and nothing can be white which is not also other than white. The Forms (i.e., Plato's ideas) we can dispense with, for they are mere sound without sense."[99]

When speaking about qualities, Aristotle does not normally distinguish between *poión* and the corresponding abstract noun *poiótēs*. If a terminological distinction is made, it does not refer to the separation of quality-particular and quality-universal as found in the Vaiśeṣika, but rather to the distinction between "qualified something" and "quality."[100] By and large, Aristotle tends to disregard the distinction between particulars and universals when dealing with the qualities and other "accidental" categories.

12. There is, however, a passage in the *Categories* where Aristotle seems to make a distinction between quality-particular and quality-universal that would be analogous to the distinction between the particular individual substance and its genus/species. Here he seems to suggest that the quality as such is as much a particular as the individual substance itself, and that we ought to speak of primary and secondary qualities, just as we speak of primary and secondary substances or "essences" (*ousía*).[101] One of the most recent translators and commentators of the *Categories*, J. L. Ackrill, has paid special attention to this passage, and he thought that Aristotle was "willing to speak of species and genera in any category."[102] But as a matter of fact, the distinction between particulars and genera/species remains irrelevant for Aristotle when it comes to the qualities and the other "accidental" categories. Ackrill, obviously somewhat disappointed, asks: "Why does Aristotle not speak of primary and secondary qualities, etc., as he does of primary and secondary substances?"[103]

In more recent times, and particularly in the twentieth century, various thinkers have been willing to pay more explicit attention to this and related issues. As one of the more prominent examples, we may mention the debate between G. E. Moore and G. F. Stout on the question: Are the characteristics of particular things universal or particular?[104] More or less explicitly, this question has played a role in some of the most exemplary presentations of modern analytic philosophy, for instance in N. Goodman's treatment of *qualia*[105] or in B. Russell's distinction between qualitative sense data and universal "sensible qualities."[106]

On the other hand, R. I. Aaron has argued that qualities, as *common* qualities, are the only type of real universals, and he states: "I observe that these two flowers share one and the same colour. It seems in this case absurd to talk of observing instances of the colour and not the colour itself. I do not observe a particular instance but the common (i.e., universal) quality itself, namely, the colour."[107] The context and orientation of such modern Western statements of the problem is obviously different from what we found in the Vaiśeṣika and Nyāya texts and in the surrounding literature of the Mīmāṃsā and philosophy of grammar. Yet it is equally obvious that there is a common stock of philosophical problems, insights, and confusions in the Indian and European traditions.

Chapter 6: Notes

1. See W. V. Quine, *From a Logical Point of View* (New York, 1963), p. 9.

2. *PEW* 4 (1954–55):259–264.

3. Ibid., p. 264.

4. *PEW* 7 (1957–58):57–60.

5. See M. Datta, "The Interpretation of the Vaiśeṣika Categories," *The Philosophical Quarterly* (Amalner) 27 (1955–56):217–225.

6. *PEW* 7:57. In addition to Viśvanātha's *Nyāyasiddhāntamuktāvalī*, Potter relies primarily on another late work, the *Padārthatattvanirūpaṇa* by Raghunātha Śiromaṇi.

7. See H. Narain, "Finding an English Equivalent for *Guṇa*," *PEW* 11 (1961–62):45–51; cf. also his *Evolution of the Nyāya-Vaiśeṣika Categoriology*, vol. 1 (Benares, 1976), pp. 128ff.

8. See *Indian Metaphysics and Epistemology*, ed. K. H. Potter (Princeton, 1977; EIPh, vol. 2), pp. 112f.

9. This is conspicuously different from the case of *dravya;* see earlier, Chapter 5, section 1.

10. See H. T. Colebrooke, *Miscellaneous Essays*, vol. 1 (London, 1837), p. 287.

11. See E. Röer, *ZDMG* 21 (1867):314 (also, "genus" and "difference"); Röer himself prefers "Allgemeines" and "Besonderes."

12. See M. Müller, *ZDMG* 6 (1851), 4; 21.

13. *Six Systems of Indian Philosophy* (Oxford, 1899), p. 586.

14. *An Indian Primer of Philosophy* (*Tarkabhāṣā* of Keśavamiśra), trans. P. Tuxen (Copenhagen, 1914), p. 48.

15. *Tarkabhāṣā*, trans. G. Jha. (Poona, 3d ed., 1967), pp. 77ff.

16. *The Vaiśeṣika Sūtras of Kaṇāda*, trans. N. Sinha (Allahabad, 1911), pp. 39ff.

17. A Winter, *ZDMG* 53 (1899):333.

18. G. Patti, *Der Samavāya* (Rome, 1955), pp. 128ff.

19. E. Hultzsch, *ZDMG* 61 (1907):794ff; *Des Viśvanātha Pañcānana Bhaṭṭācārya Kārikāvalī*, trans. O. Strauss (Leipzig, 1922), pp. 5f.

20. E. Frauwallner, *Gesch. d. ind. Phil.*, vol. 2, pp. 243ff.

21. See S. Bhaduri, *Studies in Nyāya-Vaiśeṣika Metaphysics* (Poona, 1947), pp. 19f.; B. K. Matilal, *Perception* (Oxford, 1986), pp. 379ff.; N. Smart, *Doctrine and Argument in Indian Philosophy* (London, 1964), p. 93; P. K. Mukhopadhyay, *Indian Realism* (Calcutta, 1984), passim.

22. See, for instance, S. Bhaduri, *Studies*, p. 19, n. 45; B. K. Matilal, *Perception*, p. 379: "generic properties."

23. See, for instance, S. Bhaduri, *Studies*, pp. 19f.; N. Smart, *Doctrine and Argument*, pp. 91, 93.

24. See H. Narain, *Evolution* (cited in n. 7), pp. 206ff. ("differential"); K. H. Potter, *Indian Metaphysics and Epistemology* (EIPh, vol. 2), pp. 133f.; 142f. ("individuator").

25. See earlier, Chapter 4, section 2. For further reflections on *viśeṣa*, see Appendix 2.

26. The Sūtra text does not state explicitly that it locates the "ultimate particularities" in ultimate individual substances, such as the atoms. See in this connection Jinabhadra, *Viśeṣāvaśyakabhāṣya*, ed. D. Malvania (Ahmedabad, 1966–1968), vol. 2, pp. 512ff. (v. 2666ff., with commentary). Jinabhadra refers to such "specific universals" as *manuṣyatva* and *brāhmaṇatva*. On the role of "caste universals" in Vaiśeṣika and Nyāya, see *Tradition and Reflection*, ch. 10.

27. Cf. *VS* I, 1, 17 (*Upaskāra:* 18); Candrānanda explains: *sāmānyaśabdaḥ samānaparyāyaḥ;* see also *VS* II, 2, 19 (*Upaskāra:* 17); H. Narain, *Evolution*, pp. 178ff. Narain claims that *sāmānya* was originally a synonym of *sādharmya*. On attempts to reduce *sāmānya* to similarity and on Kumārila's critique, see T. Takenaka, "*Sāmānya, sārupya*, and *sādṛśya*." *JIBSt* 26/1 (1977):500–505.

28. H. Narain, *Evolution*, p. 211 (with reference to B. Faddegon); cf. D. N. Shastri, *Critique of Indian Realism* (Agra, 1964), pp. 310ff. Narain, pp. 209f., saw a connection between *buddhyapekṣa* and Patañjali's *vivakṣā*, "intention." For another, comparable use of *buddhyapekṣa*, see *VS* VIII, p. 12 (*Upaskāra:* VIII, 2,1): *ayam, eṣa, tvayā kṛtam, bhojaya-enam iti buddhyapekṣam*. There is no reference to *apekṣābuddhi* (see later, Chapter 9, section 2) in *VS*. See also *Mahābhāṣya*, vol 1, pp. 171ff.

29. *PBh*, p. 311.

30. See ibid., p. 19.

31. *NK*, p. 19.

32. Ibid., p. 20; on "inherential" and "noninherential" causes, see E. Frauwallner, *Gesch. d. ind. Phil.*, vol. 2, pp 169ff.

33. See later, Chapter 9, section 3.

34. *Vy.*, p. 143.

35. Candrānanda says: *anuvṛttibuddhyapekṣaṃ sāmānyaṃ vyāvṛttibuddhyapekṣo viśeṣaḥ.*

36. See earlier, Chapter 5, sections 8f.; see also P. K. Mukhopadhyay, *Indian Realism* (cited in n. 21), pp. 65, 70, 294.

37. Cf. H. C. Joshi, "An Aspect of Causality according to Udayanācārya," *Proceedings of the All-India Oriental Conference* 16 (1951):322–329; R. R. David, *The Problem of Universals in Indian Philosophy* (Delhi, 1972), pp. 22ff.; P. K. Mukhopadhyay, *Indian Realism*, pp. 71ff.

38. See, for instance, Jayanta, *NM*, p. 276: *aniṣyamāṇe sāmānye nanu śabdānumānayoḥ kathaṃ pravṛttiḥ;* see also S. C. Chatterjee, *The Nyāya Theory of Knowledge* (Calcutta, 1965), pp. 209ff. (on *sāmānyalakṣaṇa*).

39. B. K. Matilal, *Perception* (cited in n. 21), pp. 382f. The Buddhist arguments are summarized by Aśoka Paṇḍita, *Sāmānyadūṣaṇadikprasāritā* (*Six Buddhist Nyāya Tracts in Sanskrit*, ed. Haraprasad Shastri. Calcutta, 1910, pp. 94–102). See also Śāntarakṣita, TS (with *Pañjikā* by Kamalaśīla), v. 707–811; especially 766ff. (Śaṅkarasvāmin; Bhāvivikta). On *jāti* and *upādhi*, cf. H. Narain, "Evolution of Upādhi as an Ontological Concept", *Proceedings of the All-India Oriental Conference* 29 (1978):430–434.

40. See *Kir.*, GOS, p. 23:

> *vyakter abhedas tulyatvaṃ saṃkaro 'tha-anavasthitiḥ /*
> *rūpahānir asambandho jātibādhakasaṃgrahaḥ.*

See also the commentary by Vardhamāna, Bibliotheca Indica (1911ff.), pp. 161f. Udayana himself provides examples for these six cases; see *Kir.*, pp. 15f. We may paraphrase as follows: A universal cannot belong only to a single individual, such as ether (*ākāśa*); the same group of individual instances cannot possess several coextensive universals (i.e., synonyms, such as *buddhi*, *upalabdhi* and *jñāna*, do not represent more than one universal); there cannot be partially overlapping extensions for universals (i.e., no real universals can belong to such partially coextensive types of motion as "going out" and "entering"); no universal can be postulated for an entity if this would involve an infinite regress (i.e., there can be no universals in universals); no universal can be postulated if this leads to a contradiction in terms (i.e., there can be no universals for the ultimate particularities); there is no universal, if there is no possible connection with its instances (i.e., no universal can be inherent in *samavāya*, inherence itself). In later Navyanyāya, "overlap" does not necessarily constitute a *jātibādhaka*.

41. Cf. BPh, p. 312: *pṛthivītvarūpatvotkṣepaṇatvagotvaghaṭatvapaṭatvādīnām*

api . . . sāmānyaviśeṣabhāvaḥ siddhaḥ. See also M. Tachikawa, *The Structure of the World in Udayana's Realism* (Dordrecht, 1981).

42. Cf. Jayanta, *NM*, p. 272 (*pūrvapakṣa*); Aśoka Paṇḍita (cited in n. 39).

43. On the Buddhist critique, see also T. Vetter, *Erkenntnisprobleme bei Dharmakīrti* (Vienna, 1964), pp. 98–110; and in general D. N. Shastri, *Critique of Indian Realism* (Agra, 1964).

44. See Vyomaśiva, *Vy.*, p. 143; this is obviously a problematic case, and there are few explicit references to it. Helārāja "defends" the Vaiśeṣika position in his commentary on *VP* III/1 (*Jātisamuddeśa*), p. 43, by suggesting somewhat ironically that the nonmanifest universals (*jāti*) do not require any substrates because there is no danger that they might fall (*na hi gurutvād adhaḥ patanam āsāṃ mā bhūd ity ādhāraḥ*). See also *VP* III/1, 41 (with Helārāja's commentary).

45. See later, Chapter 9, section 1. According to Kumārila, who did not accept the idea of *mahāpralaya*, there will always be certain individuals to exemplify their respective universals; cf. G. Jha, *Pūrva-Mīmāṃsā in Its Sources*, 2d ed. (Benares, 1964), pp. 67f.

46. B. K. Matilal, *Perception* (cited in n. 21), p. 383. On universals as "manifested" (*vyaṅgya*) and particulars as "manifestors" (*vyañjaka*), see *PBh* and *NK*, pp. 327f.

47. See Jayanta, *NM*, pp. 188ff.; especially p. 196: *piṇḍo 'bhivyañjako jāteḥ, śabdasya vyañjako dhvaniḥ*.

48. See *NM*, p. 285; *VP* III/1, 44 with Helārāja's commentary; although this is introduced as a *smṛti*, it seems to express Bhartṛhari's own view.

49. On "potentiality," see earlier, Chapter 3, section 9; and later, Chapter 8, section 12. The idea of *sarvasarvagatatva* was rejected by the Vaiśeṣika teachers. Praśastapāda called the universals *svaviṣayasarvagata*, "residing in the totality of their appropriate objects" (*PBh*, p. 314); cf. Vyomaśiva, *Vy.*, pp. 678f; Śrīdhara, *NK*, p. 317.

50. Cf. B. K. Matilal, *Perception*, p. 384; P. K. Mukhopadhyay, *Indian Realism* (cited in n. 21), pp. 101ff.; 301f.

51. Cf. *NS* II, 2, 59; 64ff.; 68f. (with certain variations in counting the Sūtras); we disregard, of course, *jāti* in the sense of "futile rejoinder."

52. In *VS* VI, 2, 16 (*Upaskāra:* 13), *jāti* appears in the sense of "birth" or "species." For Praśastapāda, see, for instance, PBh, p. 58 (*aparajātyabhāva*).

53. Cf. H. Narain, *Evolution* (cited in n. 7), pp. 184f.

54. See *NBh* II, 2, 69; in his discussion of the Nyāya theory of meaning,

Abhayadevasūri cites this Sūtra as *samānapratyayaprasavātmikā jātiḥ*; see *Sanmatitarkaprakaraṇam by Siddhasena Divākara with Abhayadevasūri's Commentary* (Ahmedabad, 1924–1931; reprint Kyoto, 1984), p. 178. See also M. Spitzer, *Begriffsuntersuchungen zum Nyāyabhāṣya* (Leipzig, 1927), pp. 43ff.

55. According to Śivāditya and others, *sāmānya* includes both *jāti*, real universals (such as "reality," *sattā*) and *upādhi*, "imposed properties" (such as "cookness," *pācakatva*); see *Saptapadārthī*, section 52 (ed. D. Gurumurti, p. 42). Cf. also Udayana, *Kir.*, GOS, p. 25: *bhūtatvam aupādhikam sāmānyam. atha jātir eva kiṃ na syāt?*

56. See *NS* II, 2, 68 (67): *ākṛtir jātiliṅgākhyā*; Patañjali, *Mahābhāṣya*, vol. 2, p. 225 (on IV, 1, 63): *ākṛtigrahaṇā jātiḥ*.

57. See Kumārila, *ŚV*, p. 438 (*Vanavāda*, v. 16): *ākṛtir jātir eva-atra saṃsthānaṃ na prakalpyate*; p. 385 (*Ākṛtivāda*, v. 3): *jātim eva-ākṛtiṃ prāhur, vyaktir ākriyate.* On *ākṛti* in grammar, see earlier, Chapter 5, section 2.

58. See Patañjali, *Mahābhāṣya*, vol. 1, p. 243 (on I, 2, 64, *Vārttika*, p. 39). This is illustrated by somewhat mythical examples.

59. See K. A. Subramania Iyer, *Bhartṛhari* (Poona, 1969), pp. 264–273.

60. Cf. Kumārila, *ŚV*, p. 389 (*Ākṛtivāda*, v. 25):

> *piṇḍeṣv eva ca sāmānyaṃ, na-antarā gṛhyate yataḥ /*
> *na hy ākāśavad icchanti sāmānyaṃ nāma kiṃcana.*

On Kumārila and the Jainas, see N. J. Shah, *Akalaṅka's Criticism of Dharmakīrti's Philosophy* (Ahmedabad, 1967), pp. 86f.

61. See *PBh*, p. 94: *rūpādīnāṃ guṇānāṃ sarveṣāṃ guṇatvābhisambandho dravyāśritatvaṃ nirguṇatvaṃ niṣkriyatvaṃ.*

62. See ibid. (with *NK*), pp. 95ff.; also E. Frauwallner, *Gesch. d. ind. Phil.*, vol. 2, pp. 212ff.

63. In particular, the quality "number" (*saṃkhyā*) depends on "relational cognition" (*apekṣābuddhi*); see E. Frauwallner, *Gesch. d. ind. Phil.*, vol. 2, pp. 190ff.; also pp. 132ff.

64. See *NV* I, 1, 23 (Calc. S. S., p. 235): *kiṃ punar atra sādhāraṇaṃ, kiṃ guṇa āho sāmānyam iti. yadi guṇaḥ sa na sādhāraṇaḥ. kasmāt? ekadravyavṛttitvāt parimāṇasya, ekadravyavṛtti parimāṇaṃ tat kathaṃ sādhāraṇaṃ bhaviṣyati-iti.*

65. Ibid., 34 (Calc. S. S., p. 284)

66. *VS* I, 1, 5 (*Upaskāra:* I, 1, 6) gives a list of seventeen *guṇas* only, which does not contain *adṛṣṭa*. Later Vaiśeṣika authors tried to justify the addition of seven more *guṇas* by referring to the *ca* used at the end of the Sūtra list. This is a conspicuously artificial procedure; cf. in this connection the Jaina Jinabhadra

(probably sixth century and apparently not familiar with Praśastapāda's work) who states explicitly that the number of *guṇas* in Vaiśeṣika is seventeen (*guṇāḥ saptadaśa: Viśeṣāvaśyakabhāṣya,* ed. D. Malvania, Ahmedabad, 1966–1968, v. 2972ff., with commentary).

67. On pleasure, pain, etc., see *PBh* (with *NK*), pp. 259ff.

68. *NK,* p. 95.

69. See Helārāja on *VP* III/1, 14; Vyomaśiva, *Vy.*, pp. 431f.; especially p. 432: *uktebhyo 'nye śeṣās te hy ekaikasmin eva dravye vartante, ekā vyaktir ekasmin eva samavetā, tathā rasādivyaktayo 'pi;* Kumārila, *Tantravārttika* I, 3, 30 (*Mīmāṃsādarśana,* ed. K. V. Abhyaṅkara and G. S. Jośī, vol. 1: I, 2–II, 1, 2d ed. Poona, 1970, p. 236): *tataḥ śuklādi tadvyaktiguṇeṣu pratitiṣṭhati; śukla* is used in the sense of *śuklatva.*

70. See *NS* (with *NBh*) II, 2, 67 (Calc. S. S.): *vyaktir guṇaviśeṣāśrayo mūrtiḥ.*

71. See Śrīdhara, *NK,* p. 95.

72. Śrīdhara himself (*NK,* p. 94) notes that the attribution of numbers to colors (as in *ekaṃ rūpam,* "one color") can be only metaphorical (*upacārāt*).

73. Vyomaśiva, *Vy.*, p. 221, quotes a modified version of Dharmakīrti, *Pramāṇavārttika* III, 200, which epitomizes this criticism: *citraṃ tad ekam iti ced, idaṃ citrataraṃ tataḥ;* see also Śrīdhara, *NK,* p. 30.

74. Cf. O. Grohma, "Theorien zur bunten Farbe im älteren Nyāya und Vaiśeṣika bis Udayana," *WZKS* 19 (1975):147–182.

75. Udayana, *Ātmatattvaviveka,* ed. Ḍhuṇḍhirāja Śāstrī (Benares, 1940), p. 274. See also *Kir.*, GOS, p. 33: *yathā śuklam iti śuklajātīyaṃ tathā citram api citrajātīyam.*

76. See, for instance, Udayana, *Kir.*, GOS, p. 15.

77. See *Mahābhāṣya* on Pāṇini V, 1, 119, *Vārttika* 5: *yasya guṇasya bhāvād. . . ;* Kaiyaṭa refers to this Vārttika in his subcommentary on II, 1, 1 (under *Vārttika* 21) and says that the word *guṇa* can also mean "universal form" (*guṇaśabdena-apy ākṛtir ucyate*).

78. See *Mahābhāṣya* on Pāṇini V, 3, 55 (vol. 2, p. 414); cf. also Bhartṛhari, *VP* III/5 (*Guṇasamuddeśa*). The question of "more or less" is also referred to by Aristotle in his discussion of qualities and specifically of colors; see *Categories,* 10 b 26f. On *guṇatāratamya,* see also Bhāsarvajña, *NBhūṣ,* p. 258.

79. *Kir.*, GOS, p. 33.

80. *Kir.*, p. 33. In the presentation of the *pūrvapakṣa,* the phrase *ekaikā eva hi śuklāruṇādirūpavyaktayo nityā api anityābhir dravyavyaktibhir vyajyante,* which has no direct precedent in the *Mahābhāṣya,* deserves special attention. On qualitative gradation, see also Bhartṛhari, *VP* I, 64 (with *Vṛtti*).

81. *Kir.*, p. 33: *astu śuklādikaṃ sāmānyam eva iti cet, na; gotvādinā parāparabhāvānupapattau jātisaṃkaraprasaṅgād iti.* J. S. Jetly's reading *śuklatvādikam* (also found in the edition by V. P. Dvivedin, Benares, 1919, p. 48) is obviously incorrect; the correct reading *śuklādikam* is found in the *Bibliotheca Indica* edition (vol. 1, Calcutta, 1911), p. 209. The issue in this context is the rejection of the *sāmānya* character of *qualities* such as "white," not of "whiteness"; this has been misunderstood by B. Bhattacharya, *A Study in Language and Meaning* (Calcutta, 1962), p. 69.

82. Vardhamāna, *Kiraṇāvalīprakāśa* on *Kir.* (Bibliotheca Indica), p. 210.

83. See Padmanābha, *Setu*, p. 202 (in *Vy.*, ChSS): *nanu na śuklādīni rūpāṇi guṇāḥ, kiṃtu jātaya eva;* in his rejection of this *pūrvapakṣa*, Padmanābha repeats Udayana's reference to an "overlap of universals" (*jātitve gotvādinā jātisaṃkaraprasaṅgāt*).

84. See Kumārila, *ŚV*, pp. 591f. (*Śabdanityatā*, v. 411ff.; especially 411: *etayā-eva diśā vācyā śuklāder api nityatā*).

85. See n. 69.

86. See Śālikanātha, *Ṛjuvimalā* on Prabhākara's *Bṛhatī*. vol. 1, ed. S. K. Ramanatha Sastri (Madras, 1934), p. 164.

87. Cf. *Ṛjuvimalā*, p. 164.

88. *Śabda* is mentioned repeatedly in *VS* (especially the first two Adhyāyas), but not included in the Sūtra list of seventeen qualities.

89. See P. F. Strawson, *Individuals* (London, 1965), pp. 69ff., on the identifiability of sounds and specifically of "sound-particulars."

90. See Jayanta, *NM*, p. 200: *ekatvād gakārasya kiṃvṛtti gatvasāmānyaṃ syāt?*

91. Ibid., p. 202; unlike Udayana, Jayanta does not refer to "subspecies" (*avāntarajāti*) of "white," etc. The suggestion that such plurality is due to the "difference of substrates" (*āśrayabheda*) is rejected.

92. Ibid., p. 201; cf. also Jayanta's distinction between the awareness of qualitative difference (*viśeṣabuddhi*) and the awareness of numerical nonidentity (*bhedabuddhi*): *anyā ca viśeṣabuddhir ucyate anyā ca bhedabuddhir iti.* Jayanta also uses the term *vicchedapratīti* to refer to our awareness of numerical difference. The Mīmāṃsā views against which Jayanta argues are found in the *Śabdanityatā* chapter of Kumārila's *Ślokavārttika*.

93. Nor is it a reason to reject "quality" as a translation for *guṇa*.

94. See earlier, Chapter 4, sections 5; 7.

95. On different versions of Aristotle's list of categories, as they appear in his own works, see *Kategorien*, trans. K. Oehler, 2d ed. (Darmstadt, 1986), pp. 352ff.; on different interpretations and applications, cf. pp. 65–95; 110–119.

96. *Guṇa* is obviously more comprehensive than *poión;* most of Aristotle's "accidental" categories could, in one sense or other, be subsumed under *guṇa.*

97. *Categories,* 3 b 10ff.; trans. J. L. Ackrill: *Aristotle's Categories and De Interpretatione* (Oxford, 1963), p. 9.

98. *Categories,* 3 b 10ff.; see also 4 a 10ff.

99. *Posterior Analytics,* 83 a 30ff. (quoted from *The Works of Aristotle,* trans. under the editorship of W. D. Ross, vol. 1, London, 1928).

100. Cf. *Categories,* 10 a 27f.

101. *Categories,* 1 a 27ff.

102. J. L. Ackrill (cited in n. 97), p. 75.

103. Ibid., p. 76.

104. Together with other relevant materials, this debate (which was first published by the Aristotelian Society in its *Supplementary Volume* of 1923) has been reprinted in *The Problem of Universals,* ed. C. Landesman (New York, 1971).

105. See N. Goodman, *The Structure of Appearance,* 2d ed. (Indianapolis, 1966).

106. See B. Russell, *The Problems of Philosophy* (London, 1951; first ed., 1912), p. 101; see also V. C. Aldrich, "Colours as Universals," *Philosophical Review* 61 (1952):377–381.

107. R. I. Aaron, "*Two Senses of the Word Universal,*" *Mind* 48 (1939):168–185; especially 184. Even Praśastapāda himself does not hesitate to illustrate the pervasive nature of universals, such as "reality" (*sattā*), by referring to the process of dyeing and the presence of "the same" color in different objects; see later, Chapter 7, section 4.

7

The Conceptualization of Being in Classical Vaiśeṣika

1. The special affinity between ontology and categoriology has often been recognized. Aristotle himself presents his list of categories as an exposition of different "meanings of being." In the philosophy of Kant, the table of categories is the central piece of his transcendental philosophy, which is supposed to replace and supersede what was formerly called *ontology.*[1] According to Nicolai Hartmann, categoriology is "the concrete execution of ontology" ("die inhaltliche Durchführung der Ontologie").[2] In modern Indian presentations of the Vaiśeṣika system, the term *ontology* itself has been rendered as *padārthaśāstra.*[3]

What then is the relation between categoriology and ontology in classical Vaiśeṣika? How does explicit ontology, explicit conceptualization of being, emerge out of the enumeration and classification of what there is? How does its development accompany and reflect the different historical layers of the system? Is the Vaiśeṣika ontology an epiphenomenon of its categoriology? Is there an understanding of being which is prior to, and the condition of, its project of categorial analysis and enumeration?

In one of the preceding chapters, we discussed E. Frauwallner's thesis that the "original beginning" of the Vaiśeṣikasūtra was an announcement to list or designate "whatever has the character of being" (*yad bhāvarūpam*).[4] An introductory and programmatic statement like this would indicate that Kaṇāda's project of enumeration and classification was guided by, and embedded in, an explicit idea of being. As we have seen, the authenticity of this statement is highly questionable. It is much more likely that the alleged "first Sūtra" represents a retrospective interpretation by the commentators Vyomaśiva and Udayana.

In those versions of the Vaiśeṣikasūtra which are extant today, being (*bhāva, sattā;* "existence," "reality") emerges as a topic of reflection and discussion in the second Āhnika of the first Adhyāya. Immediately following the introduction of the concepts *sāmānya* and *viśeṣa,* we are told in Sūtra I,2,4 (according to Candrānanda) that "existence is a universal only" (*bhāvaḥ sāmānyam eva*). Śaṅkaramiśra's expanded version of the same Sūtra tells us that this is so because *bhāva* generates nothing but inclusion (*bhāvo 'nuvṛtter eva hetutvāt sāmānyam eva*). In the remainder of the second Adhyāya, the ontological discussion is continued under the title *sattā.* In a statement that has been artificially divided into two Sūtras, we hear that *sattā,* "reality," accounts for our application of the notion "real" (*sat,* as used in I,1,7) to substances, qualities, and motions, and that it is something different (*arthāntara*) from the substances, qualities, and motions (*sad iti yato dravyaguṇakarmasu, dravyaguṇakarmabhyo 'rthāntaraṃ sattā*).[5] The versions of the *Upaskāra* and the anonymous *Vṛtti* supplement the first part of this statement as follows: *sad iti yato dravyaguṇakarmasu, sā sattā.* Unlike Aristotle, Kaṇāda does not reject the interpretation of being or reality as *summum genus.*[6] But as the supreme universal, it is also something over and above, and different from, the particular and perishable entities in which it occurs. It is, as emphasized by the ancient commentator Ātreya, imperishable and permanent (*nitya*).[7]

In later sections of the text, we again find the term *bhāva,* specifically in Sūtra IV,1,14, which states that both "reality" and "qualityness" (*guṇatva*) can be perceived by all senses (*etena guṇatve bhāve ca sarvendriyajñānaṃ vyākhyātam*).[8] The most coherent and significant section is found in Adhyāya IX. However, it does not deal with *bhāva,* but with *asat* and *abhāva,* "nonentity," "nonbeing," "nonexistence," "absence." Whereas Praśastapāda tends to neglect this topic, it becomes increasingly conspicuous and important in later Nyāya and Vaiśeṣika. It is also among the favorite topics of recent Nyāya and Vaiśeṣika studies; we may even say that it has found more attention in recent scholarship than "being" itself.[9]

2. Unlike *sattā*, both *bhāva* and *abhāva* are frequently used in a nonterminological and nonthematic sense. Also, *sat* and *asat* are not always meant to indicate the presence or absence of the universal *sattā*.[10] Obviously, these nonthematic uses cannot be taken as direct evidence for the Vaiśeṣika doctrine of reality or its explicit ontology. Yet they are by no means entirely irrelevant and negligible. They may give us clues concerning the implicit presuppositions and linguistic conditions of Vaiśeṣika ontology. The fact itself that such usages coexist, and inevitably interfere, with the doctrinal and terminological statements about being or reality, is a potential source of confusion and disagreement, but also of critical reflection and clarification.[11] We should also note that in later Nyāya and Vaiśeṣika the role of *bhāva* is more flexible than that of *sattā*; unlike *sattā*, *bhāva* may be ascribed to all six positive categories and contrasted with the seventh category, *abhāva*.[12] In another sense, it may even refer to *abhāva* itself.[13]

Various translations have been suggested for *sattā* and *bhāva*; for instance, "beingness," "existent-ness," and, most frequently, "existence."[14] *Abhāva* is often rendered as "nonexistence" and "nonbeing," but also as "absence."[15] In this presentation, *existence* will usually stand for *bhāva*, whereas *reality* will represent *sattā*.[16] This twofold translation is primarily a pragmatic device; it does not as such imply any deeper exegetic claims. The use of *existence* for *bhāva* should not suggest a contrast with "essence." Neither *bhāva* nor *sattā* establish a dichotomy between essence and existence.[17] We may also note here that the traditional verbal and actional connotations of *bhāva*, which we find emphasized by grammarians and philosophers of language, do not affect the Vaiśeṣika usage. In general, linguistic and grammatical reflections on the vocabulary of being are less significant in classical Vaiśeṣika than in the allied Nyāya system, for instance, in the work of Uddyotakara.[18]

As far as their terminological and thematic uses are concerned, *sattā* and *bhāva* appear as synonyms in the Vaiśeṣikasūtra itself and in classical Vaiśeṣika in general. The commentators take such synonymy for granted, or they state it explicitly (for instance, Candrānanda).[19] Nonetheless, the introduction of the term *bhāva* in Sūtra I,2,4 and the subsequent transition to *sattā* are conspicuous and somewhat surprising. Do these two terms reflect different sources of Vaiśeṣika ontology? How and why is *bhāva* introduced in Sūtra I,2,4? Is there any connection with the appearance of *abhāva* in I,2,1–2, with the discussion of nonbeing in Adhyāya IX, or with the old debate between Sāṃkhya and Vaiśeṣika concerning the preexistence of the product in its material cause?[20]

The commentators, beginning with Candrānanda, explain the elusive statements on *sat* and *asat* in Adhyāya IX as an exposition of the fourfold division of nonbeing into "prior," "posterior," "mutual," and "absolute" nonexistence (*prāgabhāva, pradhvaṃsābhāva, anyonyābhāva, atyantābhāva*).[21] According to Mallavādin, it would seem that this exposition has to be seen as part of the debate against the Sāṃkhya *satkāryavāda* and that it was meant to show that the rejection of origination from nonbeing applies only to "absolute nonexistence" (*atyantābhāva*).[22] May we associate the statements on causes and products in I,2,1–2 with this debate, and would the introduction of *bhāva* in I,2,4 thus be related to the *satkārya/asatkārya* controversy? The Sūtra text does not provide us with the evidence that would be necessary to answer these questions. At any rate, neither traditional commentators nor modern scholars have given a satisfactory explanation for the transition from Sūtras I,2,1–2 to the following section.[23]

3. Can we take it for granted that the category of universal (*sāmānya*) was established prior to the conception of "reality" or "existence" as one of its instances? Harsh Narain has argued that the introduction of *bhāva/sattā* as a "different object" (*arthāntara*), over and above the particular entities, may have preceded the conception and conceptualization of universals as a special category.[24] He even suggests that the notion of universals might have been derived from the conception of one existence as occurring in, and appearing through, different types of entities. In this sense, "qualityness" (*guṇatva*) would be derived from "existence in qualities" (*guṇe bhāvād*); that is, existence insofar as it is exemplified by qualities.[25]

Although a similar understanding of universals and reality is, indeed, found in Bhartṛhari and the grammatical traditions to which he is indebted, we have no evidence that early Vaiśeṣika ever adopted this view. It was explicitly rejected by some of the commentators, in particular Vyomaśiva.[26] Nonetheless, the relationship between the notions of reality and universality in early Vaiśeṣika and the problem of historical and systematic priority is an intriguing issue. Unlike Praśastapāda, Candramati presents "existence"/"reality" as a separate category (*padārtha*).[27] Its original subsumption under the category *sāmānya* should not simply be taken for granted.

Whatever the specific historical antecedents may have been, we may say that the Vaiśeṣikasūtra ascribes *sattā* or *bhāva* to the first three categories (*dravya, guṇa, karman*) only. It does not deal explicitly with the "reality" of the universals, particularities, and inherence. *Bhāva/sattā* accounts for the fact that all substances, qualities, and motions are referred to as real (*sat*) in thought and speech.[28] In this sense, the concept of existence/reality reflects and expands, but also transcends and supersedes the first historical layer of the Vaiśeṣika system.[29] *Bhāva/sattā* is the common denominator, the one universal ingredient of all concrete and particular entities. It circumscribes the totality of entities at the cosmological level of enumeration and classification, and it is added to these entities as if it were an enumerable, cosmological entity itself. It appears among those entities that constitute the second level of enumeration and classification, as a universal among other real universals.

What is the ontological status of universals (including *bhāva/sattā*), particularities, and inherence? What qualifies them as "different objects" (*arthāntara*) and as additional world constituents? In what sense can they be coordinated with the substances, qualities, and motions? In what sense can they be said to "be there"? Kaṇāda does not have an answer to these questions. The Vaiśeṣikasūtra lists the common attributes (*sādharmya*) of the first three categories;[30] it does not give a comprehensive definition of all six categories. Apart from the dubious Sūtra I,1,4, it never even lists them in their totality. For more explicit statements concerning those attributes that the universals, and so on, share with the first three categories, and specifically on the status of the supreme universal "reality"/"existence," we have to turn to Praśastapāda's *Padārthadharmasaṃgraha*.[31]

4. In accordance with the language of the Vaiśeṣikasūtra, Praśastapāda presents "reality" as a general property comparable to, though more extensive than, other universals, for instance "blueness." Paraphrasing and expanding the statements of the Sūtra, he illustrates the pervasive nature of reality in all real things by referring to the unity of the blue liquid that can impart blueness to many different particulars in the process of dyeing.

> Because of contact with one blue substance, the notion "blue" recurs with reference to mutually different particulars, such as pieces of leather and cloth, woolen blankets, etc. Likewise, the notion "real" recurs without difference in the case of substances, qualities, and motions, which are mutually different; this recurrent notion must be due to something other (than substances, etc.). It is reality which is thus established as this different something (*yathā parasparaviśiṣṭeṣu carmavastrakambalādiṣv ekasmān nīladravyābhisambandhān nīlaṃ nīlam iti pratyayānuvṛttiḥ, tathā parasparaviśiṣṭeṣu dravyaguṇakarmasv aviśiṣṭā sat sad iti pratyayānuvṛttiḥ, sā ca-arthāntarād bhavitum arhati-iti, yat tad arthāntaraṃ sā sattā-iti siddhā*).[32]

However, in addition to *sattā* and *bhāva,* Praśastapāda's work contains several conceptualizations of being not found in the Vaiśeṣikasutra. First of all, we have to mention *astitva,* "is-ness," "factuality," "objectivity." Unlike *sattā, astitva* covers not only substances, qualities, and motions, but also universals, particularities, and inherence. As a common attribute (*sādharmya*) of all six categories, it is coordinate, but not necessarily coextensive with *jñeyatva* ("knowability") and *abhidheyatva* ("nameability").[33] Its most basic connotation seems to be irreducible identity, identifiability, and accordingly, undeniability. Praśastapāda frequently justifies the assumption of enumerables by claiming them as causes or conditions (*kāraṇa, hetu, nimitta*) of occurrences in thought and linguistic usage (*pratyaya, vyavahāra*). Occasionally, he uses the word *asti* to emphasize the existential and veridical implications of such claims, for instance in the following statement concerning inherence (*samavāya*): *pratyayadarśanād asty eṣāṃ sambandha iti.*[34]

In this sense, *astitva* can be applied to anything that is an enumerable and classifiable ingredient of the world, including reality itself.[35] Like all other universals, *sattā* "is there" insofar as *astitva* can be ascribed to it. It cannot be the substrate of reality or any other real universal, as this would entail an infinite regress (*anavasthā*), which classical Vaiśeṣika regards as a fatal defect.[36]

Praśastapāda does not explain the word *astitva,* and he uses it only once in his only extant work, the *Padārthadharmasaṃgraha.* The fact that he does not explain or define it is in accordance with the basic structure of his system and with the traditional sequence of *uddeśa, lakṣaṇa,* and *parīkṣā. Astitva* is not part of the fundamental "nomenclature of the world." It is not "listed" and "named" among the categories, but used to describe and analyze them. It is a second-order concept, an abstraction. Praśastapāda sees no need to explain this instrument of analysis and description.[37]

We do not know whether Praśastapāda had predecessors as far as his terminological use of *astitva* and its coordination with *jñeyatva* and *abhidheyatva* are concerned. The testimony of Mallavādin is inconclusive. The word *astitva* as an expression of existential and veridical claims has, of course, been used in earlier Hindu and Buddhist literature (for instance, by Nāgārjuna).[38]

5. Subsequent to his introduction of the term *astitva,* Praśastapāda characterizes substances, qualities, and motions as having *sattāsambandha,* "connection with reality," and universals, particularities, and inherence as having *svātmasattva,* "being by virtue of one's identity," "being as self-identity."[39] These two terms do not signify universals, but common abstract attributes (*sādharmya*); just as *astitva,* they are neither explained nor repeated in Praśastapāda's text.[40]

The context, and specifically the attributes listed in conjunction with *sattāsambandha,* on the one hand, and *svātmasattva,* on the other, give some significant clues. The capability to produce merit and demerit, the status of cause and effect, impermanence, and so on (*dharmādharmakartṛtva, kāraṇatva, kāryatva, anityatva*)—these are features found only among those concrete and particular entities that are characterized by *sattāsambandha.*[41] Concerning the universals, and so forth, which have *svātmasattva,* Praśastapāda adds as further charcteristics that they are indicated by cognition, cannot be effects or causes, do not constitute substrates for universals and particularities, are permanent, and cannot be called *artha,* that is, concrete "objects" (*buddhilakṣaṇatva, akāryatva, akāraṇatva, asāmānyaviśeṣavattva, nityatva, arthaśabdānabhidheyatva*).[42] Quite obviously, such universals as cowness and horseness do not have the concrete actuality and causality of their particular substrates. On the other hand, they are supposed to be noncontingent and unaffected by change and destruction.

Various attempts have been made to find terminological analogies in Western thought. M. Hiriyanna, for instance, explains *svātmasat* as "intrinsically real" and contrasts it with the "borrowed being" of the particulars. He adds: "This distinction is remarkably like that between subsistence and existence."[43] He does not specify his understanding of these Western terms that were used by B. Russell and others.[44] G. Patti, who interpreted *astitva* as "essentia" in the scholastic sense, and *sattā* as "existentia," paraphrases *svātmasattva* as "Wesen, das sich selbst genügend ist."[45] Whatever the merit of these suggestions, our analysis of Praśastapāda's ontological terminology has, first of all, to consider the twofold structure of his own system.

More than once, we have referred to the distinction between *uddeśa* ("enunciation," "enumeration") and *lakṣaṇa* ("definition," "description") in Praśastapāda's system.[46] Terms from one level should not be confused with terms from the other level; the ontological commitment is different in both cases. Subject-predicate relationships at the level of *lakṣaṇa* do not reflect any cosmologically real divisions.

We found such difference exemplified by the distinction between *guṇa* and *guṇavattva*. *Guṇa* is a real enumerable; *guṇavattva* is an abstract attribute. Although they belong to the same class of entities (i.e., the substances), they do so in a different way: "In its relation to *guṇa*, 'quality', *dravya* is a cosmological substrate (*āśraya*); in relation to *guṇavattva*, 'possession of qualities', *dravya* is nothing but a logical subject (*dharmin*)."[47] Universals, particularities, and inherence can, of course, never be substrates in a cosmological sense. Of all the ontological concepts used by Praśastapāda, only *sattā/bhāva* represents a real enumerable, qualifying all those entities that can function as substrates. *Astitva*, *sattāsambandha*, and *svātmasattva* are abstract attributes.

More specifically, we may say that the distinction between *sattā* and *sattāsambandha* is analogous to that between *guṇa* and *guṇavattva*, or *dravyatva* and *dravyatvayoga*. In Praśastāpada's system, *sattā* and *sattāsambandha* define the same class of "real" (*sat*) entities; but they do so in different ways. Whatever is *sat* is the substrate (*āśraya*) of *sattā;* but it is the logical subject (*dharmin*) of *sattāsambandha*. Moreover, *sattā* as a real universal is eternal and immutable; it is not affected by the destruction of particulars. *Sattāsambandha*, on the other hand, is a temporal condition. It is the actual connection of a particular entity with the timeless universal, the fact that it "is there" as the substrate of *sattā* and that *sattā* is actually present in it.[48]

Praśastapāda avoids confusing his two levels of discourse. On the other hand, we may say that he circumvents or conceals significant problems and paradoxes.

6. At this point, we have to recall the peculiar function of "inherence" (*samavāya*); that is, the sixth and final item in Praśastapāda's list of categories. In our "introductory survey" of the categories, we referred briefly to some of the historical and systematic problems associated with this concept.[49] We noted that "classical Vaiśeṣika considers *samavāya* as a principle that is supposed to account for the cooccurrence and coalescence of different and ontologically distinct world constituents within concrete things. In a sense, it restores the unity and concreteness of things after their categorial decomposition." We also referred to M. Hiriyanna's "doubt whether its exact nature is well understood."[50] What is perhaps most frequently misunderstood or overlooked is the ontological significance of the term.

Modern surveys of the Vaiśeṣika system, as well as the classical texts themselves, describe *samavāya* as a "connection" (*sambandha*) sui generis. It "connects" relata that are *ayutasiddha*, incapable of existing separately, because they involve a relationship of "container" and "contained" or of dependence and support (*ādhāryādhārabhāva; ādhārādheyabhāva;* also *āśrayāśritabhāva* and *āśrayāśrayibhāva*).[51] In particular, it refers to the association and integration of parts and wholes, substrates and their qualities and motions, eternal substances and their ultimate particularities (*viśeṣa*), substances, qualities, motions and their respective universals (*sāmānya*). In all these cases, it "binds only those two kinds of relata, one of which must be destroyed with the severance of the relationship."[52] The very idea of a "relation" that produces and sustains one of its relata and is, according to Śrīdhara, "incompatible with its independence" (*svātantryapratirodhaka*)[53] has often been criticized and rejected, for instance, by Kumārila and his followers.[54]

Samavāya is obviously different from ordinary conjunction (*saṃyoga*), which always presupposes the separability of its relata and does not affect their very existence. As one of the "qualities" (*guṇa*), *saṃyoga* is by definition particularized; that is, it represents individual instances of conjunction that last only as long as the relata are actually conjoined. *Samavāya*, on the other hand, is never destroyed; it is always one and the same and never affected by the behavior of its relata. It does not occur in the mode of particular instances, nor is it a generic property "inherent" in such instances. Rather, it is the one pervasive structure of our universe that constitutes the condition of the possibility of concrete, qualified entities and of contingent existence.[55] Praśastapāda refers to the concept of reality or existence (*sattā, bhāva*) to illustrate the unique nature of inherence and its distinction from conjunction. Both reality and inherence are one and eternal and not affected by any changes in the realm of particulars.[56] But unlike reality, inherence is not a universal.

Inherence may be a "relation," but it also indicates a dependent mode of existence or "occurrence." It is supposed to explain the presence or "residence" (*vṛtti*), that is, the dependent occurrence, of wholes in their parts and of attributes in their substrates. Their manner of existence is, in the words of Śrīdhara, "occurrence defined by inherence" (*samavāyalakṣaṇā vṛttiḥ*).[57] According to Praśastapāda, *samavāya* itself is "of the nature of residence" (*vṛttyātmaka*) and endowed with "self-occurrence" or "residence per se" (*svātmavṛtti*),[58] allowing other entities to "occur in" their substrates and thus be actually and contingently present.

Prior to Praśastapāda, Gautama's *Nyāyasūtra* and Vātsyāyana's *Nyāyabhāṣya* use the term *vṛtti* with specific reference to the mode of presence that the whole has in its parts. In his commentary on these sections, Uddyotakara, perhaps a generation after Praśastapāda and generally a staunch advocate of the Vaiśeṣika categories, uses *samavāya* to explain this notion of *vṛtti* as "dependent occurrence."[59] Elsewhere, Uddyotakara says that inherence itself does not reside anywhere (*na ca samavāyasya vṛttir asti*) and that it is "independent" (*svatantra*) and "without substrate" (*anāśrita*).[60] This may not be fully compatible with Praśastapāda's explicit inclusion of inherence among those entities that do have a substrate.[61] Nonetheless, it illustrates in its own way what seems to be implied in Praśastapāda's concept: Inherence is the condition of the possibility of dependent presence or occurrence, not merely another dependent, inherent entity. Its status is "ontological" rather than "ontic."[62]

In its oldest uses in the Vaiśeṣika system, *samavāya* seems to have referred primarily, if not exclusively, to the relationship between material causes and their products; that is, to the "cooccurrence" of parts and wholes.[63] It may have been introduced in support of the theory that products do not preexist in their causes (*asatkāryavāda*). However, this usage was subsequently extended and extrapolated to the relationship between substrates and their attributes. In the work of Praśastapāda, this has become the most conspicuous function of *samavāya;* and once again, it illustrates his peculiar way of combining cosmology with epistemology and logic. In his system, inherence appears as the cosmological and ontological foundation of the possibility and legitimacy of predication. It is, in a sense, the hypostatized, reified copula, or the cosmic prototype of the copula.[64] Because of *samavāya,* this final item in the list of enumerables, the world is not merely a conglomeration of nameable, enumerable entities, but an integrated structure of predicative relations; because of *samavāya,* we can speak about the world in sentences and not merely in isolated words.[65]

Samavāya, as copulative being or the manner in which something "is in" something else, adds a meaning of "being" to the world that is found neither in *sattā* nor in *astitva.* It also serves to explain and justify Praśastapāda's basic understanding of the correspondence between language, thought, and reality. Its explicit presentation may appear somewhat tenuous and potentially misleading. Nonetheless, inherence is an indispensable cornerstone of the classical Vaiśeṣika system, in particular of its ontology.

7. As we have noted earlier, Praśastapāda tends to neglect the topic of nonbeing or nonexistence (*asat, abhāva*), which appears in the ninth Adhyāya of the *Vaiśeṣikasūtra* and plays a major role in later Nyāya and Vaiśeṣika. Likewise, he says very little about the debate between *satkārya-* and *asatkāryavāda.* In general, questions concerning genesis and temporal existence do not play a conspicuous role in the *Padārthadharmasaṃgraha.*[66]

However, this does not mean that questions of this kind and the background of *satkārya/asatkārya* are entirely obsolete and irrelevant in Praśastapāda's thought. He may have dealt with such matters in his lost *Ṭīkā* on the Vaiśeṣikasūtra (more precisely, on a *Vaiśeṣikabhāṣya* that is equally unavailable today). At any rate, we have evidence that questions concerning genesis and temporal existence were discussed during the "dark period" between the compilation of the Sūtra text and the *Padārthadharmasaṃgraha.* In these debates, the concept of *sattāsambandha* played a very significant role. It is also obvious that its meaning was subject to certain changes and reinterpretations.[67]

Praśastapāda's stature as a systematizer is undeniable. He is the most authoritative representative, if not the creator, of classical Vaiśeṣika and its peculiar integration of cosmology, philosophy of nature, categoriology, epistemology, and soteriology.[68] His influence in the history of the school is unequalled. In an exemplary fashion, his system combines historically divergent ingredients.

Praśastapāda tries to preserve the cosmological heritage in a new atmosphere of thought. His ontological terminology reflects this attempt. All particular, cosmologically distinct "reals" (*sat*) are assembled under the roof of *sattā*. This totality of "reals" is then integrated into a wider circle of ontologically valid enumerables under the roof of *astitva*. *Sattā* or reality itself appears as a reified universal, an entity within that wider totality circumscribed by the abstract attribute *astitva*. Any further reification and proliferation of enumerables is halted at this point. The system of enumeration has reached its limits. Only the logical-ontological subjects (*dharmin*) are enumerable, but not their predicates or abstract attributes (*dharma*). Praśastapāda concludes the *uddeśa* section of his work with the words: *evaṃ dharmair vinā dharmiṇām uddeśaḥ kṛtaḥ* ("Thus the subjects have been enumerated without their attributes"). With this short statement, Praśastapāda left a major problem to his commentators and successors. How can they uphold the ontological and cosmological validity of the distinction between *dharma* and *dharmin*, and the possibility of identifying and listing all genuine dharmins, while recognizing the functional, grammatical, relative nature of these notions?[69]

Praśastapāda tries to consolidate his system of enumeration, his inventory of all world constituents, against the arguments of the Buddhists and others who criticize any kind of illegitimate reification and hypostatic abstraction. However, his construction remains precarious. The consolidation is achieved at the expense of excluding certain crucial problems. The notion of an exhaustive inventory of all world constituents in the horizon of *astitva* and the idea of including all cosmological substrates in a complete and definitive list of ontologically valid logical subjects (*dharmin*) are as problematic and provocative as they are ingenious.

An acceptance of this construction can hardly be expected from the opponents of the Vaiśeṣika system. Praśastapāda's commentators have to deal with their questions and objections.

8. Critique comes, above all, from the Buddhists, but also from the Jainas and various Hindu schools. Vyomaśiva, Śrīdhara, and

Udayana respond to this critique in a more or less detailed fashion; and they offer different explanations and justifications for Praśastapāda's ontological ideas. Vyomaśiva's presentation is especially rich from the historical and doxographic angle. Udayana's comments and definitions have gained the greatest significance for the subsequent development of Nyāya and Vaiśeṣika thought.

First of all, the commentators have to defend the basic premises of the system of categories, the possibility of exhaustive enumeration, the fundamental understanding of being. This includes, of course, the rejection of the Sāṃkhya *satkāryavāda,* although it appears usually in rather brief and casual remarks.[70]

The greatest and most explicit challenge comes from the Buddhist doctrine of universal flux, or of the "momentariness" (*kṣaṇikatva, kṣaṇabhaṇga*) of all entities. This doctrine, which has its roots in ancient Buddhism and was systematically developed and refined in the school of Dignāga and Dharmakīrti, would obviously undermine the basic foundations of the Vaiśeṣika system.[71] The most detailed discussion and refutation is found in Śrīdhara's *Nyāyakandalī.* In particular, this text deals with the argument that momentariness is implied in the very nature of being (*sattvānumāna*); it refers explicitly to Dharmakīrti's commentator Dharmottara. According to Śrīdhara, universal momentariness would lead to absurd consequences, eliminate the distinction between being and nonbeing, and render the notions of origination (*utpatti*) and cessation (*nivṛtti*) meaningless.[72]

Authors from the allied Nyāya school, in particular Uddyotakara, Vācaspati, and once again Udayana, also argue extensively against the Buddhist theory of momentariness.[73] In earlier Nyāya literature, beginning with the Nyāyasūtra, a theory that denies any kind of independent, nonrelative identity to the entities and that we may associate with Nāgārjuna's philosophy of emptiness (*śūnyavāda*), is more significant and conspicuous.[74] It is remarkable that Vātsyāyana Pakṣilasvāmin's *Nyāyabhāṣya* invokes the Vaiśeṣika doctrine of categories in its attempt to defend the "selfhood" or identity (*svabhāva*) of entities against such universal negativism and relativism. Entities exist, and are different from each other, by virtue of their own inherent properties (*svena dharmeṇa bhāvā bhavanti*). According to Vātsyāyana, such natural division among objects (*arthabheda*), as demonstrated by the Vaiśeṣika system of classification, would be impossible if everything were ultimately negative (*abhāva*) and relative (*āpekṣika*).[75] Real distinction requires real, positive identity and identifiability. On the other hand, reality itself implies identifiability and distinguishability.

Uddyotakara's *Nyāyavārttika* adds that the universality of universals (including reality) would not be possible without real distinction (*na ca bhedam antareṇa sāmānyaṃ labdhāvakāśam*).[76] According to Vācaspati's *Ṭīkā*, this is meant to exclude the nondualistic view that only the universal is real and that the distinctions are fictitious (*sāmānyam eva tattvam, bhedas tu kālpanika iti*).[77]

9. In the Buddhist discourse about and against being, the concept of *arthakriyākāritva*, "practical efficiency," is closely related to the idea of momentariness. But there are also significant differences. In an earlier chapter, we referred to Ratnakīrti's review of various definitions of being (*sattva*) and his claim that they are all superseded by *arthakriyākāritva*.

> In his view, this definition is not just theoretically superior to the other definitions; but it is also the one which all the other schools unknowingly and unwillingly recognize: whatever somebody may say about the theoretical nature of reality, practical efficiency is the criterion he adopts when it comes to deciding what to accept as real and what not.[78]

This is typical: *Arthakriyākāritva* may be inseparable from *kṣaṇikatva*. But unlike *kṣaṇikatva*, which expresses primarily a view of the nature of the world, it also provides a criterion of reality and, moreover, a reductive explanation of what people really mean when they speak of being and nonbeing. *Arthakriyākāritva* in this sense means "making a difference," the difference that accounts for the distinction between reality and appearance.[79]

As a matter of fact, the Naiyāyikas and Vaiśeṣikas themselves accept "practical efficiency" (*arthakriyā, pravṛttisāmarthya*) as a criterion of reality;[80] but they reject emphatically the Buddhist use of this concept, that is, its role as a reductive definition of being. As a challenge to the Vaiśeṣika conceptualizations of being, specifically the concepts of *sattā* ad *sattāsambandha*, the concept of *arthakriyākāritva* plays a conspicuous and significant role in the commentaries of Vyomaśiva, Śrīdhara, and Udayana.[81]

Next to *arthakriyākāritva*, the concept of *pramāṇasambandhayogyatā*, "suitability for valid cognition," "correspondence to the means of ascertaining truth," or *pramāṇagrāhyatā*, "accessibility to valid cognition," appears as one of the most conspicuous challenges to the Vaiśeṣika conceptualizations of being. The Prābhākara school of Mīmāṃsā does not accept a universal "reality." In its view, as articulated most clearly in the works of Śālikanātha, the ideas of *sattā* and *sattāsambandha* can be reduced to the imposed property (*upādhi*) "suitability for valid cognition."[82] Although the Mīmāṃsā view of the nature of reality and the structure of the world has numerous systematic and historical affinities with the Vaiśeṣika system of categories, several Nyāya and Vaiśeṣika commentators, in particular Śrīdhara, reject the notion of *prāmaṇasambandhayogyatā* in no uncertain terms.[83]

Vyomaśiva also refers to the theory that being or reality can be explained as "connection with the present time" (*vartamānakālasambandhitva*). This theory may be associated with Maṇḍana's version of Mīmāṃsā ontology; according to Maṇḍana, reality or being (*sattva*) amounts to "being present" (*vartamānatā*); that is, to actual occurrence in time.[84] We may note here that the various explanations of being in Mīmāṃsā are associated with exegetic postitions. Whereas Kumārila adopts and modifies the Vaiśeṣika concept of *sattā*, Prabhākara and Śālikanātha propose *pramāṇasambandhayogyatā* to accommodate *kārya*, "the ought," as a reality sui generis. Maṇḍana, who rejects Prabhākara's *kārya* and wants to support his own interpretation of the nature of *vidhi*, "injunctions," criticizes *pramāṇasambandhayogyatā/pramāṇagrāhyatā* and adopts the idea of *vartamānatā*, "being present." The status of the "present time" (*vartamānakāla*) is, of course, a highly controversial one. Patañjali's *Mahābhāṣya* and Nāgārjuna's *Madhyamakakārikā* provide early highlights of the debate. Various Nyāya teachers, beginning with Gautama and Vātsyāyana, have tried to defend the notion of "present time" against its critics.[85]

Finally, we have to mention Vyomaśiva's rejection of the view that *sattā* is the only real universal whose apparent differentiation into specific universals results from a variety of associations and imposed properties (*upādhibheda*). We may connect this view with Bhartṛhari's *Vākyapadīya*.[86]

In general, the most familiar argument against the Vaiśeṣika concepts of *sattā* and *sattāsambandha* is the "dilemma about being and nonbeing" (*sadasadvikalpa*): How and when does "connection with reality" actually take place? What is it that is supposed to be connected with *sattā*? Is it something that is already real (*sat*) by itself (i.e., no longer in need of *sattā*)? Is it not yet real? But how could there be connection with the unreal (*asat*)?[87]

10. The situation is different when we come to Praśastapāda's concept of *astitva* ("is-ness," objectivity). This concept was itself a reflection of new ways of thinking, and less susceptible to charges of reification than *sattā* and *sattāsambandha.* The apologetic task was less obvious in this case. As we have seen, the concept of *astitva* is not found in the Vaiśeṣikasūtra. Praśastapāda used it only once and left it virtually unexplained. This gave a considerable measure of freedom to his three great commentators. They used this freedom by presenting rather different and somewhat personal interpretations of *astitva.*

By far the most elaborate presentation is found in Vyomaśiva's commentary. Vyomaśiva first argues that *astitva* and other abstract properties (*dharma*), such as *jñeyatva* ("knowability") and *abhidheyatva* ("nameability"), should not be construed as separable attributes and additional categories (*padārtha*), over and above the traditionally accepted six categories. Moreover, he tries to establish that a "determination" (*avadhāraṇa,* i.e., a definitive list) of all genuine world constituents is possible. Then he proposes an interpretation of *astitva* that is basically nominalistic or at least conceptualistic. What is the meaning of *astitva?* According to Vyomaśiva, the term indicates primarily a "linguistic usage" (*śābdavyavahāra*); it refers to the fact that the word *asti,* "is" (i.e., "is there," "occurs") is used or may be used. *Astitva* is (in accordance with the traditional explanation of the suffix *tva*) *aster bhāvaḥ,* the "status of *asti*"; that is, the status of affirmation in speech and thought. It means that the statement *it is* applies; and this does apply when the cognition *is* (i.e., "is there," "occurs") takes place. The use of the word *asti* does not indicate the presence of a real universal *astitva* in the objects to which it is applied. It refers to, and is the effect of, only a recurrent cognitive event. Thus our own verbal and cognitive response to the world, and not any real and enumerable constituent of the world, accounts for *astitva,* "objectivity," and its apparent universality. The impact of Buddhist nominalism is obvious in Vyomaśiva's presentation. However, the Buddhists also use such and similar reductive arguments against *sattā* and against the assumption of real universals in general.[88]

Later on in his *Vyomavatī,* Vyomaśiva discusses at length the concept of *sattā,* and he defends it against its critics.[89] In particular, he tries to explain how *sattā*, "reality," which inheres in substances, qualities, and motions only, can nevertheless be applied to the second group of categories (i.e., the universals, etc.). Here, the recurrent notion of reality is applied in a figurative, metaphorical sense (*sat sad iti jñānam upacaritam*). This conception of "metaphorical being" should, of course, not be confused with Bhartṛhari's notion of *upacārasattā* (or *aupacārikī sattā*).[90] According to Vyomaśiva, the "superimposition of reality" (*sattādhyāropa*) on universals, and so on, takes place, and has a certain legitimacy, because of their ontological contiguity. Reality itself (*sattā*) and the other universals are "cooccurrent properties" (*sādhāraṇadharma, sahacaritadharma*) in the same real substrates. However, Vyomaśiva insists that the possibility of such metaphorical use is no reason to abandon the concept of *sattā* altogether or to deny its real inherence in the first three categories.

> Concerning universals and so forth, the recurrent cognition "real" is metaphorical, because the inherence of reality would result in inconsistencies. . . . No metaphorical usage is ever found without primary usage; therefore it is established that in the case of substances and so forth the appearance of the recurrent cognition "real" is, indeed, due to the inherence of reality.[91]

Udayana and numerous later authors also invoke such "joint inherence", that is, sharing the same substrate with reality (*sattaikārthasamavāya*) or "coresidence in one object" (*ekārthavṛttitva*), as a reason to extend the usage of *sattā* to all six positive categories and specifically to the universals.[92]

11. Śrīdhara's explanation of *astitva* is conspicuously different from the one given by his predecessor Vyomaśiva. According to his *Nyāyakandalī*, the kind of "objective reality" meant by the term *astitva* is nothing but identifiability; that is, the "peculiar nature" or self-identity (*svarūpa*) of something. "That which belongs to a thing as its peculiar nature, that is its objectivity" (*yasya vastuno yat svarūpaṃ, tad eva tasya-astitvam*). Śrīdhara also substitutes the expression *svarūpavattva*, "possession of a peculiar nature" (i.e., identifiability), for *astitva*.[93] This procedure does not seem to be incompatible with the connotation of identifiability and recognizability in Praśastapāda's use of *astitva* nor with his use of the term *svarūpa* (as in the compounds *ātmasvarūpa*, *svarūpābheda, svarūpālocanamātra*).[94] Yet is is certainly not warranted by any explicit statements found in Praśastapāda's work.

Śrīdhara insists that both *astitva* and *sattā* are necessary to account for the world in which we live. Whereas we need the universal *sattā* to explain our awareness of being in its unity and universality, *astitva* as *svarūpavattva* is not superfluous either, because *sattā* as a pervasive universal could not inhere in what is without a peculiar nature of its own; that is, in nonspecific, indistinguishable entities.[95] Its pervasiveness presupposes the distinctness of its substrates. Of course, Śrīdhara does not question its restriction to the first three categories.

It would be inappropriate to equate Śrīdhara's distinction between *astitva* ad *sattā* with the relation between essence and existence or to invoke the scholastic idea of an "esse superadditum essentiae." *Astitva* as *svarūpavattva* is not essence without existence, but reality without unity and universality. A world without *sattā* would not be nonexistent; but the entities that occur in it would not have a real common denominator; that is, no "reality" apart from the fact that they are what they are. According to Śrīdhara, the "world" of universals, particularities, and inherence is, indeed, like that. They have no "reality" over and above their peculiar natures (*svarūpa*); that is, apart from the fact that they are identifiable and distinguishable essences. In this case, the awareness of unity (*ekānugama*) would be false (*mithyā*).[96]

The concept of *svarūpa* plays a crucial role in the ontology of the Prābhākara school of Pūrvamīmāṃsā. The Prābhākaras, in particular Śālikanātha Miśra, argue that the assumption of a universal *sattā* is unnecessary. In their view, there is no reality in addition to what is real; there is nothing over and above the fact that things are what they are; that is, their peculiarity and identity as things (*vastusvarūpa*). The alleged universal *sattā* can be reduced to the nonobjective property (*upādhi*) "suitability for valid cognition" (*pramāṇasambandhayogyatā*).[97] Śrīdhara rejects the ontological views of the Prābhākaras. Nonetheless, his interpretation of *astitva* as *svarūpa/svarūpavattva* shows that he has learned from them.

12. Udayana, the latest of the classical Praśastapāda commentators and the pioneer of Navyanyāya, defines *astitva* as "being the object of (i.e., accessibility to) affirmative awareness" (*vidhimukhapratyayaviṣayatva*) and, furthermore, as "ascertainability without reference to a counter-entity" (*pratiyogyanapekṣanirūpaṇatva*).[98] According to the commentary by Vardhamāna, Udayana adds the second phrase to make it clear that *abhāva,* "nonexistence," is not included in this conception of *astitva.*[99] Udayana's formula was widely accepted by later Naiyāyikas and Vaiśeṣikas. We may say that it became the leading definition or paraphrase of *astitva.* Yet it was also highly controversial and potentially conducive to an evaporation of that robust notion of reality and identifiability it was supposed to affirm and uphold against the Buddhists and other critics.

The term *vidhimukhapratyayaviṣayatva* presents "objectivity" as the correlate or domain of inherently positive, affirmative ideas. Moreover, we are told that *astitva* means identifiability that is not relative to anything else. In the history of Nyāya and Vaiśeṣika, this approach was, of course, not entirely new. Somewhat casually, Śrīdhara substitutes *vidhipratyayaviṣayatva,* "being the object of affirmative awareness," for *astitva.*[100] Elsewhere, he states that, unlike nonexistence (*abhāva*), the reality (*bhāva*) of the six positive categories is grasped in an assertive, positive manner (*vidhirūpatā*).[101] In the same context, he cites Uddyotakara's *Nyāyavārttika.* Uddyotakara, too, associates being with assertion (*vidhi*) and nonbeing with negation (*pratiṣedha*); moreover, he defines the awareness of being as independent and direct (*svatantra*) and that of nonbeing as dependent and indirect (*paratantra*).[102] As first stated in the *Nyāyabhāṣya,* both being (*sat*) and nonbeing (*asat*) are objects of valid cognition.[103] Objectivity and cognizability as such cannot establish the distinction between being and nonbeing: *sadasatoḥ pramāṇagamyatvaṃ sārūpyam.*[104]

The Nyāya-Vaiśeṣika emphasis on the inherent positivity of what there is is part of the defense against the Buddhist negativism and relativism, especially against the ideas of "negative abstraction" (*apoha*) and "voidness" (*śūnyatā*). The Naiyāyikas and Vaiśeṣikas try to anchor the concepts of "own-nature," "peculiar nature," "self-identity" (*svarūpa, svabhāva,* etc.) in the independent positivity and assertiveness of the corresponding ideas or judgments. However, this approach is obviously precarious. As noted by Vācaspati, the Buddhists themselves have emphasized the association between the concept of being and the affirmative, assertive character of positive judgments and ideas (*vidhi*).[105] Of course, they have drawn entirely different conclusions from this observation.

The idea of *svarūpa* itself, which Śrīdhara invokes to defend the inherent positivity and identifiability of *astitva,* is precarious and problematic and hardly suitable to vindicate the old realism of the Vaiśeṣika against reductionist and relativistic challenges. Udayana admits that nonbeing (*abhāva*), too, has a nature of its own: *abhāvas tu svarūpavān api.*[106] However, such *abhāva* is not entirely vacuous. It is nonbeing in the sense of real, identifiable absence of positive entities, and it implies locally or temporally specified nonoccurrences of what could be there, and does occur somewhere in time and space. Accordingly, *svarūpa* does not apply to what is utterly fictitious or even impossible (*tuccha, alīka*).[107]

Udayana's great Vedāntic opponent Śrīharṣa does not accept this attempt to limit the use of *svarūpa.* In its basic connotation of identifiability and distinguishability, it is, according to Śrīharṣa, equally applicable to the world of fictions or impossibilities, or simply to anything that is in the range of speech and thought.[108] It is obviously no problem to distinguish a hare's horn from a sky-flower or the son of a barren woman. In principle, this kind of critique had been articulated long before Udayana, for instance by Dharmakīrti.[109]

13. "All six categories possess is-ness, nameability, and knowability" (*ṣāṇṇām api padārthānām astitvābhidheyatvajñeyatvāni*).[110] Praśastapāda's short statement is elusive; its simplicity is deceptive. It does not clarify the relationship between *astitva,* on the one hand, and predicability and knowability or objectifiability, on the other. The fact that he coordinates them as common attributes (*sādharmya*) of the six categories does not necessarily mean that he considers them to be coextensive.[111] The commentators usually include nonbeing (*abhāva*) under *abhidheyatva* and *jñeyatva,* but are reluctant to do so with regard to *astitva;* although we may know and speak of nonbeing, nothing knowable or speakable exists (or "is there") apart from the six positive categories.[112]

Udayana defines all seven categories (including *abhāva*) as "nameable" (*abhidheya*).[113] Others characterize them as "objects of valid cognition" (*pramitiviṣaya*) or simply as "knowable" (*jñeya*); the distinction between being and nonbeing appears as a division of knowable objects (*prameyavibhāga*).[114] In classical Nyāya since Vātsyāyana, *tattva* has covered being and nonbeing (*sat* and *asat;* that is, positive and negative facts and occurrences) insofar as they can be objects of true knowledge and speech.[115] Praśastapāda himself does not have an explicit notion covering both being and nonbeing (although this may be implied in his *jñeyatva* and *abhidheyatva*) nor does he provide us with any explicit statements concerning the ontological status of nonbeing, the meaning of negation, and the problems and paradoxes involved in speaking about nonentities or even impossibilities. His successors in the history of Nyāya and Vaiśeṣika cannot avoid addressing these questions in a more explicit fashion.[116] Likewise, Praśastapāda shows little interest in semantic analysis and linguistic reflection. Unlike Uddyotakara, he does not pursue the question of how reality or existence function as "meanings of words" (*padārtha;* that is, the question what we actually mean when we call something *sat* or "real").[117]

We cannot discuss here the various ways in which later authors have dealt with the complex problems concerning the relationship between "is-ness," "nameability," and "knowability," or between the ontological, semantic, and epistemological spheres. Nor can we pursue the adjustments of Praśastapāda's ontological vocabulary that were introduced after Udayana. Here, Vallabha's *Nyāyalīlāvatī* and Bhaṭṭavādīndra's *Vaiśeṣikavārttika* would be of interest.[118] More radical changes (including the elimination of the universal *sattā*) were proposed in the *Padārthatattvanirūpaṇa* by Raghunātha Śiromaṇi.[119] Yet in the majority of commentaries and compendia, Praśastapāda's scheme has survived. Being as *sattā,* as reified "reality" and real universal, appears side by side with *astitva,* being as abstract "objectivity." A petrified notion of reality continues to accompany the conceptual evaporation of being.

The critique of Praśastapāda's ontology and categoriology has been deep and pervasive in the history of Indian thought. It comes from Buddhists, Jainas, and competing Hindu schools. Specific arguments have been raised not only against *sattā* and *sattāsambandha,* but also against the concept of *astitva.* We find them summarized in such works as Śāntarakṣita's *Tattvasaṃgraha* (together with Kamalaśīla's *Pañjikā*)[120] and Abhayadevasūri's *Tattvabodhavidhāyinī.*[121] In the history of Advaita Vedānta, the most devastating critique is found in Śrīharṣa's *Khaṇḍanakhaṇḍakhādya.*[122] According to the Advaita Vedāntins, an understanding of Being cannot be gained through an enumeration and classification of different entities. True, absolute being transcends and precedes all distinctions, including the distinction between being and nonbeing. No classification and conglomeration would be possible without such underlying unity; as Maṇḍana says: *saṃgraho hi na-ekam antareṇa.*[123]

In Mahāyāna Buddhism and in Advaita Vedānta, we find an intense suspicion concerning the projective power of words and the inherent futility and deceptiveness of conceptual and categorial distinctions. Classification, objectification, and representational thought in general appear as constituents of that primeval ignorance (*avidyā*), in which ordinary philosophers, such as the Naiyāyikas and Vaiśeṣikas, seem to be caught even more deeply than other ordinary people.

Chapter 7: Notes

1. See earlier, Chapter 1, section 3.

2. N. Hartmann, *Der Aufbau der realen Welt*, 2d ed. (Meisenheim, 1949), p. 2.

3. See Harimohan Jhā, *Bhāratīya darśana-paricaya*, vol. 2: *Vaiśeṣika darśana*, 2d ed. (Patna, 1964), p. 4: *Vaiśeṣika mukhyataḥ padārtha śāstra* (Ontology) *hai aur nyāya mukhyataḥ pramāṇa śāstra* (Epistemology).

4. See earlier, Chapter 4, section 1. The phrase *Vaiśeṣika scheme of ontology* appears in S. Saha, *Perspectives on Nyāya Logic and Epistemology* (Calcutta, 1987), pp. 27ff.

5. See *VS* I, 2, 7–8. Several old Jaina sources cite *VS* I, 2, 7–8 as *one* coherent statement; see Jinabhadra, *Viśeṣāvaśyakabhāṣya*, ed. D. Malvania (Ahmedabad, 1966–1968), v. 2669 (commentary; cf. also v. 2661); Siṃhasūri in Mallavādin, *DNC*, vol. 1, pp. 6; 25; 30. On the use of *arthāntara*, cf. *VS* VI, 2, 8–10 (*Upaskāra:* VI, 2, 7–8); IX, 3 (*Upaskāra:* IX, 1, 3).

6. On Aristotle, see earlier, Chapter 1, section 1.

7. See A. Thakur, "The Problem of the Vaiśeṣikabhāṣya," *Proceedings of the International Congress of Orientalists* 26, Delhi 1964, III/1 (Poona, 1969), pp. 489–493; especially pp. 491f. According to Ātreya, Sūtra I, 2, 7–8 was meant to assert and justify the permanence of the universal "reality" against the impermanence of its particular instances.

8. Cf. *VS* VII, 2, 30 (*Upaskāra:* VII, 2, 27; with variant reading) on *samavāya: dravyatvaguṇatvakarmatvapratiṣedho bhāvena vyākhyātaḥ*. Candrānanda explains: *yathā-ekadravyavattvān na dravyaṃ bhāvo guṇakarmasu ca bhāvān na karma na guṇa evaṃ samavāyo 'pi.*

9. See, for instance, B. Bhattacharya, *Negation* (Calcutta, 1965); B. K. Matilal, *The Navya-Nyāya Doctrine of Negation* (Cambridge, Mass., 1968); D. Sharma, *The Negative Dialectics of India* (East Lansing, Mich., 1970). On the treatment of *abhāva* by various Nyāya and Vaiśeṣika commentators, and their explanations why Praśastapāda did not list it as a category, see A. Thakur, *Vaiśeṣikadarśana of Kaṇāda* (Darbhanga, 1957), pp. 14f. (Introduction).

10. As a matter of fact, the nonterminological uses of *bhāva* and *abhāva* (as "occurrence" and "nonoccurrence," etc.) are more frequent than the terminological ones; see, for instance, *VS* II, 2, 10 (9); 38 (33)ff.; III, 2, 1. *Sat* may, of course, be used in the same neutral sense of "occurring" or "being the case"; see, for instance, II, 2,1 1; 29 (25)ff. *Sattva*, too, is without the terminological commitment of *sattā;* it does, however, not occur in *VS* itself.

11. See, for instance, the intriguing relationship between the "terminological" and "nonterminological" uses of *bhāva* in *VS* I, 2.

12. On the juxtaposition and contrast of *bhāvatva* and *abhāvatva*, cf. B. K. Matilal (cited in n. 9), pp. 123f.

13. See, for instance, Śrīdhara, *NK*, p. 7: *abhāvasya pṛthag anupadeśo bhāvapāratantryān, na tv abhāvāt.*

14. Cf. B. K. Matilal, *Epistemology, Logic, and Grammar in Indian Philosophical Analysis* (The Hague, 1971), pp. 71; 74f." "existence or beingness"; *Perception* (Oxford, 1986), pp. 379f. ("existent-ness"); D. H. H. Ingalls, *Materials for the Study of Navya-Nyāya Logic* (Cambridge, Mass., 1951), prefers "reality"; see pp. 53f.; 69f.; 116f.

15. Cf. D. H. H. Ingalls, *Materials*, pp. 38; 54ff.

16. This distinction applies primarily to the translations presented as Appendix 1.

17. This does, of course, not imply that the distinction between essence and existence is entirely absent in Indian thought, as suggested by M. Biardeau, *La philosophie de Maṇḍana Miśra* (Paris 1969), p. 71: "la pensée indienne ne distingue à aucun moment l'essence de l'existence."

18. See later, n. 117; on being, time, and action, see also later, Chapter 9, sections 1; 8.

19. See Candrānanda on *VS* I, 2, 4: *bhāvaḥ sattā.* The anonymous commentary edited by A. Thakur (cited in n. 9) says: *bhāvo bhavanaṃ sattā-iti yāvat.* In this version, Sūtra, I, 2, 4 is reduced to the one word *bhāvaḥ.*

20. See earlier, Chapter 3, sections 8ff.

21. In Śaṅkaramiśra's version, the first Sūtra itself reads *prāgasat* instead of Candrānanda's *asat.*

22. See Mallavādin, *DNC*, vol. 2, pp. 490ff.; 516; and later, Chapter 8.

23. Tirumalai Tātācārya, *Sugamā vaiśeṣikavṛttiḥ* (Prayāga, 1979), suggests: *kāraṇaṃ sāmānyam anumīyate.*

24. See H. Narain, *Evolution of the Nyāya-Vaiśeṣika Categoriology*, vol. 1 (Benares, 1976), pp. 157ff.; 178ff.

25. See H. Narain, *Evolution*, pp. 160ff. He also suggests that the *uktam* in *guṇeṣu bhāvād guṇatvam uktam* (*VS* I, 2, 14; cf. also 12 and 16) might be a corruption of *uktā* (as referring to *sattā*).

26. See Bhartṛhari, *VP* III/1 (*Jātisamuddeśa*); and later, Appendix 1, section 3. Much later, Vedāntic models appear in the *VS* commentary of Candrakānta Tarkālaṃkāra (nineteenth century; in *Vaiśeṣikadarśanam*, ed. R. Chaudhuri. Calcutta, 1887). In his comments on *VS* I, 1, 8 and I, 2, 3, Candrakānta, one of the universal pandits of his time, invokes the Vedāntic distinction between *vyavahāra* and *paramārtha*.

27. See H. Ui, *The Vaiśeṣika Philosophy*, pp. 99f.; 116f.; see also M. Hattori in *Indian Metaphysics and Epistemology*, ed. K. H. Potter (*EIPh*, vol. 2), p. 277.

28. This common attribute *sat* is first mentioned in *VS* I, 1, 7 (*Upaskāra:* I, 1, 8).

29. See earlier, Chapter 4.

30. *VS* I, 7 (8).

31. According to Candramati's *Daśapadārthī*, all categories are knowable (*jñeya*) and nameable (*abhidheya*); see M. Hattori, *EIPh*, vol. 2 (cited in n. 27), p. 281.

32. *PBh*, pp. 311f.; on "dyeing," cf. Bhartṛhari, *VP* III/1 (*Jātisamuddeśa*), pp. 7f.

33. See *PBh*, p. 16; on coextensiveness, see also Śrīdhara, *NK*, p. 203; and later, section 13.

34. *PBh*, p. 325; see also p. 311: *yad anugatam asti;* and later, Chapter 9, section 3.

35. See later, section 12.

36. There is no evidence for equating Kaṇāda's *bhāva* with Praśastapāda's *astitva*, as D. N. Shastri, *Critique of Indian Realism* (Agra, 1964), p. 148, would like to do.

37. See earlier, Chapter 4, sections 3; 7.

38. See Nāgārjuna, *MK* V, 8; this involves a critique of objectification and ontological commitment. In the Pali canon, we find *atthitā* and *natthitā* (cf. *Saṃyuttanikāya* II, 17; cited by Nāgārjuna, *MK* XV, 7). Cf. also Vātsyāyana, *NBh* I, 2, 6; Kumārila, *ŚV*, p. 459 (*Sambandhākṣepaparihāra*, v. 33); and the old Sāṃkhya verse quoted by E. Frauwallner, *Gesch. d. ind. Phil.*, vol. 1, p. 321 (from the *Māṭharavṛtti*).

39. *PBh*, p. 19; Śrīdhara paraphrases *svātmasattva* as *svarūpasattva;* see *NK*, p. 19.

40. However, in the section on universals, Praśastapāda uses the term *sattānusambandha*, and in the section on inherence, he speaks of *sattāyoga*; see *PBh*, pp. 312; 328.

41. Ibid., pp. 17f.

42. Ibid., p. 19; *arthaśabdānabhidheyatva* refers to VS VIII, 14 (*Upaskāra:* VIII, 2, 3): *artha iti dravyaguṇakarmasu.*

43. See M. Hiriyanna, *Indian Philosophical Studies*, vol. 1 (Mysore, 1957), p. 111.

44. See, for instance, B. Russell, *The Problems of Philosophy* (London, 1951), pp. 90ff.; 100; G. Bergmann, *Logic and Reality* (Madison, 1964), pp. 10; 248ff.

45. G. Patti, *Der Samavāya* (Rome, 1955), p. 143.

46. See earlier, Chapter 4, sections 2; 7.

47. See earlier, Chapter 5, section 6.

48. On *sattāsambandha* and temporal existence, see later, Chapter 8. For some later authors, *sattā* itself represents a temporal sense of existence, i.e., an existence which has destruction (*dhvaṃsa*) as its correlate; cf. Dinakara on Viśvanātha, *Kārikāvalī* (with *Siddhāntamuktāvalī*), v. 9 (ed. Sankara Rama Sastry. Madras, 1923, pp. 114f.).

49. See earlier, Chapter 4, section 4.

50. See M. Hiriyanna, "What Is Samavāya?" (see Chapter 4, n. 22), p. 212. Cf. also G. Patti, *Der Samavāya* (Rome, 1955); D. N. Shastri, *Critique of Indian Realism* (Agra, 1964), pp. 374–394.

51. See *PBh*, pp. 14; 324; *NK*, p. 328; *NV* IV, 2, 12 (*āśrayāśritabhāva*); Bhāsarvajña, *NBhūṣ*, p. 468 (*āśrayāśrayibhāva*).

52. K. K. Chakrabarti, art. "Vaiśeṣika," *Encyclopedia of Religion*, ed. M. Eliade, vol. 15 (New York, 1987), p. 167.

53. *NK*, p. 330. Śrīdhara paraphrases Praśastapāda's term *samavāyitva;* in Vaiśeṣika terminology, *samavāyin* usually means the substrate (*ādhāra*) in the relationship, whereas *samaveta* is that which inheres.

54. See Kumārila, *ŚV*, pp. 219f. (*Pratyakṣasūtra*, v. 146ff.). We may also recall at this point the ambivalent treatment of inherence ("Inhärenz") in Kant's *Kritik der reinen Vernunft* (for instance, B 230); Kant lists inherence among the "categories of relation," but then denies that it contains a relation ("Verhältnis").

55. For other schools, in particular the Mīmāṃsā school of Prabhākara, inherence itself is a perishable and particular phenomenon.

56. See *PBh*, pp. 328f.

57. *NK*, p. 16.

58. See PBh, pp. 328f.

59. See *NS*, *NBh*, and *NV* IV, 2, 7ff. (Calc. S. S., pp. 1045ff.); especially *NV* IV, 2, 12 (Calc. S. S., p. 1050): *vṛttir avayaveṣu āśrayāśrayibhāvaḥ samavāyākhyaḥ sambandhaḥ*. Prior to Uddyotakara, *samavāya* in its technical sense did not play a significant role in Nyāya literature. *NS* III, 2, 38 (Calc. S. S., p. 766: *anekadravyasamavāyād rūpaviśeṣāc ca rūpopalabdhiḥ*) seems to be borrowed from the Vaiśeṣikasūtra and may be spurious.

60. See *NV* I, 1, 5, (Calc. S. S., p. 158).

61. See *PBh*, p. 16: *āśritatvaṃ ca-anyatra nityadravyebhyaḥ*.

62. These terms are borrowed from the philosophy of M. Heidegger, but not necessarily used in his sense.

63. See in particular *VS* VII, 2, 29 (*Upaskāra:* VII, 2, 26): *iha-iti yataḥ kāryakāraṇayoḥ sa samavāyaḥ;* cf. also G. Patti, *Der Samavāya*, pp. 27ff.; 76ff. For an early critical reference, see Bādarāyaṇa, *Brahmasūtra* II, 2, 13: *samavāyābhyupagamāc ca sāmyād anavastiteḥ*. Bhartṛhari seems to presuppose the fully developed concept of *samavāya;* see, for instance, *VP* III/9 (*Kālasamuddeśa*); and K. A. Subramania Iyer, *Bhartṛhari* (Poona, 1969), p. 288.

64. For the role of the copula in Sanskrit, see earlier, Chapter 2, section 1 (n. 1). Our observations, of course, do not depend on the actual usage of the copula in philosophical Sanskrit.

65. On the relation between *samavāya* and *viśeṣaṇaviśeṣyabhāva* ("predicative relationship") according to Vyomaśiva, see later, Appendix 1, section 3.

66. See earlier, Chapter 3, section 9.

67. See later, Chapter 8.

68. This does not mean, of course, that he was the first to introduce the soteriological dimension or any of the other aspects of the integrated system.

69. See *Vy.*, p. 111 (and later, n. 88); *NK*, p. 16: *te eva-anyonyāpekṣayā dharmā dharmiṇaś ca bhavanti;* but cf. Vācaspati, *NVTātparyaṭīkā* III, 2, 14 (Calc. S. S., p. 843): *janakatvaṃ nāma na vastusvabhāvo 'pi tu taddharmaḥ. dharmaś ca dharmiṇo vastuto bhidyate.*

70. See earlier, Chapter 3, section 9.

71. Cf. E. Steinkellner, "Die Entwicklung des Kṣanikatvānumānam bei Dharmakīrti," *WZKS* 12–13 (1968–69; *Beiträge zur Geistesgeschichte Indiens*, Festschrift E. Frauwallner): 361–377.

72. See *NK*, 73–79.

73. See especially Vācaspati, *NVTātparyaṭīkā* III, 2, 14 (Calc. S.S., pp. 837ff.).

74. See *NS* and *NBh* IV, 1, 387ff. (Calc. S. S., pp. 977ff.).

75. See *NBh* IV, 1, 38 (Calc. S.S., p. 980); this is the first of three alternative interpretations proposed by Vātsyāyana.

76. *NV* IV, 1, 43 (Calc. S.S., pp. 991f.).

77. Ibid. (Calc. S.S., p. 992).

78. See earlier, Chapter 2, section 3.

79. On the meaning and functions of *arthakriyā*, see M. Nagatomi, "Arthakriyā," *Adyar Library Bulletin* 31–32 (1967–68):52–72; E. Mikogami, "Some Remarks on the Concept of Arthakriyā," *JIPh* 7 (1979): 79–94. Neither article explores the ontological and "inclusivistic" implications of *arthakriyā*. The concept gained major significance with Dharmakīrti; it does not play a visible role in the work of Dignāga. Nonetheless, it resumes and reinterprets older Buddhist ideas concerning the affinity of causality, practice, and being (or the false belief in it). For this, both Madhyamaka and Yogācāra provide examples. More specifically, we may refer to the Sarvāstivāda notion of *kāritra* (or *svakriyā*); cf. S Schayer, *Contributions to the Problem of Time in Indian Philosophy* (Cracow, 1938), pp. 21ff.; 38ff.; B. M. Sinha, *Time and Temporality in Sāṃkhya-Yoga and Abhidharma Buddhism* (Delhi, 1983), pp. 105–122. On *arthakriyā* and momentariness, see E. Steinkellner, "Die Entwicklung" (cited in n. 71), pp. 371ff.

80. See E. Franco, *Perception, Knowledge and Disbelief* (Stuttgart, 1987), pp. 369f. (n. 108); Franco's characterization of the Buddhist notion of *arthakriyā* as "epistemological, not ontological" is questionable.

81. See Vyomaśiva, *Vy.*, p. 127; Śrīdhara, *NK*, p. 12; Udayana, *Kir.*, GOS, pp. 95f.; and the translations presented in Appendix 1, sections 3–5.

82. See Śālikanātha, *Ṛjuvimalā* (on Prabhākara's *Bṛhatī*), ed. A. Chinnasvāmī Śāstri, (Benares, 1929; ChSS), p. 121: *bhinneṣu tu padārthasvabhāveṣu sacchabdapravṛttau pramāṇasambandhayogyatā-eva nimittam;* Maṇḍana, *Vidhiviveka*, ed. M. L. Gosvāmī (Benares, 1978), pp. 45ff., 58f., speaks of *pramāṇagrāhyatā* (and rejects it; see also his *Brahmasiddhi*, ed. S. Kuppuswami Sastri, Madras, 1937, p. 85: *pramāṇāvagamyatā;* p. 91: *pramāṇayogyatā;* p. 92: *pramāṇaviṣayatva;* etc.).

83. See later, Appendix 1, section 4.

84. On *vartamānatā/vartamānatva*, cf. Maṇḍana, *Vidhiviveka* (cited in n. 82), pp. 44ff.; 57f.; 161f. This does not necessarily imply existence at this particular time, but occurrence at some time and place; cf. later, n. 119 (on Raghunātha).

85. Cf. *Tradition and Reflection*, ch. 2, section 7; and later, Chapter 9, section 6 (especially n. 69).

86. See Vyomaśiva, *Vy.*, p. 689; and later, Appendix 1, section 3; cf. also Bhartṛhari, *VP* III/1 (*Jātisamuddeśa*), 33.

87. See later, Chapter 8; Appendix, sections 3f.

88. See Vyomaśiva, *Vy.*, pp. 110ff., 118 (for *aster bhāvaḥ, śābdavyavahāra*, etc.). In the Chowkhamba edition, this section is marred by so many misprints and inaccurate readings that it is virtually unintelligible. For an improved, but by no means fully adequate, presentation of the text, see the edition by Gaurinath Sastri, vol. 1, pp. 27ff.; 31f. On the editorial problems concerning the *Vyomavatī*, see later, Appendix, section 3.

89. See Appendix, section 3. Unlike Śrīdhara, Vyomaśiva does not respond to the Prābhākaras in this section.

90. On this concept, see K. A. Subramania Iyer, *Bhartṛhari* (Poona, 1969), pp. 209ff.; M. Biardeau, *Théorie de la connaissance et philosophie de la parole* (Paris, 1964), pp. 426ff.

91. See later, Appendix, section 3.

92. See Udayana, *Kir.*, GOS, p. 16; cf. also R. R. Dravid, *The Problem of Universals in Indian Philosophy* (Delhi, 1972), p. 41.

93. *NK*, p. 16.

94. See *PBh*, pp. 311f.; 186f.

95. See *NK*, p. 16: *yeṣāṃ tu bhāvasvarūpam eva-astitvaṃ, na teṣāṃ vyarthā sattā, svarūpasya-anuvṛttipratyayahetutvābhāvāt. na-apy astitvam anarthakaṃ, niḥsvarūpe sattāyāḥ samavāyābhāvād ity ubhayam upapadyate.*

96. See *NK*, p. 19.

97. See Śālikanātha, *Prakaraṇapañcikā*, ed. A. Subrahmanya Sastri (Benares, 1961), pp. 97ff.; *Ṛjuvimalā* (cited in n. 82), pp. 120f.

98. *Kir.*, GOS, p. 19.

99. See Vardhamāna in *Kir.*, Bibliotheca Indica), p. 137: *vidhimukhapratyaya-vedyatvaṃ svarūpam abhāve 'py asti-ity ata āha, pratiyogi-iti.*

100. See *NK*, p. 15.

101. See *NK*, p. 226; cf. also Bhāsarvajña, *NBhūṣ*, p. 538, on the distinction between being and nonbeing: *vidhipratiṣedhapradhānapratītiviṣayatvena vā tayor bhedaḥ.*

102. See *NV* I, 1, 1 (Calc. S. S., p. 26): *svatantraparatantropalabdhy-anupalabdhikāraṇabhāvāc ca viśeṣaḥ, sat khalu pramāṇasya-ālambanaṃ svatantraṃ*

bhavati, asat tu paratantram pratiṣedhamukhena pratipadyate. I adopt the reading *ālambanam* (instead of *asambandham*) from n. 1 in the text.

103. *NBh* I, 1, 1, (Calc. S.S., p. 27): *tad evaṃ sataḥ prakāśakaṃ pramāṇam asad api prakāśayati.*

104. *NV* I, 1, 2 (Calc. S.S., p. 71).

105. Cf. T. Stcherbatsky, *Erkenntnistheorie und Logik nach der Lehre der späteren Buddhisten*, trans. O. Strauss (Munich, 1924), pp. 151ff.; *Buddhist Logic* (Leningrad, 1930–1932; reprint, New York, 1962), vol. 2, pp. 199; 416f.

106. See *Kir.*, GOS, p. 4.

107. Ibid., pp. 4f.

108. See Śrīharṣa, *Khaṇḍanakhaṇḍakhādya*, ed. Laxmana Sastri Dravida (Benares, 1914; ChSS), pp. 12ff.; 44ff.; 1043ff.; cf. also S. Bhaduri, *Studies in Nyāya-Vaiśeṣika Metaphysics* (Poona, 1947), pp. 10ff.; B. K. Matilal, *The Navya-Nyāya Doctrine of Negation* (Cambridge, Mass., 1968), pp. 123f.

109. Dharmakīrti notes that those who deny that fictions or nonentities (*nirupākhya*) have their own peculiar nature (*svabhāva*) cannot explain the application of words in such cases; this implies that *svabhāva* or *svarūpa* cannot establish the distinction between being and nonbeing; cf. *The Pramāṇavārttikam of Dharmakīrti*, ed. R. Gnoli (Rome, 1960), p. 91 (autocommentary on ch. 1, v. 184).

110. *PBh*, p. 16; some manuscripts add *sādharmyam* after *padārthānām.*

111. See n. 33.

112. See earlier, section 12 (especially n. 98f.); see also Śrīdhara, *NK*, p. 230: *ṣaṭpadārthebhyo na-anyat prameyam asti.*

113. See Udayana, *Lakṣaṇāvalī* 1 (M. Tachikawa, *The Structure of the World*, pp. 56f.). Cf. also Bhaṭṭavādīndra in: *Vaiśeṣikadarśanam*, ed. A. Thakur (Darbhanga, 1985), pp. 58 ff. (on the concept of *prameya*).

114. Śivāditya opens his *Saptapadārthī* by defining the categories as *pramitiviṣaya*. For the expression *prameyavibhāga*, see *Vaiśeṣikadarśana of Kaṇāda*, ed. A. Thakur (Darbhanga, 1957), p. 2 (on *VS* I, 1, 4); also in: *Vaiśeṣikadarśanam* (Darbhanga, 1985), p. 255.

115. See *NBh* I, 1, 1 (Calc. S.S., p. 24): *kiṃ punas tattvam? sataś ca sadbhāvo 'sataś ca-asadbhāvaḥ. Tattva* in this sense is the condition of the possibility of valid representation in thought and speech, and it indicates a fundamentally epistemological perspective on being. Uddyotakara (*NV*, p. 32) defines it as that which makes the production of objectively valid, adequate ideas possible (*yathāvasthitātmapratyayotpattinimittatva, tathābhūtapratyayotpattinimitta*). In older Vaiśeṣika, *tattva* (as "identity", "essence") does not have this kind of epistemological function, nor does it imply any reference to nonbeing. In *VS* II, 1, 28 (29); II, 2, 8; 14

(12); VII, 2, 31 (28), it is used with specific reference to the "unitary essences" of ether, time, space, and inherence.

116. Cf. B. K. Matilal, *The Navya-Nyāya Doctrine of Negation* (Cambridge, Mass., 1968); see also Bhāsarvajña, *NBhūṣ*, pp. 539f., on the "being" of negations: *nañartha eva tāvad vicāryate, kim asti? na-asti vā?*

117. See, for instance, Uddyotakara, *NV* II, 2, 66 (Calc. S.S., pp. 672ff.; on the semantics of *sat*).

118. See *Nyāyalīlāvatī*, ed. Harihara Śāstrī and Ḍhuṇḍhirāja Śāstrī (Benares, 1927–1934; ChSS), pp. 691 ff. (on *sattā*); 778 ff. (on *astitva*). Vallabha (who may have lived in the twelfth century) demonstrates, above all, the elusive nature of *astitva*, by criticizing and rejecting previous attempts to define it. He rejects, for instance, the definition "denotability by the word *is*", because this would also apply to nonbeing (*astiśabdavācyatvam iti cen na, abhāve 'pi tulyatvāt*). For Bhaṭṭavādīndra, see *Vaiśeṣikadarśanam*, ed. A. Thakur (Darbhanga, 1985), pp. 68 ff. (on *sattā, astitva, bhāvatva*, etc.).

119. See *Padārthatattvanirūpaṇa*, ed. and trans. K. H. Potter, pp. 1ff.; Raghunātha proposes *vartamānatva* (actuality, being present at some time or place) as a criterion of reality. See also n. 84 (on Maṇḍana) above.

120. See *TS*, v. 571ff.

121. See *Sanmatitarkaprakaraṇam by Siddhasena Divākara with Abhayadevasūri's Commentary Tattvabodhavidhāyinī*, ed. S. Saṅghavī and B. Dośī (Ahmedabad, 1924–1931; reprint, Kyoto, 1984), p. 661. Abhayadeva cites Praśastapāda's *evaṃ dharmair vinā dharmiṇām uddeśaḥ kṛtaḥ* and discusses its problems and implications. The editors provide further relevant references. To these, we may add the two parallel passages in the *Prameyakamalamārtaṇḍa* (ed. Mahendra Kumar; Bombay, 1941, pp. 531ff.) and the *Nyāyakumudacandra* (ed. Mahendra Kumar; Bombay, 1938–1941, pp. 364ff.) by Abhayadeva's Digambara contemporary Prabhācandra.

122. See n. 108.

123. Maṇḍana, *Brahmasiddhi* (cited in n. 82), p. 89.

8

Genesis and Temporal Existence in Early and Classical Vaiśeṣika

1. As we have seen, Praśastapāda's *Padārthadharmasaṃgraha* tends to minimize the role of nonbeing and negation. Likewise, it has little to say about questions concerning genesis and temporal existence.[1] This standard text of classical Vaiśeṣika seems to be interested in entities, not processes. It tries to provide a complete inventory of what there is, without paying much attention to the relationship and possible transition between being and nonbeing. Yet this does not mean that nonbeing, genesis, and temporal existence are negligible, as far as classical Vaiśeṣika is concerned. They have their place and significance in Praśastapāda's thought, even if it is not a very conspicuous one. They constitute, moreover, a major, though elusive theme of Vaiśeṣika thought prior to the *Padārthadharmasaṃgraha*.

Among the explicit conceptualizations of being, *sattāsambandha*, "connection with reality," provides the most important point of reference. In addition to the systematic problems associated with this concept,[2] it has a complex and elusive history. Some apparently marginal modifications in its usage indicate major reorientations in Vaiśeṣika ontology, with significant implications for the history of Indian ontology in general. To trace these historical developments, we cannot limit ourselves to the extant Vaiśeṣika sources.

The term *sattāsambandha* does not occur in the Vaiśeṣikasūtra. As noted earlier, it is part of Praśastapāda's ontological vocabulary. It represents an abstract common property (*sādharmya*) of all those objects (i.e., substances, qualities, and motions) in which universals, including the supreme universal "reality" (*sattā*), inhere. As an abstract *sādharmya*, it is not to be confused with *sattā* itself.[3] In the *Padārthadharmasaṃgraha*, the term *sattāsambandha* does not answer or even address the question what being, reality, or existence is or what the words *to be* and *to exist* mean. Praśastapāda enumerates, classifies, and characterizes entities; he deals with what there is, not with the meaning of being. Furthermore, *sattāsambandha*, as used in Praśastapāda's only extant work, does not explain how or why something comes into being. It is not (certainly not explicitly) used to clarify the meaning of *genesis* or *production* (*utpatti*, *niṣpatti*, etc.) nor does it describe the state of being of entities that have been produced and come into existence; that is, of entities that have a cause and beginning and thus are impermanent. Praśastapāda distinguishes *sattāsambandha*, the state of something of which reality can be predicated, from *kāryatva*, "the state of being an effect," and *anityatva*, "impermanence."[4] Unlike *sattāsambandha*, these two abstract attributes apply only to those entities that have a cause and not to the eternal and ultimate substances, such as the atoms or ether.

2. However, there can hardly be any doubt that the *Padārthadharmasaṃgraha* was not the only text produced by Praśastapāda, who was also referred to as Praśastadeva, Praśastamati, Praśastakāra, Praśastakara, Praśastācārya, or simply as Praśasta. In addition, he seems to have written an extensive *Ṭīkā* on the Vaiśeṣikasūtras—which apparently did not deal with the Sūtra text directly, but rather with a lost *Bhāṣya* (probably on an equally lost *Vākya* on the Sūtras).[5] Although this *Ṭīkā* is no longer extant—obviously due to the great success of the *Padārthadharmasaṃgraha*, which overshadowed even the Sūtras themselves—we have at least a considerable number of references to and even quotes from it in other (primarily Jaina and Buddhist) works.

The most important indirect source on Praśastapāda's lost work, on the rather obscure phase of development between the Vaiśeṣikasūtras and the *Padārthadharmasaṃgraha*, and specifically on early Vaiśeṣika ontology, is a Jaina work, the *Dvādaśāranayacakra* or "Twelve-Spoked Wheel of Perspectives" by Mallavādin, a Śvetāmbara of the sixth century, which in its extant version is interwoven with its commentary, the *Nyāyāgamānusāriṇī* by Siṃhasūri (perhaps a century later). After two less convincing attempts, Mallavādin's text was successfully extracted from the commentary by one of the greatest modern Jaina scholars, Muni Jambuvijaya.[6]

We may say that the whole work deals with questions of being and nonbeing, presence and absence, assertion and negation. However, it does so in a very peculiar, decidedly Jaina fashion. Mallavādin, whose most important predecessor was Siddhasena Divākara,[7] does not deal with "ontology" per se; he does not try to determine or clarify the "meaning of being" as such. Instead, he surveys and classifies the various approaches to it; he uses ontology, the notions of positivity, negativity, of assertation, negation and restriction, as instruments or vehicles of doxographic classification—a classification that in his view coincides with a complete systematic survey of all perspectives on, or aspects of, one identical, but multifaceted reality. The term *naya* used in the title of the work refers to these "perspectives" or "modes of consideration." Mallavādin

> teaches three fundamental modes of considering things: general affirmation (vidhiḥ), affirmation and restriction (vidhiniyamam), pure restriction (niyamaḥ). In addition hereto each of these modes of consideration can be subject of the same three viewpoints, so that finally a total of twelve modes of consideration is brought about.

In this manner, he "believes to have exhausted all possibilities in the consideration of things."[8]

Mallavādin's scheme systematizes and radicalizes the traditional Jaina perspectivism, credits other views with a relative and limited validity, and accepts a variety of equally legitimate and limited approaches to reality. Instead of trying to establish the sheer falsity of individual doctrines, Jainism attempts to expose them in their one-sidedness and interdependence and to relegate them to their position in a totality of complementary perspectives. It does not negate them; it claims to include and transcend them in its own comprehensive framework. Mallavādin's "ontology" is thus inseparable from his inclusivistic and perspectivistic doxography. This implies that it is often difficult to distinguish between doxographic presentation and systematic reconstruction and extrapolation.

Just as the same human being may be called a father or a son, so the same being may be said to be or not to be, depending on its relation to other entities and on the perspective we choose.[9] The concrete reality of things (*vastutattva*) is such that it comprises both being and nonbeing (*sadasadātmaka*).[10] Instead of recognizing this multifaceted concreteness, the Vaiśeṣikas, as presented by Mallavādin, commit themselves to abstract and limited perspectives.

3. Among the Vaiśeṣika sources utilized by Mallavādin and his commentator Siṃhasūri, only one text is extant today: the Vaiśeṣikasūtras themselves. In addition, Mallavādin and Siṃhasūri mention, refer to, or quote from a series of commentaries and subcommentaries not available to us: the *Kaṭandī;* a *Vākya* on the Sūtras; a *Bhāṣya* on this *Vākya;* and Praśastamati's (or Praśasta's) *Ṭīkā* on the Bhāṣya.[11] Neither Mallavādin nor Siṃhasūri refer to Candramati's *Daśapadārthī.* More conspicuously, their utilization of (as well as acquaintance with) the *Padārthadharmasaṃgraha* appears extremely scanty and may be altogether dubious.[12] Among the important extant sources that Mallavādin does quote we find the *Nyāyasūtras,* Vasubandhu's *Abhidharmakośa,* Bhartṛhari's *Vākyapadīya* and Dignāga's *Pramāṇasamuccaya.*[13] Should Mallavādin have been a (younger) contemporary of Praśastapāda/ Praśastamati? Should he have known his *Ṭīkā,* but not the later *Padārthadharmasaṃgraha?* At any rate, he wrote at a time when the *Padārthadharmasaṃgraha* had not yet eclipsed the authority and popularity of earlier Vaiśeṣika's commentaries, including Praśastapāda's own earlier work.

Two issues, which are associated with the first and ninth chapters of the Vaiśeṣikasūtras, dominate Mallavādin's presentation and critique:[14]

1. Reality, *sattā,* as *sadabhidhānapratyayahetu,* as cause of the name and notion "real"; that is, as a universal inhering in whatever is real.
2. The relationship between the "real" and the "unreal" (*sat, asat*), the possibility of a transition from the one to the other, and the nature of origination or production (*utpatti*).

Mallavādin examines the thesis that *sattā* is indispensable as cause or counterpart of the predicate "real" in remarkable detail. He also discusses the problem of the application of the predicate "real" to universals, and so forth, which are supposed to be without the universal "reality" (*sattā*); and he invokes the possibility of a "metaphorical" (*aupacārika*) application and refers to the simile of a (fierce) person who is metaphorically called *lion* (*manuṣyasiṃhatva*): Could universals, too, be "real" in a metaphorical sense?[15]

However, from the number of references and the intensity of his argumentation, it is clear that the second issue, which is the issue of the ninth Adhyāya and inseparable from the controversy between *satkāryavāda* and *asatkāryavāda,* is the more important one for Mallavādin. It is in this connection that the concepts of *sattāsambandha, svakāraṇasambandha* and *svakāraṇasattāsambandha* are introduced and the "dilemma about being and nonbeing" (*sadasadvikalpa*) is presented and discussed in a variety of perspectives and applications. There is hardly any other text in which this familiar and notorious device of Indian ontological debate receives equally penetrating attention. In particular, the argumentation focuses on Sūtra IX,12 (*sadasator vaidharmyāt sadasattā na*), which Mallavādin and Siṃhasūri take as an explicit reference to the Jaina standpoint of "inclusive relativism" and to which they respond accordingly.[16] One of the most memorable discussions of the *sadasadvikalpa*—that is, of the question whether those substances, and so on, which *sattā* renders real, are real, unreal, or both real and unreal prior to their connection with reality (*prāk sattāsambandhāt satāṃ vā-asatāṃ vā sadasatāṃ vā dravyādīnāṃ satkarī sattā?*)—appears in conjunction with a citation of Sūtra IX,12.[17] In Mallavādin's presentation, this is not just a dilemma, but a trilemma: The inherence of *sattā* is equally absurd in what is real, unreal, or both real and unreal. Elsewhere, Mallavādin and Siṃhasūri cite the *Vaiśeṣikakaṭandī* and Praśastamati's *Ṭīkā* on the *Vaiśeṣikabhāṣya* in connection with Sūtra IX,12.[18]

In general, the ninth Adhyāya of the Vaiśeṣikasūtra appears as the Vaiśeṣika statement in the *satkārya-asatkārya* debate. This is why it is at the center of Mallavādin's presentation.

4. While the Vaiśeṣikasūtras leave the ontological issues discussed in the first and ninth Adhyāyas virtually unconnected, the *Padārthadharmasaṃgraha* tends to disregard altogether the topic of the ninth Adhyāya; that is, *asat* and *asatkārya*. For Mallavādin, on the other hand, as well as for the Sūtra commentators to whom he refers, this connection seems to have been a crucial issue, accounting for the significance as well as the inherent difficulties of the concept of *sattāsambandha:* What does the universal "reality," the "cause of the name and notion 'real'," as postulated in the first Adhyāya, have to do with the distinction between "real" and "unreal" and the discourse on "nonbeing" in the ninth Adhyāya, and with the explanation of production and the articulation of the *asatkārya* position?

In the *Padārthadharmasaṃgraha, sattāsambandha* does not explain "coming into being" or "production" (*utpatti,* etc.) nor does it deal with the question what *kāryatva* is; that is, the state of being of effects, of entities that have come into being.

Sattāsambandha as used in the *Padārthadharmasaṃgraha* can be paraphrased as *sattāvattva,* "having reality as a predicate." It applies to eternal, irreducible substances (including time itself) as well as to anything that has an origin (and end) in time; in this role, *sattāsambandha* is clearly distinguished from *kāryatva,* "being an effect." The terms *svakāraṇasambandha* and *svakāraṇasattāsambandha* do not occur at all in the *Padārthadharmasaṃgraha.* For Mallavādin, on the other hand, the connection between *sattāsambandha, kāryatva,* and the *asatkārya* debate is essential, and the concepts of *sattāsambandha* and *svakāraṇasambandha* form an inseparable complex: In his presentation, they constitute an attempt to explain the event of origination or production as well as the status of entities that have been produced and thus have a temporal origin.[19]

According to Mallavādin, certain Vaiśeṣika authors may have used the concept of *sattāsambandha* (or *sattāsamavāya*) to distinguish temporal, composite entities from the eternal substances, such as atoms or ether. In this view, the status of impermanent, causally dependent entities alone can be described as *sattāsambandha,* a "connection with reality" that is not part of the very nature of the entity and has a beginning (and end) in time. Eternal and uncaused substances, on the other hand, exist by virtue of their own self-sufficient reality or identity (*svasadbhāva*); they are thus credited with a mode of being (*svabhāvasattā, svarūpasattā*) that the *Padārthadharmasaṃgraha* seems to reserve for universals, and so forth:

> *nityotpannatvāt svasadbhāvena-eva santi paramāṇvākāśādīni, kāryadravyaguṇakarmaṇām eva sattāsamavāyāt sattvam iti* (Atoms, ether, and so forth, exist by virtue of their own inherent reality, since they are always present; the occurrence of causally dependent substances, qualities, and motions is due to the inherence of reality).[20]

Was this view that only effects, impermanent entities, have *sattāsambandha* actually held within the Vaiśeṣika school? Was it Mallavādin's own "constructive" addition or extrapolation? At any rate, it would seem to be a tactical and evasive suggestion, avoiding the more fundamental questions and paradoxes concerning *sattāsambandha* and the "dilemma about being and nonbeing": What is there so that it can enter into a conjunction with "reality"? What is the nature of the conjunction? What kind of reality or being does it add to what the relata "are" for themselves? What is the relationship between "coming into being," physical origination and occurrence, and "possession" of the attribute "reality"? What is the relationship between grammar and cosmology? "Is" there a merely "physical" substratum in which the universal "reality" inheres and that "has" the predicate "real"?

5. Mallavādin uses the expression *tattvopanilayana* ("descent, taking residence, of predicable essences") and Siṃhasūri speaks of *dravyatvanilayana* "descent of substanceness," etc., to describe the process of connection of a bare something (*vastumātra*) with its qualifying and predicable universals, which include in all cases "reality."[21] We do not know whether these terms were actually used in Vaiśeṣika literature, or whether Mallavādin and Siṃhasūri introduced them as devices of critical analysis.

At any rate, the idea of a something capable of serving as substratum for "reality" and other universals receives much more attention in the *Dvādaśāranayacakra* than in any extant Vaiśeṣika text; Mallavādin insists that its nature has to be accounted for. It cannot be utterly fictitious, such as a sky-flower, which will never attain "connection with reality": *prāk tat sattāsambandhāt kimātmakam iti svarūpāvadhāraṇaṃ kāryam, anyathā-asattvāt* ("One has to determine its essence, i.e., answer the question what it is like prior to its connection with reality; because otherwise it would not be there").[22]

Repeatedly, Mallavādin refers to a general distinction of two modes or meanings of being in Vaiśeṣika; that is, "self-identity" (*svabhāva*) and "connection" (*sambandha*): *dvividho hi bhāvaḥ, svabhāvaḥ sambandhaś ca, svabhāvaḥ svarūpasattā, sambandhaḥ sambandhasattā yatsambandhāt dravyaguṇakarmasu sad iti bhavati.*[23] This seems to correspond to the distinction between *sattāsambandha* and *svātmasattva* in the *Padārthadharmasaṃgraha;* yet, the differences are equally obvious. The application of *svarūpasattā/svātmasattva* to the bare substrates of "reality" and other universals is far less explicit, if not altogether elusive, in the Vaiśeṣika literature available today.[24] Does this mean that Mallavādin is unreliable? Should there have been ontological distinctions different from those in the *Padārthadharmasaṃgraha?*

Mallavādin also applies the word *astitva* to what is supposedly there as a substratum even without the universal "reality" residing in it: *atha āśrayisamavāyād ṛte 'pi kāryaṃ svena-eva astitvena-utpannam āśrayo bhavati, khapuṣpavaidharmyeṇa.*[25] Siṃhasūri paraphrases *astitva* as *svabhāvasattā,* "reality as self-identity," "self-sufficient reality."[26] He associates the distinction between "self-sufficient reality" (*svabhāvasadbhāva*) and "reality due to connection" (*sambandhasadbhāva*) with Praśastamati's response to the *sadasadvikalpa* and notes that Praśastamati did not consider products to be utterly without identity or essence (*atyantanirātmaka*) prior to the actual event of production. He adds that a product, such as a substance, is a real entity insofar as it inheres in its material causes, but that it has an identity of its own even without the connection with reality, and that it is not as essenceless as a donkey's horn (*ato dravyādi sat, tat tu svakāraṇeṣu samavetaṃ vastv eva, sattāsambandharahitam api sātmakam eva, na kharaviṣāṇādivad nirātmakam*).[27]

According to Mallavādin and Siṃhasūri, the Vaiśeṣikas also invoke a grammatical ambiguity to resolve the apparent contradiction between such quasi-being of the substrate of production and the basic premise of their *asatkāryavāda;* that is, the nonexistence of the effect or product prior to its production: There is no contradiction if *asat* (as in *prāgasat* and *asatkārya*) is taken as a *bahuvrīhi* compound. In this sense, *asat* refers to something that does not "*possess*" reality, but may well "*be*" an identifiable something (*sātmaka*); that is, a nonvacuous, nonfictitious nature or essence—just as *aputrabrāhmaṇa* means a real brahmin without a son and *aguṇaguṇa* a real quality in which no quality inheres: *katham asya sātmakatvam? na, anekāntāt, aputrabrāhmaṇavad aguṇaguṇavat. yathā na-asya putro 'sti ity aputro brāhmaṇaḥ na-asya guṇo 'sti-ity aguṇo guṇah, tathā-iha-api na-asya sad ity asat.*[28]

What is not yet, the *prāgasat,* is not simply nothing, though it is still without the qualifying, determining universals (including *sattā*) that make it accessible to identification and predication. Its being is made "complete" (*saṃpūrṇa*) in the act of production; "connection with reality" means actualization, manifestation, completion of what has a self-sufficient, yet defective "being for itself," *svabhāvasadbhāva.* Such completion is required for the "bare" substrates as well as for the universals, including *sattā*, which are "incomplete," unmanifest, as long as they are not exemplified, instantiated in particulars: *evaṃ tarhi sāmānyasattāyāḥ sattā avyaktiḥ kiñcit satī, na saṃpūrṇā satī, ekasadbhāvatvāt svasattāvat, svabhāvasadbhāvatvāt asamavetasattākāni dravyādīni yathā*.[29]

6. Are these notions of "complete" and "incomplete" being genuine Vaiśeṣika concepts? Do they imply an admission of "potentiality," nonactualized being, which the Vaiśeṣikas generally try to avoid but which is crucial for the Sāṃkhya *satkāryavāda?* Mallavādin suggests that the being of something that is not "connected" with "reality" and other universals might, indeed, be comparable to the potentiality of the Sāṃkhya *pradhāna* or primeval nature.[30] And could not *sattā* itself, insofar as it has not been manifested and exemplified through a "connection" with particular entities, be interpreted as a mere storehouse of potentialities or as potentiality par excellence? Would it, too, not be comparable to the Sāṃkhya *pradhāna?* Mallavādin says:

> In this way, *sattā*, as conceived by you (the Vaiśeṣikas), would also be primeval nature, because it is destined to bring about all sorts of experiences, just as the three guṇas function for the sake of the spirit. (*pradhānam api ca-evaṃ syād bhavatparikalpitā sattā viśvarūpopabhogapratipādanārthatvāt puruṣārthatvād guṇatrayavat*)[31]

This is obviously not what Praśastapāda or any other classical Vaiśeṣika teacher meant to say. We can readily agree with Siṃhasūri when he states: "And this is undesirable" (*aniṣṭaṃ ca-etad*).[32]

Nonetheless, Mallavādin and Siṃhasūri have proceeded from certain basic premises of Vaiśeṣika thought, and they have exploited some of its inherent problems and ambiguities. We noticed earlier the deceptive simplicity of Praśastapāda's notion of *astitva*, with its apparently clear and simple subdivision into *sattāsambandha* (for the first three categories) and *svātmasattva* (for the second group of categories).[33] Are *sattāsambandha* and *svātmasattva* mutually exclusive? Is the concept of *svātmasattva* utterly inapplicable to the first three categories? Do certain entities have *sattāsambandha* in addition to *svātmasattva?* What is the precise relationship between *astitva* and *sattāsambandha?* Are *sattāsambandha* and *svātmasattva* modes of *astitva*, or are they somehow added to it? We have seen that the *Padārthadharmasaṃgraha* does not have an explicit answer to these questions, although some relevant conclusions may be drawn from the structure of the system.

Śrīdhara's commentary *Nyāyakandalī* is more explicit. It states that *astitva* is nothing but being an identifiable nature (*svarūpa, svarūpavattva*) and that the universal reality could never inhere in what is without such identifiability or specificity. *Sattāsambandha* is thus somehow added to *astitva*.[34] This seems to imply that *astitva* (which is identified with *svarūpavattva* and thus inseparable from *svātmasattva*) and *sattāsambandha* have to be combined to account for the concrete reality and actuality of those entities which are included in the first group of categories (i.e., substances, etc.). Whatever the further implications of Śrīdhara's explanation may be, it seems to be basically compatible with Mallavādin's and Siṃhasūri's exposition and thus vulnerable to their critique.

Mallavādin unfolds the implications of Praśastapāda's ontological thought and extrapolates its potential consequences. Yet in addition, he also provides valuable doxographic information. This is most significant when it comes to the concept of *sattāsambandha* and its association with genesis and temporal existence in early Vaiśeṣika.

7. We have referred to the notion of *nilayana*, the way in which the universals, and so on, "take residence" in their particular instances. Something has to be there for the universals to take up such residence. But mere undifferentiated matter would not be enough. Specific universals are supposed to reside in specific substrates; they do not inhere at random. Substanceness will inhere only in substances, qualityness in qualities, and so forth.[35] Such "regularity of residence" (*nilayananiyama*) requires substrates that are distinguishable and specific even apart from their connection with qualifying and specifying universals (*athavā viśeṣaṇasambandham antareṇa-api vastumātrāṇāṃ parasparātiśayo 'sti, tena viśeṣaṇasambandhaniyamasiddhiḥ*). Mallavādin presents this as an explicit Vaiśeṣika teaching, even as a quote.[36]

It would certainly be uncautious to accept Mallavādin's and Siṃhasūri's account in all its details. Yet, their references and quotes seem to provide clear evidence that already the pre-Praśastapāda commentators offered different explanations of the respective functions and the relationship of *sattāsambandha* and *svakāraṇasambandha*, of their role concerning "production" (*utpatti*), and of the "dilemma about being and nonbeing" (*sadasadvikalpa*).

According to Mallavādin, "many" said that the connection with (the universal) *sattā* is, in an obviously temporal sense, posterior to the inherence of an entity in its causes, that is, its actual physical origination, and that it accounts not for its occurrence as such, but for its nameability as "real," *sat*. Others, specifically the authors of the Vākya and its Bhāṣya, said that *sattāsambandha* occurs simultaneously with the actual origination of the thing, whereas Praśastamati, as referred to by Mallavādin, held that both "connection with reality" and "connection with (or inherence in) its own causes" apply to a something (*vastu*) which is already there: *tattvopanilayanāt sadādyabhidhānārthaṃ kāraṇasamavetasya vastuna uttarakālaṃ sattāsambandha iti bahūnāṃ matam. vastūtpattikāle eva iti tu vākyakārābhiprāyo 'nusṛto bhāṣyakāraiḥ. siddhasya vastunaḥ svakāraṇaiḥ svasattayā ca sambandha iti prāśastamato 'bhiprāyaḥ.*[37]

The theory that "completion" and "connection with reality" (and the "own causes") are simultaneous (*niṣṭhāsambandhayor ekakālatvam*) had been introduced earlier as a Vaiśeṣika attempt to solve or circumvent the "dilemma about being and nonbeing." The claim is that the dilemma does not apply if the completion coincides with the connection; or rather, if the product, while being completed, is simultaneously connected with its material causes and with universals, such as reality (*na doṣaḥ, niṣṭhāsambandhayor ekakālatvāt. . . . svakāraṇasattāsambandha eva niṣṭhākālaḥ, kutaḥ? samavāyasya-ekatvāt. yasminn eva kāle pariniṣthām gacchat kāryaṃ kāraṇaiḥ sambadhyate samavāyasambandhena ayutasiddhihetunā, tasminn eva kāle sattādibhir api*).[38] According to Mallavādin, this is, of course, no solution at all, because it does not address the fundamental question: Before the "connection," there is nothing with which it could take place. And this is why Praśasta had to reinterpret the theory of simultaneity as proposed in the Vākya and Bhāṣya:

> In order to eliminate connection with what is unreal, Praśasta explains the statement in the Vākya, *niṣṭhāsambandhyor ekakālatvāt*, together with the Bhāṣya, in a different way. One connection and another connection—these are two connections (i.e., this accounts for the dual *sambandhau*); *niṣṭhāsambandhau* means two connections with what is called *niṣṭhā;*—because of their simultaneity. *Niṣṭhā*——that means *niṣṭhita*, "accomplished"; it means the completed, accomplished product, with an undefined substrate, which has attained the status of an entity because of the momentum of the causal factors. For this, the connections with reality and its own

causes take place simultaneously (*asatsambandhaparihārārthaṃ niṣṭhāsambandhayor ekakālatvāt ity etad vākyam sabhāṣyaṃ praśasto 'nyathā vyācaṣṭe—sambandhaś ca sambandhaś ca sambandhau, niṣṭhāyāḥ sambandhau niṣṭhāsambandhau, tayor ekakālatvāt. niṣṭhitaṃ niṣṭhā, kārakaparispandād vastubhāvam āpannam avyapadeśyādhāraṃ kāryaṃ niṣṭhitaṃ niṣṭhā ity ucyate, tasya svakāraṇaiḥ sattayā ca yugapat sambandhau bhavataḥ.*).[39]

8. According to Praśasta's interpretation of the formula *niṣṭhāsambandhayor ekakālatvāt, niṣṭhā,* and *sambandha* are not coordinated in a dual *dvandva* compound. Instead, there are two simultaneous "connections" with something already established as a *vastu* and capable of entering into relationships of inherence with its causes as well as the universal "reality" and an appropriate set of more specific universals. The effect has to be there, as an undefined bare substratum (*avyapadeśyādhāra*), before it can inhere in its causes and before the appropriate universals (including *sattā*) can inhere in it. And this seems to involve not only a logical, but also a temporal priority.

What Mallavādin reports seems to be a crude and futile attempt to distinguish and interrelate matters of physical or cosmological explanation and of grammatical or conceptual analysis. The "many" to whom Mallavādin refers arrange this in a temporal sequence: The thing as merely physical effect, inhering in and produced out of its causes, and the thing as correlate of speech and thought, or words and concepts, arise in temporal succession. Predicates, including "reality," are added to what is already there in a nonconceptualized mode of being. The *Vākya* and the *Bhāṣya* postulate that the two events are simultaneous, that the advent of "reality" and other universals coincides with the production of an effect out of its causes and in fact explains it in that it accounts for the *ātmalābha,* the manner in which the effect assumes its identity as a new thing; this is also meant to take care of that part of the *sadasadvikalpa,* which implies that the addition of "reality" to something that is already there would be redundant. However, it brings back the other side of the dilemma, that there cannot be connection with what is not there—a problem that Praśasta(mati) tries to resolve by his reinterpretation of the principle of simultaneity. He abandons the attempt to explain production (*utpatti*) by *sattāsambandha* or *svakāraṇasambandha;* both already presuppose some sort of entity (*vastu*). Is this begging the question? Indeed, it leaves production unexplained; but it also indicates a basic reorientation, a dissociation from older preoccupations of Vaiśeṣika thought: Praśastapāda focuses on the analysis of things as they are, on a kind of composition that is not physical composition and production; he deals with "what there is" and divides it into irreducible "categories." But the context and horizon of his "categorial analysis" of things remains that of cosmology and philosophy of nature.

Mallavādin's presentation is obviously critical and polemical; yet, it is not necessarily a misrepresentation. The tendency to construe the world out of separable constituents, to postulate bare, yet distinctive substrates, to furnish them with a garment of qualities, universals, and other attributes, and to add reality itself to what is already there—this tendency still dominates classical and even later Vaiśeṣika and accounts for some of its characteristic problems and paradoxes.[40] The universal glue of *samavāya*, "inherence," has certainly not been able to solve or cover all problems and to answer all questions.

9. The *Dvādaśāranayacakra* is a unique document. However, the problems of Vaiśeṣika ontology, and of ontology in general, are also discussed by other Jaina authors, for instance Haribhadra and Akalaṅka[41] (eighth century): Various writers refer specifically to the concept of *sattāsambandha* and the "dilemma about being and nonbeing," although usually in a much more summary and stereotyped fashion than Mallavādin. Already Jinabhadra, possibly Mallavādin's older contemporary and apparently not acquainted with Praśastapāda/ Praśastamati,[42] refers to the notion of *sattāyoga* (Ardhamāgadhī: *sattājoga;* "conjunction with reality"). He discusses the "dilemma about being and nonbeing" in connection with Vaiśeṣikasūtra I,2,8 (*dravyaguṇakarmabhyo 'rthāntaram sattā*): *sattājogād asato sato va sattam havejja davvassa / asato ṇa khapupphassa va sato va kiṃ sattayā kajjam?* His autocommentary offers a concise summary of the "dilemma" in Sanskrit (*ato dravyasya sattāyogāt sattāsamavāyāt svayaṃ sato vidyamānasya sattvam bhavati, ahosvid avidyamānasya*).[43]

This passage seems to confirm what we may conclude as well from Mallavādin's and Siṃhasūri's presentation: *Sattāsambandha* and the "dilemma about being and nonbeing" had become familiar issues of debate before Praśastapāda. It is, however, remarkable that Mallavādin's predecessor Siddhasena Divākara never refers to the problems of *sattāsambandha.* While criticizing the Vaiśeṣika theory of origination (*utpāda;* Ardhamāgadhī: *uppāya*), he mentions the idea that new substances are supposed to originate from the conjunction of causal substances (*davvaṃtarasaṃjogāhi keci daviyassa beṃti uppāyam*).[44] But it is only his tenth-century commentator Abhayadevasūri who cites the notion of *sattāsambandha* in his explanation of this passage: "Connection with reality" cannot explain the beginning of a new entity, its temporal transition from nonexistence to existence; nor does the "simultaneity of origination and connection with reality" (*utpattisattāsambandhayor ekakālatā*) provide an acceptable solution.[45]

Among the later Jaina commentators, Prabhācandra (eleventh century) devotes attention to this topic in his two works *Nyāyakumudacandra* and *Prameyakamalamārtaṇḍa*. He discusses the various possibilities of analyzing the compound *svakāraṇasattāsambandha:* Does it mean inherential connection (of an effect) with its causes *and* the universal "reality" (*svakāraṇa* and *sattā* in a *dvandva* relationship)? Does it mean connection with the reality of the causes (*tatpuruṣa*)? Or is it inherence in the causes which is connected with reality? (*kiṃ kāryasya svakāraṇaiḥ sattayā ca samavāyaḥ, kiṃ vā svakāraṇānaṃ sattayā samavāyaḥ, ahosvit sattayā yuktas tatsamavāya iti*).[46]

In the *Nyāyakumudacandra,* Prabhācandra pursues the issue into all its more or less familiar implications and ramifications. This discussion is supplemented by closely corresponding passages in the *Prameyakamalamārtaṇḍa,*[47] where Prabhācandra also addresses the fundamental problem how change and temporal events can be construed out of such static, timeless factors as "inherence," "reality," and so on.[48]

10. The Jaina texts and most other sources usually associate the "dilemma about being and nonbeing" with the concept of *sattāsambandha* (*sattāsamavāya, sattāyoga*). However, the *sadasadvikalpa* does not necessarily presuppose this concept; and as a matter of fact, it is a much older issue of debate. Vātsyāyana's *Nyāyabhāṣya,* which shows no familiarity with *sattāsambandha,* discusses the "dilemma about being and nonbeing" in the context of the *satkārya-asatkārya* debate and in connection with Sūtra IV,1,47: This Sūtra, presenting a *pūrvapakṣa,* states that prior to its production the result can neither be real nor unreal nor both. It has been suggested that this is a reference to Nāgārjuna's Madhyamaka position. At any rate, Uddyotakara's *Nyāyavārttika* develops the threefold scheme of the Sūtra and Bhāṣya into a full Madhyamaka tetralemma (*catuṣkoṭi*) by adding "neither real nor unreal."[49]

There can be no doubt that the dilemmatic structure of the *sadasadvikalpa* and its reductive application to the theories of *satkārya* and *asatkārya* reflect Nāgārjuna's method, as exemplified by the first chapter, the "Examination of Causality" (*Pratyayaparīkṣā*), in his *Mūlamadhyamakakārikā*. Nāgārjuna himself never refers to the concept of *sattāsambandha*, and the "Examination of Causality" is apparently not primarily aimed at Sāṃkhya and Vaiśeṣika, but at intra-Buddhist controversies. We have noticed earlier that the *satkārya-asatkārya* debate had its parallels and antecedents in Buddhism. The basic dilemma concerning the "existence" or "nonexistence" of the effect in its material cause, and the general ontological ambiguity of the relationship between cause and effect, could certainly be articulated before the Vaiśeṣika concept of *sattāsambandha* had been developed.

However, already Nāgārjuna's follower Āryadeva (ca. A.D. 200) seems to refer to "connection with reality" as an attempt to explain the actual occurrence of entities. In a section of his *Śataśāstra*, which is extant only in a Chinese version, he discuses and rejects the theory that an entity like a pot is real because it is combined with reality ("united with existence").[50] More than a century later, Harivarman's *Satyasiddhi* (also called *Tattvasiddhi*), a Sautrāntika text which, once again, has survived only in Chinese, lists various attempts to ascertain and define "being" or "reality," and among them, it mentions and rejects the theory that "being" consists in a connection with the attribute (*dharma;* Chinese: *fa*) "reality."[51] However, this is perhaps nothing more than a reference to the idea in *Vaiśeṣikasūtra* I,2,7–8 that to account for the recurrent notion "real" in all substances and so forth we have to assume the presence of a pervasive factor "reality," *sattā*. It seems that there is no clear evidence that either Harivarman or Āryadeva was aware of the specific role of *sattāsambandha/svakāraṇasambandha* in connection with the problems of production (*utpatti*), or of other more technical implications.

More precise references and criticisms are found in the literature of the Dignāga school. Dignāga himself was clearly aware of the attempt to explain production as "inherence (i.e., the emergence and dependent existence of the product) in its own causes" or as "inherence of reality" and other, more specific universals. He discusses it in connection with the Mīmāṃsā theory of *buddhijanma*, "birth," "production" of cognition; and he indicates that the Mīmāṃsakas (before Śabara) had to borrow this explanation of "production" from the Vaiśeṣikas, as they did not have a suitable explanation of their own.[52] The commentator Jinendrabuddhi gives two interpretations of *buddhijanma,* which illustrate this specific application of the Vaiśeṣika concepts to the production of cognition: (1) the inherence of cognition in its causal substrate, the self (*buddher ātmani svakāraṇe samavāyaḥ*); (2) the inherence of (the universals) reality, qualityness, and cognitiveness in cognition (*sattāguṇatvabuddhitvānām buddhau samavāyaḥ*).[53] Dignāga's argumentation was cited by several Mīmāṃsakas, for instance, by Kumārila's commentator Sucaritamiśra.[54]

11. The relative chronology of Praśastapāda and Dignāga has been an issue of debate. The stronger (though still inconclusive) arguments seem to support Dignāga's priority. Accordingly, his references to *sattāsambandha* and *svakāraṇasambandha* would seem to confirm what we have concluded from Mallavādin's presentation: These concepts had become both familiar and controversial prior to Praśastapāda. What is more, already Bhartṛhari, whose work was known to Dignāga, used the term *sattāsambandha* and seems to have been aware of the "dilemma about being and nonbeing."[55] Of course, Bhartṛhari's nondualistic, yet dynamic metaphysics of the word provided a comprehensive framework of ontological thought and critique that was meant to include and supersede the ontology and categoriology of the Vaiśeṣika, and to reconcile the antagonism of *satkāryavada* and *asatkāryavada*.[56]

Dignāga's argumentation was continued and expanded by Dharmakīrti and his commentators. Dharmakīrti repudiated the ideas of "connection" (*sambandha*) with reality (i.e., inherence of reality) and "union with one's causes" (*svakāraṇaśleṣa*) and suggested that *sattā* and *samavāya,* being eternal or timeless factors, could not possibly account for change and temporal events, such as production or destruction.[57] This issue, also referred to by Dignāga, is particularly significant for the Buddhists. In their view, the basic premises of the Vaiśeṣika ontology and cosmology would ultimately imply an entirely permanent (*nitya*) and static universe and provide no room for temporality and change.[58]

Yat sat tat kṣaṇikam: Whatever there is, is momentary, in a state of flux. Being itself is decay, constant loss of identity (*bhāva eva nāśaḥ*). If we do not accept impermanence, constant change, incessant production and destruction as the very heart of reality, we cannot account for it at all. We cannot construe it a posteriori out of fictions of stability, identity, and universality. No way leads back from the timeless universal, the hypostatic abstraction "reality" (*sattā*) into the real world of impermanence and constant loss of identity. *Sattā* is a convention, rooted in the false belief in the self (*ātman*). It is a projection of our thirst for identity and continuity, the empty shell of our desire and nescience. How could the idea of *sattāsambandha,* connection with such "reality," help us to understand the real world?

The Buddhists who criticize the Vaiśeṣika *asatkāryavada* do so from the angle of a much more radical *asatkāryavāda.* For the Sāṃkhya *satkāryavādins,* on the other hand, there is no real production, no coming into being. Hence, there is no need to explain it and no use for the conceptual artifice (*svakāraṇa*)*sattāsambandha.* To say that something is made, arises, or is born is just conventional linguistic behavior; ultimately, there is no production or destruction (*kriyate utpadyate jāyata ity evamādir lokasya vyavahāraḥ pravartate . . . paramārthatas tu na kasyacid utpādo 'sti na vināśaḥ*). In reality, there is only "manifestation" (*āvirbhava*), "specific arrangement" (*saṃniveśaviśeṣa*), and so forth.[59] Nothing can come from nothing; no "connection with reality" can bring into being what did not exist before; no connection is possible with what is not already there. And if being could come out of nonbeing: Why do certain alleged nonentities come into being, whereas others, such as sky flowers or hare's horns, do not? How can there be rule and regularity in what is not there?[60]

12. From the Sāṃkhya and Yoga perspective, *svakāraṇasambandha* and *sattāsambandha* (often interpreted as alternative explanations of origination, *utpatti*[61]) present equally futile attempts to avoid the notions of potency, potentiality, latency, indefiniteness, and subtleness (*avyakta, śakti, sūkṣma,* etc.) and to understand this empirical universe of identifiable and distinguishable entities without assuming primeval nature (*pradhāna, prakṛti*) as its indefinite, nonmanifest, nonactualized ground. The Vaiśeṣikas and Naiyāyikas try to construe our actual world out of manifest, definite, actualized (*vyakta, kṛtaka*) causes or constituents: "The manifest comes from the manifest" (*vyaktād vyaktam utpadyate*).[62] The atoms themselves, the ultimate causes and substrates, are irreducibly manifest, individualized, particularized in space (*vyakta, kṛtaka, paricchinnadeśa*);[63] universals and so forth are factors of qualification. Individuality, definiteness, and actuality govern the Vaiśeṣika universe. Being is well-defined, well-demarcated being; existence is actual existence. There is no world ground of potentiality, no *pradhāna* or *prakṛti.* Potentiality is relegated to the realm of (prior or posterior) nonbeing. Causation is not actualization of the nonactual, but production of new actualities out of preexisting, underlying actualities. In Sāṃkhya and Yoga, on the other hand, the causal state is a potential one; actuality is of the nature of an effect or product (*kāraṇaṃ śaktiḥ, kāryaṃ pravṛttiḥ*).[64] Past and future themselves are relegated to and explained as potential, nonmanifest, "subtle" (*sūkṣma*) modes of being.[65] Time itself, or its division into past, present, and future, appears as derivative, subordinated to the scheme of actuality and potentiality.

Indeed, there is no nonmanifest "nature" (*prakṛti, pradhāna*), no world ground of potentiality for the Vaiśeṣikas. But do they succeed in avoiding potentiality altogether? Do they in fact try to avoid it? Candramati, the "unorthodox" Vaiśeṣika teacher, adds "potentiality" and "nonpotentiality" (*śakti, aśakti*) to his list of categories.[66] Praśastapāda, of course, does not include them in his inventory of world constituents. Yet, potentiality continues to play its role, though evasive and unacknowledged, even in "orthodox" Vaiśeṣika. *Śakti* and related terms appear in various places, as the "power" of causes to produce their effects or as the "power" of particulars to "manifest" their appropriate universals.[67] In general, the ideas of "manifestation" and "actualization" have a tenacious, though highly elusive and problematic presence in the Vaiśeṣika attempts to explain the relationship between universals and particulars. Quite apart from all the technical difficulties pointed out by critics like Dharmakīrti—is this not an undesirable admission of "potentiality"? And is not *sattā* itself, if not actualized and exemplified through *sattāsambandha,* sheer potentiality and as such (as suggested by Mallavādin and Siṃhasūri) comparable to the "primeval nature" (*pradhāna*) of Sāṃkhya?[68] In spite of all objections and difficulties, classical Vaiśeṣika consistently avoids interpreting its universals as potentialities (and the highest universal, *sattā,* as potentiality per se). Unlike Bhartṛhari, it does not view the universals as cosmic matrixes, even though they constitute the eternal framework of all things that can come into existence. Bhartṛhari, on the other hand, provides us with a comprehensive reinterpretation of the Vaiśeṣika universals in terms of his philosophy of powers and dynamic potentialities (*śakti*); he may have been inspired by texts that are not available to us.[69]

13. Reciprocating the Sāṃkhya criticism, the Naiyāyikas and Vaiśeṣikas turn the "dilemma about being and nonbeing" (*sadasadvikalpa*) against the Sāṃkhya ideas of manifestation and modification: How can manifestation itself take place? Does it occur as something that did or did not exist before? Does it have to be "produced" and added to what is not yet manifest? Does it simply have to be manifested? Would this not lead to an infinite regress? Vācaspatimiśra summarizes this counterapplication of the *sadasadvikalpa* as follows:

> *āvirbhāvaḥ paṭasya kāraṇavyāpārāt prāk sann asan vā. sa ced asan prāptam asata utpādanam. atha san, kṛtaṃ tarhi karaṇena.* (Prior to the application of the causes, the manifestation of the cloth is either real or unreal. If it is unreal, then the production of something unreal is established. If, instead, it is real, then production is unnecessary).[70]

Bhārsarvajña reports that the Sāṃkhya teacher Mādhava (around A.D. 500) admitted that manifestation (*abhivyakti*) is something new, a factor or ingredient (*dharma*) that has to be added to what becomes manifest. According to Bhāsarvajña, this would amount to *asatkāryavāda* (*yadi hy abhivyaktir anyo vā kaścid dharmo 'sann eva kriyate*); and it would destroy the very fundamentals of the Sāṃkhya doctrine.[71]

However, it is not only Mādhava, the so-called destroyer of Sāṃkhya (*sāṃkhyanāśaka*), who uses such language; and what he says is perhaps not just a concession to the arguments of the Vaiśeṣikas and Naiyāyikas. The Yoga teaches the "replacement" of "modes" (*bhāva*) and so forth and the production of new dharmas—although in substrates (*dharmin*) which are supposed to remain identical: It teaches the "change of modes, characters and states" (*bhāvalakṣaṇāvasthānyathātva*). It is symptomatic that the word *utpatti,* "production," appears in its own definition of *pariṇāma,* "modification": *avasthitasya dravyasya pūrvadharmanivṛttau dharmāntarotpattiḥ.*[72] Insofar, it is understandable, though ultimately inconclusive, that W. Liebenthal saw a reference to Patañjali's Yoga in Vātsyāyana Pakṣilasvāmin's remark "what is not (yet) real comes into being" (*asad utpadyate*) in his commentary on Nyāyasūtra I,1,29.[73]

Uddyotakara tries to expose the futility of all attempts to define manifestation (*abhivyakti*) without production; that is, without something new coming into existence. The notion of an effect (*kārya*) itself implies that something is made (*kriyate*) or produced; and this is incompatible with the idea of mere manifestation. Nor does it help to say that the effect is a *dharma,* a (new) attribute or ingredient of a persistent and identical substrate. And it is equally futile to claim that manifestation is just "awareness relating to the effect" (*upalabdhiḥ kāryaviṣayā*), a state of being (*avasthāna*), a special arrangement (*saṃsthānaviśeṣa*), or an "unfolding of the own nature of the cause" (*kāraṇasya svalakṣaṇapuṣṭiḥ*). In all cases, manifestation implies that something occurs without having existed before (*abhūtvā bhavati*); that is, the advent of something new (*apūrvābhyāgama*).[74]

Manifestation has to be subsumed under production: It is just a "special case of production" (*utpatter viśeṣaḥ*).[75] There is no change or modification (*pariṇāma*) of any kind that does not imply some sort of replacement and a coming into being of what did not exist before. The concept of "permanence in change" (*pariṇāminityatā*) as found in Sāṃkhya and Yoga[76] is a loophole and an illusion. With specific reference to the formation of words, and continuing a discussion we already find in Patañjali's *Mahābhāṣya*, the *Nyāyabhāṣya* states that there is nothing permanent that is subject to modification (*vikāradharmaka*); and it advocates *ādeśa*, "substitution," "replacement," instead of *vikāra*.[77] According to the Vaiśeṣika and Nyāya, this same principle applies not only to the field of language, but to the world in general: What is truly eternal, such as the ultimate substances and the universals, does not change at all; and where there is change, there must be production, destruction, and replacement.

Buddhist literature provides us with numerous parallels and supplements to this debate between Nyāya-Vaiśeṣika and Sāṃkhya-Yoga.[78]

14. Uddyotakara's *Nyāyavārttika* also contains some intriguing references to the concepts of *sattāsambandha* and *svakāraṇasambandha*. One of these references is found in the commentary on *Nyāyasūtra* I,1,10—in a section that in the printed editions seems to be marred by a crucial misprint. In this section, Uddyotakara discusses the concept of *utpatti*, "production," in connection with the Buddhist attempt to reconcile the fact of lasting memory (*smṛti*) with their basic premise of constant flux and change; and he claims that in the Buddhist context there is no room for the very notion of "production" in the true sense, as something different from what is being produced. More specifically, "production" (and the state of being of something that has been produced) can be defined either as "connection with its own causes and reality" or as "reality qualified by connection with its own causes." Both possibilities are unacceptable in the system of the Buddhists; therefore, there is a contradiction between their premises and the true nature of production: *utpattiḥ svakāraṇasattāsambandhaḥ sattā vā svakāraṇasambandhaviśiṣṭā, ubhayaṃ ca tantre na-abhyupagatam iti virodhaḥ*.[79]

Whereas the first alternative is very familiar, the second one (*sattā svakāraṇasambandhaviśiṣṭā*) would not seem to be in good agreement with the premises of the Vaiśeṣika system and with the basic role of *sattā* as a timeless universal. However, Uddyotakara repeatedly uses *sattā* with temporal implications and in a sense that is not fully compatible with its role as a universal, for instance in his definition of permanence and impermanence (*nityatā, anityatā*): In this usage, "reality" itself can be impermanent or permanent depending on whether it is seen in relation to a "limit" or not; and impermanence is the "reality" of something that is limited from both sides (i.e., prior and posterior nonexistence), whereas permanence is the reality of something that is not limited in this manner (*avadhyapekṣānapekṣabhedāt sattā-eva-ubhayathā* (i.e., *anityā* or *nityā*). *yā-ubhayāntaparicchinnavastusattā, sā-anityatā-iti. yā tu-ubhayāntānavacchinnavastusattā, sā nityatā*).[80] Impermanence is also defined as "junction with reality which is not endless" (*anātyantikasattāyoga*).[81]

In his commentary on *Nyāyasūtra/Nyāyabhāṣya* II,2,6, Uddyotakara discusses problems concerning "inherence"; and referring to the polemical question whether "cowness" takes residence in what is a cow by itself or not, he says that this dilemma has no basis: only if we are dealing with a concrete entity (*vastu*) can we say that it is connected with "cowness" (*yadā-eva vastu, tadā-eva gotvena-abhisambadhyate ity anāspado vikalpaḥ*).[82] He adds that this also takes care of the "dilemma about being and nonbeing" as it relates to "connection with reality." Such "connection with reality" is neither with what is real nor with what is unreal; only if there is a concrete entity (*vastu*) can it be connected with reality. Thus the defect relating to the concepts "real" and "unreal" does not apply (*etena sattāsambandhasya sadasadvikalpo vyākhyātaḥ. na sataḥ sattāsambandhaḥ, na-asataḥ. yadā-eva tad vastu, tadā-eva sattayā sambaddham iti sadasadāśrayo doṣo 'nupapanna iti*).[83]

Earlier in the second Adhyāya, Uddyotakara distinguished the connection between an effect and its material cause (i.e., inherence) from the conjunction between separable entities. An effect or product never occurs unconnected with its material cause; the time of production is the same as the time of connection. Therefore, the effect and its material cause are not merely conjoined (as separable entities): *na punaḥ kāryam kāraṇāsambaddhaṃ vidyate, jātaḥ sambaddhaś ca-ity ekaḥ kālaḥ. tasmān na kāryakāraṇe saṃyukte.*[84] Vācaspatimiśra's *Tātparyaṭīkā* paraphrases the principle of the simultaneity of production and connection by referring to the relationship between the whole and its parts, the thing qualified by a universal and the universal itself, qualities and motions and their underlying substance (*jātaḥ sambaddhaś ca-ity ekaḥ kālaḥ. tathā hi, na-avayavy avayavāsambaddho 'sti, na hi jātimān jātyasambaddho 'sti, na guṇakarmaṇī dravyāsambaddhe staḥ*).[85]

15. Jayantabhaṭṭa refers to the same principle of simultaneity in the variant formulation *jātaṃ ca sambaddhaṃ ca-ity ekaḥ kālaḥ* and attributes it to the "Ācāryas": *tad api parihṛtam ācāryaiḥ jātaṃ ca sambaddhaṃ ca-ity ekaḥ kāla iti vadadbhiḥ.*[86] Who were these "Ācāryas?" Their identity, as well as that of the *vyākhyātāraḥ* also mentioned by Jayanta, has been a matter of debate. As pointed out by A. Wezler, the newly discovered *Nyāyamañjarīgranthibhaṅga* by Cakradhara contains valuable information that allows us to go beyond the assumptions of E. Frauwallner and B. Gupta. According to Cakradhara, the *vyākhyātāraḥ* were commentators of the *Nyāyabhāṣya*, whereas the *ācāryāḥ* were "commentators of Uddyotakara, beginning with Rucikāra" (*uddyotakaravivṛtikṛto rucikāraprabhṛtayaḥ*).[87] There is no good reason to question Cakradhara's reliability. But does the information provided by him settle the issue once and for all?

In the passage under discussion, Jayanta's reference to the "Ācāryas" would seem to include also Uddyotakara himself, since he was one of those who invoked the principle of simultaneity. However, Jayanta's use of the word *parihṛta*, "excluded," seems to indicate an argumentative procedure of "exclusion" (*parihāra*) that we do not find in the *Nyāyavārttika.* Was this more formal argumentation added in the Nyāyavārttika commentaries mentioned by Cakradhara? Uddyotakara's own casual reference to the formula *jātaḥ sambaddhaś ca-ity ekaḥ kālaḥ* obviously implies that it was already well known in his day. Do we have evidence for an earlier use and interpretation of this formula?

As we have seen, Mallavādin presents the phrase *niṣṭhāsambandhayor ekakālatvāt*[88] (or *pariniṣṭhānasambandhayor ekakālatvāt*[89]) as a formula going back to the lost *Vākya* on the Vaiśeṣikasūtras. In a passage which Jambuvijaya ascribes to Siṃhasūri, but which may contain Mallavādin's own words, we read: "Being completed and being connected,—this is one and the same time" (*parinișṭhitaṃ sambaddhaṃ ca-ity ekaḥ kālaḥ*).[90] Is this also a quote from, or a paraphrase of, a Vaiśeṣika text? Do the more familiar formulations of Uddyotakara and Jayanta go back to the same source? Do they simply replace the word *parinișṭhita* ("fully completed"), which seems to have been a technical term in early Vaiśeṣika, with the more neutral word *jāta* ("born," "produced")? The old term *completion* (*niṣṭhā*) appears in Vyomaśiva's use of the formula *niṣṭhāsambandhayor ekakālatvāt;* but elsewhere, he says: *niṣpādasambandhayor ekakālatvāt.*[91] Around A.D. 1000, the phrase *niṣṭhāsambandhayor ekakālatvāt* emerges once again in Helārāja's commentary on Bhartṛhari's *Vākyapadīya.*[92] At any rate, Mallavādin's and Siṃhasūri's statements support the conclusion that the idea of "simultaneity," as expressed by Uddyotakara and his successors, goes back to older sources, probably an old Vaiśeṣika text.

There is another intriguing and significant parallel or connection. Uddyotakara says: "Only if there is a concrete entity (*vastu*) can it be connected with reality" (*yadā-eva tad vastu, tadā-eva sattayā sambaddham*).[93] How does this correspond to what Mallavādin presents as Praśastamati's reinterpretation of the formula *niṣṭhāsambandhayor ekakālatvāt;* that is, the thesis that an entity which is already established is connected (simultaneously) with its material causes and its reality (*siddhasya vastunaḥ svakāraṇaiḥ svasattayā ca sambandha iti*)?[94] Is this the same idea, only presented in different contexts and perspectives?

16. Mallavādin's Praśastamati seems to postulate an intermediate entity that has to be there in order to be connected with its material causes and its reality. Uddyotakara, on the other hand, seems to dismiss the temporal and genetic perspective: There is no actual composition or assemblage; *sattāsambandha* is a device of analyzing a concrete and complex entity insofar as it is there; it does not describe a temporal event. Did Uddyotakara give a more faithful and positive presentation and interpretation of a theory that Mallavādin tried to ridicule? Did Uddyotakara refer to Praśastamati's/Praśastapāda's own theory? Could he have referred to it? The precise dates, and even the relative chronology of Uddyotakara and Praśastapāda, continue to be debated. E. Frauwallner dates Uddyotakara around 650 A.D., clearly later than Praśastapāda. B. K. Matilal suggests 550, but claims that he referred to Praśastapāda. Jambuvijaya believes that Mallavādin was aware of Uddyotakara, which would imply that Uddyotakara was *not* later than Praśastapāda. There is no conclusive evidence for any of these views.[95]

Uddyotakara's citation of the formula *jātaḥ sambaddhaś ca-ity ekaḥ kālaḥ* shows that he was familiar with the "theory of simultaneity" that Mallavādin attributes to the *Vaiśeṣikavākya* and its *Bhāṣya*. Should this also be the source of his statement that something is "connected with reality" only if and when (and as soon as) it is there as a concrete entity (*vastu*)? How exactly does he use the word *vastu*? The perspective of the *vastu* as a complex conglomerate of aspects (including "real" and "unreal"), or as the totality and transcendence of its qualifications, is certainly not what we would normally expect to find in Uddyotakara's *Nyāyavārttika,* a work that usually advocates the additive way of thinking found in the Vaiśeṣika system. It is much more characteristic of Jainism and perhaps of Kumārila. At any rate, it is obvious that (for tactical or dialectical reasons) Uddyotakara tries to avoid the temporal, genetic implications of *sattāsambandha,* the idea of an actual addition of reality to a separable substrate.

The question whether Uddyotakara was aware of Praśastamati's/ Praśastapāda's peculiar reinterpretation of the "simultaneity theory" or only of its earlier version in the *Vaiśeṣikavākya* and *Bhāṣya* has to remain open. Concerning the relative chronology, it may be worth mentioning that, according to Vyomaśiva, Praśastapāda responded to Uddyotakara in his own understanding of *anityatva,* "impermanence." Referring to what is basically Uddyotakara's definition of impermanence (i.e., *prāgabhāvapradhvaṃsābhāvopalakṣitā vastunaḥ sattā,* "an entity's reality which is marked by prior and posterior nonexistence"),[96] Vyomaśiva says that the "Bhāṣyakāra" (i.e., Praśastapāda?) thought that this theory might be unnecessarily complex and took impermanence simply as "destruction" (*udyotakarakalpanāyāṃ kalpanāgauravaṃ syād iti pradhvaṃsa eva-anityatvam iti-iṣṭaṃ bhāṣyakāreṇa*).[97] It seems, however, unlikely that Vyomaśiva is a reliable chronological witness in this case.

In the *Padārthadharmasaṃgraha* itself, the terms *kāryatva, anityatva,* and *utpatti* appear without becoming thematic. "Being an effect" and "impermanence" are presented as common abstract attributes of whatever has a cause (*karyatvānityatve kāraṇavatām eva;* "being an effect and impermanence belong to such entities only which have causes"), and they are not further explained. *Production* is mentioned in the section on time (*kāla*), which is called "the basis of the production, persistence and destruction of all effects" (*sarvakāryāṇām ca-utpattisthitivināśahetus*).[98]

Time and space together function as distributors or regulators of causal processes and events of production that according to Śrīdhara would otherwise take place at random.[99] The *Padārthadharmasaṃgraha* does not explicate the nature of this relationship between time and production. The role of time as universal "cause of production, persistence and destruction" has implications of dynamic and active power that are obviously not fully accounted for in the "official" and explicit presentation of *kāla* as one of the nine "substances" (*dravya*). This, too, seems to indicate unrecorded changes and reinterpretations.

17. We have seen that the relationship between (*svakāraṇa*) *sattāsambandha, kāryatva, anityatva,* and *utpatti,* which is among the most crucial issues in Mallavādin's presentation of early Vaiśeṣika, is not explicitly discussed in the *Padārthadharmasaṃgraha.* But this is different in its commentaries, most significantly those by Vyomaśiva and Śrīdhara. On the one hand, these commentators accept and develop the application of *sattāsambandha* to *all* substances, qualities, and motions, including the eternal, unproduced substrates, as we find it in the *Padārthadharmasaṃgraha.* But on the other hand, they refer to it as a potential explanation for *utpatti* and *kāryatva*—something for which there is no basis in the *Padārthadharmasaṃgraha.* However, they may have had the support of the same sources that had been accessible to Mallavādin. This seems to be true at least for Vyomaśiva, the author of the oldest extant Praśastapāda commentary.

Vyomaśiva used the "theory of simultaneity" that Mallavādin had ascribed to the *Vākya* and *Bhāṣya* to reject the *sadasadvikalpa:* The dilemma does not apply, because production and connection are simultaneous. The production of objects is precisely their connection with their own causes and reality (*tad asan, niṣpādasambandhayor ekakālatvāt. tathā hi, padārthānāṃ svakāraṇasattāsambandha eva-utpattiḥ*).[100] Subsequently, Vyomaśiva used the notion of "connection with one's causes and reality" to define the status of products (*kāryatva*) and asserted its superiority over such definitions as *abhūtvā bhavanam,* "(coming into) existence after prior nonexistence."[101] Accordingly, *akāryatva,* "not being an effect," is defined as "absence of connection with its causes and reality" *svakāraṇasattāsambandhābhāva*).[102] Is this compatible with the fact that Vyomaśiva, just like Praśastapāda, elsewhere ascribes *sattāsambandha* to the eternal substances that are *not* effects? Should we read *svakāraṇasattā* as *tatpuruṣa* ("reality of its causes") to avoid such potential incompatibility? But in the section on universals (*sāmānya*), Vyomaśiva invokes again the "theory of simultaneity" and leaves no doubt that he construes *svakāraṇasattā-* as a *dvandva* compound: *niṣṭhāsambandhayor ekakālatvād iti svakāraṇaiḥ sattādibhiś ca piṇḍasya-abhisambandha eva-ātmalābhaḥ.*[103] Unlike the earlier reference, this articulation of the "theory of simultaneity" would seem to agree with Praśastamati's reinterpretation as presented by Mallavādin—provided that Vyomaśiva's *piṇḍa* corresponds to what Mallavādin's Praśastamati calls *siddhaṃ vastu.*[104]

Did Vyomaśiva himself vacillate between different interpretations of *svakāraṇasattāsambandha?* Was he aware of such different interpretations? His references are much more casual than those of Mallavādin; if he was aware of different versions of the "theory of simultaneity," he did not take these differences very seriously. Had this whole debate and the texts in which it was laid down become obsolete in his days? As to the compound *svakāraṇasattā-*, Vyomaśiva obviously reads it in accordance with its traditional interpretation, as a *dvandva;* and he seems to disregard the problem of reconciling the association of *sattāsambandha* with *utpatti,* on the one hand, and its application to the eternal substances, on the other hand. He does not explicate how exactly *sattāsambandha* applies to uncaused substances; that is, how it can occur outside and apart from *svakāraṇasattāsambandha.* In his view, this seems to be quite unproblematic; and he sees no room for the *sadasadvikalpa* in this case.

Vyomaśiva uses *svakāraṇasattāsambandha* to define or explain both *utpatti* (or *ātmalābha,* "acquisition of identity") and *kāryatva.* The difference may be one of emphasis only. Whereas *utpatti* means primarily the actual event of "coming forth" or "production," it can also refer to a continued "standing out," "having come forth" in the sense of "existence," "ex-sistentia."[105] Even if *svakāraṇasattāsambandha* is used to define *kāryatva,* "being an effect," the connotation of temporality, "existence" in the sense of a temporal act (*bhavana*), is still obvious.[106]

18. Śrīdhara, who was familiar with Vyomaśiva's commentary, tried to illustrate the simultaneity or coincidence of "being born by the power of one's causes" and "connection" (with reality and other universals) in his own way, comparing it with the application of the action of cutting or splitting to what is to be cut (*svakāraṇasāmarthyād upajāyamānam eva tatra sambadhyate, yathā chidikriyā chedyena*).[107] The term *sāmarthya* occurs also in Śrīdhara's reference to the "dilemma about being and nonbeing." He notes that only those "previously unreal" (*prāgasat*) entities can be connected with reality, for which there is a causal power (*kāraṇasāmarthya*) to do so. No such power exists with reference to utterly fictitious objects, such as donkey's horns (*kharaviṣāṇa*).[108]

Unlike Vyomaśiva, Śrīdhara does not accept "connection with one's causes and reality" as a definition of "being an effect," since this would not apply to destruction and in general to effects that are absences or nonentities (*svakāraṇe samavāyaḥ prāgasataḥ sattāsamavāyo vā kāryatvam ity eke. tad ayuktaṃ pradhvaṃse tadabhāvāt*). Śrīdhara also rejects Uddyotakara's definition of impermanence (*anityatva*) as "reality which is marked by prior and posterior nonexistence" (*prākpradhvaṃsābhāvopalakṣitā sattā*).[109]

Nonbeing obviously had more weight and independence for Śrīdhara than for Vyomaśiva. According to his way of thinking, it is more fully integrated in the world and in its network of causality, production, and destruction. No definition or explanation of causality or of "being an effect" can be complete without reference to nonbeing. Our world is a world of absences and presences; absences are real states of affairs. Such increasing emphasis on nonbeing, negation, and absence corresponds to the general development of thought in Vaiśeṣika and Nyāya.[110] More specifically, we may also refer to such Nyāya authors as Śaṅkarasvāmin and Trilocana who in their argumentation against the Buddhist idea that destruction and cessation are immanent in reality (*svarūpanivṛtti*) tend to reify destruction as well as production and to treat it as something that requires a causal explanation of its own. Similar arguments were proposed by Uddyotakara and Aviddhakarṇa.[111]

Udayana's *Kiraṇāvalī* cuts the whole discussion short. "Being an effect" is simply the state of being of something that did not exist before; and "impermanence" is the fact that something that did exist does not continue to exist: *kāryatvam abhūtvā bhāvitvam, anityatvaṃ ca bhūtvā-abhāvitvam iti hi vivakṣitam*.[112] Among the classical Praśastapāda commentators, Udayana seems to be least interested in the old debates about production and destruction in which the concepts of *sattāsambandha* and *svakāraṇasambandha* once had their place. Nonetheless, various casual references show that he was quite familiar with the notion of *svakāraṇasattāsambandha* (or *svakāraṇasattāsamavāya*).[113] Udayana was on the way to Navyanyāya and a leading representative of a development during which the old cosmogonic and cosmological preoccupations were finally superseded by epistemology, logic, and problems of definition. To a certain extent, the term and concept of *sattāsambandha* remains in use and preserves its connotations of temporality. We find it, for instance, in Bhāsarvajña's *Nyāyabhūṣaṇa*, where it refers to an essentially temporal state of being, to actuality or being present.[114] Other later authors used *sattā* itself in this sense: being as temporality and as the condition and counterpart of destruction. But this does not lead to a full and radical reexamination of the question of "being and time."[115]

Of course, the textbooks of classical and later Vaiśeṣika continue to describe specific processes of production among substances, qualities, and motions.[116] But the old cosmogonic questions have faded away. Time itself is an eternal, petrified substance, one basic entity among others. "Connection with reality" is no longer a process or event, but a condition that eternal and irreducible substances may share with transitory entities. The meaning of genesis or production is no longer a central issue. Temporality itself is of minor importance, as far as the existence and basic structure of the universe is concerned.

Chapter 8: Notes

1. See earlier, Chapter 7, section 7.

2. Cf. ibid., sections 4; 9.

3. *Sattāsambandha* appears within a list of abstract nouns, such as *sāmānyaviśeṣavattva* (*PBh*, p. 17). Praśastapāda's predilection for such nouns distinguishes his style from that of the Sūtras. For instance, *VS* I, 7 (8) lists a number of attributes (such as *sāmānyaviśeṣavat*), but does not refer to the abstract status of possessing them which is implied in Praśastapāda's use of the suffix *tva*. Generally, the Sūtra text does not show Praśastapāda's clear and consistent distinction between the levels of "enumeration" (*uddeśa*) and "definition" and "analysis" (*lakṣaṇa*, *parīkṣā*).

4. See *PBh*, p. 17: *kāryatvānityatve kāraṇavatām eva*.

5. Cf. G. Chemparathy, "Praśastapāda and His Other Names," *Indo-Iranian Journal* 12 (1969–70): 241–254; see also "The Various Names for the Famous Vaiśeṣika Work of Praśastapāda," *Ṛtam* (Lucknow) 1 (1969–70): 23–27.

6. Other important Jaina sources include Jinabhadra's *Viśeṣāvaśyakabhāṣya* (probably sixth century and apparently not familiar with Praśastapāda's *Padārthadharmasaṃgraha*).

7. See *Siddhasena Divākara's Sanmatitarka* with a critical introduction and an original commentary by S. Saṅghavi and B. Doshi (Bombay, 1939), especially pp. 10 and 72, on the tradition that Mallavādin wrote a commentary on Siddhasena's work.

8. See E. Frauwallner in Mallavādin, *DNC*, vol. 1, p. 2; cf. also K. K. Dixit, *Jaina Ontology* (Ahmedabad, 1971), pp. 92f.; 114–122.

9. *DNC*, vol. 2, pp. 436, 497f.

10. *DNC*, p. 501: *sadasadātmakavastutattvapratyakṣīkaraṇārtham jaināḥ ekam eva-ātmānaṃ paramārthaṃ dravyārthaparyāyārthobhayalakṣaṇam upavarṇayanti.*

11. See A. Thakur, Introduction to *VS*, ed. Jambuvijaya, GOS, especially pp. 10ff; cf. also G. Chemparathy (cited in n. 5).

12. For possible correspondences with the *Padārthadharmasaṃgraha*, see *DNC*, vol. 2, pp. 463; 471; 524ff. The most conspicuous correspondences occur on p. 524. Yet, the agreement is only partial, and the parallel passages are continued by statements not found in the *Padārthadharmasaṃgraha*. It seems that this entire *pūrvapakṣa* section was taken from the *Ṭīkā*, which may have contained many arguments of the *Padārthadharmasaṃgraha* in a more extensive and elaborate form. This is also the view of the editor, Jambuvijaya; see his note on p. 524.

13. For a helpful list of quotes, see vol. 3, pp. 887f. (Mallavādin) and 890ff. (Siṃhasūri). On p. 771, Siṃhasūri cites a verse from Vasubandhu's *Triṃśikā*.

14. Most of the relevant discussions are found in the seventh *Ara* ("spoke") of the work.

15. *DNC*, p. 520. Later, this simile plays a significant role in Vyomaśiva's work; see later, Appendix, section 3.

16. See *DNC*, pp. 459; 498f.; 502f.

17. *DNC*, p. 459.

18. Ibid., pp. 498ff.

19. On the general importance of genesis and evolution in older thought, see earlier, Chapter 3.

20. *DNC*, p. 457; see also pp. 455f. (Siṃhasūri): *āśrayabhūtaṃ svena-astitvena svabhāvasattayā-eva-utpannam.*

21. *DNC*, p. 516; see also pp. 847; 481 (Siṃhasūri: *dravyatvanilayana; dravyatvaṃ nilīyate*).

22. Ibid., p. 459; cf. Siṃhasūri: *sattāsambandhaśūnyatvād na-eva-asti tat, anavadhṛtātmakatvāt, khapuṣpavat.*

23. Ibid., pp. 441f.; see also p. 462 (Siṃhasūri): *dvividho hi bhāva uktaḥ. svabhāvasadbhāvaḥ sambandhasadbhāvaś ca.*

24. See *PBh* and *NK*, p. 16. Śrīdhara's definition of *astitva* as *svarūpavattva* would seem to imply the applicability of *svātmasattva/svarūpasattva* to "bare" substances, etc. On the other hand, Praśastapāda seems to reserve *svātmasattva* for universals, etc. (i.e., the second group of categories; see *PBh*, p. 19).

25. *DNC*, p. 456.

26. See Siṃhasūri, *DNC*, p. 456: *svena-eva-astitvena svabhāvasattayā-eva-utpannam.*

27. See ibid., p. 462.

28. Ibid., p. 462.

29. Ibid., p. 464; see also p. 463 (Mallavādin and Siṃhasūri on a "surplus" (*atiśaya*) or gradation (*sat, sattara, sattama*) with regard to being.

30. Cf. ibid., p. 462: *sattāsambandhād ṛte 'pi yathā parapakṣe pradhānādīnāṃ sātmakatvam.*

31. Ibid., p. 479; Siṃhasūri paraphrases: *sāṃkhyaparikalpitaṃ sakalajagatkāraṇaṃ pradhānādiparyāyaṃ syād bhavatā vaiśeṣikena parikalpitā sattā.*

32. See Siṃhasūri, *DNC*, p. 479.

33. See earlier, Chapter 7.

34. See *NK*, p. 16.

35. *DNC*, p. 481: *yat tulyajātīyāvayavārabdhaṃ vastumātraṃ kāryaṃ tad dravyatvena sambadhyate, yat tu kāraṇaguṇārabdhaṃ vastumātraṃ tad guṇatvena sambadhyate.* Siṃhasūri speaks of a *dravyatvanilayananiyama*, etc.

36. Ibid., p. 486.

37. Ibid., pp. 516f.

38. Ibid., pp. 508f.; see also p. 510: *pariniṣṭhānasambandhayor ekakālatvāt.*

39. Ibid., pp. 512f.; cf. Bhartṛhari, *VP* III/9 (*Kālasamuddeśa*), p. 33; and Siṃhasūri, *DNC*, p. 513.

40. See earlier, Chapter 5–6.

41. See Haribhadra, *Śāstravārttāsamuccaya* (Bombay, 1929), v. 248ff.; Akalaṅka, *Tattvārthavārttika*, ed. and trans. into Hindi, M. K. Jain (Benares, 1952–1957), p. 96 (on Sūtra, I, 33): *sattādvayaprasaṅgaś ca, ekā-ābhyantarī, aparā bāhyā.* Such "duplication of being" is, of course, a constant theme of Mallavādin's critique.

42. Jinabhadra lists only seventeen qualities (*guṇa*), instead of Praśastapāda's twenty-four; see *Viśeṣāvaśyakabhāṣya*, ed. D. Malvania (Ahmedabad, 1966–1968), v. 2972ff. (with autocommentary). The relative chronology of Mallavādin and Jinabhadra is still open to debate; cf. K. K. Dixit, *Jaina Ontology* (Ahmedabad, 1971), p. 10; however, Dixit's date for Mallavādin (fifth century) seems too early.

43. *Viśeṣāvaśyakabhāṣya*, v. 2669.

44. *Sanmatitarka* (cited in n. 7), p. 152 (III, 38).

45. See *Sanmatitarkaprakaraṇam with Abhayadevasūri's Commentary Tattvabodhavidhāyinī* (see earlier, Chapter 7, n. 121, p. 648).

46. See Prabhācandra, *Nyāyakumudacandra*, ed. Mahendra Kumar (Bombay, 1938–1941), p. 220. The *dvandva* construction is the most common one; cf. Vācaspati, *Bhāmatī* on *BSBh* II, 1, 18; *Tattvakaumudī* on *SK*, v. 9.

47. *Prameyakamalamārtaṇḍa*, ed. Mahendra Kumar, 2d ed. (Bombay, 1941), p. 271: *prāgasataḥ svakāraṇasamavāyāt sattāsamavāyāt vā tatsiddhiś ca.*

48. Ibid., pp. 618ff.

49. *NBh* and *NV* IV, 1, 4 (Calc. S.S., pp. 996f.); Uddyotakara adds *ubhayaviparīta*, "the opposite of both being and nonbeing" (i.e., "neither real nor unreal") to complete the tetralemma. See also the threefold scheme of exclusion in *VS* IX, 12.

50. See *Śataśāstra*, English trans., pp. 44ff.; in *G. Tucci, Pre-Diṅnāga Buddhist Texts on Logic from Chinese Sources* (Baroda, 1929, GOS; reprint San Francisco, 1976). The authenticity of the text has been questioned. Cf. also Āryadeva, *Catuḥśataka* XI, 15 (*satkārya* and *asatkārya*).

51. See S. Katsura, *A Study of Harivarman's Tattvasiddhi* (Diss. University of Toronto, 1974), pp. 39f.

52. See M. Hattori, *Dignāga, On Perception* (*Pramāṇasamuccaya*, ch. 1) (Cambridge, Mass., 1968), p. 69; see also E. Frauwallner, *Materialien zur ältesten Erkenntnislehre der Karmamīmāṃsā* (Vienna, 1968), pp. 101f.

53. See Hattori, *Dignāga*, p. 170, n. 6. 47.

54. Ibid., p. 170, n. 6. 47; see also n. 6. 45: *vaiśeṣikoktasvakāraṇasamavāya.*

55. See Bhartṛhari, *VP*, III/3 (*Sambandhasamuddeśa*), 48; Bhartṛhari invokes his distinction between "primary" and "figurative" being (*mukhyā sattā, upacārasattā*) to make the transition from "nonbeing" (as absence of primary being) to "being" intelligible. For Dignāga's critique of Bhartṛhari, see E. Frauwallner, *Kl. Schr.*, pp. 785ff.; 856.

56. Cf. *VP* III/3, 43; 79ff. (with Helārāja's commentary); see also later, Chapter 9, section 1 (Bhartṛhari on time).

57. Cf. Dharmakīrti, *Pramāṇavārttika* III, 111ff.; 115f. (ed. Y. Miyasaka, II, 111ff.).

58. Cf. *Pramāṇavārttika* III, 116: *nityaṃ viśvam idaṃ tataḥ;* see also later, Chapter 9, on the Vaiśeṣika concept of time; and K. Mimaki, *La réfutation bouddhique de la permanence des choses* (Paris, 1976). For a different kind of critique of the "static" sense of being in Vaiśeṣika, see Śālikanātha, *Ṛjuvimalā* on Prabhākara's *Bṛhatī,* ed. A. Chinnaswami Sastri (Benares, 1920), pp. 120 f.; *Prakaraṇapañcikā,* ed. A. Subrahmanya Sastri (Benares, 1961), pp. 97ff.

59. *YD,* ed. R. C. Pandeya, p. 54; see also p. 48 (*saṃniveśaviśeṣamātratvād asata utpattiḥ pratiṣiddhā*).

60. See ibid., p. 55: *nirātmakatvād asatāṃ sarveṣām aviśiṣṭatā;* cf. also p. 52: *saty asati vā sambandhe doṣaprasaṅgāt;* and Śaṅkara, *BUBh* I, 2, 1 (*Works,* vol. 1; Delhi, 1978, p. 616): *prāgutpatteḥ śaśaviṣāṇavad abhāvabhūtasya ghaṭasya svakāraṇasattāsambandhānupapattiḥ, dviniṣṭhatvāt sambandhasya.*

61. See, for instance, Vācaspati, *Tattvakaumudī* on *SK,* v. 9: *tasmād iyaṃ paṭotpattiḥ svakāraṇasamavāyo vā svasattāsamavāyo vā.*

62. Ibid., on *SK,* v. 15 (introduction).

63. Cf. *YD,* p. 69.

64. Ibid., p. 65.

65. See *YBh* IV, p. 13; being manifest (*vyakta*) corresponds to the present.

66. See earlier, Chapter 4, section 4.

67. See earlier, Chapter 3, n. 39; and especially *PBh* and *NK,* pp. 327f.; Praśastapāda and Śrīdhara refer to the "power" of the particulars to manifest their respective universals (*vyaṅgyavyañjakaśakti*). Cf. also Jayanta, *NM,* vol. 2, pp. 64f., for a critical discussion of the concept of *śakti.*

68. See earlier, section 6 (n. 30ff.).

69. See especially *VP* III/9 (*Kālasamuddeśa*); and later, Chapter 9, section 1.

70. *Tattvakaumudī* on *SK,* v. 9; see also the critical presentation of the *satkāryavāda* by Śrīdhara, *NK,* pp. 143f.

71. See *NBhūṣ,* p. 569; and earlier, Chapter 3, n. 38.

72. *YBh* III, 13 (conclusion); the same formula appears in *NBh* III, 2, 15 as part of a Sāṃkhya *pūrvapakṣa*. However, the *Yuktidīpikā* presents this as a hostile interpretation of the *asatkāryavāda* (see YD, p. 49: *pariṇāmo hi nāma-avasthitasya*

dravyasya dharmāntaranivṛttiḥ dharmāntarapravṛttiś ca, tatra dharmāntarasya nirodhābhyupagamād, asataś ca-utpattipratijñānād . . .) and insists that no reference to "production" or "destruction" is needed for the definition of "modification" (*YD*, p. 53: *dharmāntarasya-āvirbhāvaḥ pūrvasya ca tirobhāvaḥ pariṇāmaḥ*).

73. See W. Liebenthal, *Satkārya in der Darstellung seiner buddhistischen Gegner* (Stuttgart, 1934), p. 44, n. 43; and *NBh* I, 1, 29: *asad utpadyate utpannaṃ nirudhyate iti yogānām.* Here, as elsewhere, the "Yogas" may be Vaiśeṣikas.

74. See Uddyotakara, *NV* IV, 1, 48 (Calc. S.S., p. 998).

75. See *NV* III, 1, 33 (Calc. S.S., p. 761).

76. Cf. *YBh* IV, 33.

77. See *NBh* II, 2, 53 (Calc. S.S., p. 650); also II, 2, 57 (653); and Patañjali, *Mahābhāṣya* I, 1, 56 (on *Vārttika* 11f.; vol. 1, pp. 136f.): *ādeśo hi nāma yo 'bhūtvā bhavati.*

78. See W. Liebenthal, *Satkārya* (cited in n. 73); cf. also P. M. Williams, "On the Abhidharma Ontology," *JIPh* 9 (1981): 227–257.

79. See *NV* I, 10. Not only the editions in the Bibliotheca Indica (p. 69) and Calc. S.S. (p. 191) read *tantreṇa-abhyupagatam;* A. Thakur's edition (Darbhanga, 1967, p. 390) has *svatantreṇa-abhyupagatam.* However, this is incompatible with the context as well as with Vācaspati's *Tīkā.* One could also consider the reading *tantreṇa-anabhyupagatam.*

80. *NV* II, 2, 12 (Calc. S.S., p. 592; Bibliotheca Indica: II, 2, 13; p. 286). See also Śrīdhara, *NK,* p. 18: *prākpradhvaṃsābhāvopalakṣitā vastunaḥ sattā-eva-anityatvam iti kecit.* This may be a reference to Uddyotakara. Uddyotakara is mentioned explicitly in Vyomaśiva's discussion of "impermanence"; see *Vy.*, p. 129.

81. See *NV* V, 1, 36 (Calc. S.S., pp. 1149f.).

82. Ibid. II, 2, 64 (Calc. S.S., p. 669); cf. also Mallavādin, *DNC,* pp. 508f.: *sadādir anāspado vikalpaḥ.*

83. *NV* II, 2, 64 (669).

84. Ibid., II, 1, 33 (Calc. S.S., pp. 494f.).

85. See *Tātparyaṭīkā* on *NV* II, 1, 32 (Calc. S.S., p. 476).

86. See Jayanta, *NM,* p. 285.

87. See A. Wezler, "Zur Identität der 'Ācāryāḥ' und 'Vyākhyātāraḥ' in Jayantabhaṭṭas Nyāyamañjarī," *WZKS* 19 (1975): 135–146; and Cakradhara, *Nyāyamañjarīgranthibhaṅga,* ed. N. J. Shah (Ahmedabad, 1972), pp. 44, 135ff. (see the editor's reference to Vyomaśiva on p. 135).

88. See Mallavādin, *DNC,* pp. 512f.

89. Ibid., p. 510.

90. Siṃhasūri (?), *DNC,* p. 510.

91. See Vyomaśiva, *Vy.,* pp. 690; 126.

92. See Helārāja on *VP* III/9 (*Kālasamuddeśa*), 19. In his commentary on *VP* III/9, p. 33, Helārāja paraphrases *niṣṭhā* as *samāpti,* "completion" (*kartavyasya samāptir niṣṭhākālaḥ*); cf. Mallavādin and Siṃhasūri, *DNC,* p. 509: *niṣṭhānaṃ samāptiḥ.*

93. See n. 83.

94. Mallavādin, *DNC,* pp. 516f.

95. See E. Frauwallner, *Gesch. d. ind. Phil.,* vol. 2, p. 22; B. K. Matilal, *Nyāya-Vaiśeṣika* (Wiesbaden, 1977), pp. 64, 85; Jambuvijaya, "Mallavādi: The Great Jaina Logician," *Kanakura kinenronbunshū* (Kanakura Festschrift) (Tokyo, 1966), pp. 73–78; especially p. 76: "Thus it appears that M. may have examined Uddyotakara's philosophical views." There is, however, no sufficient evidence to support this suggestion. It would certainly not be compatible with the early date (i.e., fourth century) that Jambuvijaya proposes for Mallavādin.

96. For Uddyotakara's definition, see earlier, section 14 (n. 80).

97. Vyomaśiva, *Vy.,* p. 129.

98. See *PBh* and *NK,* pp. 63ff.

99. Cf. *NK,* pp. 25, 32; on the Vaiśeṣika concept of time, see later, Chapter 9.

100. *Vy.,* p. 126; for an English translation of the section in which this passage appears, see Appendix 1, section 3.

101. *Vy.,* p. 129.

102. Ibid., p. 143.

103. Ibid., p. 690.

104. Cf. *NDC,* pp. 516f.; see also above, earlier, section 7.

105. We may recall here Mallavādin's expression *nityotpannatva,* "being always present," "eternal existence/*utpatti*"; see *DNC,* p. 457; and earlier, section 4.

106. For the use of *ātmalābha,* "acquisition of identity," "coming into existence," cf. Kumārila, *ŚV,* p. 45 (*Codanāsūtra,* v. 48): *ātmalābhe hi bhāvānāṃ kāraṇāpekṣitā bhavet / labdhātmānāṃ svakāryeṣu pravṛttiḥ svayam eva tu.* The verse is quoted by Śāntarakṣita, *TS,* v. 2848.

107. *NK*, p. 15.

108. Ibid., p. 17. Śrīdhara seems to respond to the critique of Śālikanātha; see later, Appendix 1, section 4 (n. 40f.).

109. *NK*, p. 18; cf. Prabhācandra, *Nyāyakumudacandra*, ed. Mahendra Kumar (Bombay, 1938–1941), pp. 220ff. (on *kāryatva*, *svakāraṇasattāsambandha*, etc.).

110. See, for instance, D. N. Shastri, *Critique of Indian Realism* (Agra, 1964), pp. 395–418; B. K. Matilal, *The Navya-Nyāya Doctrine of Negation* (Cambridge, Mass., 1968).

111. Cf. K. Mimaki, *La réfutation bouddhique de la permanence des choses* (Paris, 1976), especially pp. 141ff.; 26ff.; 125ff.

112. *Kir.*, GOS, p. 20; see also p. 78 (on *utpatti* and *ātmalābha*).

113. See, for instance, *Kir.*, GOS, p. 227 (with somewhat doxographic references to the *satkāryavāda*).

114. See Bhāsarvajña, *NBhūṣ;* and later, Chapter 9, section 7.

115. See, for instance, Dinakara on Viśvanātha, *Kārikāvalī* (with *Siddhāntamuktāvalī*), v. 9 (ed. Sankara Rama Sastry; Madras, 1923, pp. 114f.). On "being and time" in general, see later, Chapter 9.

116. For some details and technicalities, cf. H.-G. Türstig, *Entstehungsprozesse in der Philosophie des Nyāya-Vaiśeṣika-Systems* (Wiesbaden, 1982).

9

The Vaiśeṣika Concept of Time

1. Bhartṛhari opens the chapter on time (*Kālasamuddeśa*) in his *Vākyapadīya* with the following statement: "Some consider time to be one single, eternal, all-pervading substance, apart from activities and processes (i.e., the topic of the preceding chapter, *Kriyāsamuddeśa*), the measure of entities involved in action" (*vyāpāravyatirekeṇa kālam eke pracakṣate | nityam ekam vibhudravyaṃ parimāṇaṃ kriyāvatām*).[1]

He also mentions the view that this one time-substance is, by virtue of self-differentiation (*vibhaktena-ātmanā*), the cause of the "origin, duration and destruction" (*utpatti, sthiti, vināśa*) of temporal beings; and he cites the idea that it is the "wire-puller of this world-machine" (*asya lokayantrasya sūtradhāraḥ*), differentiating and regulating the universe through its powers of "prevention" (*pratibandha*) and "permission" (*abhyanujñā*), or withholding and releasing. Thus it produces "priority and posteriority" (*paurvāparya*) or temporal sequence (*kramarūpatā*).[2] It regulates the production and manifestation (*janmābhivyakti*) of different entities, by releasing them into actual existence or preventing them from emerging. It does so by activating or actualizing those powers and potentialities (*śakti*) that constitute the condition of the possibility of all actual, particularized existence.[3] More specifically, this means that the "eternal act" (*kriyā nityā*), that is, reality itself (*sattā*), the highest universal, is unleashed and manifested in those lower universals (*jāti*) which are the eternal prototypes and potentialities of all particulars (*vyakti*).[4] Subsequently, these universals themselves develop their own drive towards concrete, temporal, individual existence; that is, they affect the production of appropriate particulars in which they take residence and to which they impart a specific identity and class membership.[5] The "power" (*śakti*) of inherence (*samavāya*) then supersedes the distinctness of the causal factors that constitute a thing and produces the appearance of a concrete unity and identity with its causes (*ekatvam iva tā vyaktīr āpādayati kāraṇaih*).[6] In all these processes, time (*kāla*) is present and indispensable as the first and foremost "power," and as the regulating principle for the other powers.[7]

Although time itself is eternal (*nitya*) and unchanging, it seems to be divided into many different "times." It assumes the appearance of temporality and seems to coincide with the processes and changes it administers. Accordingly, time is called a "process" or "act" (*vyāpāra iti kathyate*).[8] And because of time, the entire universe which is in its ultimate reality devoid of sequence appears to possess temporal sequence.[9]

In loose association, Bhartṛhari discusses other aspects and interpretations of time and its "phases": past, present, and future. In this context he cites and rejects (according to Helārāja) a strictly cyclical view of time that would imply that we can and will return to an identical past. Ultimately, temporal occurrences are irreversible and nonrecurrent.[10] He presents a preliminary summary and conclusion in verse 62: There are different perspectives on time (*bhinnaṃ kālasya darśanam*); some see it as a power (*śakti*), others as the soul or self (*ātman*) or as a deity (*devatā*). Bhartṛhari's own view is clearly stated by Helārāja: Time is the first and foremost *śakti*, the "independent power" (*svātantryaśakti*) of *brahman*. As such, it is the first stage in the unfolding of the cosmic illusion, the dispersal of absolute unity into particularity and multiplicity.[11]

In the remaining section of his "chapter on time," Bhartṛhari produces further observations concerning the relationship between time and temporality; that is, the principle of *kāla* itself and the character and sequence of temporal phenomena. He presents various reflections on the status of past, present, and future and refers specifically to the relationship between language and time. He also discusses the meaning of "being" itself, as it relates to his analysis of temporality and time.

How does "being" in a verbal sense, that is, as an act (*kriyā*), relate to "being" as a noun? How does the verb *be* (*bhū*), how does the noun *reality* (*sattā*) refer to time (for instance, to the past in the expression *bhūtā sattā*)?[12] In some detail, Bhartṛhari deals with ancient problems and paradoxes concerning the status of the present as an apparently evanescent phenomenon between past and future. How can an evanescent act "be there"? How can "being" itself in its verbal sense, as an act or process, be there? Questions of this kind are recorded not only in early Nyāya literature, but also in Patañjali's *Mahābhāṣya*. Related paradoxes are found in Nāgārjuna's *Madhyamakakārikā*.[13]

The commentator Helārāja, at least five centuries after Bhartṛhari, associates Bhartṛhari's introductory verse, and perhaps some of the following verses, with the Vaiśeṣika theory of time.[14] But another author from Kashmir, Bhaṭṭotpala (possibly Helārāja's contemporary) in his commentary on Varāhamihira's *Bṛhatsaṃhitā*, does not suggest any connection with the Vaiśeṣika. Instead, he refers to a somewhat mythical *kālavāda*.[15]

What then is the relationship or resemblance between Bhartṛhari's "chapter on time" and the Vaiśeṣika theory of time and temporality? Bhartṛhari and Helārāja provide a broad background and intriguing synthesis of various Indian views of time. Where in this scheme does the Vaiśeṣika have its place?

2. Kaṇāda as well as Praśastapāda list time (*kāla*) as one of the nine substances. It usually appears in close company with the other two unitary and ubiquitous substances, ether (*ākāśa*) and space (*diś*). In the Vaiśeṣikasūtra, three short sections provide some scanty details: II, 2, 6–11 (according to Candrānanda; II, 2, 6–9 in Śaṅkaramiśra's *Upaskāra*); V, 2, 23–28 (V, 2, 21–26 in the *Upaskāra*); VII, 2, 25–28 (VII, 2, 21–25 in the *Upaskāra*).

From these sections, we learn the following about the "substance" time: It is an eternal (*nitya*) and unitary essence (*tattva*).[16] Its "marks" or indicators (*liṅga*) are such notions and linguistic expressions as "prior" (*para;* i.e., more remote), "simultaneous" (*yugapad*), "long" (*cira*), "quick" (*kṣipra*).[17] Candrānanda's version has an additional Sūtra which states that the (apparent) multiplicity of time is due to the variety of its effects (*kāryaviśeṣeṇa nānātvam*). The same idea is obviously taken for granted in Śaṅkaramiśra's version.[18] Just like space and ether, time is "inactive" and "without motion" (*niṣkriya*); yet it is, in a somewhat elusive manner, involved with causality.[19] It contributes, for instance, to the production of the "qualities" priority (*paratva*) and posteriority (*aparatva*) in objects which are more or less remote in time; that is, it accounts for the sequential character in things and events.[20]

Praśastapāda deals with time in a somewhat more explicit and coherent fashion, but does not provide entirely new perspectives. According to his general classification of substances, time shares the following attributes with ether, space, and souls: It possesses omnipresence (*sarvagatatva*), ultimate dimension (*paramamahattva*), and provides a common abode for all conjoined, that is, composite entities (*sarvasaṃyogisamānadeśatva*).[21] With space alone, it shares the following two characteristics: possession of five qualities (*pañcaguṇavattva*) and regulative causality for everything that has an origin (*sarvotpattimatāṃ nimittakāraṇatvam*).[22]

In the brief chapter dealing specifically with time, Praśastapāda cites and expounds the statements of the Sūtra text. He also tries to provide arguments to establish their validity. Time itself, that is, real time, has to be the cause or basis (*nimitta*) of such notions (*pratyaya*) as prior, posterior, simultaneous, nonsimultaneous and so on, because it is impossible to account for them otherwise. It is also the cause (*hetu*) of our conventional reference (*vyavahāra*) to different units and periods of time, from such minute segments as *kṣaṇa* (the smallest "moment") and *lava* (a subdivision of the twinkling of the eye) to the month (*māsa*) and year (*saṃvatsara*), and finally to the ultimate cosmic cycles (*pralaya, mahāpralaya*).[23]

In between, Praśastapāda notes somewhat casually that time is the cause of the origin, duration, and destruction of all effects or products because of such (temporal) designation (*sarvakāryāṇāṃ ca-utpattisthitivināśahetus, tadvyapadeśāt*). Furthermore, we are told that the five qualities of time are number (*saṃkhyā;* i.e., numerical unity), dimension (*parimāṇa*), separateness (*pṛthaktva*), conjunction (*saṃyoga*), and disjunction (*vibhāga*); and we are assured once again that time, just like ether (*ākāśa*), is an eternal substance.[24] Finally Praśastapāda explains how time, in spite of its fundamental unity, may assume a figurative diversity and multiplicity (*nānātvopacāra*): This is due to a variety of superimposed functions with which it is associated (*upādhibheda*); that is, to its association with the different phases of existence of temporal entities. Similarly, one and the same person, in accordance with his different functions, may be called a cook, and so forth; and a crystal may assume different imposed colors, in accordance with different objects placed in its proximity.[25]

Further characteristic details are provided by the more elaborate section dealing with the qualities *paratva* and *aparatva*, two qualities potentially inherent in all substances which exist in space and time. They are relational qualities; this means that they require an actual reference to an observer and his location in space or time. The observer's relational cognition (*apekṣābuddhi*) establishes the spatial or temporal distance of an object; that is, its remoteness or proximity, and its priority or posteriority. Though dependent on cognition these qualities are, nonetheless, really present in their respective objects as along as such presence is warranted by the actuality of the "relational cognition."[26] Praśastapāda illustrates temporal distance and proximity by referring to the case of a young man, of youthful appearance, and an old man, with beard, wrinkles, and so on. The characteristics of the young person produce in us the idea of nearness in time, i.e., of posteriority (*aparatva*) in relation to the older person; the old man, on the other hand, produces the notion of greater distance in time, i.e., of priority (*paratva*).[27]

Although Praśastapāda's treatment of *paratva* and *aparatva* is far more elaborate and technical than the corresponding statements in the Vaiśeṣikasūtra, it does seem to follow certain clues provided by Kaṇāda. A precise determination of the meaning of the Sūtras is, however, further hampered by textual inconsistencies.[28]

3. Although we may agree with B. Faddegon's statement that Praśastapāda's chapter on time "does not contain much that is new in comparison to the Sūtras,"[29] there are, nevertheless, some new perspectives and problems. At the very least, they are now much more explicit and conspicuous than in the Sūtras. Among these, the relationship between time and causality deserves special attention. In Bhartṛhari, time appeared as the causal power (*śakti*) par excellence, the "sovereign power" (*svātantryaśakti*) of *brahman* that is capable of unleashing or suppressing all other causal factors.[30] Compared to Bhartṛhari's statements, Kaṇāda's references to the connection between time and causality are extremely brief and elusive. How does Praśastapāda's treatment relate to Kaṇāda, on the one hand, and to Bhartṛhari, on the other hand?

As we have seen, Praśastapāda describes both time and space as the *nimittakāraṇa* of everything that has an origin. Later on, he states that time is the "cause of the origin, duration and destruction" (*utpattisthitivināśahetu*) of all effects or products. Why does he not repeat this second statement with reference to space? What exactly does he mean by the term *hetu* in this context? And what exactly does he mean by *nimittakāraṇa* in his earlier reference to the "regulative causality" (*nimittakāraṇatva*) of both time and space?

Nimittakāraṇa is usually translated as "efficient cause" or "instrumental cause." This is certainly too strong and potentially misleading, as far as the terminology of Praśastapāda and his commentators, such as Vyomaśiva and Śrīdhara, is concerned. The word *kāraṇa* itself can be used in a very weak sense; even universals (*sāmānya*), which have no causal power in any strict sense of the word, may be called "causes of cognitions" (*pratyayakāraṇa*). Vyomaśiva and Śrīdhara explain that a cause in this sense can be only a *nimittakāraṇa*, as other types of causality, such as material or "inherential" causes (*samavāyikāraṇa*), are excluded in this case.[31] Universals have to be there to make certain ideas possible as well as valid. As we have seen, Praśastapāda believes in the fundamental correspondence between language, thought, and reality. In this scheme of correspondence, universals provide certain words and ideas with an objective "basis." They are indispensable conditions or occasions for their factual occurrence as well as their validity.[32]

Praśastapāda also refers commonly to the objective "causes of linguistic usage" (*vyavahārahetu*, etc.). All legitimate expressions are effects or reflections of real entities. They call for a "causal" explanation within Praśastapāda's basic framework of correspondence. Although this procedure is not entirely unknown in the Vaiśeṣikasūtra, it is far less conspicuous and pervasive than in Praśastapāda's work.[33] As a matter of fact, the term *vyavahāra* never even occurs in the Sūtras. Likewise, the three fundamental features of *astitva* ("is-ness," objectivity), *jñeyatva* (knowability), and *abhidheyatva* (speakability), which Praśastapāda lists and coordinates as common attributes of all categories, are never explicitly mentioned in the Sūtra text.

The "causal" argument, which postulates an objective basis or support for linguistic and cognitive occurrences, plays a very significant role in the Vaiśeṣika presentation of time. Temporal notions, such as "posterior," "simultaneous," "quick," and so forth are indicators (*liṅga*) of time insofar as they are "caused" or conditioned by it. The commentators Vyomaśiva and Śrīdhara make this implication quite explicit. Such notions represent a "specific effect" (*viśiṣṭaṃ kāryam*) that presupposes an equally specific cause.[34] No such effect can arise without an appropriate basis—and this basis must be time itself (*na ca nimittam antareṇa kāryasya-utpattir asti, tasmād yad atra nimittam, sa kāla iti*).[35] Udayana, too, defends the premise that a specific cognition (*viśiṣṭapratyaya*) requires the presence of a regulating principle (*nimitta*) that serves as the specifying, defining factor (*viśeṣaṇa*) of the cognition.[36]

We may now return to Praśastapāda's statement that time is the cause of the origin, duration, and destruction of all effects or products, because of such (temporal) designation (*sarvakāryāṇāṃ ca-utpattisthitivināśahetus, tadvyapadeśāt*). Śrīdhara explains the phrase *tadvyapadeśāt* by referring to such expressions as "time of origin" (*utpattikāla*) and "time of destruction" (*vināśakāla*).[37] Udayana refers to the use of words like "today" (*adya*) and "tomorrow" (*śvas*) in statements concerning production or destruction.[38]

Vyomaśiva is more explicit. He mentions expressions which associate processes of origination, duration, and destruction with specific times, such as "midday" (*madhyānha*), the early morning (*prātar*), the end of the rainy season (*varṣānta*), and so forth; and he adds that here as in analogous cases (for instance, such phrases as *cākṣuṣaṃ vijñānam*, "visual cognition") the linguistic association reflects a causal connection.[39]

Quite obviously, Praśastapāda and his commentators once again use linguistic phenomena to make inferences concerning the metaphysical reality of time. But in this case, we are dealing not only with the sheer existence of time as the "cause" of words and cognitions, but also with its causal role in the extramental world. "Cognitive" causality is invoked to infer physical and metaphysical causality. Moreover, we are not dealing with time as a mere "condition of the possibility" of human experience, or as a "form of apprehension" ("Anschauungsform") in the Kantian sense. Nor is causality itself one of the "categories" or forms of synthesis through which we organize the material of experience. Praśastapāda and his commentators were not transcendental philosophers. Causality is a real force and structure of the extramental world; and time is a real causal factor. But once again, we have to ask: What precisely is its causal role?

4. In a work published in 1921, A. B. Keith noted: "But the term cause must not be understood in the sense that the Vaiśeṣika adopted the popular view that time was a great cosmic power which caused movement of things; this is wholly contradictory to the view of the Sūtra, which never attributes the origin of motion to time, as well as to the harmonious tradition of the school."[40] In 1956 E. Frauwallner observed that the atomistic and mechanistic world-view of old Vaiśeṣika, which tried to explain the production of things by assigning specific causes to them, did not leave room for time as a universal "cosmic cause" (*Weltursache*").[41] These observations are obviously justified. The network of causal explanation in Vaiśeṣika, and the later idea of causal aggregates (*kāraṇasāmagrī*), can hardly be reconciled with the notion of time as an independent creative power (*svātantryaśakti*) or as a cosmic "wire-puller."[42] In general, it does not seem to be compatible with any kind of active, dynamic cosmic force. This is certainly the conclusion drawn by some commentators. They tend to interpret time, just like space, as an indispensable condition or basis (*ādhāra*) of motion and causal processes, as a structured medium of their occurrence that determines their basic sequential character, but does not by itself produce any effects or initiate any motions. Śaṅkaramiśra's *Upaskāra* uses the concept of *ādhāra* to explain the role of time as "occasional cause" (*nimittakāraṇa*) of motion: *nimittakāraṇatvena-ādhāramātraṃ karmaṇaḥ kālaḥ*.[43] Śrīdhara uses the term *ādhāra* to paraphrase Praśastapāda's statement that time and space provide a common abode for all composite entities (*sarvasaṃyogisamānadeśatva*).[44]

Śrīdhara also notes that time and space have an indispensable "supplementary function" (*aṅgatva*) in all processes of causation or production. Their regulative causality (*nimittatva*) is implied in the fact that the production of an effect has to occur at one particular place in time and space (*idam eva ca deśasya kālasya ca nimittatvaṃ, yad ekatra kāryotpattir, anyatra-anutpattir iti*).[45] Udayana calls this rule that an effect always takes place at some particular time (*kadācit*) its *kādācitkatva*.[46]

Occurrence in time and space is an inherent condition of causal processes. More specifically, the relationship between cause and effect would not be possible without the sequential nature of time. Time regulates and distributes the appearance of products. It is not their dynamic and creative matrix. Praśastapāda's and Śrīdhara's views are quite different from those of the mythical *kālavāda*, the theory that time is a supreme cosmic power. This *kālavāda* is documented in the Atharvaveda, the later Upaniṣads, and the Mahābhārata.[47] It is present in Bhartṛhari's chapter on time and in the *Yuktidīpikā*, and discussed in even greater detail in Jaina literature, for instance in Mallavādin's *Dvādaśāranayacakra* (together with Siṃhasūri's commentary) and again, much later in Guṇaratna's commentary *Tarkarahasyadīpikā* on Haribhadra's doxography *Ṣaḍdarśanasamuccaya*.[48] It is also familiar from various Buddhist texts, such as the *Mahāprajñāpāramitāśāstra* attributed to Nāgārjuna and Vasu's commentary on Āryadeva's *Śataśāstra*.[49] In a number of instances, the concept of *kāla* appears in association, but also in competition with the concept of *niyati;* that is, cosmic fate.

To be sure, reminiscences and adaptations of this ancient mythology of time are clearly recognizable in several Vaiśeṣika texts, most conspicuously in Vyomaśiva. Here, we get much more detailed references to certain specific regulative and generative powers of time or a regular association between recurrent times and certain events in nature. For instance, flowers appear invariably at certain times of the year. A causal relationship (*kāryakāraṇabhāva*) between such recurrent times and the appropriate seasonal phenomena can thus be ascertained by means of "positive and negative concomitance" (*anvayavyatireka*).[50]

Yet in general, it remains true that the Vaiśeṣika concept of time is only a faint and distant echo of the ancient mythology of time as a universal cosmic power and as the matrix of all entities. In classical Vaiśeṣika, time has been stripped of its dynamic and creative aspects. It is still a medium and framework of causal processes, and it may be invoked to account for certain regularities in nature. But its own causal power has become elusive and deeply ambiguous. For the most part, it serves to explain cognitive and linguistic phenomena and to provide a foundation for our linguistic behavior (*vyavahāra*). This is the kind of causality that is also ascribed to universals and other timeless and nonproductive entities. Time itself is an ultimate substance among other ultimate, irreducible substances. It is just one item in the list of basic world constituents.

5. As we have seen, Praśastapāda ascribes five qualities (*guṇa*) to time as well as space: *saṃkhyā* (number), *parimāṇa* (dimension), *pṛthaktva* (separateness), *saṃyoga* (conjunction), and *vibhāga* (disjunction). Among these, *saṃyoga* and *vibhāga* are the most important ones, as far as the relationship between time itself and the temporal phenomena is concerned. However, Praśastapāda's short chapter does not provide any details. For further clues, we have to turn to the sections on "remoteness" (*paratva*) and "proximity" (*aparatva*) in time and space, and on *saṃyoga* and *vibhāga* themselves.

As we noted earlier, the actual occurrence of *paratva* and *aparatva* depends on "relational cognition" that relates spatial or temporal objects to the standpoint of an observer. Referring to the case of spatial distance and proximity, Praśastapāda (as explained by Śrīdhara) tells us that such cognition reflects a larger or smaller number of interconnected "space points" (*dikpradeśa*) between the observer and the object. Due to its conjunction with the further points in space and based on the "relational cognition" of the observer the object that is further removed then acquires the quality "remoteness" (*tatas tām apekṣya pareṇa dikpradeśena saṃyogāt paratvasya-utpattiḥ*). Likewise, the object that is less remote is equipped with "proximity" (*aparatva*).[51] Remoteness and proximity in time, that is, priority and posteriority, are explained in an analogous fashion. An older man, with the characteristic marks of old age, causes the relational cognition of greater distance in time. On the basis of such cognition, and because of his conjunction with a more distant point in time (*kālapradeśa*), the quality *paratva* appears in this older person (*tatas tām apekṣya pareṇa kālapradeśena saṃyogāt paratvasya-utpattiḥ*). Likewise, the quality *aparatva* takes residence in the younger person—by virtue of the appropriate relational awareness and because of this person's conjunction with a less remote point in time.[52]

Conjunction is possible only if at least one of the conjoined entities is of limited size and has the capability of separate, independent motion (*pṛthaggatimattva*). Accordingly, there can be no conjunction between ubiquitous entities (*vibhūnāṃ tu parasparataḥ saṃyogo na-asti*).[53] This implies that ether, space, and the souls (*ātman*), as ubiquitous substances, can neither be conjoined with nor contained in time. In a literal sense, they exist apart from time or side by side with it. This would not eo ipso exclude the atoms from existence in time or from temporality. However, Praśastapāda and his commentators tend to exclude permanent (*nitya*) entities altogether from the domain of time and temporality. Both Vyomaśiva and Śrīdhara take such exclusion simply for granted when they note somewhat casually that the distinction between priority and posteriority (*pūrvāparabhāva*) does not apply to permanent entities.[54]

We may note here that later authors often defined the concepts of past, present, and future in terms of (or more specifically, as "correlates," *pratiyogin*, of) "prior" and "posterior nonbeing" (*prāgabhāva, pradhvāṃsābhāva*) of particular entities. For any entity, the past time (i.e., the time of its being in the past) is that time which is specified by its "posterior nonbeing" or disappearance, whereas its future (i.e., the fact that it is still "in the future") is determined by its "prior nonbeing," the fact that it is not yet there.[55] Accordingly, permanent entities, which are without prior and posterior nonbeing, would be without past and future. They would either be timeless or confined to an eternal present. The groundwork for this new type of definition was laid by Udayana himself. In his *Kiraṇāvalī*,[56] he defines the future (*bhaviṣyattā*) of an entity (*dharmin*) as the "factuality of its prior nonbeing" (*prāgabhāvāstitā*) and its past (*atītatva*) as the state of its destruction (*pradhvaṃsasthiti*) or its cessation (*nivṛtti*). Time itself is called "past," "present," or "future" only in a secondary, derivative sense. Although this may be basically compatible with Praśastapāda's approach, it certainly introduces a new perspective and goes, moreover, clearly beyond Vyomaśiva's and Śrīdhara's explanations of the same passage.[57]

It is obvious that in Praśastapāda's theory of remoteness and proximity time appears as a precise analogue, if not replica, of space. It is equally obvious that his notions of "conjunction with time" (*kālasaṃyoga*) and of points or segments of time (*kālapradeśa*) are not thoroughly worked out. Their exact meaning remains elusive. How can things "move" in time, so that an increasing number of conjunctions or contacts with time can be accumulated? Of course, there is the familiar association with cyclical events and recurrent movements of the sun and other celestial bodies. The commentators propose various forms of association with such cycles, especially the revolution of the sun (*ādityaparivartana*), to measure distance in time.[58] But how does the idea of an extent, or measurable dimension, relate to the time substance as such? What precisely is a point or segment of time (*kālapradeśa*)? How does it relate to the concept of a "moment" (*kṣaṇa*) that Praśastapāda lists among the conventional indicators of time?

6. Time itself, in its timeless essence, is not "momentary" (*kṣaṇika*). It is the cause (*hetu*) or condition of our conventional reference (*vyavahāra*) to "moments" and other units of time. But it is in no way defined or affected by such conventional notions. The terms *kṣaṇika* and *kṣaṇikatva*, as well as the word *kṣaṇa* itself, do not even appear in the Vaiśeṣikasūtra.[59] In Praśastapāda, they are introduced in a somewhat casual fashion. Their role is limited, if not marginal; yet the fact that they do find their way into the system has a certain symptomatic significance.

According to Praśastapāda, "momentariness" (*kṣaṇikatva*) characterizes all motions (*karman*) and some qualities (*guṇa*). Śrīdhara explains momentariness as "being subject to very fast destruction" (*āśutaravināśitva*).[60] Among the qualities, those of ether and the souls, that is, sound (*śabda*) and such mental attributes as cognition (*buddhi*), desire (*icchā*), and effort (*prayatna*), provide examples of momentariness.[61] Disjunction (*vibhāga*), too, is always momentary and, moreover, not even embedded in a series of consecutive moments.[62] In addition to this general association with "momentariness," the concept of *vibhāga* and its counterpart *saṃyoga* have a special affinity with the notion of "wholes" (*avayavin*); that is, composite substances which owe their existence and continuity to the conjunction of their parts. If anything changes in this respect, that is, if there is any destruction (*vināśa*) or production (*utpatti*) of pertinent conjunctions or disjunctions, then their identity is jeopardized, and they are exposed to a potential "momentariness" sui generis.[63] However, the Vaiśeṣika idea of momentariness does not amount to the radical Buddhist identification of existence and flux. Even the momentary existence of sounds, and so forth, still covers phases of several moments (including the moment of destruction).

In Praśastapāda's system the qualities *saṃyoga* and *vibhāga* are real entities whose occurrence, that is, production and destruction, calls for a causal explanation. In his attempt to provide this explanation, Praśastapāda used the terms *utpatti* and *vināśa* as tools of description and analysis. He did not present them as objects of analysis, nor did he reify them in any way comparable to the reification of *saṃyoga* and *vibhāga*. Yet his treatment of *saṃyoga* and *vibhāga* provides a model for the subsequent thematization and reification of *utpatti* and, more specifically *vināśa,* which is associated with the Nyāya authors Aviddhakarṇa and Uddyotakara. In confronting the Buddhist claim that destruction (*vināśa, vināśitva*), constant loss of identity, is inherent in the nature of reality itself, these authors argued that its occurrence requires a causal explanation. The debate between the schools of Buddhist logic and Nyāya-Vaiśeṣika on this thesis that destruction or impermanence must have a cause (*vināśasya sahetukatvam*) was carried on for a number of centuries.[64] Among the Vaiśeṣika commentators, Śrīdhara was one of its most vigorous participants.[65]

In spite of the general rejection of Buddhist "impermanence" by the "orthodox" Hindu schools, the idea of the moment (*kṣaṇa*) did gain increasing significance in Hindu thought, most conspicuously in the Yoga school.[66] At this point, we do not have to discuss the details of these developments or the more specific attempts made by the Nyāya and Vaiśeṣika teachers to respond to the challenge of Buddhism, to reinterpret or neutralize its radical theory of momentariness, and to provide their own definition of *kṣaṇa, kṣaṇikatva,* and so on.[67] Nor do we have to discuss the various ways in which the increasing emphasis on, and reification of, nonbeing (*abhāva*) relates to these developments.[68]

We may now return to our earlier question concerning the relationship between the substance *kāla* and the phenomena of temporality and change. Praśastapāda pays little attention to the details of this relationship. He tends to disregard the problems and paradoxes of past, present, and future that have occupied not only the Buddhist schools, but also the grammarians and the Naiyāyikas. It may suffice here to recall Patañjali's *Mahābhāṣya,* Nāgārjuna's *Madhyamakakārikā,* and Vātsyāyana Pakṣilasvāmin's *Nyāyabhāṣya.*[69]

E. Frauwallner has referred to the following curious observations in connection with Praśastapāda's treatment of temporal "remoteness" and "proximity" (*paratva, aparatva*): These notions are discussed with exclusive reference to the present; that is, to two persons of different age who exist contemporaneously with an observer whose "relational cognition" (*apekṣābuddhi*) ascertains and actualizes their respective priority and posteriority.[70] The ontological status of what is no longer present (i.e., "in the past") or not yet present (i.e., "in the future") is not explicitly discussed. Frauwallner considers the possibility that this might be a deliberate disregard or omission. Whether it was deliberate or not, we may certainly say that this kind of omission reflects and reinforces Praśastapāda's attempt to objectify and essentialize time and temporality and to neutralize and domesticate them in his system of categories.

7. The Vaiśeṣika concept of time, as presented in the Vaiśeṣikasūtra and Praśastapāda's *Padārthadharmasamgraha,* was questioned and criticized not only from the outside, by competing and hostile schools. Even within the Vaiśeṣika and Nyāya tradition, the status of *kāla* as a special substance was not universally accepted. It was questioned and reinterpreted not only by the radical innovator Raghunātha Śiromaṇi, who identified space, time, and ether with God,[71] but also by the generally rather conservative Śivāditya. In his *Saptapadārthī,* Śivāditya suggests that ether, time, and space are in reality one and the same substance, and that they appear to be different only because they are associated with different functions and superimposed properties: *ākāśāditrayaṃ tu vastuta ekam eva upādhibhedān nānā bhūtam.*[72]

Unlike Praśastapāda, Śivāditya does not use the word *hetu*, "cause," in his definition of time. Instead, he says: "Time is of three kinds—i.e., characterized by production, duration, and destruction: (*kālas tu-utpattisthitivināśalakṣaṇas trividhaḥ*).[73] According to Mādhava's commentary on this passage, *utpatti* corresponds to the future, *sthiti* to the present, and *vināśa* to the past (*utpattyā bhaviṣyan, sthityā vartamānaḥ, vināśena bhūtakālo lakṣyate iti trividhaḥ*).[74] However, Śivāditya's identification of ether, time, and space is usually disregarded by the authors of other familiar handbooks of the combined Nyāya and Vaiśeṣika systems, for instance Keśavamiśra's *Tarkabhāṣā*, Laugākṣi Bhāskara's *Tarkakaumudī*, and Annaṃbhaṭṭa's *Tarkasaṃgraha*.

The most elaborate and explicit critique of Praśastapāda's description and explanation of time is found in Bhāsarvajña's *Nyāyabhūṣaṇa*. Bhāsarvajña quotes verbatim a good deal of Praśastapāda's section on time[74] and then proceeds to refute his arguments. According to Bhāsarvajña, real, absolute time can be established neither as the indispensable cause or condition of certain cognitive and linguistic phenomena nor as a universal cosmic or physical cause. The Lord (*īśvara*) alone deserves to be recognized as the cause of all cognitive and noncognitive effects (*bhagavān īśvaras tāvat sarveṣāṃ jñānājñānātmakānāṃ kāryāṇāṃ nimittam asti*).[76] Bhāsarvajña also rejects Praśastapāda's theory of the apparent or figurative diversification of time, as well as his explanation of distance and proximity (*paratva, aparatva*).[77] In general, time cannot be established as the substrate of qualities. "Therefore, time is not a substance" (*tasmān na dravyaṃ kālaḥ*).[78] If time and space were to be credited with universal cosmic causality (*jagannimittatva*), then this would be nothing but a reference to the Lord "under a different name" (*nāmāntareṇa*). However, because time and space are considered to be unconscious (*acetana*), they would not constitute appropriate objects of devotion.[79]

Bhāsarvajña is a decidedly theistic thinker, a theologian as well as philosopher. The concept of God emerges not only in his treatment of time and space, but also in connection with the notion of being itself. In an earlier section of his *Nyāyabhūṣaṇa*, he discusses the idea of "divine cognition" (*īśvarajñāna, parameśvarajñāna, maheśvarajñāna*) and its relation to being and time and presents the following observations: Entities in all three time phases, not only those in the present, are objects of divine awareness. If something loses its status of being present and becomes a matter of the past it does not therefore abandon its connection with divine cognition (*vartamānasvabhāvaṃ hitvā-atītabhāvam upagacchan na-īśvarajñānasambandhaṃ jahāti*).[80] "Association with divine cognition" thus provides a wider horizon of being than *sattāsambandha*, "connection with (the universal) reality." *Sattāsambandha* applies to entities that exist in the present; it lasts as long as an entity is actually present. *Īśvarajñānasambandha*, on the other hand, preserves those entities that have lapsed into the past and anticipates those that have not yet arrived and are still "in the future." Divine cognition thus provides a framework and receptacle of reality in its widest sense—wider than the highest universal, *sattā*, and encompassing also *astitva*, the common denominator of all six categories.

Through this juxtaposition with his theological notion of *īśvarajñānasambandha*, Bhāsarvajña exposes the temporal dimension and limitation of the concept of *sattāsambandha* that Praśastapāda left unexplained and unexplored. In a sense, the *Padārthadharmasaṃgraha* seems to avoid or suppress the earlier temporal implications of the concept, its association with *utpatti* ("production", "genesis") and so forth. As we have seen in the preceding chapter, Mallavādin and others provide us with some historical insight concerning these hidden and forgotten implications.[81] We have also seen that Praśastapāda tends to disregard the entire thematic syndrome of actuality and potentiality, manifestation and latency, and of the ontological status of past, present, and future. He does not refer to the extensive Buddhist and Hindu debates on these issues. Nor does he contribute to the ontological defense and phenomenological analysis of the present time, which is so conspicuous in Vātsyāyana Pakṣilasvāmin's *Nyāyabhāṣya* and other Nyāya works.[82] In general, Praśastapāda does not respond explicitly to the Buddhist notion of momentariness, nor to the radical critique and denial of time and being-in-time that we find in Nāgārjuna's Śūnyavāda.[83]

8. The Vaiśeṣika concept of time, on the one hand, and its treatment of temporality and impermanence, on the other hand, illustrate once again its basic ontological orientation. They exemplify its commitment to a definitive enumeration, classification, objectification, and identification of what there is. These objectives determine its understanding of what there is, and its conception of being itself. *Sattā* and *astitva* are horizons of enumeration and classification, common denominators of what there is in a sense of "being" that implies, above all, enumerability and identifiability—and that is supposed to provide definitive and unambiguous support for objectifying, representational thought and speech.

Time itself is an enumerable, juxtaposable entity, "an ultimate substance among other ultimate, irreducible substances. It is just one item in the list of basic world constituents."[84] Temporality has been marginalized. Impermanence, change, and the loss of identity have been neutralized and domesticated in the system of ultimate enumerables and irreducible world constituents. The verbal connotations of the words for "being," especially the root *bhū*, do not play any role in this system. The notion that being itself might be an act or process (*kriyā*) is not taken into consideration. This applies not only to the radical Buddhist identification of being-becoming (*bhūti*) as sheer temporality, that is, as a substrateless process (*kriyā*),[85] but also to less radical verbal interpretations of *bhāva* in other schools of Indian grammatical and philosophical thought; here, existence appears not just as a process occurring in time, but as the "activity" of upholding oneself or one's own identity (*ātmadhāraṇa*).[86] *Bhāva*, as used by Kaṇāda and Praśastapāda, is simply a synonym of *sattā;* that is, another term for the highest among the timeless universals.[87]

The *Vaiśeṣikasūtra* uses the word *kriyā* commonly as a synonym of its technical term *karman*, as another word for the category of (primarily physical) motion.[88] Praśastapāda uses *kriyā* less frequently. His discussion of *karman* also focuses on various types of physical motion; in addition, it refers to the mental and physiological initiation of such motions.[89] Obviously, the Vaiśeṣika category of *karman/kriyā* covers only a segment of what is called *act* or *process* in other schools and correlated with the semantic domain of the verb. Nonetheless, it is here where classical Vaiśeṣika accommodates, above all, the idea of momentariness; any *karman* is by definition *kṣaṇika*.[90] In spite of his fundamental belief in the correspondence of language, thought, and reality, Praśastapāda generally avoids specific grammatical arguments and references. In particular, he does not refer to the grammatical connotations of his terms *karman/kriyā* and *bhāva*. In this regard, his procedure is conspicuously different from that of Uddyotakara, whose arguments are often based on grammatical observations, and who refers specifically to the verbal associations of *bhāva*.[91]

The combination of grammar and metaphysics which we found in the *Vākyapadīya* has no parallel in the *Padārthadharmasaṃgraha.* In general, there is not much resemblance between Bhartṛhari's and Praśastapāda's expositions of time. Bhartṛhari's presentation is far more comprehensive and inclusive. He attempts a synthesis of earlier views on being and time, which takes into account the Buddhist theory of momentariness, while anchoring all verbal and temporal being in the unity and permanence of *brahman.* Of course, Bhartṛhari himself has been exposed to Buddhist and Jaina criticism, for instance in Dignāga's *Traikālyaparīkṣā*[92] and Mallavādin's *Dvādaśāranayacakra.* Mallavādin and his commentator Siṃhasūri try to include (and supersede) Bhartṛhari's views within a wider panorama of perspectives on being and time.[93]

In Buddhism, the tendency is an increasingly radical and explicit fusion of being and time or temporality. In other schools, specifically in Advaita Vedānta, time appears as fundamentally incompatible with reality in the true sense, that is, with the unbroken identity of *brahman;* accordingly, it is relegated to the status of *māyā,* cosmic illusion.[94] In the classical Vaiśeṣika system, time is marginalized and superseded not by being presented as an appearance or illusion, but by being raised to the status of an eternal, "timeless" substance. It appears side by side with other irreducible substances and timeless entities and is thus relegated to a small and somewhat marginal segment of what there is.[95]

Chapter 9: Notes

1. *VP* III/9, 1.

2. *VP* III/9, 3–5; see also 30; 42 (*kramarūpatā*); II, 22 with *Vṛtti;* K. A. Subramania Iyer, *Bhartṛhari;* pp. 112f., and in general on this chapter, P. S. Sharma, *The Kālasamuddeśa of Bhartṛhari's Vākyapadīya* (Delhi, 1972). H. Coward, "Time (Kāla) in Bhartṛhari's *Vākyapadīya,*" *JIPh* 10 (1982): 277–287, presents some basic and general observations.

3. VP III/9, 9f. See also Gaurinath Sastri, *The Philosophy of Word and Meaning* (Calcutta, 1959), pp. 28ff.

4. VP III/9, 16: *kriyā-abhivyajyate nityā;* that *sattā* is meant follows from the context and from the general structure of Bhartṛhari's thought; on *sattā* and *kriyā,* see also III/8 (*Kriyāsamuddeśa,* 22ff. (with Helārāja); and G. Cardona, "A Path Still Taken: Some Early Indian Arguments Concerning Time," *JAOS* 111 (1991): 445–

464. This richly documented article contains much valuable information on our topic, specifically on problems and debates concerning the status of the "present time" and "present action."

5. *VP* III/9, 17 (with Helārāja); see also III/1 (*Jātisamuddeśa*), 27, on the drive of the universals towards the "production of their substrates" (*svāśrayābhiniṣpatti*); and III/3 (*Sādhanasamuddeśa*), 81 (*ātmatattvaṃ prakāśate*).

6. VP III/9, 18.

7. Time is the *svātantryaśakti* of *brahman;* see later, n. 11.

8. *VP* III/9, 12; time thus seems to coincide with different times or phases of time, such as the seasons, the world periods, and more generally past, present, and future.

9. *VP* III/9, 46.

10. *VP* III/9, 51ff. The irreversibility is stated more explicitly and categorically by Helārāja in his commentary on v. 53. Helārāja attributes the view that the same entities pass again and again through the phases of past, present, and future (i.e., emerge from, and disappear in, *prakṛti* in endless cycles) to the Pañcādhikaraṇa school of Sāṃkhya.

11. See Helārāja on III/9, 62; see also *VP* I, 3 (on *brahman's* "power of time," *kālaśakti*).

12. *VP* III/9, 79 (with Helārāja); see also III/1, 36f. (on Vārṣyāyaṇi's "six modifications of being", *bhāvavikāra,* known from Yāska's *Nirukta,* and on sequence as the very essence of such being).

13. Cf. *VP* III/9, 85; and the detailed discussion and documentation of these problems by G. Cardona (cited in n. 4).

14. See Helārāja on III/9, 1.

15. See Bhaṭṭotpala on *Bṛhatsaṃhitā* I, 7 (ed. A. V. Tripāṭhī, Benares, 1968, p. 9); Bhaṭṭotpala also cites *VP* III/9, 76, and refers to the view that time is the cause of the world (*jagataḥ kālaḥ kāraṇam*).

16. Cf. *VS* II, 2, 7–8; see also B. Faddegon, *The Vaiçeṣika System,* pp. 208ff.

17. VS II, 2, 6; the *Upaskāra* version has the variant reading *aparasmin aparam.*

18. Cf. *VS* II, 2, 9 (with Candrānanda); II, 2, 15 (13 in the *Upaskāra*) makes an analogous statement about space.

19. Cf. *VS* V, 2, 23 (21); *dikkālāv ākāśaṃ ca kriyāvadbhyo vaidharmyān niṣkriyāni;* but cf. also II, 2, 11 (9): *kāraṇe kālākhyā;* V, 2, 28 (26): *kāraṇena kālaḥ.* Candrānanda explains: *pratyayabhedasya kālo nimittakāraṇaṃ vyākhyātaḥ.*

20. Cf. *VS* VII, 2, 25 (21).

21. *PBh*, p. 22.

22. Ibid., p. 25.

23. Ibid., pp. 63f.; see also J. Sinha, *A History of Indian Philosophy*, vol. 1 (Calcutta, 1956), pp. 377–385.

24. Cf. *PBh*, p. 64: *tasya-ākāśavad dravyatvanityatve siddhe.*

25. Cf. ibid., p. 64: *maṇivat pācakavad vā nānātvopacāra iti*; see also *NK*, p. 66, on this passage.

26. On the role of *apekṣābuddhi*, see E. Frauwallner, *Gesch. d. ind. Phil.*, vol. 2, pp. 132ff.; 190ff. (*apekṣābuddhi* and numbers, *saṃkhyā*).

27. Cf. *PBh*, pp. 164ff. (with *NK*).

28. See n. 17 (on *VS* II, 2, 6); and E. Frauwallner, *Gesch. d. ind. Phil.*, vol. 2, n. 160 (on another variant: *param aparam*); see also *VS* VII, 2, 25f. (21f.).

29. *The Vaiçeṣika System*, p. 214.

30. See earlier, section 1. On the analogy between different functions (*kriyā*) of time and different human occupations, see also *VP* III/9, 32.

31. See *Vy.*, p. 143: *kāraṇānām abhāvo 'kāraṇatvam samavāyyasamavāyikāraṇatvābhāvaḥ. nimittakāraṇatvaṃ ca jñanotpattāv iṣyata eva; NK*, p. 20: *akāraṇatvaṃ samavāyyasamavāyikāraṇatvābhāvah, na tu nimittakāraṇatvapratiṣedho buddhinimittatvābhyupagamāt.* See also Uddyotakara, *NV* II, 1, 39: *parāparādipratyayānāṃ ca sanimittatvāt kālapratiṣedho na yuktaḥ.*

32. The Buddhist Abhidharma schools classify such "cognitive causes," or objective conditions for phenomena of awareness, as *ālambanapratyaya* (Pali: *ārammaṇapaccaya*). There is no explicit classification like this in the Vaiśeṣika theory of causality.

33. See, for instance, *VS* II, 2, 6. Praśastapāda adds the term *pratyaya* to the list of indicators of time (cf. *PBh*, p. 63). Although this term is not entirely absent in *VS*, it does not play any comparable role.

34. Vyomaśiva's presentation is very elaborate; cf. *Vy.*, pp. 342ff. (ed. Gaurinath Sastri, pp. 120ff.); specifically p. 344: *viśiṣṭakāryotpattau viśiṣṭena nimittena bhavitavyam.*

35. Śrīdhara, *NK*, p. 64.

36. Cf. *Kir.*, GOS, p. 78; the Bibliotheca Indica edition, p. 353, has some variant readings.

37. Cf. *NK*, p. 65.

38. *Kir.*, p. 78.

39. Cf. *Vy.*, p. 349; in his *Upaskāra* on *VS* II, 2, 9, Śaṅkaramiśra refers to such "seasonal" terms as *vernal* and *hibernal*.

40. *Indian Logic and Atomism*, p. 233.

41. *Gesch. d. ind. Phil.*, vol. 2, p. 111.

42. See earlier, section 1. The Vaiśeṣika does not have one single "cosmic cause" of the "origin, duration and destruction" of things, such as *brahman* (cf. Śaṅkara, *BSBh* I, 1, 2) or *prakṛti* (cf. the phrase *sthityutpattipralaya:* Īśvarakṛṣṇa, *SK*, 69).

43. On *VS* V, 2, 26; likewise, Jayanārāyaṇa's *Vivṛti* uses the expression *ādhārādheyabhāva* to explain the "causality" of time.

44. Cf. *NK*, p. 22.

45. Ibid., p. 25.

46. Cf. Udayana, *Nyāyakusumāñjali* (with four commentaries), ed. Padmaprasāda Upādhyāya and Ḍhuṇḍhirāja Śāstrī (Benares, 1957), p. 53.

47. See, for instance, *Atharvaveda* XIX, 53–54; *Śvetāśvatara Upaniṣad* I, 1–2 (*kāla* and other "first causes); J. Scheftelowitz, *Die Zeit als Schicksalsgottheit in der indischen und iranischen Religion* (Stuttgart, 1929), specifically pp. 12ff., on the Mahābhārata; F. O. Schrader, *Über den Stand der indischen Philosophie zur Zeit Mahāvīras und Buddhas* (Leipzig, 1902), pp. 16–30 (epic and systematic *kālavāda*); S. Schayer, *Contributions to the Problem of Time in Indian Philosophy* (Cracow, 1938), pp. 4–12; also K. K. Mandal, *A Comparative Study of the Concepts of Space and Time in Indian Thought* (Benares, 1968), pp. 3–53; Satyavrat Sastri, *Essays on Indology* (Delhi, 1963), pp. 149ff.

48. See Mallavādin, *DNC*. vol. 1, pp. 192ff.; 205–219; in Mallavādin's panorama of viewpoints, the *Kālavāda* (*kālakāraṇavāda, kālādvaita*) appears between the theories of "fate" (*niyati*) and "own-nature" (*svabhāva*); see also *Ṣaḍdarśanasamuccaya* by Haribhadra with Guṇaratna's commentary *Tarkarahasyadīpikā*, ed. L. Suali (Calcutta, 1905), pp. 10ff.; and *YD*, p. 131, on the interaction between time, the "material cause" (*upādāna*), and "fate" (*bhāgya*).

49. See É. Lamotte, *Le traité de la grande vertu de sagesse de Nāgārjuna* (*Mahāprajñāpāramitāśāstra*) (Louvain, 1944; reprint, 1981), pp. 76ff.; G. Tucci, *Pre-Diṅnāga Buddhist Texts on Logic from Chinese Sources* (Baroda, 1929, GOS; reprint, San Francisco, 1976), part I (*Śataśāstra*), pp. 76f.

50. See *Vy.*, p. 349. Much later, Viśvanātha Pañcānana, *Kārikāvalī*, v. 45, says: *janyānāṃ janakaḥ kālo jagatām āśrayo mataḥ;* Jayanārāyaṇa, *Vivṛti* on *VS* II, 2, 9, refers to scriptural statements on the cosmic role of time.

51. See *PBh*, p. 164; *NK*, p. 168; and E. Frauwallner, *Gesch. d. ind. Phil.*, vol. 2, pp. 228ff.

52. See *PBh*, pp. 164f.; *NK*, pp. 168f. Later on, distance in time was characterized as "restrictive," irreversible distance (*niyataparatva*), and distinguished from the *aniyataparatva* in space; cf. M. Tachikawa, *Structure of the World*, pp. 95f.; and *EIPh*, vol. 2, p. 524.

53. *PBh*, p. 141; on the possibility of an indirect conjunction, see Vyomaśiva, *Vy.*, p. 494.

54. See Vy., p. 126 (*pūrvāparabhāvānupapatti*); *NK*, p. 17 (*pūrvāparabhāvābhyupagama*); see, on the other hand, *YBh* IV, 33. Vyāsa, who distinguishes the absolute eternity (*kūṭasthanityatā*) from the *pariṇāminityatā* of *prakṛti*, ascribes sequence, as the flow of moments, also to eternal, permanent entities (*nityeṣu ca kramo dṛṣṭaḥ*).

55. See, for instance, Laugākṣi Bhāskara, *Tarkakaumudī*, ed. and trans. P. I. Gradinarov, *The Moon-Light of Logic* (Delhi, 1991), section 8; see also J. Sinha, *A History of Indian Philosophy*, vol. 1 (Calcutta, 1956), p. 382.

56. Cf. *Kir.*, GOS, pp. 80f.; Bibliotheca Indica, p. 357 (with some variant readings).

57. See *NK*,p. 66; *Vy.*, p. 351.

58. See *Vy.*, p. 343: *janmanaḥ prabhṛty ekasya ādityaparivartanāni bhūyāṃsi-iti paratvam, anyasya ca alpīyāṃsi-ity aparatvam;* see also *Kir.*, GOS, pp. 76f. (*pratyāsatti*).

59. See, on the other hand, *YS* III, 9; 52; IV, 33. The flow of such moments applies to permanent as well as impermanent entities.

60. Cf. *PBh* and *NK*, p. 290.

61. Cf. *PBh*, p. 25: *ākāśātmanāṃ kṣaṇikaikadeśavṛttiviśeṣaguṇavattvam.*

62. Cf. ibid., p. 152: *vināśas tu sarvasya vibhāgasya kṣaṇikatvād . . . kṣaṇika iti.*

63. See earlier, Chapter 5.

64. Cf. K. Mimaki, *La réfutation bouddhique de la permanence des choses* (Paris, 1976), pp. 26ff.; 125ff.

65. Cf. *NK*, pp. 75ff.

66. Cf. *YBh* III, 52. Vyāsa rejects the notion that time as such is a real entity; see also B. M. Sinha, *Time and Temporality in Sāṃkhya-Yoga and Abhidharma Buddhism* (Delhi, 1983), pp. 82ff.

67. For a definition of *kṣaṇa*, see Śivāditya, *SP*, sections 130f. (ed. Gurumurti, pp. 95f.). Raghunātha Śiromaṇi, who rejected the idea of time as a substance, added the concept of *kṣaṇa* to his list of categories; see *Padārthatattvanirūpaṇa*, ed. and trans. K. H. Potter (Cambridge, Mass., 1957), pp. 14f.; 73ff.

68. See, for instance, D. N. Shastri, *Critique of Indian Realism* (Agra, 1964), pp. 395–418.

69. Cf. Patañjali, *Mahābhāṣya*, vol. 2, pp. 123f.; *NS* and *NBh* II, 1, 39ff. (Calc. S.S., vol. 1, pp. 517ff.); Nāgārjuna, *MK*, ch. 2 (*Gatāgataparīkṣā*); cf. also G. Cardona (cited in n. 4); and M. Hiriyanna, "An Indian View of Present Time," *Indian Philosophical Studies* (Mysore, 1957), pp. 121–126 (on the present time as "duration", according to the Nyāya interpretation).

70. Cf. E. Frauwallner, *Gesch. d. ind. Phil.*, vol. 2, p. 112.

71. Cf. *Padārthatattvanirūpaṇa* (cited in n. 67), p. 23: *tatra dikkālau na-īśvarād atiricyete, mānābhāvāt.*

72. See Śivāditya, *SP*, section 18 (ed. Gurumurti, p. 19); Candrakānta, *Vaiśéṣikadarśanam* (Calcutta, 1887), p. 4. This view is also found in later Sāṃkhya literature, for instance Aniruddha's *Sāṃkhyasūtravṛtti* and Vijñanabhikṣu's *Sāṃkhyapravacanabhāṣya* on *Sāṃkhyasūtra* II, 12. By contrast, older Sāṃkhya and Yoga simply reject the notion of time as a separate entity; see n. 66. H. Ui's claim (see *The Vaiśeṣika Philosophy*, pp. 136f.) that Praśastapāda, too, regarded ether, time, and space as ultimately one and the same entity is based on his misunderstanding of the phrase *ākāśakāladiśām ekaikatvād* (*PBh*, p. 58).

73. Cf. *SP*, section 16 (ed. Gurumurti, p. 18).

74. Cf. *SP*, ed. A. M. Bhattacharya (Calcutta, 1934), p. 22. For Śivāditya's own definition of *utpatti, sthiti, vināśa*, etc., see *SP*, sections 128ff. (ed. Gurumurti, pp. 94ff.); also sections 188 ff. (ed. Gurumurti, pp. 144ff.).

75. See *NBhūṣ*, p. 590 (with some obvious errors and variations from Praśastapāda's text); the quotation was not identified as such by the editor, Yogīndrānanda.

76. Ibid., p. 591.

77. Ibid., p. 592.

78. Ibid., p. 593.

79. Ibid., p. 593; Bhāsarvajña seems to reduce time to a measure and property (*viśeṣaṇa*) of motions and actions (*kriyā*) and refers specifically to its ultimate units, the moments (*kṣaṇa*).

80. Ibid., p. 468. This may remind us of Christian and Islamic ideas concerning the presence of all things in the mind of God (as, for instance, in Avicenna/ibn Sīnā).

81. See earlier, Chapter 8.

82. See earlier, n. 69 (on *NS* and *NBh* II, 1, 39ff.).

83. See Nāgārjuna, *MK*, ch. 2 (*Gatāgataparīkṣā*) and ch. 19 (*Kālaparīkṣā*).

84. See earlier, section 4.

85. We may refer here to a familiar Buddhist verse that seems to go back to the *Paramārthagāthā* attributed to Asaṅga (cf. A. Wayman, *Buddhist Insight*, ed. G. Elder; Delhi, 1984, p. 336, v. 5), and that appears with a number of variant readings in Buddhist, Hindu, and Jaina literature. L. de La Vallée Poussin's edition of Nāgārjuna, *MK* (with Candrakīrti), p. 116, n. 1, gives the following version: *kṣaṇikāḥ sarvasaṃskārā, asthirānāṃ kutaḥ kriyā | bhūtir yā-eṣāṃ kriyā sā-eva kārakaṃ sā-eva ca-ucyate*. For other occurrences, see, for instance, Mallavādin, *DNC*, vol. 3, pp. 801, 807; Vācaspati, *Tattvavaiśāradī* on *YS*/*YBh* IV, 20; *Bhāmatī* on *BS*/*BSBh* II, 2, 20; and numerous later texts. In all its versions, the verse identifies being as a pure act or process and leaves no room for a separate agent.

86. See, for instance, Yāska, *Nirukta* I, p. 2 (on Vārṣyāyaṇi's "six modifications of being"); and the detailed presentation by G. Cardona (cited in n. 4). The phrase *ātmadhāraṇaṃ* (or *svarūpadhāraṇaṃ*) *karoti* is used by Bhaṭṭoji Dīkṣita (as quoted by H. Narain, *Evolution of the Nyāya-Vaiśeṣika Categoriology*, vol. 1; Benares, 1976, p. 166). It follows the traditional interpretation of *asti* in Yāska I.2; cf. Bhartṛhari III/3 (*Sambandhasamuddeśa*), p. 47: *ātmānam ātmanā bibhrad asti;* Helārāja says: *ātmānam ātmanā dhārayati-ity aster arthaḥ;* see also III/8 (*Kriyāsamuddeśa*), 26 (with Helārāja).

87. But notice the temporal connotation in *bhāvitva*, as used in such compounds as *yāvaddravyabhāvitva*, *PBh*, p. 103.

88. Cf. *VS* I, 1, 14 (Candrānanda paraphrases *kriyā* as *karman*); II, 1, 12; V, 2, 23; etc.

89. Cf. *PBh* (with *NK*), pp. 290–311. Bhāsarvajña does not accept *karman* as an independent category and subsumes it instead under *guṇa;* see *NBhūṣ.*, p. 158.

90. See earlier, section 6.

91. Cf. *NV* I, 1, 10 (Calc. S. S., vol. 1, p. 191): *sarvo hi bhāvo bhavitāram apekṣate, kriyātvād utpattivad iti;* see also *NV* IV, 1, 21 (vol. 2, p. 948: *dvayī hi naḥ kriyā, utkṣepaṇādikā ca-ākhyātaśabdavācyā ca*.

92. Cf. E. Frauwallner, *Kl. Schr.*, pp. 785ff.

93. Mallavādin and Siṃhasūri discuss the philosophy of the grammarians in the fifth *Ara;* cf. *DNC*, vol. 2, pp. 377–415. The verbal, dynamic interpretation of being gains great significance in the Pratyabhijñā school of Śaivism. Being (*sattā, bhavattā*) itself appears as a divine act, as the "vibration" (*sphuraṇa, spandana*) of the absolute; see, for instance, Utpaladeva, *Pratyabhijñākārikā* I, 45 with his own *Vṛtti* (*sphurattā mahāsattā; bhavanakartṛtā*); see also Abhinavagupta's *Vimarśinī* and *Vivṛtivimarsinī* on this verse (= I, 5, 14).

94. For some general observations, see A. N. Balslev, *A Study of Time in Indian Philosophy* (Wiesbaden, 1983), pp. 57–72. In *BSBh* II, 3, 7, Śaṅkara ascribes the nature of eternal presence (*vartamānasvabhāva*) to the self (*ātman*).

95. Numerous modern studies on time and temporality in Indian thought have been compiled by H. S. Prasad in two recent anthologies: *Essays on Time in Buddhism* (Delhi, 1991); and *Time in Indian Philosophy* (Delhi, 1991; essays on non-Buddhist schools). However, few of these contributions deal explicitly with the ontological meaning of time or the fundamental question of "being and time."

10

Epilogue

1. In his article "Heidegger and Vedānta: Reflections on a Questionable Theme," J. L. Mehta speaks of the "metaphysical," that is, "representational" and "concept-generating," dimension of the Sanskrit tradition and of the "ontological speculation" it has produced. He suggests that Sanskrit and the Indian philosophical tradition (unlike the East Asian languages and traditions) failed to attract Heidegger's attention, because they were too close to the language and thought of the Greeks. "Since *this* possibility of thinking has been fulfilled in its amplest and purest form in the Greek tradition, Heidegger is not interested in how Sanskrit speaks (in the sense in which, according to Heidegger, it is language that speaks, not man), nor in the tradition that has evolved out of it."[1]

Mehta adds the following long note to these observations and suggestions:

> Granting the metaphysical component in Sanskrit, however, it may be instructive to investigate the correctives it has developed against this representational or objectifying element, thus exhibiting its

> own unique genius: a mode of utterance in which representation and the cancellation of the representative force are held in tension and balance. Perhaps the uniqueness of Indian philosophy and religion lies in the simultaneous deobjectification of the objectified, in the iconoclastic moment which is never for long absent from its iconism. If, as Heidegger admits (*Discourse on Thinking*, New York: Harper and Row, 1966, 46), thinking is of two kinds, calculative and meditative or representational and nonrepresentational, it may yet be of significance to his concern to see how Indian thought took notice of the problem which it so explicitly recognized as crucial, the forms in which the problem presented itself as a haunting, ever-present task for thinking, and the solutions offered. Looked at from this point of view, the history of Indian philosophy may prove to be not just an antiquarian, humanistic pursuit but a treasure house of direct promise to the Heideggerian quest.[2]

Mehta's suggestion that an assumed lack of "otherness" accounts for Heidegger's failure to respond to Indian thought is intriguing in spite of the fact that Heidegger asserted the uniqueness of the Greek tradition against the Indian tradition no less than against any other non-European tradition. In his view, Greece alone has produced philosophy, metaphysics, and the basic conditions of science and technology. Heidegger rejects the very idea of "Indian philosophy." The tradition of philosophy and metaphysics is, by definition, that very tradition which has produced modern science, technology, and the "atomic age." The commitment to the "question of being" as well as the most radical "oblivion of being" are in a unique way associated with Europe, with its peculiar development of calculation, representation, and objectification, and a will to power that has led to nihilism and relativism as well as to the domination of the earth. Heidegger does not pursue the question whether or how the "question of being" may have been asked *and* forgotten in India or other non-European traditions. He does not explore or even consider the possibility that representational and objectifying thought, and the intellectual will to power, may have evolved in such traditions, without dominating them as they did in Europe and without producing the same results of science, technology, and modernity.

It has not been the purpose of our investigations, nor is it the purpose of this brief epilogue, to test or refute Heidegger's grand and provocative vision of the "question of being" and the uniqueness and coherence of the Greek-European tradition. Nor do we have to discuss the elusive question to what extent this vision is susceptible to empirical, that is, historical and philological, refutation.[3] But in accordance with J. L. Mehta's suggestions, we may certainly propose the following diagnosis: "Representational," "objectifying" thought is fully present in the Vaiśeṣika system of categories, in its enterprise of enumerating and classifying whatever there is, and above all, in its conceptualizations of being. To be sure, it is not a Cartesian attempt to establish man as the master and owner of nature; but it is an attempt to put the world at our intellectual and conceptual disposal, to explain it once and for all through a process of comprehensive enumeration and classification. Being itself is either objectified and appears as an entity among entities or it accompanies the process of enumeration as its receding horizon or expanding shadow. Temporality, change, and evanescence are neutralized and "mastered" by positing time itself as a timeless substance.

2. In the traditional Indian ranking of the systems of philosophy, especially in the doxographies inspired by Advaita Vedānta, the place of the Vaiśeṣika is not very high.[4] In fact, it usually appears as the lowest among the "orthodox" (*āstika*) systems. We do not have to discuss here the extent of its "orthodoxy," i.e. its adherence to the Veda, and of its soteriological commitment. Both the "theism" and the soteriological relevance of the Vaiśeṣika have been questioned by traditional Indian opponents as well as modern scholars.[5] Śaṅkara called the Vaiśeṣikas "semidestructionists" or "seminihilists" (*ardhavaināśika*).[6] This is obviously meant to suggest a certain proximity to Buddhism. However, in the course of his presentation and critique of the Vaiśeṣika system, Śaṅkara did not pursue its relationship with Buddhism. Instead, he questioned the very nature and possibility of "categories," of establishing ultimate types or classes of entities, and of objectifying and conceptualizing being itself. Classification and categorization may work in various contexts of ordinary practical life. But they cannot be brought to the level of the "totality" of what there is nor can they be applied to an absolute truth and reality beyond all contexts of practical, pragmatic orientation.[7]

The Vaiśeṣikas coordinate and juxtapose their "categories," their basic divisions of what there is, as if they were natural species, "such as humans, horses, and rabbits" (*yathā manuṣyo 'śvaḥ śaśa iti*).[8] On the other hand, they admit that all other categories depend on substance and could not exist without it (*dravyādhīnatvaṃ śeṣāṇām abhyupagacchanti*) They cannot deny the fact that they have a shared essence, an essential unity with the substance (*dravyātmakatā*). So how can qualities, motions, and other abstract attributes be coordinated with the underlying substance? Furthermore, once we start objectifying, reifying, and enumerating abstractions, why should we list only six? Why not a hundred or a thousand?[9]

As we noted earlier, the question of the completeness of categorial, ontological enumeration and the potential proliferation of enumerables has been associated with Praśastapāda's statement that he had listed the subjects without their attributes (*evaṃ dharmair vinā dharmiṇām uddeśaḥ kṛtaḥ*).[10] Among the Vaiśeṣika commentators, it is, above all, Vyomaśiva who addresses this problem; likewise, he tries to deal with the nondualistic invocations of a potential collapse of all categorial distinctions and of the merger of all categories with a single category "substance" (*dravya*).[11]

For Śaṅkara, the enumerative approach, that is, the attempt to produce a finite and definitive list of categories or types of entities, is an equally artificial and futile attempt to subdivide and objectify what is one "without a second" (*advaita*) and transcends the dichotomy of being and nonbeing as well as that between subject and object.[12]

Later Advaita Vedāntins criticize, above all, the notion of difference and particular identity (*viśeṣa, bheda, svarūpa*), which is the most fundamental premise of the Vaiśeṣika enterprise. Such authors as Śrīharṣa and Ānandabodha[13] argue against the very possibility of defining entities, of establishing them in their individual identity, and of defining and establishing being itself in its distinction from nonbeing. Their efforts are continued by Citsukha (a commentator of Śaṅkara as well as Śrīharṣa and Ānandabodha),[14] Madhusūdana Sarasvatī, and many others. Madhusūdana tells us that even God Brahmā himself would inevitably fail in the attempt to grasp the totality of what there is "in a specific manner" (*viśeṣākāreṇa*); that is, by identifying all its subdivisions. These are by definition endless and they depend, in fact, on the groundless, endless, and meaningless differentiation and proliferation of thought and language itself.[15]

3. Beyond the critique of objectification, differentiation, and enumeration, the Advaita Vedāntins see the ever-present goal of final liberation or transcendence, the nondual state of *ātman/brahman* that is prior to, and the condition of, all apparent dichotomies and alternatives, including those between being and nonbeing: *sad asat sadasac ca-iti vikalpāt prāg yad iṣyate tad advaitam.*[16] This is, in a sense, the primeval, precosmogonic unity of the Vedic-Upaniṣadic texts.[17] Soteriology appears as the reversal of cosmogony, a return to that transcendent unity of being and nonbeing which is supposed to precede the "first dharmas" (*dharmāni prathamāni*); that is, the first ritual and cosmogonic acts of establishing entities in their separate identities.[18]

The Buddhists, especially the Mahāyāna Buddhists, may be heterodox *vaināśika* and *nāstika* according to Śaṅkara's orthodox school, but they are certainly in full agreement with him as far as the basic assessment of objectification, enumeration, and classification is concerned. In its various manifestations in the Vaiśeṣika system of categories, or in the Abhidharma lists of *skandha, dhātu,* and *āyatana,*[19] enumeration and objectification are part of the conventional world of *saṃvṛti* and *vyavahāra.* They are symptoms of an acute cognitive defect and affliction (*avidyātimiropaghāta*), of an attachment to phenomena whose nature and identity is vacuous and inauthentic (*sāṃvṛta*).[20] "One should not enumerate dharmas."[21] One should not, above all, try to grasp, define, and objectify being and nonbeing and then, in turn, be enslaved and afflicted by this distinction. One should not be attached to the "identity" (*svabhāva*) of any particular entity nor to the dichotomy of being and nonbeing. Nobody has expressed this in more memorable formulations than Nāgārjuna. Those who are "seized by the monstrous belief in being" (*bhāvagrahagṛhīta*) require some kind of medical treatment (*cikitsā*).[22] The transcendence of *is* and *is not* (*astināstivyatikrama*), of nonbeing and being, or negativity and positivity (*nāstyastitvavyatikrama*), the quiescence of *is not* and *is* (*nāstyastitāśānti*) has to be achieved.[23] The calming down of verbal and conceptual proliferation, of the urge to objectify (*prapañcopaśama; draṣṭavyopaśama*), the disappearance of our preoccupation with being and nonbeing is *nirvāṇa.*[24]

Earlier in this study, we suggested that such radical rejection or transcendence of enumeration, categorization, objectification, and ontological conceptualization has, nevertheless, ontological implications. Negative ontology, deliberate silence about being and nonbeing, radical critique of worldly notions of being and identity may, indeed, be reflections and expressions of an intense search for, and commitment to, being and identity. In this context, we referred to the "soteriontology" of Advaita Vedānta and Mahāyāna Buddhism.[25]

Exploring the role and significance of "negative ontology" and "soteriontology" in the Indian tradition, and its search for nonrepresentational, nonconceptual, nonpossessive ways of thinking, has not been the purpose of this study. Nonetheless, we may agree with J. L. Mehta's statement that the Indian tradition has produced a unique "tension and balance" between representational and nonrepresentational thought[26] or between objectification and its transcendence. We may also suggest that any transcendence of, or withdrawal from, ontological conceptualization and objectification presupposes and requires that kind of honest and stubborn, though perhaps futile, conceptualization which we found exemplified by the Vaiśeṣika ontology and categoriology. There can be no meaningful silence about being without such efforts of speaking about it.

Chapter 10: Notes

1. See J. L. Mehta, *India and the West: The Problem of Understanding* (Chico, Calif., 1985), p. 236. Mehta's article was originally published in *International Philosophical Quarterly* 18 (1978) and also reprinted in *Heidegger and Asian Thought*, ed. G. Parkes (Honolulu, 1987).

2. Ibid., p. 265, n. 24.

3. Likewise, we have abstained from exploring the question of how the linguistic peculiarities of the Sanskrit language may have influenced or guided Indian thought about being; for some general reflections concerning the relationship between language and ontological thought, see earlier, Chapter 1 (especially the reference to the assessment by C. Kahn in n. 36). On Heidegger, India, and the "Europeanization of the earth," see also *India and Europe*, ch. 24.

4. Cf. *India and Europe*, ch. 19.

5. See earlier, Chapter 4; cf. also A. Thakur, "Kaṇāda—Āstika or Nāstika," *Journal of the Ganganatha Jha Kendriya Sanskrit Vidyapeetha* (Allahabad; formerly G. Jha Research Institute) 32 (1976): 121–135.

6. See *BSBh* II, 2, 18.

7. Cf. Śaṇkara on *Chāndogya Upaniṣad* VI, 2, 1 (critical references to the notion of being as highest universal); see also *Gītābhāṣya* XIII, 12 (reality, knowability, and the evaporation of the concept of being).

8. See *BSBh* II, 2, 17. Praśastapāda himself suggests that the juxtaposition

of substances qualities and motions is comparable to that of "hides, garments, blankets, and so forth" (*carmavastrakambalādi*; see *PBh*, pp. 311 f.

9. See ibid. (*Works*, vol. 2, p. 237): *na ca vaiśeṣikaiḥ kalpitebhyaḥ ṣaḍbhyaḥ padārthebhyo 'nye 'dhikāḥ śataṃ sahasraṃ vā-arthā na kalpitavyā iti nivārako hetur asti*).

10. See earlier, Chapter 7, section 7 (especially n. 69).

11. See *Vy.*, ChSS, p. 111. The idea of an open-ended doctrine of categories (*aniyatapadārthavāda*) has been suggested by some modern Naiyāyikas. But its meaning and origin are elusive, and it has no significance for traditional Nyāya and Vaiśeṣika; cf. P.K. Mukhopadhyay, *Indian Realism* (Calcutta, 1984), pp. 168; 226f.

12. See later, n. 16; on the meaning of *advaita*, cf. T. Vetter, *Studien zur Lehre und Entwicklung Śaṅkaras* (Vienna, 1979), pp. 30–34. *Chāndogya Upaniṣad* VI, 2, calls being (*sat*) itself "one without a second" (*ekam eva-advitīyam*).

13. Cf. Śrīharṣa, *Khaṇḍanakhaṇḍakhādya* (especially section 4: *Bhāvatvalakṣaṇakhaṇḍana*, a systematic refutation of all attempts to define being and nonbeing); also Ānandabodha, *Nyāyamakaranda*.

14. Cf. V. A. Sarma, *Citsukha's Contribution to Advaita* (Mysore, 1974), pp. 119–134 (a comprehensive refutation of the notions of difference and distinctive identity, as conceived in the Nyāya-Vaiśeṣika tradition); cf. also Sādhu Śāntinātha, *Māyāvāda* (Poona, 1938).

15. Cf. *Vedāntakalpalatikā*, ed. and trans. R. D. Karmarkar (Poona, 1962), p. 40: *sarveṣāṃ padārthānāṃ tena rūpeṇa* (i.e., *viśeṣākāreṇa*) *jñanaṃ brahmaṇo 'py aśakyam, anantatvāt*. Madhusūdana's most important work, the *Advaitasiddhi*, is a systematic response to the pluralistic metaphysics and ontology of Madhva's Dvaita Vedānta.

16. Śaṅkara, *Upadeśasāhasrī* XVI, 33.

17. Cf. Śaṅkara, *BUBh* I, 4, 7 (*Works*, vol. 1, p. 654; on the concepts of *avyākṛta*, *vyākṛta*, and *saṃsāra*).

18. See earlier, Chapter 2; cf. also *India and Europe*, ch. 17; and *BU* III, 8, 9 (*dyāvāpṛthivyau vidhṛte tiṣṭhataḥ . . .*) with Śaṅkara's commentary.

19. See earlier, Chapter 3, section 6.

20. Prajñākaramata on Śāntideva's *Bodhicaryāvatāra* (Bibliotheca Indica), p. 364 (as quoted by T. R. V. Murti, *The Central Philosophy of Buddhism*, 2d ed. London, 1970, p. 246): *yad etat skandhadhātvāyatanādisvarūpam upalabhante, tad eṣāṃ sāṃvṛtaṃ rūpam*.

21. See earlier, Chapter 3, section 6, and n. 27.

22. See *Acintyastava*, v. 52; cf. C. Lindtner, *Nāgārjuniana* (Copenhagen,

1982), pp. 140ff.; cf. also F. Tola and C. Dragonetti, "Nāgārjuna's Catustava," *JIPh* 13 (1985): 1–54 (especially p. 18).

23. See *Ratnāvalī* I, 62f.; I, 45.

24. See ibid., I, 42: *bhāvābhāvaparāmarśakṣayo nirvāṇam ucyate; MK* V, 8: *astitvaṃ ye tu paśyanti nāstitvaṃ ca-alpabuddhayaḥ / bhāvānāṃ te na paśyanti draṣṭavyopaśamaṃ śivam;* the term *prapañcopaśama* appears in the dedication (perhaps not by Nāgārjuna himself) which opens this work.

25. See earlier, Chapter 2, section 14.

26. See earlier, section 1.

Appendix 1: Selected Ontological Texts

1. Introduction

The following selections from Candrānanda's *Vṛtti* on the Vaiśeṣikasūtra, Vyomaśiva's *Vyomavatī,* Śrīdhara's *Nyāyakandalī,* and Udayana's unfinished *Kiraṇāvalī* are representative of classical Vaiśeṣika ontology. As a matter of fact, they are among the most coherent and explicit statements concerning the Vaiśeṣika concepts of being prior to the period of Navyanyāya. With the exception of Śrīdhara's *Nyāyakandalī,* these texts have so far not been translated into any Western language.[1]

Candrānanda's *Vṛtti* is without question the most ancient extant commentary on the Vaiśeṣikasūtra, although its precise date remains elusive. A terminus post quem is provided by the fact that Candrānanda cites Uddyotakara's *Nyāyavārttika* (probably seventh century).[2] He also seems to have known the work of Praśastapāda. On the other hand, Bhartṛhari's commentator Helārāja (tenth century) may have been familiar with the *Vṛtti.*[3] Hypothetically, we will assume a date around, or somewhat prior to, A.D. 900.

Vyomaśiva's *Vyomavatī* is the oldest extant commentary on Praśastapāda's *Padārthadharmasaṃgraha.* Vyomaśiva was familiar with the work of Dharmakīrti (seventh century) and perhaps Śaṇkarasvāmin (eighth century). On the other hand, the *Vyomavatī* precedes the work of Śrīdhara (tenth century). Accordingly, we may suggest a date around 800, or in the ninth century.[4] By his own testimony, Śrīdhara completed his *Nyāyakandalī* in 991.[5] Udayana's *Kiraṇāvalī* may have followed several decades later and belongs to the eleventh century.[6] Udayana's work concludes the period of classical Nyāya and Vaiśeṣika and paves the way for Navyanyāya. The treatment of Praśastapāda's ontological discourse is characteristically different in the three commentaries. For instance, whereas Vyomaśiva provides a very elaborate and coherent discussion of *sattāsambandha,* Udayana tends to neglect it. The choice of texts reflects these differences.

The three Praśastapāda commentaries refer extensively to opposing views (*pūrvapakṣa*). In addition, Vyomaśiva's text is interspersed with "internal dialogues" in which the author raises critical questions and potential objections for himself. In such cases, the alternation between standpoints (or questions and answers) is indicated by a dash (-). In general, the translation is meant to illustrate the style and method of the classical Vaiśeṣika discussions about being. It does not provide a full analysis. Parentheses indicate paraphrases or explanatory supplements to the text.

2. Vaiśeṣikasūtra *with Candrānanda's* Vṛtti, *ed. Jambuvijaya, GOS, 1,2,1–18; IX, 1–12.*

The Jaina scholar Jambuvijaya, who also edited Mallavādin's *Dvādaśāranayacakra,* published his edition of Candrānanda in 1961 (Baroda, GOS). Until 1957, the oldest available commentary on the Vaiśeṣikasūtra was the *Upaskāra* by Śaṇkaramiśra, written around 1500. Most of the older editions of the Sūtra text (since 1860) are accompanied by it. In 1957, Anantalal Thakur published an anonymous commentary which may be several centuries older than the *Upaskāra.*[7] The Sūtra texts used by these three commentaries vary significantly; Jambuvijaya's edition provides useful concordances.[8]

The edition is based upon two manuscripts: a Śāradā manuscript from the Oriental Institute, Baroda, and a Jaina Devanāgarī manuscript from the possession of the Jaina Muni Punyavijaya.[9]

TRANSLATION

a. 1, 2, 1–18

1: The nonexistence of the effect follows from the nonexistence of the cause.

The terms *effect* (or *product, kārya*) and *cause* (*kāraṇa*) have been mentioned previously.[10] (Kaṇāda) makes (this) statement in order to define them. The cause—inherential causes, for instance threads, as well as noninherential causes, such as their conjunctions—is such that a substance which is its effect, for instance a cloth, does not come into being if it is not there, or disappears with the destruction of (the cause). The effect is the opposite (of this).

2: But the nonexistence of the cause does not follow from the nonexistence of the effect.

However, if the substance (which is the effect), for instance the cloth, is not present, this does not mean that the threads or their conjunctions cannot occur.

The three attached (*ānuṣaṅgika*) categories, i.e., universals, (particularities, and inherence) have been mentioned.[11] Among these, he (now) explains the universals.

*3: Depending on (the mode of) cognition (*buddhyapekṣa*) (the universal appears as) universal or specific factor.*[12]

This means that it appears as a universal factor relative to the cognition of inclusion and as a specific factor relative to the cognition of exclusion—in the following sense: (On the one hand), it relates to an inclusive cognition, (such as the general notion) "cow" that recurs with reference to different individual (cows); (and on the other hand, it relates to a cognition such as) "this (cow) is different from that (other animal)" that is mutually exclusive insofar as these same individuals are concerned.

*4: Existence (*bhāva*) is a universal only.*[13]

Existence, that is, reality (*sattā*), is a universal only and not a specific factor, because it is inclusive with reference to all three (categories), substances, (qualities, and motions).

5: Substanceness, qualityness, and motionness are universals as well as specific factors.

These (factors) substanceness, qualityness, and motionness are universals, because the recurrent cognitions "substance", relating to (all substances, i.e.) earth and so forth, "quality," relating to (all qualities, i.e.) color and so forth, and "motion," relating to (all motions, i.e.) throwing upwards and so forth, are due to them. They are (also) specific factors, as they exclude one another.

6: (This ambiguity applies) except for the ultimate particularities.

"Particularities"—being factors of particularization (i.e., ultimate distinction) for those (accomplished yogins) who are capable of seeing them—are inherently present in the eternal substances, such as the atoms and ether, causing cognitions of ultimate exclusion (of the type) "this is one (ultimate individual), and this is another one" with reference to entities with equal shapes and qualities. Thus the particularities have been explained.

Reality (*sattā*), however, is

7: That which produces (the notion) "real" with reference to substances, qualities, and motions.

That which produces the recurrent cognition "real" with reference to the three different categories, substances and so forth, is reality.

If (it is said that reality) is destroyed once its substrates are destroyed, (we say): No, because

*8: Reality is something different (*arthāntara*) from substances, qualities, and motions.*

Because reality is distinct from substances and so forth, therefore it is not destroyed if the substances and so forth are destroyed.[14]

(Now there is) an argument for the distinctness (of reality) from substances and so forth:

9: It is not a substance, because it occurs in single (ultimate) substances.

A (single ultimate) substance, such as an atom or ether, is without (underlying) substance, because there is no substance that would be its (material) cause. And a (composite substance), for instance a pot, occurs in (i.e., consists of) more than one substance, because it is combined with those substances which are its inherential causes (*samavāyikāraṇa*). Reality, on the other hand, which is present without restriction in each individual entity, "is not a substance, because it occurs in single (ultimate) substances."

10: And because it exists in qualities and motions, it is not a motion or quality.

Reality cannot be a quality or a motion, because there are neither qualities in qualities nor motions in motions, but reality is present in qualities and motions.

11: Also, because there is no specific universal (inherent in it).

If reality were one among the substances and so forth, then specific universals, such as substanceness, would also be present in reality, just as in substances and so forth. But this is not so. Therefore, reality is not a substance, quality or motion.

12: Substanceness has (already) been established by (the criterion) "occurrence in single (ultimate) substances."[15]

Just as reality cannot be a substance, because it is fully present in each individual substance, so substanceness cannot be a substance, "because it occurs in single (ultimate) substances."

13: Also, by (the criterion) "that there is no specific universal (inherent in it)."

If substanceness were a substance, quality, or motion, then some specific universal, from among substanceness and so forth, would be present in substanceness, just as in substances and so forth. Therefore, (as this is not so,) substanceness is not a substance, (quality, or motion).

14: Qualityness is established because (of the fact that) it exists in qualities.[16]

Qualityness is not a quality, because there are no qualities in qualities, but qualityness is present in qualities.

15: Also, by (the criterion) "that there is no specific universal (inherent in it)."

If qualityness were a substance or motion, then substanceness or motionness would exist in it as specific universals. But this is not so. Therefore, qualityness is not a substance or motion.

16: Motionness is established because (of the fact that) it exists in motions.

Motionness is not a motion, because there is motionness in motions, but there is no motion in a motion.

17: Also, by (the criterion) "that there is no specific universal (inherent in it)."

Substanceness or qualityness would exist in motionness, if it were a substance or quality. Therefore, (as this is not so,) motionness is not a substance or quality.

18: Existence is one (and the same), because its indicator, (the notion) "real," is without distinction, and because there is no (other) indicator of distinction.[17]

The word *one* means nondifferentiation (*abheda*), not a number. The "indicator" (*liṅga*), that is, "that which indicates" (reality), is a notion. By means of this "indicator," that is, the recurrent notion "real," we become aware of reality. Because (this notion) is without distinction in all (its instances), and because there is no (other) notion containing (such) distinction, reality is without differentiation.

b. IX, 1–12[18]

Because (Kaṇāda) wants to clarify inference,[19] he now shows its domain (of application).

1: Because it does not have a function, quality, or designation, (an effect) is not real (prior to its production).

Not only sense perception, but inference, too, is unable to discover an effect prior to its production: There is inference if there is an indicator (i.e., an inferential mark); but there is no such indicator (of the effect prior to its production), because we do not notice any function or quality belonging to it; nor is there another (potential) indicator, referred to by the word *designation* (*vyapadeśa*). Therefore, (the effect) is not real prior to its production (*prāg utpatter asat*).

Afterwards—

2: What is real, (becomes) unreal.[20]

And an effect that has become real (*sat*), is nothing but unreal, once it has been destroyed (*pradhvasta*) at a later time; there is not just concealment of (something that remains) real, as it has, indeed, no function, quality, or designation.

In the time between (production and destruction), however—

3: The real is something different from the unreal, because it has function, quality, and designation.[21]

Prior to its destruction (*pradhvaṃsa*) and for the time after its production, a thing that has come to be something different from what is unreal is called *real* because there is function, quality, and designation.

4: Yet, (even what is) real "is not."

A thing, even if it is real, "is not" in a secondary sense,[22] insofar as it excludes what is different, as in "the ox is not a horse," or if it does not fulfill its function, as in "this is not a (real) ox, because it does not pull (the cart)."

5: And what is (entirely) different from the real, that, too, is unreal.

And what is different from (any) real thing in the sense that its nature is absolute (i.e., unqualified) nonexistence (*atyantābhāva*), so that it cannot be subsumed under prior, secondary, or posterior nonexistence (*prāgupādhipradhvaṃsābhāva*)—for instance, a hare's horn—that, too, is unreal, indeed.[23] If (the question is raised): "Since there is no differentiation of what is unreal—why do (productive) factors operate in the case of prior nonexistence only, but not in other cases?" (Then we respond):

"No, (this does not apply), because we are aware of (such) differentiation."

Concerning this (nonbeing)—

6: The cognition "unreal" (arises) because the perception of a past entity is no longer there, because of the recollection of (this) past entity, and because there is perception of something that contradicts (its continued existence).

The cognition "unreal" arises with reference to (a "posterior nonentity," i.e.) something that is unreal due to destruction (*pradhvaṃsāsat*) once we have determined its disappearance (for the following reasons): at present, we no longer perceive a past thing as we did before; we remember this past thing; we perceive something that contradicts (its continued existence), such as potsherds (which are incompatible with the continued existence of the pot of which they were parts). Otherwise, how could it be that we no longer perceive it—as (we assume that) its nature (and condition of visibility) has not changed?[24]

Concerning "prior nonexistence", however, (such cognition arises)—

7: Because likewise, there is perception of existence with reference to (what was) nonexistence.

Concerning prior nonexistence, the ascertaining cognition (that something was) "unreal" (arises) in the following manner: There was no perceptual cognition having a pot as object at the time of its prior nonexistence, when there was (only) a lump of clay, but now, distinctive cognition with a pot as object has emerged, which is incompatible (with the prior absence of such cognition); and we remember the state of nonexistence (of the pot). Therefore, (we conclude that) this entity has just now come into being, and previously, it was indeed without existence.

8: This (also) explains (the negative particle a-, *as in)* aghaṭa, *"non-pot,"* ago, *"non-cow," and* adharma, *"non-dharma" (i.e., demerit or violation of sacred duty).*[25]

When for some additional reason the correct understanding "this is not a pot, it is a pan" occurs to somebody who had developed the (erroneous) notion "pot" in connection with a pan—then it should be recognized (that this is) due to the (subsequent) absence of the awareness (of the entity as) pot, to its recollection and to the perception of something incompatible (with it), such as a pan. Likewise, (we account for the notion) "non-cow" (i.e., the corrective awareness, "it is not a cow") as applied to a horse. So also, (the notion) "demerit" (or "violation of sacred duty") occurs (as a correction) if a (false) way of seeing analogies has led somebody to respect bathing at night and so forth as sacred duty. Thus there are three types of examples, corresponding to the division of conscious, unconscious, and transempirical (entities; *cetanācetanātīndriya*).

*9: There is no difference of meaning (between subject and predicate) in (the statement) "a nonentity (i.e., what is never present) does not exist" (*abhūtaṃ na-asti*).*

What is different from prior, posterior, and secondary nonexistence, in the sense that its nature is absolute nonexistence,[26] for instance a hare's horn—that is referred to without distinction by the two synonymous expressions (*paryāyaśabda*) "nonentity" and "does not exist." Nothing different (from itself) is said of it by its synonymous designations. So it is only pointed out, defined by these very synonyms. It is not negated in terms of place, time, and so forth (i.e., its negation is not, like that of other subjects, an exclusion from particular locations in space, time, and so forth).

But in other cases (we say, for instance)—

10: "There is no pot in the house." This denies the connection of a real pot with the house.

"There is no pot at this place or time": This negates the pot and so forth with reference to (a particular) place and so forth; it does not negate it with reference to its own nature.

11: "There is no other (i.e., second) moon": This excludes the moon from (having a) universal.[27]

"There is no second moon." This denial of a number (i.e., the number two) excludes the moon from (having a specific) universal, namely "moonness." Based on this premise, it has been stated that there is no universal "moonness." (Some) explain this as follows: Because there is no (specific) place, time, condition, capability, or secondary application (involved in this case), the negation of the universal "moonness" is just a special case of what is absolutely unreal (*atyantāsat*).

"Sour milk is not produced from sand; it is produced from milk. But we do not perceive it (there). Therefore, (this) effect is both real and unreal (*sadasat*) in its cause." (Against this view, Kaṇāda says:)

12: Because the real and the unreal are heterogeneous, reality and nonreality cannot coexist in the effect (prior to its production).

Because reality and nonreality are incompatible (in the same substrate) at the same time, the effect cannot be both real and unreal in its cause. Therefore, it is unreal only.[28]

3. *Vyomaśiva, Vyomavatī, ed. Gaurinath Sastri, vol. 1, p. 33, line 20, to p. 37. line 19 (Vy., ed. Gopinath Kaviraj and Dhundhiraj Shastri, ChSS, p. 124, line 22, to p. 127, line 30; Ms. Mysore, No. C-1575, folio 22a, line 9, to folio 25a, line 3).*

The edition by Gopinath Kaviraj and Dhundhiraj Shastri (Benares, 1924–1930, ChSS; reprinted, 1983) is based on one single manuscript, written in 1916 and kept in the Sarasvati Bhavan Library in Benares. This edition is full of misprints and erroneous readings and sometimes simply unintelligible. Gaurinath Sastri, the editor of the new edition (Benares 1983–1984; Śivakumāraśāstrī-Granthamālā), reexamined the Benares manuscript and revised the entire text. He has succeeded in correcting numerous mistakes and closing various gaps. One of the most significant gaps appears in the section on *sattāsambandha,* which the following pages present in English translation. The Chowkhamba edition, p. 124, omits the long passage that appears in Gaurinath Sastri's edition on p. 34 (from *sat sad iti* in line 6 to *sāmānyādiṣu* in line 20) and on folio 22 b (lines 4 to 9) of the Mysore manuscript.[29] However, numerous problems remain in the revised edition. Neither Gaurinath Sastri nor the editors of the first edition consulted the original from which the Benares manuscript was copied. This ancient manuscript in Devanāgarī is preserved in the collection of the Oriental Research Institute at the University of Mysore (Ms.

No. C-1575).[30] It solves numerous problems and is generally of great help for a better understanding of the *Vyomavatī*.

The translation follows Gaurinath Sastri's text. But in a number of instances, readings provided by the Mysore manuscript were found to be preferable. The following is a list of cases where I differ from Gaurinath Sastri. "Mys." indicates that I am adopting a reading from the Mysore manuscript.

p. 33, line 24: *san guṇaḥ* (instead of *sadguṇaḥ;* cf. Mallavādin, *DNC*, p. 458; Candrānanda on *VS* I, 1, 7; Śaṅkara on *Chāndogya Upaniṣad* VI, 2, 1).

p. 34, line 1: *sat sad ity jñānam* (Mys.; instead of *sad ity jñānam*).

p. 34, line 4: *viśeṣyajñāna* (Mys.; instead of *viśiṣṭajñāna-;* Vyomaśiva himself does not always distinguish between these two terms).

p. 34, line 8: *-sannikarṣodbhāve* (Mys.; instead of *sannikarṣodbhāvane*).

p. 34, line 11: *yadi vā* (Mys.; instead of *yad vā*).

p. 34, line 24: *satā sattvam* (Mys.; instead of: *sattāvattvam*).

p. 35, line 1: *-sādhāraṇadharmād* (required by the context; instead of *-asādhāraṇadharmād*).

p. 35, line 4: *samavetā sattā* (instead of *samavetatvena;* Mys.: *samavetā; sattā* is required by the context).

p. 35, line 7: *-pratibaddho* (Mys.?; instead of *-pratibandho*).

p. 35, line 16: *vakṣyāmas* (Mys.; instead of *pravakṣyāmas*).

p. 35, line 18: *rajatasādharmyopalabdhe(ḥ)* (Mys.; instead of *rajatasādharmye upalabdhe*).

p. 35, lines 19–20: *samavāyābhāvenānubhavābhāvāt . . . rajatatvāsamavāyenānubhavābhāvāt* (Mys.; instead of *samavāyenānubhavābhāvāt . . . rajatatvasya samavāyenānubhavābhāvāt*).

p. 36, lines 2–3: *jñāne 'navasthādibādhakam* (Mys.; instead of *jñānam, na cāsya bādhakaṃ*).

p. 36, line 5: *vikalpyate kiṃ satām* (Mys.; instead of *vikalpate, kim sattā satām*).

p. 36, line 6: *veti* (Mys.; instead of *ceti*).

p. 36, line 19: *japādhi* (instead of *cakrādi;* considered as possible emendation by Gaurinath Sastri himself).

p. 36, line 20: *upādhīyamāno 'samavetaḥ kvacit* (Mys.; as amended; instead of: *upādhīyamānaḥ samaveto vā, kvacit*).

p. 36, line 24: *avyapadeśyatāprasaṅgaḥ* (Mys.; as amended; instead of *apy adṛśyatāprasaṅgaḥ*).

p. 36, line 25: *dravyatvena satā* (Mys.; instead of *dravyatvena;* Chowkhamba ed.: *dravyatvena sattā*).

p. 37, line 9: *arthakriyākāritvena* (Mys.; instead of: *arthakriyākāritve*).

p. 37, line 11: *arthakriyāntareṇa* (Mys.?; instead of *arthakriyām antareṇa*).[31]

TRANSLATION

Now (Praśastapāda) presents the common attributes (*sādharmya*) of the three (categories) beginning with substance, i.e., of those (entities) the first of which is substance. Because it is not understood how many they are, (he adds) "of three altogether." Of these a common attribute is "connection with reality" (*sattāsambandha*). "Connection of reality" (with its substrate)—that means "inherence having reality as a qualifying adjunct" (*sattopalakṣitaḥ samavāyaḥ*).[32]

But what is the proof that reality is really present in substances and so forth?

The awareness of substance, quality, and motion as "real." To be more explicit, reality is really present, because the recurrent cognition "real" is the cognition of something qualified and would not be possible without a qualifying factor (i.e., reality).

But in this case, (the limitation of connection with reality to) "three" (categories) would be incorrect, because the recurrent cognition "real" (*sat sad ity jñānam*) arises also with reference to universals and so forth. To be more explicit, because we find the specific cognition "real" also with regard to universals, ultimate particularities, and inherence, connection with reality has to be ascribed (to them, too).

Well, then (how would you respond) if (we say): As far as universals and so forth are concerned, the recurrent cognition "real" is due to their intrinsic identity (*svātmasattva;* i.e., being in the sense of having an identifiable nature)?

If it were so, exactly this should also be the case, as far as substances and so forth are concerned. What would be the use of "reality?" Either (the universal) "reality" or "intrinsic identity" should be accepted in all cases, because in the absence of any distinction in the recurrent cognition "real" there is no proof that it arises under the influence of two different causes. To be more explicit, in the case of substances and so forth, the recurrent cognition "real" is also due to intrinsic identity, simply because it is recurrent cognition "real," just like the recurrent cognition "real" referring to universals and so forth. Or rather, the recurrent cognition "real" in the case of universals and so forth is also caused by (the universal) reality, simply because it is recurrent cognition "real," just like the cognition "real" referring to substances and so forth.

This is not right, because an inconsistency would result if there were "connection with reality" also in the case of universals and so forth. To be more explicit, if we assume that "connection with reality" applies also to universals, then the fact that we find the recurrent cognition "real" also with reference to "reality" itself would imply that there, too, we would have another "connection with reality"; and this would amount to an infinite regress. And as far as the ultimate particularities (*viśeṣa*) are concerned, their association with (the universal and general factor) reality would result in doubt (as to their individual identity), and to ascertain (this identity), there would have to be another ultimate particularity, and there again another connection with reality; in this sense, there would (again and again) be room for doubt, and to bring about certainty, there would have to be (always) another ultimate particularity. This means there would be an infinite regress of doubt, certainty, and ultimate particularity. And reality cannot be present (i.e., inhere) in inherence itself (as this would lead to another infinite regress). Therefore, there is no connection with reality for universals and so forth, as this would result in inconsistencies.

But would this not be similar in the case of "being as intrinsic identity" ("own-nature", "self-identity"; *svarūpasattva*)? To be more explicit: If there is one single intrinsic identity in the universals and so forth, then we would have in this case, too, the defect of an infinite regress and so forth, just as with (the universal) reality.—But then (one might say that intrinsic identity) is confined to individual entities.—(If this were so), its nature would be exclusive, and it could not produce the recurrent cognition "real," because that is inclusive.

No (this is not so), because it can be explained otherwise. To be more explicit, concerning universals and so forth, the recurrent cognition "real" is metaphorical, because the inherence of reality would result in inconsistencies.—Metaphorical application, too, requires—if it actually takes place (*pravartamāna*)—a basis (*nimitta*).—There is production of the recurrent notion "real" (*sat sad iti pratyayajanakatvam*) insofar as the own nature (of universals and so forth), (which is) a "cooccurrent attribute" (*sādhāraṇadharma;* i.e., an attribute inhering in the same substratum as reality), provides the basis for this metaphorical application.[33] Where there is reality, there (i.e., in the same substratum) the "cooccurrent attribute" is found; and it is because of its perception that the superimposition of reality (*sattādhyāropa*) does indeed take place. Since the recurrent cognition "real" with reference to universals and so forth can (thus) also be explained otherwise, it is an inconclusive reason (for establishing the presence of the universal "reality"). And one should not say that also in the cases of substances and so forth the recurrent cognition "real" results merely from a "cooccurrent attribute"; because here, no inconsistency arises if (we assume) primary (i.e., non-metaphorical) application. Moreover, no metaphorical usage is ever found without primary usage; therefore it is established that in the case of substances and so forth the appearance of recurrent cognition "real" is, indeed, due to the inherence of reality.

Others, however, say: Since the recurrent cognition "real" is produced by the qualifying factor (*viśeṣaṇa*) "reality," there is primary usage in both cases; that means that "reality" functions as qualifying factor by virtue of inherence in one case, and through a "predicative relationship" (*viśeṣaṇaviśeṣyabhāva*) in the other. To be more explicit, "predicative relationship" does not merely amount to conjunction (*saṃyoga*) and inherence (*samavāya*) because this would imply that it cannot occur in the case of "absence" (*abhāva*—where *viśeṣaṇaviśeṣyabhāva* is thought to be specifically appropriate). Rather, it is invariably related (*pratibaddha*) to the cognition of something qualified (*viśiṣṭajñāna*). Wherever there is cognition of something qualified, there is a "predicative relationship." Consequently, since the recurrent qualified cognition "real" arises also with reference to universals and so forth, "predicative relationship" is indeed the (appropriate) relationship, and therefore, the recurrent cognition "real" is primary in both cases (i.e., universals and so forth as well as substances and so forth).

This is also incorrect. Wherever qualities, motions, and universals are recognized as qualifying factors by both (sides of the debate), there it is found to be by virtue of inherence. Because inherence of reality, that is, the "pervader" (*vyāpaka,* the more comprehensive inferential element), is to be ruled out as far as universals and so forth are concerned, its role as a qualifying factor, that is, the "pervaded" (*vyāpya,* the less comprehensive inferential element), is also to be ruled out. Therefore it is appropriate to say that there is only superimposition of reality (*sattādhyāropa*), which is due to the perception of an attribute accompanied by it (i.e., inhering in the same substratum as reality). Otherwise figurative understanding, as well as false cognition, would be eliminated in all cases. To be more explicit, in (the figurative expression) "the young man is a lion," "lionness" would be a qualifying factor also with reference to the young man, just as with reference to the lion; and there would be primary (i.e., nonfigurative) cognition only. Likewise, in the case of the (false) cognition "there is silver," where there is (only) mother-of-pearl, "silverness" would be a qualifying factor, just as with reference to (real) silver, and there would be no falsity. But there *is* false cognition, as we shall explain in the appropriate section.

Well, then (how do you respond) if (we say): (The cognition has a) figurative status, because it arises by means of superimposition of "lionness"—which is due to the perception of an attribute usually accompanied by it (i.e., "lionness")—on the young man, who has no (real) connection with "lionness"? Likewise, there is falsity (in the perception of "silver" in mother-of-pearl), because (this cognition) arises by means of superimposition of "silverness," which is due to the perception of attributes which (mother-of-pearl) has in common with silver.[34]

(But then you have to explain) *how* this (superimposition is supposed to take place), because without the inherence of "lionness" in the young man there cannot be any actual experience of it; and likewise, we cannot experience "silverness" in mother-of-pearl when it is not actually inherent in it.

Well, then (let us say): It is "lionness" from memory that functions with reference to the young man; and likewise, it is "silverness" (from memory) in the case of mother-of-pearl. Thus, figurative application as well as falsity are accounted for.—In this case, it is (also) correct (to say) that in relation to universals and so forth the recurrent cognition "real" is due to superimposition of (the universal) "reality," because the inherence of reality would involve inconsistencies.

But how can there be metaphorical application, because no connotation of *as* or *like* (*ivārtha*) appears, if the recurrent cognition "real" refers to universals and so forth? For that is metaphorical cognition, where the connotation of *as* or *like* occurs. In the absence of any differentiation in superimposition (as such), there would otherwise be no distinction (of metaphorical application) from false cognition.

This is not so. Although being aware that a human person has no connection with "lionness," somebody can still have the (metaphorical) idea "this (person) is a lion"; (but) somebody who is aware that (a particular piece of) mother-of-pearl has no connection with silver does not in the same way conceive of it as silver (because he has become aware that this was an illusion). Thus in false cognition the inconsistency is to be discovered later; but in figurative cognition, (the awareness of an) inconsistency is right there even earlier. It is only to illustrate his courage that (people) conventionally refer to a young man as a "lion." But in false cognition, they believe that an object is something different from what it (really) is. And in the recurrent cognition "real," as it refers to universals and so forth, inconsistencies such as infinite regress are there in all three times (i.e., past, present, and future, and yet the cognition persists). What remains (to be said) in this connection, can be (easily) inferred.

Well then, let us admit that the recurrent cognition "real" is metaphorical in the case of universals and so forth, and primary (i.e., nonmetaphorical) with reference to substances and so forth. But then there is a dilemma about "connection with reality." Does it apply to what is real or what is unreal (i.e., to entities or nonentities)? If it applies to what is (already) real, then this prior "being real" (*sattva*) is either due to "connection with reality," or it occurs without "connection with reality." If you assume "connection with reality," there would again be the same dilemma, and thus an infinite regress. If (you say that it is) without "connection with reality"), what (then) is the use of (the universal) reality?—Well, then (let us say that) there is real existence for what is unreal because of "connection with reality."—In this case, it would not be real existence in an absolute sense (*pāramārthika*), because it depends on a superimposed condition (*upādhi*). And if nonentities could become real by means of "connection with reality," then donkey's horns and so forth could also be real, as nonreality is without differentiation. Moreover, because (the universal) reality has no real existence itself, there could be no real existence in substances and so forth that would be due to a connection with it. If (you say that reality) is real by virtue of its own nature (and identity; *svarūpa*), then this should apply equally to substances and so forth; and if by virtue of "connection with reality," then there is an infinite regress.[35]

Hence the Buddhists believe that "being real" can be explained as "practical efficiency" (*arthakriyākāritva*). Others (take it) in the sense of "having a connection with the present time" (*vartamānakālasaṃbandhitva*).[36]

That (dilemma) which we mentioned in this context—that is, the question whether "connection with reality" produces real existence for what is real or not real (entities or nonentities)—that is incorrect, because origination and "connection with reality" are simultaneous. To be more explicit, the production of objects is precisely their connection with their own causes and (the universal) reality. There is no prior "being real," as the "theory of the preexisting effect" (*satkāryavāda*) has been rejected.[37] And the assumption that there is such "connection with its own causes and (the universal) reality" for what is not (previously) real does not imply that this is so also in the case of donkey's horns and so forth; as the fact that there are no causes for their production is ascertained by the very fact that they do not exist. In the case of eternal entities, this dilemma does not apply, because the relationship between prior and posterior does not apply.

And it is not (so as was claimed earlier) that this is not real existence in an absolute sense, since "connection with reality" has absolute validity. Nor is this existence externally conditioned (and superimposed; *aupādhika*) in substances and so forth, like the color of the *japā* flower in a crystal and so forth, because reality *inheres* in them.—Yet a superimposed condition, though being superimposed and not inherent, sometimes overshadows the inherent color (of a thing).[38] To be more explicit, the color of a crystal and so forth may, for instance, be overshadowed by the proximity of a red substance; in this situation, the presence of a superimposed condition is established by the fact that one has the impression "the crystal is red." Reality, however, does not in this way overshadow the essential nature (and identity; *svarūpa*) of substances and so forth, since "substanceness" and so forth are also manifest. Nor is it noninherent in them, as we are aware of its inherence.

But then, if "substanceness" and so forth are distinct (from substances and so forth), the consequence would be that substances (as such) cannot be named, because they would not have an essential nature (and identity) of their own.—This is not so, because (a universal such as) "substanceness" is confined to (its appropriate particulars, such as) substances. To be more explicit: The designation "substance" refers to a substance by virtue of the presence of "substanceness" (in it); and to qualities and so forth, (the appropriate designation refers) by virtue of "qualityness" and so forth. Consequently, although there is no difference in the separation (of universals from particulars) as such, substanceness inheres in substances only; and therefore, it causes the (appropriate) linguistic usage only with regard to them, and not with regard to qualities and so forth. In this manner, we can also say about "qualityness" that its inherence in certain specific (restricted, *niyata*) substrates is a restrictive factor (i.e., regulates the corresponding linguistic usage).[39] However, in spite of the distinction (between universals and particulars), inherence becomes manifest through the relationship between a substrate and what inheres in it, and thus causes the (linguistic) usage (that something is) "inherent" (i.e., occurs *in* something else). But if there were no such distinction (of universals and particulars), then there would be no difference between essential natures (inhering in the same particular substrate), since they would all be identical with one (and the same) substrate and could not produce differentiated (linguistic) usage. Or if they were different, then (such multiplicity) should also apply to the substrate, because otherwise there would no longer be identity (of universals and particulars).

And one should not say that the cognition of substances and so forth is fictitious, because then (something) that in positive and negative concomitance (*anvayavyatireka*) is coextensive with "effectivity" (*arthakriyā;* the criterion of reality according to the Buddhists) would be fictitious, and that would be a highly undesirable consequence. So it is established that the recurrent cognition "real" with regard to substances and so forth is due to "connection with reality."

If one assumes that there is reality by virtue of "practical efficiency" (*arthakriyākāritva*), then (one has to deal with) the same kind of objection (that was raised against the Vaiśeṣikas): Does practical efficiency apply to what is real or unreal (entities or nonentities)? Provided that there is reality, if there is practical efficiency of what is (already) real, then it is difficult to avoid a vicious circle. To be more explicit, if you say that being real is due to producing effects (and fulfilling purposes; *arthakriyājanakatva*), and on the other hand, that (only) what is real produces effects, then (this implies that) if the one is not established, the other cannot be established.

Well, then (let us say that) "producing effects" applies to something that is (already) real by virtue of another "effectiveness."—(But) then again, we would have this dilemma, and therefore an infinite regress. And if the nonreal (nonentities) were to produce effects, then this would also apply to donkey's horns and so forth, and if "effectiveness" were real by means of another "effectiveness," (then again there would be) an infinite regress.—Well, then (how do you respond) if (we say that effectiveness is real) by virtue of its own essential nature (*svarūpa*)?—Then this would also apply to the objects (as such, and we would not need *arthakriyā* to account for their reality).

With this (argumentation) the theory that "being real" is due to a "connection with the present time" is also refuted.[40]

Well, then (let us say that) "being real" is the *capability* (*sāmarthya*) of producing effects (i.e., not necessarily *actual* effectiveness).—If this ("capability") is supposed to produce the recurrent cognition "real" by pervading many objects—then there is only a difference in name (between it and *sattā*, "reality"). But without being pervasive, it would not produce a recurrent cognition. Moreover, with regard to "producing effects," the (appropriate) linguistic usage would be "capable to produce effects" and not the recurrent (expression) "real," because the characteristics (and meaning) of these are different.

That may be enough. So this is established: Substances and so forth have "connection with reality" (*sattāsambandha*).

4. *Śrīdhara,* Nyāyakandalī *(with the relevant sections of Praśastapāda's* Padārthadharmasaṃgraha*), ed. V. P. Dvivedin, Vizianagram Sanskrit Series, p. 11, line 12, to p. 12, line 25; p. 16, lines 1–8; p. 17, lines 5–14.*

Unlike Vyomaśiva's *Vyomavatī*, Śrīdhara's *Nyāyakandalī* has been copied many times and is preserved in a number of manuscript collections.[41] There are, moreover, several subcommentaries (including the *Pañjikā* by Maladhārin Rājaśekharasūri), although none of them has been published so far.[42] The work has also been translated into English (by Ganganatha Jha) and, more recently, into Hindi.[43] For the following translation samples, the edition of the text by Vindhyeśvarī Prasāda Dvivedin (or Dviveda; Benares, 1895; Vizianagram Sanskrit Series) has been adopted. It has become the basis for several subsequent editions and was reprinted in 1984. A few minor errors in V. P. Dvivedin's text have been corrected. Unlike the *Vyomavatī*, the *Nyāyakandalī* does not pose any major textual problems.

TRANSLATION

a. p. 11, line 12, to p. 12, line 25

[Praśastapāda:] Universals[44] are of two kinds, ultimate and nonultimate, and they cause the awareness of recurrence (or inclusion; anuvṛtti*). Of these (two kinds), reality (*sattā*) is the ultimate (universal), because of its wide domain (of instances); because it produces only inclusion (i.e., inclusive awareness), it is a universal only (i.e., the universal par excellence). Substanceness and so forth are nonultimate (universals), because of their smaller domain of instances. Because they produce distinction (or exclusion;* vyāvṛtti*), too, they are also called particularities, even though they are universals.*

[Śrīdhara:] (Praśastapāda) describes the universals: "Universals are of two kinds." He describes this division into two kinds: "ultimate and nonultimate." The word "and" implies restriction (*avadhāraṇa*); that is, there are only ultimate and nonultimate (and no other universals).[45] He describes their character: "They cause the awareness of recurrence (or inclusion)." The reason why one perceives a mutual correspondence of the natures of concrete entities which are completely separate is the universal. He answers the question what this ultimate universal is: "Reality is the ultimate (universal)." For this, he presents an argument: "because of its wide domain of instances." This means: because of its large number of instances, as compared to substanceness, and so forth. "Because it produces only inclusion, it is a universal only." Substanceness, and so forth, on the other hand, are also particularities, since they also cause the distinction of their substrates from heterogeneous ones. But reality causes only the inclusion of its substrates; therefore, it is a universal only. Although this (reality) is excluded from (i.e., does not occur in) the universals, and so forth, it cannot (be said to) produce the distinction of its own domain of substrates from these (universals, and so forth), because they can also be recognized through the awareness of their own "essential reality" (and self-identity; *svarūpasattā*). The production of inclusion (i.e., inclusive awareness) is meant to apply to positive entities (*vastu*). Therefore, there is no inconsistency, although (reality) accounts for the distinction (of its substrates) from nonbeing.

Some[46] (hold the following view): Ordinary linguistic usage applies the notion "it exists" (*asti*) to anything that is apprehended by a means of knowledge; and in the opposite case, it applies "it does not exist" (*nāsti*). Therefore, reality is nothing but "accessibility to the means of knowledge" (*pramāṇagamyatā*).[47] This is not correct for the following reason: Prior to the occurrence of the means of knowledge, the entity would, as an undesirable consequence, be unreal. And because something unreal, such as a donkey's horn, cannot be apprehended, we would have mutual dependence (i.e., a vicious circle of reality depending on apprehension and the possibility of apprehension depending on reality). And furthermore, because (only) a real means of knowledge can apprehend (its object), and because reality is defined as being apprehended by a means of knowledge (*pramāṇagrāhyatā*), the apprehending means of knowledge would always entail another apprehending factor; and accordingly, an infinite regress (*anavasthāna*) would occur.

(The opponent may qualify his view as follows:) Well, then we do not hold the view that reality is (actual) connection with a means of knowledge, but rather, that reality is nothing but the (individual) nature (and identity; *svarūpa*)[48] of the entities, which is capable of being connected with the means of knowledge. Even those who postulate the universal "reality" have to admit the individual identity of objects, because reality does not inhere in what does not have a nature (and identity), such as a hare's horn. So let us say that just this (individual identity) is there. What would be the use of reality (*sattā*)?

Here, we respond: The individual natures of objects are different in each single case. How can there be the awareness of one common form with regard to the (individual natures) or the application of one common term, as one cannot apprehend the connection (with a means of knowledge) with reference to an infinite number (of objects)?—Well, then (let us say that) there is one (identical) factor (for such application) present in them.—So you have admitted what we are looking for.

(The opponent may say:) Somebody, who has seen one individual cow and then sees another one, will have an experience that reproduces the previous content. But for somebody, who perceives a grain of mustard after he has seen a mountain, there is no such reappearance of a previous content (of awareness). Why then should we imagine a universal (common to the mountain and the grain of mustard)?—Our response would be: Is it the recurrence of a complete set of characteristics that is absent in (the example of) the mountain, and so on, or is (such recurrence) not even found in a partial sense? If you deny (the presence of) a universal because not all characteristics recur, then you should reject cowness, too; because we do not find similarity in every respect between two (cows) that are brindled or spotted in different ways (*śābaleya, bāhuleya*).

(The opponent may suggest:) Well, then the recurrence of characteristics is not even found in a partial sense. This is not tenable, because all these (various entities) appear equal insofar as their nature is distinct from nonbeing. However, that much is different: In the case of individual cows, the cognition of membership in the appropriate class (*tajjātīyatā*) takes place immediately, because the likeness pervades a large number of parts. With regard to the mountain, and so on, (such cognition appears) with delay, because the likeness pervades only a small number of parts and, accordingly, the genus is not conspicuous. Likewise, the perception of a water jar leads us to the (delayed) recognition that its genus "earth" is (also present) in a platter.

Hereby, we have also rejected (the explanation of) being as "effectiveness" (or "practical efficiency"; *arthakriyākāritva*).[49] The reason (for the rejection) is: What is unreal does not have effectiveness; it would have reality only, if effectiveness were real, and effectiveness would be real by virtue of (other) effectiveness. This would imply an infinite regress (*anavasthāna*),[50] and the undesirable consequence would be that everything is unreal.

b. p. 16, lines 1–8

[Praśastapāda:] All six categories possess is-ness (objectivity), nameability, and knowability.

[Śrīdhara:] Although the abstract attributes (*dharma*) are not separate from their subjects (*dharmin*) and although these same (attributes) may, indeed, be attributes and subjects relative to each other, nonetheless he mentions them separately, to clarify them in their role as subjects. "Isness" ("objectivity"), that is, possession of a peculiar nature (and identity; *svarūpavattva*), is the common attribute of all six (categories). That which belongs to a thing as its peculiar nature, that is its objectivity (*astitva*). "Nameability" is suitability for the application of a name; and this is nothing but the nature of the thing. [Knowability is suitability to be grasped by cognition; this, too, is nothing but the peculiar nature].[51] Because of a difference of aspects, the self-identity of what there is (*bhāvasvarūpa*) is called *knowability* and *nameability*.

c. p. 17, lines 5–14

[Praśastapāda:] The three (categories) beginning with substance (i.e., substances, qualities, and motions) have connection with reality . . .

[Śrīdhara:] "The three (categories) beginning with substance have connection with reality (*sattāsambandha*)"; in other words, inherential connection with the universal reality is a common attribute of substances, qualities, and motions. How connection with reality applies to them, has (already) been explained.[52] But now, the following problem is considered: Is "connection with reality" for something real or unreal? If it is for something real, then this would be real prior to its connection with reality, and reality would be useless. If, instead, the connection would be with something unreal, then reality would also apply to donkey's horns, and so forth. (We respond:) We do not admit priority and posteriority in the case of permanent entities. Concerning impermanent entities, reality applies only to "prior nonbeing" (*prāgasat*), because of the capability of the causes (to bring it into existence); and there is no unwarranted extension (of this application of reality) to donkey's horns, and so forth, because nothing has the potential to accomplish their production.

5. Udayana, Kiraṇāvalī, *ed. J. S. Jetly, GOS, p. 15, line 14, to p. 16, line 21.*

Udayana initiates the transition from classical Nyāya and Vaiśeṣika to Navyanyāya. He shows a new commitment to the formal criteria of definition and classification. His conceptual orientation is characteristically different from that of Vyomaśiva and Śrīdhara; this is reflected by his discourse on "being." Whereas *sattāsambandha* is at the center of Vyomaśiva's presentation, Udayana almost disregards it.[53] In India, the *Kiraṇāvalī* is considered as the culmination of the classical Vaiśeṣika commentaries. It has been copied many times. Various authors have composed subcommentaries; among them, Vardhamāna and Padmanābha. Vardhamāna's *Prakāśa* has a further subcommentary by Raghunātha Śiromaṇi.[54] After a paraphrase in Bengali, Gaurinath Sastri has presented a free rendering and extensive paraphrase in Hindi.[55] Only a minor segment of the work is available in English translation.[56]

The first printed edition appeared between 1897 and 1919 (Benares

Sanskrit Series). An edition with Vardhamāna's *Prakāśa*, Rucidatta's *Prakāśavivṛti* and Bhaṭṭa Vādīndra's *Dravyakiraṇāvalīṭīkā* was published between 1911 and 1956 (Bibliotheca Indica).[57] The following translation sample is based on the edition by Jitendra S. Jetly (Baroda, 1971; GOS). This edition lists a number of variant readings. However, numerous misprints and problematic readings require caution and the consultation of the other editions.

TRANSLATION

With the words "universals", and so on (Praśastapāda)[58] classifies the universals. A universal (or "uniformity", *sāmānya*), that is "the essence of what is uniform" (*samānānāṃ bhāvaḥ*), an intrinsic, nonaccidental attribute (*dharma*) of a plurality (of entities). With this reference to a plurality of subjects (*dharmin*) and the fact that their attribute is nonaccidental, the definition of the universal as "eternal, unitary, and present in many particulars" (*nityam, ekam, anekavṛtti*)[59] has been indicated. (The universals are) of two kinds. He shows this twofold nature with the words "ultimate and nonultimate" ("superior and inferior"). The word "and" is used in the sense that (these different universals) reside in one and the same particular (*ekavyaktisamāveśa*).[60]

There is no universal that has only one particular instance; this will be explained with reference to ether, and so forth. There is no universal that has no less and no more particular instances (than another universal, i.e., that would be coextensive with it), as, for example, in the juxtaposition of the synonymous terms[61] *buddhi, upalabdhi, jñāna* (all meaning "cognition" or "awareness"). There is no universal with mutual deviation (*mitho vyabhicāri;* i.e., partially overlapping with another, coordinate universal), as in the case of the "confusion of genera" (*jāti-saṃkara*) that occurs for such (types of motion) as "going out" and "entering."[62] Nor is there a universal that has a universal, and so forth (i.e., a universal, particularity, or inherence) as its particular instance, because then we would have an infinite regress (for universals inhering in universals), a contradiction in terms (for universals inhering in ultimate particularities), or a lack of (inherential) connection (for universals inhering in inherence).[63] Therefore, a universal that stands in a relationship of mutual exclusion is incompatible (*viruddha;* i.e., cannot coexist with another one of coordinate rank in the same particular). If it is compatible, it must stand in a relationship of subordination (*parāparabhāva;* "superiority and inferiority"); such is the rule. This means: the superior (universal; i.e. ultimately reality) includes (the others); the inferior ones are included (*vyāpya*). He suggests an argument: "It causes the awareness of recurrence (or inclusion)." If there were no universals, there would be no uniform awareness with reference to separate particulars. All substances, qualities, and motions can produce inclusive awareness with the help of universals only. He mentions the superior (i.e., ultimate) one: "Of these (universals), reality (*sattā*) is the ultimate one." The universal reality is to be treated as superior (and ultimate). Why? "Because of its wide domain (of instances)." This means because it has a larger domain than substanceness, and so forth. So it is also in other cases: If something has a larger domain in relation to something else, then it is to be treated as "superior" (and "ultimate," *para*); this applies likewise to "reality." And this reality is "a universal only" (*sāmānyam eva,* the universal par excellence). Unlike substanceness, and so forth, it is not also a particularity. Why? "Because (it produces) only inclusion."

Now (there is the following problem): Reality is excluded from (i.e., does not occur in) universals, and so forth. If it would, nonetheless, fail to produce the distinction of its domain of substrates from these (universals, and so forth), then substanceness and other (nonultimate universals) would also fail to produce any distinction, since there is no difference (between these cases).[64] (We say:) No, because reality may be manifested through all particular entities merely as such, and because there is no restriction concerning its manifestors.[65] It is, however, excluded from universals, and so forth, because of inconsistencies (i.e., reasons that contradict its presence). For the other universals, there is no manifestation in all entities, because they are to be manifested by (specific) shapes, qualities, effects, causes, and so on,[66] and because these are restricted (to specific entities).

(The opponent[67] suggests:) Then let us say that reality is nothing but the individual nature of the entities (*vastusvarūpa*). And one should not argue as follows: If the recurrent notion "cow" would be due to "individual nature" and would occur even in the absence of such (universals) as cowness, then it could also occur in the presence of horses, and so on. Likewise, if we would have the recurrent notion "real" because of "individual nature," and without "reality," then it would apply everywhere. (One should not draw this parallel), because the (indiscriminate) recurrence of this (notion "real"), even in the absence of the (universal reality), would be quite acceptable.—(Here we say:) No, there is no recurrence of notions without a proper basis (*nimitta*). And the specific entities (*viśeṣa*) as such cannot be this basis; nor can it be the defining characteristic (*lakṣaṇa*), because then the universals as such[68] (including the nonultimate universals, such as "cowness," which the opponent accepts) would be eliminated. For (one could) never (be certain that) there is a manifestation of a universal over and above the specific entities and the characteristic mark.

In this case (i.e., if recurrent awareness requires a universal), how do you explain the recurrent notion "real" with respect to universals, and so forth (where reality does not inhere)? This is because they inhere in the same objects as reality (*sattaikārthasamavāya*).[69] It is like the awareness of number and other (qualities) in qualities (where they cannot actually inhere). If you say that this might then also apply to nonbeing, we respond: No (this is not so), because its conception implies incompatibility with (the predicate) real.[70]

Appendix 1: Notes

1. The English translation of the *Nyāyakandalī* by G. Jha was first published in *The Pandit*, vols. 25–37 (1903–1915); reprints appeared in 1916 and 1982. There are complete Hindi translations, or rather paraphrases, of the *Nyāyakandalī* (by Durgadhar Jha, Benares, 1963) and of the *Kiraṇāvalī* (by Gaurinath Sastri, Benares, 1980). Some excerpts from the *Kiraṇāvalī* are found in M. Tachikawa, *The Structure of the World in Udayana's Realism* (Dordrecht, 1981). W. Slaje, *Die Wahrnehmungslehre bei Vyomaśivaḥ* (Diss. Vienna, 1983), gives a German translation of Vyomaśiva's analysis of sense perception (*Vy.*, ChSS, pp. 554–62).

2. See Candrānanda on *VS* III, 2, 4.

3. Cf. A. Aklujkar, "Candrānanda's Date," *Journal of the Oriental Institute* (Baroda) 19 (1969–70): 340–341. The Candrānanda mentioned by Abhinavagupta (cf. U. P. Shah, "A Reference to Bhaṭṭa Candrānanda by Abhinavagupta," *Sambodhi* 4, 1975: 7–8) is apparently not identical with our Vaiśeṣika commentator.

4. See W. Slaje, *Die Wahrnehmungslehre*, pp. 7–21; Slaje suggests ca. A.D. 900 as the most likely date. It is remarkable that Vyomaśiva does not respond to the definition of reality as *pramāṇasambandhayogyatā* (or *pramāṇagrāhyatā*), which is associated with the Prābhākara school and above all with Śālikanāthamiśra. This seems to support an earlier date.

5. Śrīdhara himself mentions "913 Śaka" (i.e., A.D. 991) as the date of the completion of his work; cf. *NK*, p. 331.

6. For a discussion of the date of Udayana, see G. Chemparathy, *An Indian Rational Theology* (Vienna, 1972), pp. 19ff. Chemparathy suggests the earlier part of the eleventh century for Udayana's mature works. The unfinished *Kiraṇāvalī* may have been his last work. There are no clearly identifiable quotes from, or references to, Śrīdhara in the *Kiraṇāvalī*. On the other hand, the editor of the *Nyāyakandalī*, Vindhyeśvarī Prasāda Dvivedin, found apparent references to Udayana in Śrīdhara (cf. *NK*, Sanskrit preface, p. 21; especially n. 3). However, it is by no means certain that the views mentioned by Śrīdhara were first introduced by Udayana, or specifically associated with him. Śrīdhara's acquaintance with Vyomaśiva seems to be much less questionable; it was taken for granted by his commentators; see V. G. Parikh (cited in n. 42), p. 210.

7. *Vaiśeṣikadarśana of Kaṇāda with an anonymous commentary*, ed. A. Thakur (Darbhanga, 1957).

8. Cf. also M. Nozawa, "The Vaiśeṣikasūtra Referred to in the Padārthadharmasaṃgraha," *JIBSt* 24 (1976): 1006–1000 (32–38). According to Nozawa, the Sūtra text used by Praśastapāda was different from any currently available text.

9. See the introduction by A. Thakur to *VS*, ed. Jambuvijaya, GOS.

10. The first reference is I, 1, 7. Among the later sections dealing with causality and inference, see, for instance, IV, 1, 1ff.

11. Cf. Candrānanda on I, 1, 6: *tadanuṣaṅgāt sāmānyaviśeṣasamavāyā api vakṣyante* ("Universals, particularities, and inherence will also be mentioned, insofar as they are attached to these"; i.e., substances, qualities, and motions). The first appearance of *sāmānya* and *viśeṣa* is in I, 1, 7 (Śaṅkaramiśra's I, 1, 4 is missing in Candrānanda's version). In I, 1, 17; 22; 24, *sāmānya* is unterminological. In the version edited by A. Thakur (1957), Sūtras I, 2, 1–2 appear also as I, 1, 13–14.

12. The translation follows Candrānanda's commentary.

13. *Bhāvaḥ sāmānyam eva;* i.e., existence/reality is the universal par excellence, as it is not limited in its application to substances, qualities, and motions. The *Upaskāra* version has *bhāvo 'nuvṛtter eva hetutvāt sāmānyam eva.*

14. For different versions and citations of Sūtras 7 and 8 (especially their appearance as a single Sūtra), see earlier, Chapter 7, section 1 (especially n. 5). Likewise, I, 2, 9 appears in a number of variant readings. It is missing in the *Upaskāra*.

15. In this Sūtra, as well as in Sūtras 14 and 16, we have to supply the

phrase "as something different from substances, qualities, and motions" (*dravyaguṇakarmabhyo 'rthāntaram*) from Sūtra I, 2, 8.

16. See earlier, Chapter 7, section 3, for the interpretation of this section (and the suggestions of H. Narain).

17. Several later Sūtras make reference to this statement; see II, 1, 18; II, 2, 8; II, 2, 14 (*tattvaṃ bhāvena*); III, 2, 31 (*tattvaṃ ca*).

18. The division of each Adhyāya into two Āhnikas is abandoned after Adhyāya 7; in the *Upaskāra* version, it is continued through the entire text.

19. "Inferential" (*laiṅgika*) knowledge is referred to in Sūtra IX, 18.

20. This was generally taken as a direct rejection of the premises of the *satkāryavāda*. The Sūtra is missing in the anonymous commentary edited by A. Thakur (1957).

21. We adopt the reading *kriyāguṇavyapadeśabhāvād*. On *kriyā*, *guṇa*, and *vyapadeśa* as criteria of reality, see also *YD*, ed. R. C. Pandeya, pp. 48ff.

22. The text says: *asat ity upacaryate*.

23. For the interpretation of this section and the fourfold division of nonbeing, see earlier, Chapter 7, section 2 (especially n. 21ff.); cf. also B. Gupta, "Story of the Evolution of the Concept of Negation," *WZKS* 12–13, (1968–69; *Beiträge zur Geistesgeschichte Indiens, Festschrift E. Frauwallner*): 115–118 (with reference to *VS* IX, 5).

24. See Candrānanda's analogous explanation of the recognition and correction of erroneous awareness in his commentary on Sūtra IX, 8.

25. Cf. the detailed discussion of the function of the negative particle *a* by Bhartṛhari, *VP* III/14 (*Vṛttisamuddeśa*), 253ff. (with Helārāja's commentary).

26. We have to read *yad anyad atyantābhāvarūpam* instead of *yad atyantābhāvarūpam* in the printed text.

27. This would correspond to the first item in Udayana's list of factors that exclude genuine universals (*jātibādhaka*); see earlier, Chapter 6, n. 40.

28. This Sūtra was often quoted by the opponents and critics of the system; see, for instance, Mallavādin and Siṃhasūri, *DNC*, pp. 459, 498, 460, 465, 490. Cf. also *NS* IV, 1, 47: *na asan na san na sadasat sadasator vaidharmyāt* (together with *NBh*).

29. In general, the "ontological" sections of the *Vyomavatī* seem to be among the most corrupt in the Chowkhamba edition.

30. I want to thank Dr. Elliot Stern for providing me with a copy of the Mysore manuscript.

31. This illustrates that there is still need for a critical edition of this important text.

32. *Upalakṣaṇa* is an incidental, or at least nonessential, indicator. We have to remember that there is only one eternal *samavāya*, the condition of the possibility of all dependent, contingent occurrence, and that it is not really affected by any of the relata that it combines and unifies; see earlier, Chapter 7, section 6. Cf. also *Vy.*, p. 149 (Gaurinath Sastri, p. 42): *dravyatvena yogo dravyatvopalakṣitaḥ samavāyaḥ;* p. 151 (44): *guṇopalakṣitaḥ samavāyaḥ samavetā vā guṇāḥ.*

33. See earlier, Chapter 7, section 10 (especially n. 90ff.). On the use of the dash (-) in this translation, see Appendix 1, Introduction.

34. The example of the silver and mother-of-pearl is a stock example in Indian debates on error and illusion; for Mallavādin's use of the example of the young man and the lion, see *DNC*, p. 520; and earlier, Chapter 8, n. 15.

35. On the "dilemma about connection with reality," commonly referred to as *sadasadvikalpa*, see earlier, Chapter 8, sections 9ff.

36. We may associate this view with the philosophy of Maṇḍanamiśra; see earlier, Chapter 7, n. 84.

37. The casual nature of this reference to the Sāṃkhya *satkāryavāda* seems typical; see earlier, Chapter 3, section 9.

38. For the image of the crystal and the *japā* flower, see Bhartṛhari, *VP* III/3 (*Sambandhasamuddeśa*), 40f. (with commentary by Helārāja).

39. Cf. the expression *nilayananiyama*, "regularity" (or "restriction") of "residence," see Mallavādin and Siṃhasūri, *DNC*, p. 481; see also p. 486; and earlier, Chapter 8, section 7.

40. See n. 36.

41. It was, however, generally neglected in Śrīdhara's native Bengal; cf. Gopinath Kaviraj, *Gleanings from the History and Bibliography of the Nyāya-Vaiśeṣika Literature* (Calcutta, 1961; first published 1924–1927), pp. 23f.

42. On Maladhārin's *Pañjikā*, see B. G. Parikh, *Journal of the Oriental Institute* (Baroda) 24 (1974):206–210.

43. See n. 1.

44. The text has the singular: *sāmānyaṃ dvividham.*

45. See, on the other hand, *PBh* and *NK*, p. 10; here, the *ca* at the end of the *VS* list of seventeen qualities is credited with the implication of seven further qualities.

46. The opponents in this case are followers of Prabhākara, most notably Śālikanātha.

47. The printed text (*NK*, 12, 1. 5) reads: *pramāṇagamyā-eva sattā;* instead, we have to read: *pramāṇagamyatā-eva sattā.*

48. For the use of *svarūpa, svarūpamātra,* etc., in the Prābhākara school, see Śālikanātha, *Prakaraṇapañcikā,* ed. A. Subrahmanya Sastri (Benares, 1961), pp. 97ff.; 289ff.

49. The brevity is conspicuous, if compared with Vyomaśiva's treatment of *arthakriyākāritva.* On the other hand, Vyomaśiva does not deal with the Prābhākara concept of *pramāṇagamyatā* (*pramāṇagrāhyatā; pramāṇasambandhayogyatā*).

50. See earlier, for the invocation of an "infinite regress" against the concept of *pramāṇagrāhyatā.*

51. We adopt the additional statement given in n. 2 of the edition.

52. See earlier, section 4a.

53. See earlier, Chapter 8, section 18.

54. The commentary by Vardhamāna, together with the subcommentary by Rucidatta, is found in the Bibliotheca Indica edition of the *Kiraṇāvalī* (see later, n. 57). Parts of other commentaries were published in the Princess of Wales Saraswati Bhavana Texts, among them Raghunātha's *Dīdhiti* (Benares, 1932). See also Mathurānātha, *Kiraṇāvalīrahasya,* ed. G. Sastri (Benares, 1981).

55. See n. 1; the Bengali paraphrase appeared in two volumes (Calcutta, 1935–1957).

56. See M. Tachikawa, *The Structure of the World in Udayana's Realism* (Dordrecht, 1981).

57. Edited by Siva Chandra Sarvabhouma and Narendra Chandra Vedantatirtha.

58. See earlier, section 4a.

59. Cf. P. K. Mukhopadhyay, *Indian Realism* (Calcutta, 1984), pp. 101ff.; 301f.; B. K. Matilal, *Perception* (Oxford, 1986), p. 384.

60. This corresponds to what is otherwise known as *sāmānādhikaraṇya,* "concurrence," "cooccurrence" in the same substrate (or, grammatically, in the same subject). The universal *sattā* invariably accompanies all lower universals.

61. The printed text (GOS, 16, 1.1) has *paryavasthitau;* instead, we have to read *paryāyasthitau* (as in n. 1) or, preferably, *paryāyāvasthitau* (with Gaurinath Sastri, *Kiraṇāvalī;* Benares, 1980, p. 180).

62. This example is the only instance of a *jātisaṃkara* mentioned by Praśastapāda himself; see *PBh,* p. 293.

63. This exemplifies Udayana's list of six criteria which exclude genuine universals (*jātibādhaka*); see Chapter 6, n. 40; and *Kir.*, GOS, p. 23.

64. See section 4a (Śrīdhara).

65. We adopt the variant reading *vyañjaka-* given in n. 6; it is also found in the Bibliotheca Indica and in Gaurinath Sastri's edition.

66. We adopt the reading given in n. 8: *saṃsthānaguṇakārya.*

67. That is, a follower of Prabhākara.

68. See the variant reading *sāmānyamātroccheda* (n. 10); and Vardhamāna, Bibliotheca Indica, pp. 127f.: *viśeṣās tattadvyaktayaḥ.*

69. We adopt the simplified reading *sattaikārthasamavāyāt* from n. 12, instead of *sattayā-ekārthasamavāyāt* in the text.

70. We read *pratīter* instead of *pratītir;* cf. the edition by Gaurinath Sastri (1980), p. 190; and Bibliotheca Indica (1911), p. 228.

Appendix 2: The Concept of Viśeṣa *and the Name of the* Vaiśeṣika *System*

Viśeṣa, or more precisely *antyaviśeṣa* ("ultimate particularity"), the fifth category of classical Vaiśeṣika, has often been associated with the very name of this system. and it is commonly considered as one of its most peculiar and characteristic concepts.[1] According to Praśastapāda's *Padārthadharmasaṃgraha*, "ultimate particularities" are factors of irreducible individual identity. They reside exclusively in the eternal, noncomposite substances, that is, in the individual atoms, souls, and mental organs, and in the unitary substances ether, time, and space, and they account for the ultimate distinctness of these fundamental ingredients of the universe.[2] Without these factors of distinction, so we are told, even accomplished yogins would not be able to identify individual atoms.[3]

This familiar doxographic outline and the stereotyped descriptions found in the traditional compendia of Nyāya and Vaiśeṣika as well as in modern surveys of Indian philosophy avoid or conceal various significant problems. How is Praśastapāda's exposition of *viśeṣa* related to the treatment of this topic in the *Vaiśeṣikasūtra?* What is the connection between "ultimate particularities" (*antyaviśeṣa*) and "specific universals" (*sāmānyaviśeṣa*) or "intermediate species"? What is the role of generic identity and distinctness on the one hand and of numerical identity on the other? What distinguishes "ultimate particularity" from the distinctness and numerical identity of "ordinary" and composite individuals (*vyakti, piṇḍa*)? What is the connection of the term *viśeṣa* with the name of the Vaiśeṣika system? What is the correlation between the concept of ultimate particularity and the basic structure and fundamental ontological orientation of this system?

The special association of ultimate particularity with the identity and distinctness of individual atoms, minds (*manas*), and souls or selves (*ātman*) has led some modern interpreters to the assumption that *viśeṣa* is basically a notion of numerical identity, or some kind of principle of individuation (*principium individuationis*). Harsh Narain suggests that the concept of universal (*sāmānya*) in Vaiśeṣika was originally meant to explain why different individuals can be classified as members of one class ("Why are they two *cows?*"), whereas the concept of *viśeṣa* was supposed to explain why they are nevertheless numerically distinct and distinguishable individuals ("Why are they *two* cows?").[4] Subsequently, the domain of this principle of numerical identity would have been limited to the realm of permanent substances, excluding all other (i.e., composite and impermanent) individuals. The translation "individuator" used by K. H. Potter and some other scholars also suggests a special association between *viśeṣa* and the problems of individuation and numerical identity.[5] However, both Potter and Narain also describe *antyaviśeṣa* as "infima species". Narain even speaks of "infima species or individual" and suggests that these terms are simply interchangeable.[6] Such usage blurs the conceptual distinction between the lowest, most specific species (i.e., the ultimate unit of generic identity) and the numerical identity of its individual instances. Nonetheless, this is a symptomatic and potentially suggestive confusion. It reflects an unclarified ambiguity inherent in the Vaiśeṣika concept of *viśeṣa* itself, a peculiar combination and overlap of questions concerning generic and numerical identity.

The *Vaiśeṣikasūtra* does not explicitly specify the status of the ultimate particularities. It does not tell us whether *antyaviśeṣa* means infima species as the lowest generic unit, or the particularity and numerical identity of ultimate (or other) individuals. Praśastapāda clearly associates *viśeṣa* with ultimate individuals. But does this mean that he is dealing with numerical identity as opposed to generic identity? What kind of identity and distinctness does he postulate for the atoms and other ultimate substances? At this point, a curious and inconspicuous historical variant may provide us with a systematic clue. We find it in Candramati's *Daśapadārthaśāstra*.[7] Candramati (as translated by Hsüan-tsang) reserves *viśeṣa/antyaviśeṣa* (Chinese: *i; pien*) for the three unitary substances ether, time, and space. Unlike Praśastapāda, he does not associate it with individual atoms or selves. Evidently, this interpretation is equally compatible with the elusive statements found in the *Vaiśeṣikasūtra*. The entire complex of *sāmānya* and *viśeṣa*, as presented by the Sūtra text, left room for variations. Candramati himself divided *sā-*

mānya into two distinct categories, that is, the highest universal reality (*sattā*) and the specific universals (*sāmānyaviśeṣa*). Similar ideas were ascribed to other authors, such as Rohagupta.[8] Many centuries later, Śivāditya defined *sāmānya* as "threefold" (*trividha*) instead of Praśastapāda's "twofold" (*dvividha*).[9]

Candramati does not justify or explain his presentation of ultimate particularity. Nonetheless, we may paraphrase its basic implications as follows: Ether, time, and space constitute a special case and pose special problems within the enumeration and classification of substances, qualities, and motions. Though they are subdivisions of the class of substances (*dravya*) and appear side by side with the elemental substances, souls, and mental organs, they are different insofar as they are classes constituted by one single instance. Their identity is clearly a generic one; they are genuinely different types or species of entities. But such generic identity coincides with the numerical identity of unique, unitary individuals. In this case, the concept of *sāmānyaviśeṣa*, which implies inclusion (of different individuals or subordinate species) as well as exclusion (of other species), would not be appropriate. Accordingly, one should speak of exclusion only. Clearly, this meaning of *antyaviśeṣa* implies a special case of generic identity which, according to Candramati, would not apply to numerically different atoms or souls. Candramati does not address the problem of numerical identity as such in this context.

The relative chronology of Candramati and Praśastapāda has not yet been established in a conclusive manner. Moreover, it seems quite unlikely that the application of *viśeṣa* to individual atoms and so forth was Praśastapāda's personal innovation.[10] Accordingly, we are not in a position to postulate historical priority for Candramati's version or to explain Praśastapāda's model as a later and derivative development. Nonetheless, we may say that Candramati provides us with a systematic nucleus and that Praśastapāda's interpretation is an extension and extrapolation of this nucleus. Whatever the historical developments may have been, Praśastapāda's notion of ultimate particularity is a systematic extension of generic identity to the level of ultimate individuality, that is, to the individual noncomposite substances, the indestructible and irreducible ingredients of the universe. Of course, in addition to this cosmologically privileged and fundamentally timeless identity and distinctness, the ultimate substances are also endowed with the quality "separateness" (*pṛthaktva*).[11] This is the ordinary kind of distinctness and numerical identity which is found in composite, impermanent substances or individuals (*vyakti, piṇḍa*) as well. It is, however, not of any significance in the present context; it is not used to establish a systematic relation or distinction between generic and numerical identity or to clarify the more general problems of classification, identification, and instantiation.

Viśeṣa is neither numerical identity as such, nor is it a *principium individuationis*. Praśastapāda does not need such a principle; the problem does not arise in his way of thinking. Ultimate individuals are always there; the concept of *viśeṣa* asserts their irreducible identity and distinctness. Once again, the Sāṃkhya and Yoga metaphysics provides a symptomatic contrast. These systems do not recognize any actuality, distinctness, and individuality in *prakṛti*, the underlying substance of the world, nor do they recognize any permanent atoms. There are no ultimate ingredients of the world that would have an identity apart from their actuality and distinctness in time and space. Even accomplished yogins or the Lord (*īśvara*) himself can identify homogeneous individual entities only with reference to their position in a spatiotemporal framework. In this connection, Vyāsa's *Yogabhāṣya* cites and dismisses the Vaiśeṣika concept of *viśeṣa*.[12] Vārṣagaṇya's statement that there is no distinctness in the primal cause (*mūlapṛthaktva*) appears as an implicit response to the Vaiśeṣika concept of ultimate, irreducible particularity.[13]

Numerous Western and Indian authors have suggested that the very name of the Vaiśeṣika system is derived from its fifth category, *viśeṣa*. We find this view among traditional doxographers (for instance, Guṇaratna)[14] as well as modern scholars (for instance, Nandalal Sinha and K. H. Potter).[15] However, this explanation is by no means generally accepted. Various other explanations have been suggested.[16] Instead of associating the name Vaiśeṣika with the technical meaning of *viśeṣa* as "ultimate particularity", several scholars have emphasized the commitment of the system to *viśeṣa* in a more general sense, that is, to pluralism and particularity, or more specifically to demarcation, characterization, and differentiation. According to B. Faddegon, the word Vaiśeṣika "denotates the system as a doctrine of characterization".[17] This would seem to agree with the explanation of Udayana who paraphrases *viśeṣa* as *vyavaccheda* (i.e., "demarcation", "distinction").[18]

We do not have sufficient evidence to determine the historical origin and the original meaning of the name of the Vaiśeṣika system. We may, nevertheless, present some general and partly negative observations. As we have seen, the concept of *viśeṣa* was not very conspicuous in the *Vaiśeṣikasūtra;* nor was its meaning well clarified. The literature of the following centuries demonstrates that it was open to different interpretations. Kaṇāda's system was probably known as *Vaiśeṣika* before the definition of the fifth category was finalized. Although this name does not appear in the *Vaiśeṣikasūtra,* it is taken for granted by Praśastapāda[19] and several authors who may have been his contemporaries, such as Jinabhadra and Mallavādin,[20] or even his predecessors, such as Bhartṛhari.[21] Other early names of the system are *Kāṇāda* and *Aulūkya,* which is used by Nāgārjuna.[22] It would certainly seem rather unlikely that the Vaiśeṣika authors themselves should have derived the name of their system from its fifth category. Those commentators who address the question of derivation usually disregard this possibility.[23]

But whatever the actual derivation and the original meaning of the name *Vaiśeṣika* may have been, we may say that *viśeṣa* in its role as "ultimate particularity" is a central and symptomatic concept. It illustrates the basic ontological orientation of the classical Vaiśeṣika system, its commitment to identifiability, distinctness, and comprehensive enumeration. Without ultimate particularity, the whole edifice of distinct, enumerable entities would not have a secure basis. Reality itself, as conceived in the Vaiśeṣika system, would collapse or evaporate without individual identity and distinctness. The ultimate, permanent substances have an irreducible numerical identity which is at the same time generic identity. There is no permanent numerical identity which is not eo ipso timeless generic identity. Once again, this indicates the marginalization of time and temporality in classical Vaiśeṣika thought.[24] Ultimate individual identity itself is removed from the very possibility of temporality and change; it is also utterly abstract and transempirical. Those ideas of enumeration and classification which were at the center of the Vaiśeṣika enterprise lose their meaning and applicability in this realm of ultimate particularities.[25]

Appendix 2: Notes

1. See later, n. 14 f.

2. See *PBh,* pp. 321 f.

3. Ibid.; see also Candrānanda on *VS* I, 2, 6.

4. See H. Narain, *Evolution of the Nyāya-Vaiśeṣika Categoriology,* vol. 1 (Benares, 1976), p. 215; Narain also suggests that *viśeṣa* might have originated as a radicalization of the quality *pṛthaktva,* "separateness."

5. See K. H. Potter, *Indian Metaphysics and Epistemology* (*EIPh,* vol. 2), pp. 142 f.; see also K. K. Chakrabarti, art. "Vaiśeṣika", *Encyclopedia of Religion,* ed. M. Eliade, vol. 15 ("ultimate differentiator"; "ultimate individuator"). H. Narain prefers the translation "differential."

6. See H. Narain, p. 214; K. H. Potter, p. 142. For a somewhat idiosyncratic discussion of *viśeṣa* and its roles in the Vaiśeṣikasūtra and Praśastapāda, see V. S. Gajendragadkar, *Kaṇāda's Doctrine of the Padārthas* (Delhi, 1988), pp. 131–141.

7. See H. Ui, *The Vaiśeṣika Philosophy;* and M. Hattori in *Indian Metaphysics and Epistemology,* ed. K. H. Potter (*EIPh,* vol. 2), p. 280. Cf. also U. R. Jha, *Daśapadārthī* (Jammu, 1977; a Sanskrit "reconstruction" and commentary).

8. See H. Ui, ibid.; A. Thakur, Introduction to *VS,* ed. Jambuvijaya (GOS), pp. 6 ff.; especially p. 8.

9. See Śivāditya, *SP,* p. 7 (section 7): *sāmānyaṃ param aparaṃ parāparaṃ ca-iti.* In Śivāditya's terminology, the lowest (*apara*) universal seems to correspond to the concept of *infima species.*

10. See earlier, Chapter 4, sections 3–4; specifically the reference to Ātreya.

11. On *pṛthaktva,* see *PBh* and *NK,* pp. 138 ff.; on the "separateness" and numerical unity (*ekatva*) of a unitary substance like time, see pp. 63 ff.

12. See *YBh* III, 53.

13. Ibid.; see also the *Vivaraṇa* attributed to Śaṇkara and the commentaries by Vācaspati and Vijñānabhikṣu on this section.

14. Cf. A. Thakur (cited in n. 8), p. 2. See also Candrakānta, *Vaiśeṣikadarśanam* (Calcutta, 1887), p. 2.

15. See Nandalal Sinha, Introduction to *The Vaiśeṣika Sūtras of Kaṇāda* (Allahabad, 1911), pp. VI f.; K. H. Potter (cited in n. 5), p. 142.

16. See A. Thakur (cited in n. 8), pp. 2 ff.; H. Ui, *The Vaiśeṣika Philosophy,* pp. 3 ff.

17. B. Faddegon, *The Vaiçeṣika System,* p. 18; see also pp. 118 ff.; and H. Narain (cited in n. 4), pp. 23 ff.

18. See Udayana, *Kir.,* GOS, p. 227 (referring to the word *vaiśeṣika*): *viśeṣo vyavacchedaḥ tattvaniścayaḥ, tena vyavaharati-ity arthaḥ.*

19. See *PBh*, p. 234. *VS* X, 18 (X, 2, 7 *Upaskāra*) uses the word *vaiśeṣika* in the sense of "specific attribute."

20. See Jinabhadra, *Viśeṣāvaśyakabhāṣya*, ed. D. Malvania (Ahmedabad, 1966–1968), p. 24; Mallavādin, *DNC*, vol. 1, pp. 87; 291. Siṃhasūri uses the term more frequently.

21. See Bhartṛhari, *Mahābhāṣyadīpikā*, ed. V. Swaminathan (Benares, 1965), p. 25.

22. See Nāgārjuna, *Ratnāvalī* I, 61; cf. also Uddyotakara, *NV* I, 2, 4 (Calc. S. S., p. 367).

23. See Udayana, *Kir.*, GOS, p. 227 (cited in n. 18).

24. See Chapter 9.

25. The applicability of number to the ultimate substances and the idea of a totality of such substances are elusive; various more or less explicit suggestions may be found in the history of Nyāya and Vaiśeṣika. Concerning the number of selves (*ātman*), Śrīdhara states that it is endless. Even if there is an infinite number of selves that have reached final liberation, the number of those still in bondage will not be exhausted and not even diminished. Absolute freedom has always been there; nonetheless, *saṃsāra* will never be over (see *NK*, pp. 87 f.). Although this is part of Śrīdhara's rejection of nondualism, it may also be seen as an implicit concession to Advaita Vedānta. On the "innumerability" (*aparisaṃkhyeyatva;* not necessarily infinity in a strong sense) of living beings, see also *NBh* and *NV* I, 1, 1 (Calc. S. S., p. 22).

Glossary: Ontological Terms in Classical Vaiśeṣika

The purpose of this glossary is to facilitate the use of the book and to provide a convenient survey of some of the more prominent and significant terms used and discussed in the preceding chapters. The glossary is limited to ontological and categoriological terms found in the classical Vaiśeṣika texts and commentaries (including *pūrvapakṣa* sections and pertinent doxographic sources) and some allied Nyāya works. It does not include Navyanyāya terminology. In general, the translations or paraphrases correspond to those used in the text of the book. They indicate only those meanings and connotations which are relevant in the context of Vaiśeṣika ontology. For further explanations and interpretations, as well as for additional terminology, the index has to be consulted.

abhāva	nonexistence, nonentity, absence (the seventh category in later Nyāya-Vaiśeṣika)
adhidheyatva	nameability, semantic identifiability
abhivyakti	manifestation, actualization
abhūtvā bhāvaḥ (bhavanam)	(coming into) existence after prior nonexistence
ādhāra	basis, substrate

alīka	void, utterly fictitious
anityatva	impermanence
anyonyābhāva	mutual absence, reciprocal nonexistence
artha	a) object, meaning; b) technical term for the first three categories of the Vaiśeṣika system
arthakriyākāritva	bringing about an efficient action, effectiveness (i.e., fulfilling a purpose or producing an effect); making a difference in practice (used as a reductive definition of reality, *sattā*, by the Buddhist critics of the Vaiśeṣika)
arthakriyāsāmarthya	capacity for efficient action, capability of fulfilling a purpose or producing an effect
asat	unreal, nonbeing, nonentity
asatkāryavāda	theory that the effect (or product) does not preexist in its material cause (Nyāya-Vaiśeṣika)
āśraya	substrate
astitva	"is-ness," objectivity, identifiability, factuality
ātmalābha	"acquisition of identity," production
atyantābhāva	absolute nonexistence, permanent absence
aupacārikī sattā	see: *upacārasattā*
avayava—avayavin	part—whole
āvirbhāva	manifestation, appearance, actualization (Sāṃkhya-Yoga)
bhāva	existence, reality, presence (in its most specific usage, *bhāva* is a synonym of *sattā;* as opposed to *abhāva*, it refers to the six positive categories)
bhāvatva	status of being a real entity, belonging to the positive categories
bhāvin	having existence or reality, existent

bhavitṛ	subject of existence
bheda	distinction, division, separate occurrence
bhūta	(matter of the) past, matter of fact, real; creature; element
bhūti	becoming, being (in a verbal sense, as process)
dharma	property, (abstract) attribute, unit of identification
dharmin	substrate, subject, or locus of a property
dravya	substance (the first category of the Vaiśeṣika
ekārthavṛttitva	cooccurrence in the same object (i.e., substrate)
guṇa	quality (the second category of the Vaiśeṣika system)
guṇavattva	possession of qualities
jāti	genus, species, real universal (see also: *sāmānya*)
jñeyatva	knowability, cognitive identifiability
kāla	time (one of the nine substances of classical Vaiśeṣika)
kāraṇa(tva)	(the status of being a) cause
karman	motion, action involving motion (the third category of the Vaiśeṣika system)
kārya(tva)	(the status of being an) effect or product
kṣaṇa	moment, smallest unit of time
kṣaṇikatva	momentariness, flux, discontinuity of existence (primarily in Buddhism)
niṣpāda, niṣpatti	origination, production
niṣṭhā(na)	completion, complete production

nityatva	eternity, permanence
nivṛtti	cessation, disappearance
padārtha	a) meaning of a word; b) basic topic; c) category (in Vaiśeṣika)
pariṇāma	modification, transformation
piṇḍa	(concrete) individual
pradhvaṃsābhāva	nonbeing due to destruction, posterior (subsequent) nonexistence
prāgabhāva	prior nonexistence, nonbeing prior to production
pramāṇagamyatā	(*-grāhyatā;—viṣayatā*) accessibility to valid cognition
pramāṇasambandhayogyatā	suitability for valid cognition, capacity to validate cognition (used as a reductive definition of reality, *sattā,* in the Prābhākara school of Mīmāṃsā)
pravṛttisāmarthya	practical efficiency, capacity to make a difference in practice
sadasadvikalpa	"dilemma about being and nonbeing"; dialectical problem whether (the universal) reality inheres in what is real or unreal by itself
sadbhāva	reality (in a veridical sense), real occurrence
sādharmya	homogeneity, similarity, common attribute
śakti	capacity, potentiality
sāmānya	universal, generic property (the fourth category of the Vaiśeṣika system; see also *jāti*)
samavāya	inherence, cooccurrence, copulative being (the sixth category of the Vaiśeṣika system)
samavāyikāraṇa	inherential cause, substrate in which something inheres

sambandha	connection, relation
sambhava	production, occurrence, possibility
sanmātra	an entity merely as such, being as such
sat	being, entity, real
satkāryavāda	theory that the effect (or product) preexists in its material cause (Sāṃkhya-Yoga)
sattā	"beingness," reality (as the highest universal in Vaiśeṣika)
sattādhyāropa	superimposition of reality
sattaikārthasamavāya	coinherence in the same object with *sattā*; sharing the same substrate with reality
sattāsamavāya	inherence of (the universal) reality
sattāsambandha	connection with (the universal) reality
sattāvat	possessing reality; something of which reality can be predicated
sattāvattva	the state of possessing reality; being something of which reality can be predicated
sattva	being, entity, reality (unlike *sattā*, *sattva* is not used as a technical term in Vaiśeṣika)
śūnya	void, empty, devoid of identity
svabhāva	"own-being," identity, self-sufficient essence (and/or existence)
svabhāvasadbhāva	self-sufficient reality, reality as identifiable essence
svakāraṇasambandha	(inherential) connection with the material causes
svakāraṇasattāsambandha	(inherential) connection with the material causes and (the universal) reality
svarūpa	"own-form," specific nature, peculiarity, what something is as such
svarūpasattva	(-*sattā*) reality as (or by virtue of) specific

	nature, reality coinciding with what something is as such
svarūpavattva	possession of a peculiar nature, identifiability
svasadbhāva	"own-reality," self-sufficient reality
svātmasattva	being as self-identity, reality coinciding with what something is as such, reality per se
tattva	suchness (as truth-condition), true state of affairs
tirobhāva	disappearance, withdrawal into potentiality (Sāṃkhya-Yoga)
tuccha, tuchya	void, utterly fictitious
udbhava	origination, production
upacārasattā	reality in a metaphorical, figurative sense
upādhi	imposed property, nonauthentic (nonobjective) attribute
utpatti	genesis, production, occurrence in time
vartamānakālasambandhitva	(the status of) being connected with the present time (as definition of reality)
vartamānatā	being present (as definition of reality according to Maṇḍana)
vastu	real thing (as "abiding," independently existing)
vastumātra	mere something, a real thing merely as such
vidhi (mukha) pratyayaviṣayatva	accessibility to (or being the object of) directly affirmative awareness, correspondence to positive modes of cognition
vināśa	disappearance, destruction
viśeṣa	(ultimate) particularity (the fifth category of the Vaiśeṣika system); in a less technical

	sense: specific factor, specific type, distinction
viśeṣaṇa	qualifier, distinguishing mark, predicate
viśeṣaṇaviśeṣyabhāva	relation of qualifier and qualificand; relation between subject and predicate
vṛtti	(actual) occurrence
vyakti	a) manifestation, actualization; b) individual, particular instance
vyañjaka	manifestor, manifesting factor

Abbreviations

ABORI	*Annals of the Bhandarkar Oriental Research Institute.*
AKBh	Vasubandhu, *Abhidharmakośabhāṣya.*
Ak. Wiss. (Lit.)	Akademie der Wissenschaften (und der Literatur).
BSBh	Śaṅkara, *Brahmasūtrabhāṣya.*
BU (Bh)	*Bṛhadāraṇyaka Upaniṣad (Bhāṣya).*
Calc. S.S.	Calcutta Sanskrit Series.
ChSS	Chowkhamba Sanskrit Series.
Diss.	Ph.D. dissertation.
DNC	Mallavādin, *Dvādaśāranayacakra;* quoted from: *Dvādaśāraṃ nayacakram,* ed. Jambuvijaya, 3 vols. (Bhavnagar, 1966–1988).
EIPh	*Encyclopedia of Indian Philosophies,* ed. K. H. Potter.
Gesch.d.ind.Phil.	E. Frauwallner, *Geschichte der indischen Philosophie,* 2 vols. (Salzburg, 1953–1956); the translation by V. D. Bedekar: *History of Indian Philosophy,* 2 vols. (Delhi, 1973) is not always adequate.
GOS	Gaekwad's Oriental Series.
Hist. Wb. Phil.	*Historisches Wörterbuch der Philosphie,* ed. J. Ritter and K. Gründer (Basel, 1971ff.).

India and Europe	W. Halbfass, *India and Europe: An Essay in Understanding* (Albany: SUNY Press, 1988).
JAOS	*Journal of the American Oriental Society.*
JIBSt	*Journal of Indian and Buddhist Studies* (Tokyo).
JIPh	*Journal of Indian Philosophy.*
Kir.	Udayana, *Kiraṇāvalī,* ed. J. S. Jetly (Baroda, 1971; GOS); with additional or alternative references to the edition by M. S. Chandra Sarvabhouma and Narendra Chandra Vedantatirtha (Calcutta, 1911–1956; Bibliotheca Indica).
Kl. Schr.	*Kleine Schriften.*
Mahābhāṣya	Patañjali, *The Vyākaraṇa-Mahābhāṣya,* ed. F. Kielhorn, 3d ed., revised by K. V. Abhyankar, 3 vols. (Poona, 1962–1972).
MK	Nāgārjuna, *(Mūla-) Madhyamakakārikā.*
Mys.	Mysore manuscript of Vyomaśiva's *Vyomavatī.*
NBh	Vātsyāyana Pakṣilasvāmin, *Nyāyabhāṣya;* see *NV.*
NBhūṣ	Bhāsarvajña, *Nyāyabhūṣaṇa,* ed. Yogīndrānanda (Benares, 1968).
NK	Śrīdhara, *Nyāyakandalī;* see *PBh.*
NM	Jayanta, *Nyāyamañjarī;* if not marked otherwise, quoted from *The Nyāyamañjarī of Jayanta Bhaṭṭa,* ed. S. N. Śukla, 2 vols. (Benares, 1934–1936; Kashi Sanskrit Series).
NS	*Nyāyasūtra;* see *NV.*
NV	Uddyotakara, *Nyāyavārttika;* if not marked otherwise, quoted from *Nyāyadarśanam* with Vātsyāyana's *Bhāṣya,* Uddyotakara's *Vārttika,* Vācaspati Miśra's *Tātparyaṭīkā* and Viśvanātha's *Vṛtti,* ed. Taranatha Nyaya-

	Tarkatirtha and Amarendramohan Tarkatirtha, 2 vols. (Calcutta, 1936–1944; Calc.S.S.; reprint Kyoto, 1982).
PBh	Praśastapāda, *Padārthadharmasaṃgraha* (*Praśastapādabhāṣya*); if not marked otherwise, quoted from *The Bhāṣya of Praśastapāda*, together with the *Nyāyakandalī* of Śrīdhara, ed. V. P. Dvivedin (Benares, 1895; Vizianagram Sanskrit Series; reprint Delhi, 1884 under the title *The Praśastapāda Bhāshya*).
PEW	*Philosophy East and West*.
SK	Īśvarakṛṣṇa, *Sāṃkhyakārikā*.
SP	Śivāditya, *Saptapadārthī*; if not marked otherwise, quoted from *Saptapadārthī of Śivāditya*, ed. and trans. D. Gurumurti (Madras, 1932).
ŚV	Kumārila, *Ślokavārttika*; quoted from *Ślokavārttika* with the commentary *Nyāyaratnākara* by Pārthasārathi Miśra, ed. Dvārikadāsa Śāstrī (Benares, 1978; Prācyabhāratī Series).
Tradition and Reflection	W. Halbfass, *Tradition and Reflection: Explorations in Indian Thought* (Albany: SUNY Press, 1991).
TS	Śāntarakṣita, *Tattvasaṃgraha* (with *Pañjikā* by Kamalaśīla).
v.	verse.
Verhaar, vols. 1–6	*The Verb 'Be' and Its Synonyms*, ed. J. W. M. Verhaar (Dordrecht, 1968–1973).
VP	Bhartṛhari, *Vākyapadīya*; usually cited in conjunction with Bhartṛhari's own *Vṛtti*, with Helārāja's *Prakāśa*, or with other commentaries, in accordance with the editions by K. A. Subramania Iyer, 1963ff.
VS	*Vaiśeṣikasūtra*; cited according to the edition by Jambuvijaya (Baroda, 1961; GOS) or as indicated.

Vy. Vyomaśiva, *Vyomavatī*, ed. Gopinath Kaviraj and Dhundhiraj Shastri (Benares, 1924–1930; in *The Praśastapādabhāshyam by Praśastadevāchārya with commentaries;* ChSS; reprint, 1983); with additional or alternative references to the edition by Gaurinath Sastri, 2 vols. (Benares, 1983–1984; Śivakumāraśāstrī-Granthamālā); see also Mys.

Works, vols. 1–3 *Works of Śaṅkarācārya in Original Sanskrit*, Delhi. 1: *Ten Principal Upaniṣads with Śāṅkarabhāṣya*, (reprint, 1978; originally Delhi, 1964); 2: *Bhagavadgītā with Śāṅkarabhāṣya* (reprint, 1978, of the 2d ed. by Bhagavat; Poona, 1929); 3: *Brahmasūtra with Śāṅkarabhāṣya*, n.d. (unacknowledged reprint of the edition by V. S. Paṇśīkar; Bombay, 1915).

WZKS *Wiener Zeitschrift für die Kunde Südasiens.*

YBh Vyāsa, *Yogabhāṣya.*

YD *Yuktidīpikā*, ed. R. C. Pandeya (Delhi, 1967).

YS *Yogasūtra.*

ZDMG *Zeitschrift der Deutschen Morgenländischen Gesellschaft.*

Index

The index lists proper names, as well as a selection of relevant terms, from the text of the book. With the exception of important anonymous works, titles of works are usually not listed. Names and concepts from the notes appear only if they are of special thematic relevance and go beyond the information provided by the text. Names which are found in bibliographical references (i.e., primarily names of modern scholars) have usually been omitted. Entries do not necessarily appear in the form in which they occur in the text. Some terminological entries refer to exemplary usages only. Subheadings have been generally avoided. All references, if not marked otherwise, are page references. Timothy Cahill, Ph.D. candidate in the Department of Oriental Studies, University of Pennsylvania, deserves special recognition for his contribution to this index.